Sympathy

OXFORD PHILOSOPHICAL CONCEPTS

OXFORD PHILOSOPHICAL CONCEPTS

Christia Mercer, Columbia University
Series Editor

PUBLISHED

Efficient Causation
Edited by Tad Schmaltz

Memory
Edited by Dmitri Nikulin

The Faculties
Edited by Dominik Perler

Sympathy
Edited by Eric Schliesser

FORTHCOMING

Health
Edited by Peter Adamson

Eternity
Edited by Yitzhak Melamed

Evil
Edited by Andrew Chignell

Self-Knowledge
Edited by Ursula Renz

Dignity
Edited by Remy Debes

Pleasure
Edited by Lisa Shapiro

Animals
Edited by G. Fay Edwards and Peter Adamson

Consciousness
Edited by Alison Simmons

Space
Edited by Andrew Janiak

Moral Motivation
Edited by Iakovos Vasiliou

OXFORD PHILOSOPHICAL CONCEPTS

Sympathy
A HISTORY

Edited by Eric Schliesser

OXFORD
UNIVERSITY PRESS

OXFORD
UNIVERSITY PRESS

Oxford University Press is a department of the
University of Oxford. It furthers the University's objective
of excellence in research, scholarship, and education
by publishing worldwide.

Oxford   New York
Auckland   Cape Town   Dar es Salaam   Hong Kong   Karachi
Kuala Lumpur   Madrid   Melbourne   Mexico City   Nairobi
New Delhi   Shanghai   Taipei   Toronto

With offices in
Argentina   Austria   Brazil   Chile   Czech Republic   France   Greece
Guatemala   Hungary   Italy   Japan   Poland   Portugal   Singapore
South Korea   Switzerland   Thailand   Turkey   Ukraine   Vietnam

Oxford is a registered trade mark of Oxford University Press
in the UK and certain other countries.

Published in the United States of America by
Oxford University Press
198 Madison Avenue, New York, NY 10016

© Oxford University Press 2015

All rights reserved. No part of this publication may be reproduced,
stored in a retrieval system, or transmitted, in any form or by any means,
without the prior permission in writing of Oxford University Press,
or as expressly permitted by law, by license, or under terms agreed with
the appropriate reproduction rights organization. Inquiries concerning
reproduction outside the scope of the above should be sent to the
Rights Department, Oxford University Press, at the address above.

You must not circulate this work in any other form
and you must impose this same condition on any acquirer.

Library of Congress Cataloging-in-Publication Data
Sympathy : a history / Edited by Eric Schliesser.
pages cm.—(Oxford philosophical concepts)
ISBN 978-0-19-992889-7 (pbk. : alk. paper)—
ISBN 978-0-19-992887-3 (hardcover : alk. paper)
1. Sympathy.
BJ1475.S96   2015
177'.7—dc23   2014040336

1 3 5 7 9 8 6 4 2
Printed in the United States of America
on acid-free paper

Contents

LIST OF ILLUSTRATIONS ix

CONTRIBUTORS xi

SERIES EDITOR'S FOREWORD xvii

EDITOR'S ACKNOWLEDGMENTS xix

Introduction: On Sympathy 3
ERIC SCHLIESSER

1 Stoic Sympathy 15
RENÉ BROUWER

2 Plotinus on *sympatheia* 36
EYJÓLFUR K. EMILSSON

Reflection Galen's Sympathy 61
BROOKE HOLMES

3 Sympathy in the Renaissance 70
ANN E. MOYER

Reflection Music and Sympathy 102
GIUSEPPE GERBINO

4 Seventeenth-Century Universal Sympathy: Stoicism, Platonism, Leibniz, and Conway 107
CHRISTIA MERCER

Reflection "Take Physic, Pomp": King Lear Learns Sympathy 139
SARAH SKWIRE

5 Spinoza's Parallelism Doctrine and Metaphysical Sympathy 146
KAROLINA HÜBNER

6 The Eighteenth-Century Context of Sympathy from Spinoza to Kant 171
RYAN PATRICK HANLEY

Reflection The French Theater of Sympathy 199
JULIE CANDLER HAYES

7 Hume and Smith on Sympathy, Approbation, and Moral Judgment 208
GEOFFREY SAYRE-MCCORD

Reflection Tracing a Line of Sympathy for Nature in Goethe's *Wahlverwandtschaften* 247
ELIZABETH MILLÁN

8 Sympathy in Schopenhauer and Nietzsche 254
BERNARD REGINSTER

9 From *Einfühlung* to Empathy: Sympathy in Early Phenomenology and Psychology 286
REMY DEBES

10 Sympathy Caught between Darwin and Eugenics 323
    DAVID M. LEVY AND SANDRA J. PEART

11 Fair and Impartial Spectators in Experimental Economic Behavior:
    Using Sympathy to Derive Action 359
    VERNON L. SMITH AND BART J. WILSON

BIBLIOGRAPHY 387

INDEX 423

List of Illustrations

Figure 6.1. Recognitions in La Chaussée's plays may come about through either the "call of blood" or emotionally-based sympathy 202
Figure 10.1. "Am I not a man and a brother?" 331
Figure 11.1. A Two-Person Trust Game in Extensive Form 375
Figure 11.2. Private Knowledge of Payoffs in the Trust Game 379
Figure 11.3. Another Two-Person Trust Game in Extensive Form 383

Contributors

RENÉ BROUWER is a lecturer at the University of Utrecht, where he teaches law and philosophy in the Faculty of Law. He works on theory of law and topics in ancient philosophy, with a special focus on Stoicism, its origins and reception, and the tradition of natural law. He recently published *The Stoic Sage: The Early Stoics on Wisdom, Sagehood and Socrates* (Cambridge University Press).

REMY DEBES is associate professor of philosophy at the University of Memphis. His research is in ethics and the history of ethics, with an emphasis on the Scottish Enlightenment, human dignity, and moral psychology. He is currently editing *Dignity: History of a Concept* (forthcoming in the Oxford Philosophical Concepts series) and (with Karsten Stueber) *Ethical Sentimentalism* (forthcoming from Cambridge University Press).

EYJÓLFUR K. EMILSSON was born in Reykjvík, Iceland, in 1953. He studied philosophy and ancient Greek at the University of Iceland and received his Ph.D. from Princeton University in 1984. After some years of research and teaching at the University of Iceland, since 1993 he has been professor of ancient philosophy at the University of Oslo. In addition to numerous articles, mostly on Plotinus and late ancient philosophy, Emilsson has published two books on Plotinus: *Plotinus on Sense-Perception: A Philosophical Study* (Cambridge University Press, 1988) and *Plotinus on Intellect* (Oxford University Press, 2007).

GIUSEPPE GERBINO is associate professor of music at Columbia University. His research interests include the Italian madrigal, the relationship between music and language in the early modern period, early opera, and Renaissance theories of cognition and sense perception. He is the author of *Canoni ed Enigmi: Pier Francesco Valentini e l'artificio canonico nella prima metà del Seicento* (Torre d'Orfeo, 1995), and *Music and the Myth of Arcadia in Renaissance Italy* (Cambridge University Press, 2009), winner of the 2010 Lewis Lockwood Award of the American Musicological Society.

RYAN PATRICK HANLEY is Mellon Distinguished Professor of Political Science at Marquette University. He is the author of *Adam Smith and the Character of Virtue* (Cambridge University Press, 2009) and editor of the Penguin Classics edition of *The Theory of Moral Sentiments* (2010) and *Adam Smith: His Life, Thought, and Legacy* (forthcoming from Princeton University Press). His latest book is *Love's Enlightenment: Rethinking Charity in Modernity* (forthcoming from Cambridge University Press).

JULIE CANDLER HAYES is professor of French and dean of the College of Humanities and Fine Arts at the University of Massachusetts, Amherst. Her research focuses primarily on literary and philosophical texts of the French Enlightenment; she has also written extensively on contemporary literary theory and the history and theory of translation. Her most recent book is *Translation, Subjectivity, and Culture in France and England, 1600–1800* (Stanford University Press, 2009). Her earlier books study French theater and Enlightenment concepts of "systematicity" in literature, philosophy, and science. Her current scholarly work looks at seventeenth- and eighteenth-century women moral philosophers.

BROOKE HOLMES is professor of classics at Princeton University. Her first book, *The Symptom and the Subject: The Emergence of the Physical Body in Ancient Greece*, appeared in 2010, and a second book, *Gender: Antiquity and Its Legacy*, was published in 2012. She has also coedited volumes on Aelius Aristides and the reception of Epicureanism, and published widely on subjects from the river Scamander in Homer to the medical analogy in Plato to Deleuze's reading of Lucretius. She is currently at work on a book manuscript entitled "The Tissue of the World: Sympathy in Greco-Roman Antiquity."

KAROLINA HÜBNER is assistant professor of philosophy at the University of Toronto. She is the author of a number of articles on Spinoza's metaphysics.

DAVID M. LEVY is a professor of economics at George Mason University and a Distinguished Fellow of the History of Economics Society. His Ph.D. in economics is from the University of Chicago, where he wrote his dissertation under George Stigler. Sandra Peart and he revived the doctrine of analytical egalitarianism from classical economics. They have codirected the Summer Institute for the Preservation of the History of Economics for fifteen years.

CHRISTIA MERCER is Gustave M. Berne Professor of Philosophy at Columbia University. She is the author of *Leibniz's Metaphysics: Its Origins and Development* (Cambridge University Press) and most recently of "The Philosophy of Anne Conway: Radical Rationalism and the Feminization of Nature." She is the general editor of Oxford Philosophical Concepts.

ELIZABETH MILLÁN is a professor of philosophy at DePaul University in Chicago. In 2004, she was awarded a fellowship from the Alexander von Humboldt Foundation. Her publications include a book on Schlegel, edited volumes on romanticism and Goethe, and several articles on aspects of Alexander von Humboldt's work. She is currently finishing a book on "The Romantic Roots of Alexander von Humboldt's Presentation of Nature."

ANN MOYER is associate professor of history at the University of Pennsylvania. She specializes in the intellectual and cultural history of Renaissance Europe, especially sixteenth-century Italy. Moyer is an executive editor of the *Journal of the History of Ideas*, and serves as executive director of the Renaissance Society of America.

SANDRA J. PEART is dean of the Jepson School of Leadership Studies at the University of Richmond. She obtained her Ph.D. in economics at the University of Toronto and is president of the International Adam Smith Society, codirector of the annual Summer Institute for the History of Economic Thought, and a former president of the History of Economics Society. She has written or edited eight books and more than fifty refereed articles, many with David M. Levy.

BERNARD REGINSTER is professor in and chair of the Department of Philosophy at Brown University. He has published extensively on issues in nineteenth-century ethics, particularly in German thought. His most recent book, *The Affirmation of Life: Nietzsche on Overcoming Nihilism*, was published by Harvard University Press in 2006. He is currently working on another book on the genealogical critique of ethical outlooks, "The Will to Nothingness," as well as on issues from psychoanalytic psychiatry.

GEOFFREY SAYRE-MCCORD is the Morehead-Cain Alumni Distinguished Professor of Philosophy at the University of North Carolina at Chapel Hill. He is the director of the University's Philosophy, Politics, and Economics Program. Sayre-McCord works primarily in metaethics, moral theory, and the history of moral philosophy.

ERIC SCHLIESSER is BOF Research Professor in Philosophy and Moral Sciences at Ghent University. In 2015 he joined the University of Amsterdam as professor of political theory in the Department of Political Science. He has published widely in early modern philosophy and the sciences, philosophy of economics, and philosophical methodology. He has edited volumes on Adam Smith and Isaac Newton.

SARAH SKWIRE is a Fellow at Liberty Fund, Inc., and the author of the college writing textbook *Writing with a Thesis*. Skwire has published on subjects from Shakespeare to zombies and the broken window fallacy, and her work has appeared in journals as varied as *Social Philosophy and Policy*, *Literature and Medicine*, the *George Herbert Journal*, and the *Journal of Economic Behavior and Organization*. She writes a regular book review column, Book Value, for the *Freeman Online* and blogs at *Bleeding Heart Libertarians*. Her poetry has appeared, among other places, in *Standpoint*, the *New Criterion*, and the *Vocabula Review*.

VERNON L. SMITH was awarded the Nobel Prize in Economic Sciences in 2002 for his groundbreaking work in experimental economics. He has joint appointments with the Argyros School of Business and Economics and the School of Law at Chapman University. Smith has authored or coauthored more than 250 articles and books on capital theory, finance, natural resource economics, and experimental economics. In 1991, Cambridge University Press published *Papers in Experimental Economics*, and in 2000, a second collection of more recent essays, *Bargaining and Market Behavior*. Cambridge published his *Rationality in Economics: Constructivist and Ecological Forms* in 2008. Smith has received an honorary doctor of management degree from Purdue University, and is a Fellow of the Econometric Society, the American Association for the Advancement of Science, and the American Academy of Arts and Sciences.

BART J. WILSON is the Donald P. Kennedy Endowed Chair in Economics and Law at Chapman University's Economic Science Institute. He has published articles in the *American Economic Review*, the *Proceedings of the National Academy of Sciences*, and *the Journal of Law, Economics and Organization*. His research has been supported with grants from the National Science Foundation, the Federal Trade Commission and the Institute for Justice.

Series Editor's Foreword

Oxford Philosophical Concepts (OPC) offers an innovative approach to philosophy's past and its relation to other disciplines. As a series, it is unique in exploring the transformations of central philosophical concepts from their ancient sources to their modern use.

OPC has several goals: to make it easier for historians to contextualize key concepts in the history of philosophy, to render that history accessible to a wide audience, and to enliven contemporary discussions by displaying the rich and varied sources of philosophical concepts still in use today. The means to these goals are simple enough: eminent scholars come together to rethink a central concept in philosophy's past. The point of this rethinking is not to offer a broad over-view, but to identify problems the concept was originally supposed to solve and investigate how approaches to them shifted over time, sometimes radically.

Recent scholarship has made evident the benefits of reexamining the standard narratives about western philosophy. OPC's editors look beyond the canon and explore their concepts over a wide philosophical landscape. Each volume traces a notion from its inception as a solution to specific problems through its historical transformations to its modern use, all the while acknowledging its historical context. Each OPC volume is *a history* of its concept in that it tells a story about changing solutions to specific problems. Many editors have found it appropriate to include long-ignored writings drawn from the Islamic and Jewish traditions and the philosophical contributions of women. Volumes also explore ideas drawn from Buddhist, Chinese, Indian, and other philosophical cultures when doing so adds an especially helpful new perspective. By combining scholarly innovation with focused and astute analysis, OPC encourages a deeper understanding of our philosophical past and present.

One of the most innovative features of *Oxford Philosophical Concepts* is its recognition that philosophy bears a rich relation to art, music, literature, religion, science, and other cultural practices. The series speaks to the need for informed interdisciplinary exchanges. Its editors assume that the most difficult and profound philosophical ideas can be made comprehensible to a large audience and that materials not strictly philosophical often bear a significant relevance to philosophy. To this end, each OPC volume includes Reflections. These are short stand-alone essays written by specialists in art, music, literature, theology, science, or cultural studies that *reflect on* the concept from other disciplinary perspectives. The goal of these essays is to enliven, enrich, and exemplify the volume's concept and reconsider the boundary between philosophical and extra-philosophical materials. OPC's Reflections display the benefits of using philosophical concepts and distinctions in areas that are not strictly philosophical, and encourage philosophers to move beyond the borders of their discipline as presently conceived.

The volumes of OPC arrive at an auspicious moment. Many philosophers are keen to invigorate the discipline. OPC aims to provoke philosophical imaginations by uncovering the brilliant twists and unforeseen turns of philosophy's past.

Christia Mercer
Gustave M. Berne Professor of Philosophy
Columbia University in the City of New York
June 2015

Editor's Acknowledgments

This volume was first conceived on a beautiful fall day in upstate New York back in 2005. My then-senior colleague Fred Beiser had invited Christia Mercer to Syracuse University for a lecture and had assigned me the pleasing task to show her around. During a walk through Cazenovia, she persuasively tried out the idea of an Oxford Philosophical Concepts series on me. I enthusiastically and spontaneously offered to edit "formal causation" and "sympathy"; I volunteered not because I was an expert on either topic, but rather because I had long been frustrated by the absence of a philosophical-historical-cultural source to help me navigate the complex issues that these concepts had generated in the course of my own research.

I am very grateful to Christia for trusting me with "sympathy," despite my lack of credentials for the task. Her vision animates not just the series but also this particular volume. She has been instrumental in getting a number of the distinguished contributors to participate in the volume, and she had a decisive hand in the choice of topics. In particular, she encouraged me to put together a truly interdisciplinary volume; alongside chapters by professional philosophers, it also contains indispensable contributions by economists, historians, political scientists, classicists, musicologists, and literature scholars.

The Adam Smith Program at the Jepson School of Leadership Studies at Richmond University and Liberty Fund generously sponsored two back-to-back workshops in Virginia that allowed most of the contributors to this volume to get together and share drafts of their chapters and work through some of the key texts discussed in this volume. At Richmond University, I am especially grateful to Dean Sandra J. Peart and Shannon Best for being such gracious, efficient, and generous hosts. At Liberty Fund I am especially grateful to Doug Den Uyl, Christine Henderson, and Elizabeth Letson for their indispensable efforts.

Since this volume was conceived, I owe considerable debts to three employers, Syracuse University, Leiden University, and Ghent University as well as three grant agencies (NWO: Netherlands Organisation for Scientific Research, FWO: The Research Foundation—Flanders, and BOF: Bijzonderonderzoeksfonds at Ghent University), which have facilitated and sponsored my research. They have helped make me a winner in an unfair lottery—not the least of which is the joy of learning so much from the stellar and generous contributors to this volume. The highlight was an impromptu, unrecorded recital by Eyjólfur Kjalar Emilsson.

In addition, I thank Peter Ohlin, Lucy Randall, and Gwen Colvin at Oxford University Press; I cannot imagine a better editorial team.

Finally, I thank Sarit and Avi for teaching me how love and sympathy mutually reinforce each other.

Sympathy

Introduction: On Sympathy

Eric Schliesser

1. Introduction and Overview of the Volume

"Sympathy" is derived from the Greek συμπάθεια, the state of feeling together (derived from the composite of fellow [συν]-feeling [πάθος]). A solid Latin translation would be *compassio*. Unfortunately, whatever is exactly meant by "sympathy," to English ears, "compassion," that is, to quote a dictionary, "a feeling of wanting to help someone," would seem to denote merely a subset of sympathy, perhaps the paradigmatic feeling consequent of "empathy." So, we cannot simply equate sympathy and compassion. "Empathy" (from the Greek ἐν (*en*), "in, at") is a word that was coined only in the twentieth century in order to capture the meaning of the German *Einfühlung*, which means to enter into somebody's feelings (see chapter 9 in this volume for the details).

Both in the vernacular as well as in the various specialist literatures within philosophy, psychology, neuroscience, economics, and history, "sympathy" and "empathy" are routinely conflated. In practice, they are also used to refer to a large variety of complex all-too-familiar social phenomena: for example, simultaneous yawning or the giggles. But "sympathy" is also deployed to understand the otherwise mysterious, coaffective bond within an individual's mind and body, for example, in order to explain how our emotions are accompanied by distinct bodily states. "Sympathy," or more often "sympathies," is also used to refer to the "network" or "interconnected" quality of the nervous system, sometimes with the vibration of musical strings as a metaphor, sometimes more literally. In addition, there are many natural phenomena that invite sympathetic explanations: the distant action of magnets, the spread of contagious diseases (see Holmes's Reflection), the resonance of musical strings (Gerbino's Reflection) and the co-occurrences of some natural phenomena with natural and human disasters (see Moyer's chapter). From the start sympathy is also a tool in divination (see the chapters by Brouwer or Emilsson).

Moreover, sympathy also addresses another kind of issue altogether: the moral problem associated with social dislocation and political conflict. It is, then, turned into a vehicle toward generating harmony among otherwise isolated individuals and a way for them to fit into a larger whole, be it society or the universe (see Mercer's, Hanley's, and Sayre-McCord's chapters, especially). The fact that sympathy is often (e.g., Brouwer, Emilsson) understood as an active principle, that is, as something that is a source of change or causal power (or energy, etc.), means that it is not only deployed as an explanation but that it can be a means in generating connections where previously linkages had been latent.

While "sympathy" does appear (with related concepts like harmony, natural friendship, pity, etc.) in Plato and Aristotle, it tends to be identified as originating in Stoic thought (see René Brouwer's chapter) in the western, philosophical tradition. It was also taken up and developed in nontrivial ways by Plotinus (Emilsson), Pliny, Vitruvius, and Galen (Holmes's reflection), among others. A use for the concept was rediscovered in the Renaissance and promoted not so much as one might expect, by the most famous Platonizing philosopher, Marsilio Ficino, but by Erasmus and, especially, Girolamo Fracastoro (see Ann Moyer's chapter). The concept does useful work in Shakespeare (Skwire's Reflection) and musicology (Gerbino's Reflection). Even though, as Moyer argues in chapter 3, in Fracastoro's account of sympathy, sympathy itself had a properly atomistic explanation, the concept was banished by Descartes and lumped in with the to-be-discarded occult (see, especially, Descartes's *Principles of Philosophy* 4.187).

Despite the enduring influence of Descartes and fellow travelers in the mechanical philosophy, some philosophers of the early modern period found the concept too useful to forego (e.g., the contributions below by Mercer, Hanley, and Sayre-McCord and Hayes's Reflection). During the eighteenth century, sympathy plays a central role in the great moral psychologies of Hume, Adam Smith, and Sophie de Grouchy; sympathy is not just made respectable physiologically in the work of David Hartley, but also accorded a central role in his natural theology (see Hanley). At the end of the early modern period, sympathy had moved from an occult quality hidden to the senses to a crucial concept in capturing the manner in which human understanding involves a certain sort of sympathetic recognition (see Millán on Goethe in her Reflection). The complex entwinement of recognition and sympathy plays a central role in both Reginster's chapter on Schopenhauer's embrace of compassion and Nietzsche's criticism not of compassion as such, but on the way it is understood, as well as in Debes's chapter on how *Einfühlung* (or empathy) was developed in theoretical philosophy (in questions over the existence of other minds) and then applied in practical philosophy and the newly emerging scientific discipline of psychology.

But the impulse to banish sympathy recurs throughout history and across disciplines. For example, David Levy and Sandra Peart describe one such episode from the history of economics in chapter 10, on the role of eugenics in displacing the moral practice of sympathizing with others and "sympathy" from the vocabulary of late nineteenth-century political economy.[1] While social psychologists remained interested in sympathy, behavioral psychologists, and economists banished it. Some recent economists have rediscovered sympathy in part experimentally and, in part, as Vernon Smith and Bart Wilson show in chapter 11, by careful rereading of the classics of the field.

Of course, with the discovery of mirror neurons by a group of researchers with experiments on macaque monkeys at the University of Parma, interest in sympathy and empathy has exploded across many disciplinary boundaries.[2] These "neurons respond both when a particular action is performed by the recorded [brain] and when the same action, performed by another individual, is observed."[3] It has become impossible to keep abreast of all the fast-moving developments.[4] Sympathy's past is fascinating for many intrinsic reasons; the conceptual and explanatory moves of this past linger on in contemporary practices, and they are also often rediscovered in modern science.

2. Sympathy—an Analysis

Given the diversity of usages of "sympathy" within the context of very different theoretical aims, one might doubt that there is a single, underlying concept rather than a host of family resemblances. Even so, one can identify five features that are incorporated in or presupposed by most usages of the term "sympathy." I start with the following four:

---

[1] This is not to deny that sympathy could also be used to codify racist prejudices at the origins of scientific sociology and behavioral psychology. See John A. Mills, *Control: A History of Behavioral Psychology* (New York: New York University Press, 2000), 26–27, on Franklin Giddings's "sympathy scale."

[2] G. Rizzolatti, L. Fogassi, and V. Gallese, "Mirrors in the Mind," *Scientific American*, 295.5 (2006): 54–61.

[3] V. Gallese and A. Goldman, "Mirror Neurons and the Simulation Theory of Mind-Reading," *Trends in Cognitive Sciences* 2.12 (1998): 493–501, at 493.

[4] For a very fine philosophical introduction, which contains some of the relevant history, see A. I. Goldman, *Simulating Minds: The Philosophy, Psychology, and Neuroscience of Mindreading* (Oxford: Oxford University Press, 2006). For recent, sober analysis see, for example, S. Spaulding, "Mirror Neurons and Social Cognition," *Mind and Language* 28.2 (2013): 233–57; and R. Cook, G. Bird, C. Catmur, C. Press, and C. Heyes, "Mirror Neurons: From Origin to Function," *Behavioral and Brain Sciences* 37.2 (2014): 177–92.

1. Sympathy is used to explain *apparent* action at a distance.
2. The very possibility of sympathy presupposes that it takes place among things/events/features that are in one sense or another alike, often *within* a single being/unity/organism (which can be the whole universe); these are to be contrasted with the antipathy (ἀντιπάθεια) of unalikes.
3. The cause(s) of sympathy is/are invisible to the naked eye.
4. The effect(s) of sympathy can be (nearly) instantaneous.

All four features, taken individually or combined, are neutral among cosmological, physical, and psychological accounts of sympathy. The second feature is emphasized in Emilsson's chapter below. This second condition of the possibility of sympathy I call the "likeness principle," or the LP. It is a metaphysical background commitment that is presupposed in nearly all applications of the concept. Admittedly, in some cases it is *by virtue* of taking place within a unity that sympathy is possible; on my account of the LP, this is sufficient for the possibility of sympathy (even among things that are otherwise very unalike).[5]

Obviously, in the hands of different thinkers there will be a great deal more fleshing out and linkage to other important commitments and concepts. Even so, these four features allow what we might call very "naturalistic" analyses of sympathy—for they can be made compatible with nonmiraculous mechanisms. There is, thus, despite Descartes's strictures, no necessary connection with the occult or magic when one deploys a sympathetic explanation. This fact helps explain the remarkable revival of the fortunes of sympathy in otherwise sober thinkers like Hume, Adam Smith, Sophie de Grouchy, and Mill (etc.).

In fact, reflection on these four features suggests that sympathy is a concept that might be put to work as a useful, innocent placeholder while one is searching for underlying explanations for many different kinds of causal processes. Of course, even if one is comfortable with

---

5 I have benefited from reading an unpublished draft paper by Sorana Corneanu on Bacon.

causes spread out over great distances with simultaneous effects, the LP is open to various abuses. In particular, one might be tempted to treat the LP not so much as a condition of possibility or as a constraint on explanation but as itself the *explanans* of instances of apparent "sympathy." One might discern in such abuses the reasons for Descartes's suspicion of the concept. To be sure, the LP as *explanans* is neither an appeal to a supernatural cause nor itself invoking anything unintelligible. But explaining by way of the LP does seem to fall short in specificity (say, of the mechanism, force, etc.).

Yet even granted the concern, we should not underestimate the heuristic fruitfulness of invoking the LP as *explanans*—doing so might well call attention to the existence of an unsuspected, unitary phenomenon. Of course, sometimes an appeal to sympathy where at bottom the LP does the explanatory work might be the best one can do for a whole range of naturally recurring phenomena. This fact might help explain why sympathy is an explanatory concept that, in fact, regularly gets banished and reinvented in a whole range of serious intellectual enterprises, including literary ones. If nothing else, the invocation of sympathy is evidence of the desire to discern intelligible patterns of connection even among spatially distant features.

In the four listed features above, I emphasize that sympathy is a concept that is invoked in the context of spatially distant, yet somehow connected events. Sympathy may also be invoked to characterize connections among temporarily distant events or things (etc.). For example, Kenelm Digby's once celebrated, seventeenth-century mechanical analysis of sympathy allows for this. Moreover, some such role for sympathy may well be an essential ingredient (as R. G. Collingwood and Walter Benjamin suggest along very differing lines) in historical practice (on Benjamin see Hayes's contribution). Even so, temporal symmetry tends to be asymmetrical in that it is backward looking and tends to piggyback on other mechanisms (for example, the imagination). Reflection on this aspect reveals that the LP also has a kind of symmetry requirement built into it. We can articulate, thus, a fifth feature of sympathy:

5. Sympathy is, in principle, bidirectional even if the elements or agents that enter into a sympathetic relationship vary in their power to do so.

By this I mean to capture the fact that sympathy is not just introduced to capture distant action but generally meant to capture *mutual* action or at least the capacity for coaffectability (which itself might be a fine translation for συμπάθεια). In a sympathetic relation, all the relata participate or engage; this is why sympathy is thought to be an active principle.[6] It's the presence of both the LP (2) and this bidirectional aspect (5) that makes sympathy an attractive concept to philosophers as dissimilar as Anne Conway, Leibniz, Smith, de Grouchy, and John Stuart Mill, who wish to stress the natural moral equality and connectedness of all (see especially the chapters by Mercer, Sayre-McCord, and Levy and Peart below).

So, to sum up: sympathy is a concept that picks out a structurally distinct step in a causal process. Its presence may, but need not, invite further inquiry. Given that the natural and moral phenomena it helps make salient are ubiquitous and important, we should expect that interest in deploying a concept akin to sympathy will not be extinguished in any possible future.

3. Early Modern Philosophy, Reconsidered

This volume does not aim to offer a comprehensive historical and cross-cultural survey of sympathy. Rather, the aim is to create a useful starting place for scholars and students alike interested in the origin and development of sympathy in (western) philosophy and closely associated disciplines. This is why the volume is genuinely interdisciplinary in character:

---

6 This is not to deny that there are cases of sympathy where one of the relata is not really active: Adam Smith has a famous example of sympathizing "with the dead" in *The Theory of Moral Sentiments*; see Smith, *The Theory of Moral Sentiments*, ed. D. D. Raphael and A. L. Macfie (1759; Oxford: Clarendon Press, 1976), 1.1.10.13: 12. But in most such cases, the inactive relatum is conceived as or imagined as active somehow. I thank Kathryn Pogin for discussion of this point.

the contributors are not just distinguished historians of philosophy but also historians, classicists, economists, political theorists, and literary theorists.

While a couple of chapters synthesize active research (Sayre-McCord and Reginster), most are very much invitations to future research. I conclude this introduction by giving an example of what I have in mind for early modern philosophy. Descartes's injunction against sympathy had been so powerful that when Newton published *Principia* (1686), which contained his new law of universal gravity, many informed readers believed that Newton had deployed something akin to sympathy in implying that there exists action at a distance in Newtonian gravity. In a letter to Christian Huygens, Leibniz compares Newton's account of gravity to sympathy, as a kind of "inexplicable quality." (See Mercer's chapter for context.)

Some figures in Newton's circle unambiguously embraced action at a distance. For example, after reading the *Principia*, Locke treated it as a quality superadded to matter by God:

> The gravitation of matter towards matter, by ways inconceivable to me, is not only a demonstration that God can, if he pleases, put into bodies powers and ways of operation, above what can be derived from our idea of body, or can be explained by what we know of matter, but also an unquestionable and every where visible instance, that he has done so. ("Second Reply to the Bishop of Worcester", 1699, *The Works of John Locke*, 4.467)[7]

In his letter to Edward Stillingfleet, bishop of Worcester (and reflecting the doctrines of the first edition of the *Essay*), Locke accepts the mechanical philosophers's assertion that theirs is the only intelli-

---

7 Quoted in Hylarie Kochiras, "Locke's Philosophy of Science," *The Stanford Encyclopedia of Philosophy* (Fall 2013 ed.), ed. Edward N. Zalta, http://plato.stanford.edu/archives/fall2013/entries/locke-philosophy-science/.

gible philosophy. He takes Newton's results to offer empirical evidence for the idea that the world is in a nontrivial sense unintelligible and, thus, inconceivable. The only cause that can produce inconceivable effects is God, hence God superadds gravity to matter (and this opens the door to Leibniz to claim, familiar to us from his famous correspondence with Samuel Clarke, that action at a distance is not just a violation of the principle of sufficient reason but a perpetual miracle).

Similar arguments for superaddition were popular in Newton's circle in order to explain phenomena other than gravity. Stewart Duncan called my attention to the following argument by Richard Bentley:

> For this Sympathetical Union of a Rational Soul with Matter, so as to produce a Vital communication between them, is an arbitrary institution of the Divine Wisdom: there is no reason nor foundation in the separate natures of either substance, why any Motion in the Body should produce any Sensation at all in the Soul; or why This motion should produce That particular Sensation, rather than any other. (Richard Bentley (1692–93), *The Folly and Unreasonableness of Atheism*)[8]

Here, rather than using sympathy and the LP as an argument to explore the materiality of the soul, the existence of sympathy in conjunction with what is taken to be—given a strong commitment to substance dualism—an evident violation of the LP (recall point 2, above), is evidence for God's (providential) intervention.

Due to the correspondence between Newton and Bentley after the first edition of the *Principia*, modern scholarship on Newton has been less willing to attribute to Newton a commitment to action at a distance.

---

[8] Richard Bentley, *The Folly and Unreasonableness of Atheism Demonstrated from the Advantage and Pleasure of a Religious Life, the Faculties of Human Souls, the Structure of Animate Bodies, and the Origin and Frame of the World: in Eight Sermons Preached at the Lecture Founded by the Honourable Robert Boyle*, Esquire, London: H. Mortlock, 1692-3. See also Jennifer A. Herdt, "The Rise of Sympathy and the Question of Divine Suffering," *Journal of Religious Ethics* 29.3 (2001): 367–99. I thank Charles Wolfe for calling my attention to this article.

Newton writes, "You sometimes speak of gravity as essential & inherent to matter: Pray do not ascribe that notion to me; for the cause of gravity is what I do not pretend to know, and therefore would take more time to consider of it." Given that in context, Newton talks of an "intelligent agent," John Henry has defended attributing a superaddition thesis to Newton.[9] But this has not been the dominant approach; many recent scholars rely on this passage to claim that Newton rules out action at a distance altogether.[10] By contrast, I have argued for a more limited interpretation of the claim in Bentley's letter: that Newton only denies that gravity is essential and inherent to matter (a view that, as John Henry has emphasized, Newton associates with Epicureanism).

I have argued that in the suppressed version of book 3 of the *Principia*, the "Treatise on the System of Nature," which was published posthumously shortly after Newton's death, Newton was willing to endorse the disposition to act at a distance as a relational (nonessential) quality of matter. To make my case I relied on these (connected) passages: "And although, in a pair of Planets, the action of each on the other can be distinguished and can be considered as paired actions by which each attracts the other, yet inasmuch as these are actions between two bodies, they are not two but a simple operation between two termini.... In this way conceive that a simple operation, arising from the concurring nature of two Planets, is exerted between them."[11]

---

9 John Henry, "Isaac Newton and the Problem of Action at a Distance," *Revista de Filozofie KRISIS* 8–9 (2009): 30–46, and "Gravity and *De gravitatione*: The Development of Newton's Ideas on Action at a Distance," *Studies in History and Philosophy of Science Part A* 42.1 (2011): 11–27.

10 Andrew Janiak "Newton and the Reality of Force," *Journal of the History of Philosophy* 45.1 (2007): 127–47; Hylarie Kochiras, "Gravity and Newton's Substance Counting Problem," *Studies in History and Philosophy of Science Part A* 40.3 (2009): 267–80; Steffen Ducheyne, *The Main Business of Natural Philosophy: Isaac Newton's Natural-Philosophical Methodology* (Dordrecht: Springer, 2011).

11 Here, I am using a new, unpublished translation by George E. Smith. I am grateful for permission to reproduce this passage. For the detailed argument, see Eric Schliesser, "Without God: Gravity as a Relational Quality of Matter in Newton's Treatise," in *Vanishing Matter and the Laws of Motion: Descartes and Beyond*, ed. Peter Anstey and Dana Jalobeanu (London: Routledge, 2011), 80–102. My argument has not won widespread agreement; the only thing that scholarship agrees on is that Newton denies that gravity is an essential quality of matter in the Third Rule of Reasoning of the *Principia* (see Kochiras, "Locke's Philosophy of Science.")

What matters for present purposes, however, is that Newton's wording in the "Treatise" echoes William Gilbert's treatment of action at a distance of celestial bodies (that is, the moon and the earth) in his posthumously published (1651) *De mundo nostro sublunari philosophia nova* (307). Like Newton later (in addition to the quoted passage from the "Treatise," see *Principia*, book 3, proposition 7, cor. 1, and proposition 7 of part 3 of book 2 of the *Opticks*), Gilbert treats the conspiring or concurring nature of celestial bodies as analogous to magnetism. He explicitly treats this conspiring attraction as an instance of sympathy (which he had always distinguished from magnetism in his more famous work *On the Magnet*). Along the way, Gilbert appeals to an instance of LP.[12]

So while sympathy was certainly not part of "mainstream" post-Cartesian natural philosophy, influential natural philosophers like Gilbert and Newton flirted with it in their physics (and, perhaps, Gilbert influenced Newton's "Treatise"). This should encourage more research into the views of other important natural philosophers who we know did not reject action at a distance out of hand (e.g., Kepler, Margaret Cavendish, Hooke).

Finally, one reason why this volume has two chapters in which Spinoza figures prominently (Hübner on metaphysics in chapter 5 and Hanley on moral philosophy in chapter 6) is that against Descartes's strictures, Spinoza had insisted in his *Ethics* that "nobody as yet has determined the limits of the body's capabilities: that is, nobody as yet has learned from experience what the body can and cannot do" (part 3, proposition 2, scholium). This agnostic stance on the body's capacity reopens the door to an active conception of the body's activity and, thus, a conception of sympathy as not merely a placeholder for our ignorance of the world's causal nexus when confronted by apparent action at a distance but as a potential explanation of existing phenomena. I hope that

---

12 For an excellent treatment, see Pierre Duhem, *La Théorie physique: Son Objet, sa structure* (Paris: Vrin, 1997), 358. Unfortunately, Duhen is unaware of Newton's "Treatise."

the combined effect of the contributions by Mercer, Hanley, Hübner, Sayre-McCord, and the related Reflections inspire scholars of early-modern philosophy to explore the ways in which variants of sympathy cross the more familiar divisions among empiricists and rationalists or experimentalists and speculative philosophers of the period.[13]

---

[13] I thank Christia Mercer, Nicole Osborne, Sandrine Berges, David M. Levy, Charles Wolfe, Kathryn Pogin, Daniel Schneider, Michael Deckard, and Sorana Corneanu for comments on earlier drafts. Special thanks to René Brouwer for assistance with Greek. In addition, I have benefited from suggestions by Farah Focquart, Remy Debes, Sharon Spaulding, Alva Noë, and Jason Stanley. The usual caveats apply.

CHAPTER ONE

Stoic Sympathy

René Brouwer

1. Introduction

Explanations of the causes of sympathy or "common feeling" can be fascinating. Here is a recent one, offered by the Dutch-American primatologist Frans de Waal: "The way our bodies are influenced by surrounding bodies is one of the mysteries of human existence, but one that provides the glue that holds entire societies together. It is also one of the most underestimated phenomena, especially in disciplines that view humans as rational decision makers.... We occupy nodes within a tight network that connects all of us in both body and mind."[1] For de

---

[1] Frans de Waal, *The Age of Empathy* (New York: Harmony Books, 2009), 63. Since de Waal speaks of empathy, a terminological remark is appropriate here. The distinction between sympathy and empathy is blurred. See, e.g., Douglas Chismar, "Empathy and Sympathy: The Important Difference," *Journal of Value Inquiry* 22 (1988): 257–66, an attempt to disentangle the two. For de Waal sympathy differs from empathy in the sense that sympathy would be "proactive," with the purpose of improving someone's situation; empathy is the process by which we gather information about someone else (see de Waal, *Empathy*, 88, cf. Stephen Darwall, "Empathy, Sympathy, Care," *Philosophical Studies*

Waal this mystery is solved in terms of blind bodily attractions, which he calls "preconcerns." To these preconcerns layers of complexity are added by learning and intelligence, and so—still according to de Waal—we arrive at what is usually understood by sympathy.

In this chapter I go back to some of the earliest naturalistic accounts of sympathy that can be found in the Greco-Roman classical tradition. As I show, de Waal's account, which he summarizes as "bodily connections come first—understanding follows" (72), bears clear similarities to the conception of sympathy as it made its debut in the history of thought, that is as referring to interactions or coaffections that have a natural cause. I pay attention to some early occurrences of sympathy, starting out with its tentative use by Plato and Aristotle (section 2), before moving on to the more elaborate accounts in the Hellenistic period (section 3). By then both Epicurus and the Stoics assigned an important role to sympathy. Epicurus uses sympathy in his account of the relation between body and soul. Cleanthes, the second head of the Stoic school, does so, too, but above all the Stoics apply sympathy to the world as a whole. It is here that sympathy, as a "cosmological" notion, obtains the widest possible scope. In section 4 I discuss two topics related to this cosmic understanding of sympathy: the first, divination, is in the ancient sources standardly connected with sympathy, the other, cosmopolitanism, foreshadows its modern usage.

2. Plato and Aristotle

In one of his dialogues Plato (c. 429–347 BCE) makes a first hesitant reference to sympathy. In the *Charmides*, Socrates, Charmides, and Critias search for the definition of "moderation" (*sophrosunē*). In the manner typical for a Socratic dialogue, in which Socrates's interlocutor proposes a definition, which will turn out to be deficient, in the *Charmides*

89.2–3 (1998): 261–82, at 261). As we will see, the classical use of sympathy is closer to his understanding of empathy.

Socrates and Critias arrive at a deadlock or aporia, too. This is how Plato's Socrates describes what happens: "Now when Critias heard this and saw me at a loss—just as those people who see people yawning opposite them are suffering with them [*sumpaschousin*] in the same manner, so he appeared to be compelled by me being at a loss and to be drawn into a state of loss himself" (169C). In discussing a proposed definition of moderation Socrates is in his characteristic manner at a loss: he finds out that the proposal cannot stand a critical examination. By hearing and seeing Socrates, Critias arrives "sympathetically" at the same aporetic state. Typical for Plato, there is a subtle irony involved here: whereas Socrates's aporia is the result of his awareness that the definition of moderation must be wrong, Critias's state of confusion has another cause. Plato's Socrates compares Critias's getting into this state with the urge to yawn that is brought about by seeing others yawning. Plato's use of the word "compelling" suggests that Critias's being at a loss has a cause beyond his control. As we will see, this explanation of sympathy in terms of an involuntary cause, or perhaps better in terms of a physiological reaction, is an important characteristic in the ancient interpretation of this phenomenon.

Whereas Plato used this conception of sympathy only in passing, in one of the chapters of the *Problems* traditionally ascribed to Aristotle (384–322 BCE) sympathy is the main topic. Of course, in modern times Aristotle's authorship of the *Problems* has been problematized.[2] In antiquity, however, the work was attributed to Aristotle, as for example in the second century CE by Aulus Gellius, *Attic Nights*, at 19.4. Nowadays the common view is that Aristotle started writing the work, and that after his death some of his texts were reworked and new material was added.[3] The chapter on sympathy is thought to

---

2 For an overview see Pierre Louis, ed., *Aristote: Problèmes* (Paris: Les Belles Lettres, 1991), 1.xxii–xxiii.
3 See Louis, *Problèmes*, 1.xxvi–xxvii; Robert Mayhew, trans., *Aristotle: Problems: Books 1–19* (Cambridge, MA.: Loeb, 2011), xxi. However, Hellmut Flashar, *Aristoteles: Problemata physica* (Berlin: Akademie Verlag 1991), 356–57, argues for the post-Aristotelian origins of the work, placing it in the third century BCE.

belong to its earliest parts. According to some scholars, Aristotle would even have written this chapter while still working with Plato in the Academy.[4] It is indeed remarkable that "Aristotle" among the many examples that he discusses under the heading of sympathy starts off with the phenomenon that we encountered in the *Charmides*, yawning in response to others' yawning (at 7.1–3, 6). Another example Aristotle includes is the urge to pass urine in the vicinity of water, to which, perhaps in a later edition, the variant of urinating together is added, which should remind us of the fact that at least from the Hellenistic period onward this social activity was institutionalized in the form of multiseated latrines, and later brought to perfection by the Romans.[5] Other instances of sympathy are shuddering in response to unpleasant sounds (in section 5), as well as suffering when seeing others suffer (in section 7). As elsewhere in the *Problems*, these sympathetic occurrences are above all understood in a physiological manner.[6] A telling example is the explanation of shuddering in response to unpleasant sounds (7.5). These sounds, according to Aristotle, are rough breaths, which strike the roots of our hair. As they move in the opposite direction, they make the hairs stand upright. The thrust of these examples will be clear: under the heading of sympathy Aristotle discusses a set of instances of a coaffection over which one has apparently no control and of which the cause is best set out in physiological terms.

For Aristotle, just as for Plato, these instances of coaffections are special cases: sympathy remains restricted to isolated phenomena. The place of sympathy changes radically with Epicurus and above all the Stoics, who both use "sympathy" in a systematic way.

---

4 See already Émile Egger, *Essai sur l'histoire de la critique chez les Grecs* (Paris: Durand, 1850), 128; Louis, *Problèmes*, xxviii–xxxix.
5 See Gemma C. M. Jansen, Ann Olga Koloski-Ostrow, and Eric M. Moormann, eds., *Roman Toilets* (Leuven: Peeters, 2011), 131–34.
6 See Mayhew, *Problems*, xxii.

3. Epicurus and the Stoics

Epicurus (341–270 BCE) discusses sympathy in two contexts: in his account of perception as well as with regard to the nature of the soul. First, in his account of perception, which can be found in his *Letter to Herodotus*, Epicurus uses the term "sympathies."[7] An external object at high speed throws out a thin outer layer of atoms and thus brings about an image of these external objects in us. This would in turn bring sympathies or coaffections back to the external objects. Epicurus does not further elaborate on the coaffections, and their exact role remains thus unclear: for example, does Epicurus refer to the affections created by the image in us, or to the change in the external objects themselves?[8] The second context in which Epicurus uses sympathy is in his discussion of the corporeal nature of the soul. A bit further in the *Letter to Herodotus*, at Diogenes Laertius 10.64 (LS 14A), Epicurus asserts that the soul, like the body, is corporeal, consisting of fine particles going through the rest of the body, which makes affinity between soul and the rest of the body possible. Again the precise details remain obscure. What is clear here, however, is that Epicurus uses sympathy in the context of his mechanistic particle physics, and uses it to explain perception as well as the interaction between body and soul.[9]

It is also in the context of the relation between body and soul that one of the first extant references to sympathy in Stoicism occurs. As any discussion of Stoicism ought to emphasize, what is left over of one of the most influential schools of thought in antiquity are scattered references in later authors, often hostile to Stoic doctrine. Only from

---

7 The letter survived in Diogenes Laertius's *Lives of Eminent Philosophers*, 10.35–83. "Sympathies" is mentioned at 48 (LS 15A). On Diogenes Laertius see *infra*, section 3.
8 According to Anthony A. Long and David N. Sedley, *The Hellenistic Philosophers* (Cambridge: Cambridge University Press, 1987), vol. 1, 76, the interactions relate to the changes in the external objects, which would affect the impressions, too. According to Lucretius, *On the Nature of Things* 3.168–70 (LS 14B), the coaffections are in fact caused in the mind.
9 See also Christof Rapp, "Interaction of Body and Soul: What the Hellenistic Philosophers Saw and Aristotle Avoided," in *Common to Body and Soul*, ed. Richard A. H. King (Berlin: De Gruyter, 2006), 186–208, at 188–92.

the "late" Stoics, who lived between four and six centuries after the school had been founded, such as Seneca (4 BCE/1 CE–65), Epictetus (second half of the first century CE), or Marcus Aurelius (121–80), have complete treatises come down to us.[10] With regard to the early Stoics we should thus always keep in mind that any account of their doctrines is above all a reconstruction based on second- or third-hand sources from authors writing on the Stoics.[11] Important non-Stoic sources include Cicero, Diogenes Laertius, Sextus Empiricus, and Alexander of Aphrodisias.

The first Stoic explicitly brought in connection with sympathy is Cleanthes (331–232 BCE), the second head of the school. There is a preliminary point that needs to be emphasized in relation to this passage. If Cleanthes already used the term, sympathy should not be considered as a new doctrine added to Stoicism by the "middle" Stoic Posidonius (around 90 BCE), as an influential modern commentator argued.[12] In fact, in Edelstein and Kidd's collection of what has remained of his wide-ranging scholarship there is little that suggests that sympathy is a typically "Posidonian" topic. In his *On Divination*, at 2.33–5 (fr. 106.26, Edelstein and Kidd), Cicero (106–43 BCE) brings sympathy in connection with Posidonius, but not without mentioning the early Stoics Chrysippus (c. 280–207) and Antipater (second century BCE), too; otherwise Posidonius is explicitly mentioned in relation to sympathy in a discussion of the explanation of the tides, in a crude Latin translation of a sixth-century treatise, written by Priscianus Lydus, a pupil of Damascius, the last head of Plato's Academy before it was closed on the orders of Emperor Justinian.[13] It thus seems safe to conclude that sympathy is a common Stoic doctrine held from the early Stoics onward, a

---

10 Epictetus is a special case: he left us his short *Manual*. Otherwise we possess notes of his lectures made by his student Arrian, in English usually referred to as the *Dissertations*.

11 Useful collections of these sources include *SVF* for the early Stoics, *FDS* for Stoic logic, Alesse for the "middle" Stoic Panaetius of Rhodes, and Edelstein and Kidd for the middle Stoic Posidonius of Apameia. For the abbreviations see the list at the beginning of the bibliography.

12 See Karl Reinhardt, *Kosmos und Sympathie* (Munich: Beck, 1926), 111–15.

13 Fr. 219.18, Edelstein and Kidd.

conclusion confirmed by the simple fact that most of our extant sources attribute sympathy to the Stoics in general.

Cleanthes's account survived in the treatise *On the Nature of Man*, written by Bishop Nemesius of Emesa toward the end of the fourth century CE.[14] As the title of his book indicates, Nemesius's focus is on the nature of man, and it is in chapter 2 that he offers an account of various pagan views. Here Nemesius pays considerable attention to Cleanthes's views, of whom he records a syllogism, a favorite way by which the early heads of the Stoic school presented and justified their doctrines.[15] The syllogism goes like this: only bodies are affected by each other. The soul "is affected" (*sumpaschei*) by the body, when for example the body is sick or being cut. Also, and here Cleanthes uses *sumpaschei* again, is the body affected by the soul, so that when the soul feels shame or fear, the body turns red and pale respectively. Cleanthes's conclusion is that the soul is thus corporeal, too.[16] Even if in this argument sympathy plays only a subordinate role, in order to prove the corporeality of the soul, it does make clear that Cleanthes used the term with some emphasis, and that like Epicurus he did so in the context of the interaction between body and soul.

Both Epicurus and Cleanthes thus make sympathy play a constructive role in their understanding of the corporeal nature of the soul. But here their agreement ends. Whereas Epicurus explains the nature of the interaction between body and soul in mechanical terms as a relation between atomic particles, for Cleanthes, or the Stoics in general, the interaction is one of complete pervasion. A second difference between

---

14 For a translation with extensive notes, see Robert W. Sharples and Philip J. van der Eijk, trans., *Nemesius: On the Nature of Man* (Liverpool: Liverpool University Press, 2008).

15 See p. 21.6–9 Morani (*SVF* 1.518; LS 45C). For the syllogisms of Zeno of Citium (335–263 BCE), the founder of the school, see Malcolm Schofield, "The Syllogisms of Zeno of Citium," *Phronesis* 28 (1983): 31–58; for Cleanthes see Malcolm Schofield, *The Stoic Idea of the City*, 2nd ed. (Chicago: University of Chicago Press, 1999), 130–35.

16 Tertullian, *On the Soul* 5 (*SVF* 1.518), offers a Latin translation of the argument, in which the reference to sympathy appears in the manuscripts as *passionum commutatione*. Modern editors, puzzled by the expression, suggested either *communicatione* (von Arnim), or *communione* (Waszink). On the argument see further Heinrich Dörrie, *Porphyrios' "Symmikta zetemata"* (Munich: Beck, 1959), 134–36.

Epicurus and the Stoics relates to the scope of the application of the notion of sympathy: for Epicurus sympathy plays a role in the context of his psychology, whereas for the Stoics sympathy is above all a feature of the world as a whole. In the remainder of this chapter I focus on the Stoics' cosmological understanding of sympathy, first by presenting the evidence on how broadly they understood the scope of sympathy, and second by setting out their explanation for this interconnection.

In a text by Alexander of Aphrodisias, a commentator on Aristotle's works living in the second century CE who was hostile toward Stoic doctrine, we find that Chrysippus "first holds that the whole...is sympathetic with itself [*sumpathes hautōi*]."[17] In a text that survived in the corpus of the biographer and philosopher Plutarch (50–120), but which is considered spurious, this Stoic doctrine can be found, too: "The world...is in sympathy with itself [*sumpathē hautōi*]."[18] In the second place, and this should perhaps be considered an implication of the first doctrine that sympathy is a feature of the world itself, the Stoics maintain that the entities within the world are in sympathy with each other. The point is made explicitly by the Stoic Cleomedes (second century CE), who at the beginning of his treatise *The Heaven* speaks of "sympathy of the parts in the cosmos for each other."[19] The most common examples of sympathy in the world that are given in our sources deal with the interaction between heaven and earth. In the account that survived via the skeptic Sextus Empiricus (probably second century CE) some typical examples can be found, in which the sun, the moon, and the stars are said to exercise their influence over the earth:

> The world exhibits sympathies: in accordance with the waxings and wanings of the moon many sea and land animals wane and wax, and

---

17 See *On Mixture* 216.14–16 (*SVF* 2.473; LS 48C).
18 Ps.-Plutarch, *On Fate* 574D (*SVF* 2.912).
19 See 1.1.13 Ziegler/Todd (not in *SVF*), cf. 1.1.69–71 (*SVF* 2.534). Alan C. Bowen and Robert B. Todd, trans., *Cleomedes' Lectures on Astronomy* (Berkeley: University of California Press, 2004) offer a modern translation with commentary.

ebb and flood occur in some parts of the sea. And in the same way, too, in accordance with certain risings and settings of the stars alterations in the surrounding atmosphere and all varieties of change in the air take place, sometimes for the better, but sometimes fraught with pestilence.[20]

In *On the Nature of the Gods*, at 2.19 (not in *SVF*), Cicero, in his typical, rhetorical style, offers the Stoic examples as follows:

Furthermore, who will this continuous, harmonious, and united connection between things [*rerum consentiens, conspirans, continuata cognatio*] not force to agree with the things said by me? Could otherwise the earth at one time blossom, then again be rigidly barren, or, while so many things themselves change, the lengthening and shortening of the days at the summer and winter solstices be recognized, or the tides of the sea and the narrow straits be moved by the rising and setting of the moon, or the diverse courses of the stars be maintained in the encompassing rotation of the entire heaven?

Most of the examples are related to the influence of the heaven on earth, but some with regard to interactions on earth are extant, too. One of these, yet again preserved by Cicero, is the striking of the "strings of a lyre" (*nervi in fidibus*), which makes other strings sound.[21] Another is the influence of climate on health, and even mental strength, and is ascribed to Chrysippus: since the air quality in Athens is better than in Thebes, the Athenians are sharp witted, and the Thebans stupid, but strong.[22]

How did the Stoics explain both forms of sympathy? For that we need to turn to the two principles of Stoic physics. Our fullest exposition of

---

20 *Against the Professors* 9.79 (*SVF* 2.1013).
21 *On Divination* 2.33 (*SVF* 2.1211).
22 *On Fate* 7 (*SVF* 2.950; LS 55Q).

Stoic physics can be found in the compendium known under the title *Lives of Eminent Philosophers*, by Diogenes Laertius, who probably lived in the third century CE.[23] At 7.134 (*SVF* 1.85; LS 44B) Diogenes Laertius starts off his account of Stoic physics with these two principles, "the active" (*to poioun*) and "the passive" (*to paschon*). The passive principle the Stoics described as "matter," or "substance without quality." The active principle, which the Stoics held to be corporeal, too, was identified with "reason" (*logos*), but they gave it a host of other names, too. In the account in Diogenes Laertius, these other names for the active principle include "god," "Zeus," "intellect," and "fate," and elsewhere he adds "providence,"[24] whereas in other sources than Diogenes Laertius "law" is included, too.[25] The active principle is mixed with the passive principle, and in this way the cosmos is formed. The Stoics explained this process of mixture in terms of an all-pervasive "breath" (*pneuma*), by which reason can permeate matter.[26] With the help of this notion of breath the Stoics were able to explain the diversity in the world as well as the unity of the world.[27]

Let us first take a closer look at diversity. In materialist terms the Stoics identified the active principle in its purest form with a special kind of fire, which they called "creative fire" (*pur technikon*) and distinguished from ordinary, destructive fire.[28] Through condensation fire

---

23 For the Greek text of Diogenes Laertius see now the splendid version edited by Tiziano Dorandi, *Diogenes Laertius: Lives of Eminent Philosophers* (Cambridge: Cambridge University Press, 2013). For modern discussions of Stoic physics see David N. Sedley, "Stoic Physics and Metaphysics," in *The Cambridge History of Hellenistic Philosophy*, ed. Keimpe A. Algra et al. (Cambridge: Cambridge University Press, 1999), 382–411; David Furley, "Cosmology," in *The Cambridge History of Hellenistic Philosophy*, ed. Keimpe A. Algra et al. (Cambridge: Cambridge University Press, 1999), 412–51; Michael J. White, "Stoic Natural Philosophy (Physics and Cosmology)," in *The Cambridge Companion to the Stoics*, ed. Brad Inwood (Cambridge: Cambridge University Press, 2003), 124–52.
24 Diogenes Laertius 7.138 (*SVF* 2.634; LS 47O), with reference to Chrysippus, *On Providence*.
25 Plutarch, *On the Fortune of Alexander* 329B (*SVF* 1.262; LS 67A), Chrysippus, *On Law*, which survived in Emperor Justinian's *Digest* 1.3.2 (*SVF* 3.314; LS 67R).
26 Sextus Empiricus, *Against the Professors* 9.78–80 (*SVF* 2.1013); Alexander of Aphrodisias, *On Mixture* 216.14–28 (*SVF* 2.473).
27 See further Valéry Laurand, "La sympathie universelle: Union et séparation," in *Les Stoïciens et le monde*, ed. Thomas Bénatouïl and Pierre-Marie Morel (Paris: Presses universitaires de France, 2005), 517–35.
28 Preserved in Stobaeus's fifth-century anthology, at 1.213.15–21 (*SVF* 1.120; LS 46D).

dissolves into air, then water, and "still more compressed" into earth.[29] The mixtures of these elements can account for the different entities in the world, with each entity consisting of a particular mixture of the active element and the passive elements.[30] The Stoics discerned five different basic levels of mixtures among the entities in the world. On the lowest level of this scale of nature, furthest removed from the highest level of fiery breath, the mixture results in the level called "tenor" (*hexis*), with stones as the standard example. One level up, with a bit more of the active breath, plants can be found. With regard to plants the active principle manifests itself in matter as "nature" (*phusis*), or the "power to grow." It is this characteristic that distinguishes plants from stones. On the third level, that of living beings, breath manifests itself in the characteristic of "soul" (*psuchē*), which brings the power to perceive and to act, whereas with regard to human beings at a particular age this soul becomes rational (level 4), which brings the power of reason. Finally, on the highest level we find entities that are in possession of perfect reason, notably gods and sages.[31]

With their doctrine of breath in matter the Stoics not only explained the diversity in the world, they also made it account for its unity. The passages by Alexander of Aphrodisias and ps.-Plutarch, which we encountered already above, can now be quoted in full:

> [Chrysippus] first holds that the whole is unified by a breath [*pneuma*], which pervades it completely, and by which the universe is held together and stabilized and is sympathetic with itself. (Alexander of Aphrodisias, *On Mixture* 216.14–16)

> The world is governed by nature, is breathing [*sumpnous*], and is in sympathy with itself. (ps.-Plutarch, *On Fate* 574D)

---

29 Stobaeus 1.129.2–30.13 (*SVF* 2.413; LS 47A).

30 The position of air is ambiguous: in some sources, e.g. Nemesius, *On the Nature of Man* 52.19–20 (*SVF* 2.418; LS 47D), air is presented as an active element too.

31 See further René Brouwer, *The Stoic Sage* (Cambridge: Cambridge University Press, 2014), 72–73.

The sympathy of the world with itself is thus explained in terms of "breathing" or "breath." This is also how Cicero's Stoic spokesman Balbus in *On the Nature of the Gods* 2.19, put it, in the continuation of the passage already quoted above: "What is certain is that these processes could not take place through harmonious activity in all parts of the universe, unless they were pervaded by one single, divine, all-pervading breath [*uno divino et continuato spiritu*]." The underlying explanation is apparently that the Stoics considered the world itself as a living being, with its breath as the force that pervades it, as Diogenes Laertius at 7.142–43 (*SVF* 2.633) has it: "The doctrine that the world is a living being, rational, animate and intelligent, is laid down by Chrysippus in the first book of his treatise *On Providence,* by Apollodorus in his *Physics,* and by Posidonius." For this doctrine the Stoics could fall back on respectable thinkers like Heraclitus (around 500 BCE) as well as Plato, especially in the *Timaeus* 34B and the *Laws,* book 10.

The notion of sympathy is closely related to the Stoics' understanding of causation, fate and providence. Although this cannot be the place to deal with these notions in detail, a brief comparison between each of these notions on the one hand and sympathy on the other may be helpful to elucidate Stoic sympathy somewhat further. Just as "fire" and "reason," so "fate," "providence," and "sympathy" relate to a different aspect of the active principle. The active principle is the ultimate cause, which diversifies into various different bodily causes along with the pervading breath of the universe. "Fate" (*heimarmenē*) can thus be explained as the chain of causes.[32] The metaphor "chain," however, is somewhat misleading. It might make us think of the simpler "mechanical" understanding of causation in terms of events, as in event A is the cause of event B, whereas what the Stoics had in mind is causation in the sense of bodily interaction. The standard example that survived in Sextus Empiricus, *Against the Professors* 9.211 (*SVF* 2.341; LS 55B), is of

---

32 See Cicero, *On Fate* 11–13 (*SVF* 2.945–46). However, sometimes "fate" is simply identified with the active principle. See e.g. Stobaeus 1.79.1 (*SVF* 2.913): "Fate is a pneumatic power [δύναμιν πηευματικήν] governing the order of the whole."

the knife cutting the flesh: according to the Stoics, the knife is the cause to the flesh being cut, rather than that the event of the cutting causes the effect of the incision of the flesh.[33] The other Stoic image of a "web" (*sumplokē* or *epiplokē*) of interacting bodily causes is hence more appropriate.[34] Providence brings out yet another aspect of the active principle. It refers to the divine, overall plan, according to which the series of causes is brought about.[35] Human beings with their rational faculties are in principle able to discover this divine plan, or at least that part that is relevant to them. In practice, however, they fall back on notions like luck or fortune. With everything in the world determined and planned for, luck or fortune cannot play a substantial role in Stoicism. Only human beings to whom the course of things are as of yet unclear fall back on fortune or luck, whereas human beings who did gain full insight into the course of the divine breath are able to explain this course in terms of interconnected causes.[36] In short: fate, providence, and sympathy all bring out a particular aspect of the active principle. Providence relates to the overall divine plan, and fate to the aspect of the web of causes, whereas sympathy brings out the physical interconnectedness of the world with itself and the entities in it.[37]

The Stoic doctrine of cosmic sympathy had considerable influence in antiquity, as Plotinus's engagement with it shows.[38] The origins of

---

33 See Susan Sauvé-Meyer, "Chain of Causes: What Is Stoic Fate?" in *God and Cosmos in Stoicism*, ed. Riccardo Salles (Oxford: Oxford University Press, 2009), 71–90, esp. 76–77.

34 συμπλοκή is used in ps-Plutarch, *On the Opinions of the Philosophers* 885A (*SVF* 2.976); ἐπιπλοκή is in Aulus Gellius, *Attic Nights* 7.2.3 (*SVF* 2.1000; LS 55K).

35 See Calcidius (fourth century CE), *Commentary on the Timaeus* 183.6–14 Waszink (*SVF* 2.933; LS 54U).

36 See René Brouwer, "Polybius on Stoic *tyche*," *Greek, Roman, and Byzantine Studies* 51 (2011): 111–32; Jan Opsomer, "Virtue, Fortune, and Happiness in Theory and Practice," in *Virtues for the People*, ed. Geert Roskam and Luc Van der Stockt (Leuven: Peeters, 2011), 151–73.

37 See Myrto Dragona-Monachou, *The Stoic Arguments for the Existence and the Providence of the Gods* (Athens: University of Athens, 1976), 287; and R. Jim Hankinson, "Stoicism, Science, and Divination," *Apeiron* 21.2 (1988): 123–60, at 149.

38 While rejecting the immanentism of the Stoics' single force, and offering the transcendentalist hierarchy of the one, the intellect, and the world soul instead, Plotinus would make sympathy (and divination) a characteristic of the world soul only, the last and lowest level on this scheme. See chapter 2 *infra*.

this remarkable theory are far less clear. They can perhaps be found in the reflection on the relation between the human body and soul. Above we already saw how Cleanthes used sympathy in this context. The inference appears to have been that a relation similar to the one between the human body and the human soul should exist in the world too.[39] A passage that supports such an explanation survived in Diogenes Laertius 7.143 (*SVF* 2.633; LS 53X): "The world [*kosmos*] is a living thing in the sense of an animate substance endowed with sensation; for animal is better than non-animal, and nothing is better than the world, *ergo* the world is a living being. And it is endowed with soul, as is clear from our several souls being each a fragment of it." Just as in Cleanthes's syllogism, with which we started out, the human body is affected by the human soul (and vice versa), so, we may infer, cosmic matter is affected by the world soul. The origin of the doctrine of sympathetic interaction in the world would thus have to be found in the parallel between human being and world, or between micro- and macrocosm.

4. Divination and Cosmopolitanism

With the Stoics sympathy became thus above all a feature of the world. For human beings cosmic sympathy obviously plays a role too, if only because they live in this interconnected world. As we have already seen, the position of human beings in this world is special: different from all other entities in the world, apart from the gods that is, human beings can participate on the highest levels on the scale of nature, since they develop reason in themselves (or, in the Stoics' materialist terms, a spark of fire).

With a system of thought that is as integrated as that of the Stoics, it will not be possible to elaborate on all possible aspects of the role of sympathy with regard to human beings. Here I like to highlight divination and cosmopolitanism. Divination is in relation to sympathy one

---

39 "This most dubious step," as Long and Sedley, *Hellenistic Philosophers*, vol. 1, 287, formulate it.

of the most discussed topics in the sources. Although this is different for cosmopolitanism (the sources simply do not explicitly discuss sympathy in relation to it), the connection can nevertheless be made, and this allows us to reflect on the relation between Stoic cosmic sympathy and the modern use of sympathy as common feeling.

For the modern reader divination is perhaps the most intriguing topic the Stoics bring up in relation to their theory that the world and the parts in it are in sympathy. To begin with, we should be aware of the fact that for the ancients divination was part of everyday life,[40] and that the Stoics dealt with this fact of life, too.[41] The Stoic definition, transmitted via Cicero's *On Divination*, our most important source on Stoic divination, is "the prediction and presentiment of things that are thought to occur by luck."[42] As we have seen, for the Stoics the relations between things cannot be a matter of luck, but of sympathy. Divination is based on this interconnectedness: specific signs can be understood as tokens on the basis of which the future course of the divine breath in matter can be predicted. In Greek antiquity these signs are traditionally oracles and dreams,[43] and those indeed the Stoics relate to their doctrine of natural connectedness. In his *On Dreams* Chrysippus offers us an amusing example. According to Chrysippus, someone who dreams of an egg may well be the lucky winner of a jackpot, since this dream could indicate that a treasure consisting of gold and silver (referring to the yoke and the white of the egg respectively) is buried under

---

[40] See Sarah I. Johnston, *Ancient Greek Divination* (Oxford: Wiley-Blackwell, 2008); as well as Sarah I. Johnston and Peter T. Struck, eds., *Mantikê: Studies in Ancient Greek Divination* (Leiden: Brill, 2005).

[41] See esp. Friedrich Pfeffer, *Studien zur Mantik in der Philosophie der Antike* (Meisenheim am Glan: Hain, 1976), 43–112; David Wardle, *Cicero: On Divination Book 1* (Oxford: Oxford University Press, 2006).

[42] See 1.9. Cf. Chrysippus's definition in the traditional terms of gods and men at *On Divination* 2.130 (*SVF* 2.1189), as "the power to understand, see and explain the signs, which the gods give to human beings."

[43] Next to these natural types of divination the Romans, mainly under the influence of the Etruscans, would add some more technical types of divination, like examining entrails (haruspicy) and bird watching (auspicy). For the distinction see Cicero, *On Divination* 1.34 (not in *SVF*; LS 42C).

the bed of the dreamer.[44] The connection between sympathy and the interpretation of this particular dream is explicitly made in the (critical) comments Cicero presents at *On Divination* 2.142 (not in *SVF*):

> Is there some such natural interconnectedness [*continuatio coniunctioque naturae*], which, as I said before, the Greeks call *sumpatheia*, that the finding of a treasure must be deduced from dreaming of an egg?... But by which natural connection [*naturalis cognatio*] are treasures, legacies, honours, victory, and many other things of the same kind connected with dreams?

The indignant tone makes clear that the predictability of future events based on sympathy in the world was a controversial issue. Already in antiquity the Stoics were heavily criticized for it: the critics apparently turned their attention not so much to the underlying doctrine of cosmic sympathy (which they may have accepted for the sake of argument), but rather to the idea that the traditional signs could be interpreted as signs of sympathy, which they rejected.[45] Even among the Stoics themselves the status of divination became a contentious issue. Whereas early Stoics, like Zeno, Cleanthes, and Chrysippus, accepted it,[46] Panaetius declared it "unsupported" (*anupostaton*).[47] The precise nature of Panaetius's criticism is difficult to assess, however: does "unsupported" mean that Panaetius rejected divination full stop, or did he rather consider divination useless for nonperfect human beings, since the interpretations of dreams and oracles in this web of causes could in fact only by performed by perfect human beings?[48] If the former, Panaetius would

---

44 See Cicero, *On Divination* 2.134 (*SVF* 2.1201).
45 See Cicero, *On Divination* 2.33 (*SVF* 2.1211), *On the Nature of the Gods* 3.28 (not in *SVF*).
46 See Diogenes Laertius 7.149 (*SVF* 2.1191); Cicero, *On Divination* 1.6 (*SVF* 1.173, 2.1187).
47 See (again) Diogenes Laertius 7.149 (fr. 139 Alesse); cf. Cicero, *On Divination* 2.89 (fr. 140 Alesse), and *Lucullus* 107 (fr. 136 Alesse).
48 As Cicero takes his arguments against astrology from Panaetius too (see his *On Divination* 2.87–98, fr. 140), Francesca Alesse, ed., *Panezio di Rodi: Testimonianze* (Naples: Bibliopolis, 1997), 269, argues for the former. However, Panaetius often takes the stance that the early Stoics focus on the as of yet

have distanced himself from the early Stoics; if the latter, Panaetius would still have agreed with the founders of his school, who in their usual austere fashion indeed declared that only a human being who has brought his reason to perfection can be a true diviner.[49]

Here we touch on an aspect of Stoicism that cannot be stressed enough: all ordinary human beings have reason, after it has naturally developed in each of them between the age of seven and fourteen years.[50] However, this rational faculty is not yet perfect. Each human being will have to develop this faculty further in order to bring it to perfection. Whereas in principle perfection is possible, in practice the many "perversions" around (*diastrophai*; see Diogenes Laertius 7.89 [*SVF* 3.228]) prevent this from happening.[51] Panaetius concludes from this that in cases where this high-level perfection cannot be achieved, it is best to concentrate on "perfection" at a lower level. It is at this lower level that the influential notion of *humanitas* kicks in, picked up and developed by Cicero, the idea that all human beings as rational beings, without being sages, share this characteristic of reason and on this basis form a community of mankind.[52]

This brings us to the second topic, the social implications of cosmic sympathy. The closest we can get to sympathy in relation to the affect of common feeling in Stoicism is cosmopolitanism, rather than "pity"

---

nonexistent sage, and that he therefore decided to resort to a second-rate type of perfection that can be applied to ordinary human being. See e.g. Cicero, *On Proper Functions* 1.146, 3.12 (fr. 75 Alesse), and cf. *On Friendship* 18. He might thus have argued that divination is useful for the sage, but not for those who like most of us have only limited insight into the interconnections in the world. See also Teun Tieleman, "Panaetius' Place in the History of Stoicism with Special Reference to His Moral Psychology," in *Pyrrhonists, Patricians, Platonizers*, ed. Anna-Maria Ioppolo and David N. Sedley (Naples: Bibliopolis, 2007), 103–41; and René Brouwer, "On the Ancient Background of Grotius's Notion of Natural Law," *Grotiana* 29 (2008): 1–24.

49 See Stobaeus 2.114.16–21 (*SVF* 3.605), *On Divination* 2.129 (*SVF* 3.607).
50 See Iamblichus (c. 245–c. 325), *On the Soul* as preserved in Stobaeus 1.317.21–24 (*SVF* 1.149, 2.835).
51 See on the achievability of perfection Brouwer, *Stoic Sage*, 92–135.
52 See Wolfgang Schadewaldt, "Humanitas romana," in *Aufstieg und Niedergang der römischen Welt*, 1.4, ed. Hildegard Temporini (Berlin: De Gruyter, 1973), 52–61; Ingo Gildenhard, *Creative Eloquence* (Oxford: Oxford University Press, 2011), 201–16.

(*eleos*), as is sometimes suggested.[53] For the Stoics pity is one of the "bad" emotions, a disease of the soul resulting from an incorrect response to a particular event.[54] (The incorrectness of the response here is of course measured by the standards of perfect reason.) Although the origin of cosmopolitanism can perhaps already be traced back to the sophist Hippias or to Socrates in the late fifth century BCE,[55] the Stoics played an important role in the history of its development. The term is clearly attested for the fourth-century Cynic Diogenes of Sinope,[56] who surely inspired the early Stoics on this point. They developed it in a manner that shows a close affinity to their naturalist understanding of sympathy, which comes out most clearly with regard to the sage. The sage participates on the highest level of the active principle, possessing as a perfectly rational human being that pure, undiluted fiery disposition. The sage's reason is fully in line with cosmic reason, or even an active part of it. Since becoming an active part of the cosmic process is all that matters, the life of a sage need not be a life with friends, as Seneca tells us: "What kind of life will the sage have, if he be left without friends? ... His life will be that of Jupiter, who, amid the dissolution of the world, when the gods are confounded together and nature rests for a space from her work, can retire into himself and give himself over to his own thoughts."[57] The sage's participation in this world order even has mystical overtones. Cleanthes compares the sage with an "initiate" (*telestēs*) into one of the mystery religions, someone who is

---

53 Margarita Kranz and Peter Probst, "Sympathie," in *Historisches Wörterbuch der Philosophie*, ed. Joachim Ritter, Karlfried Gründer, and Gottfried Gabriel, vol. 10 (Basel: Schwabe, 1998), 752.

54 See e.g. Cicero, *Tusculan Disputations* 4.18 (*SVF* 3.415), Lactantius (c. 240–c. 320), *Divine Institutions* 3.23 (*SVF* 1.213).

55 Eric Brown, "Socrates the Cosmopolitan," *Stanford Agora: An Online Journal of Legal Perspectives* 1 (2000): 74–87, accessed 15 July 2013, http://agora.stanford.edu/agora/issue1/index.html; Max Hossenfelder, "Oikeiosis," in *Der Neue Pauly*, ed. Hubert Cancik and Helmuth Schneider, vol. 8 s.v. (Leiden: Brill, 2003).

56 Diogenes Laertius 6.63 (fr. 335 Giannantoni); cf. Marie-Odile Goulet-Cazé, "Un Syllogisme stoïcien sur la loi dans la doxographie de Diogène le Cynique: À propos de Diogène Laërce VI 72," *Rheinisches Museum* 125 (1982): 214–40; Marie-Odile Goulet-Cazé, *L'ascèse cynique* (Paris: Vrin, 1986).

57 Seneca, *Letters* 9.16 (*SVF* 2.1065; LS 40O); cf. Mario Vegetti, *L'etica degli antichi*, 4th ed. (Rome: Laterza, 1996), 288.

"filled with the divine,"[58] whereas Chrysippus compares discovering the final truth on the gods as initiations "when the soul has found its stability, is in control and is capable of keeping silent towards the uninitiated."[59] However, if there are any sages, and more than one, they will affect each other, as they are by their very nature also active particpants in the highest level of the breath permeating the world. The manner in which this happens is literally far-reaching. This is how Plutarch in *On Common Conceptions* 1068F (*SVF* 3.627) states it: "If a single sage anywhere extends his finger prudently, all the sages throughout the world will benefit. This is the work of their friendship, into which the virtues of the sages for their common benefit end."[60] Sages related in this way are therefore also said to form a community, a Stoic doctrine preserved by Arius Didymus (first century CE), a philosopher and presumably also adviser to Augustus: "A community exists amongst them, because they participate in reason, that is the law by nature."[61] A similar formulation can be found in ps.-Plutarch, *On Homer* 119 (not in *SVF*): "This is the familiar doctrine of the Stoics, that there is one cosmos, in which by nature gods and men rule together participating in justice."[62] Note the expression "to rule" here, a clear reference to the highest level of the active principle. The Stoics' ideal community of sages thus does not refer to a political utopia in the sense of a group of sages that set up and form a community together.[63] Once a human being will have perfected his or her own rational capacities, he or she will

---

58 See Epiphanius of Salamis (fourth century CE), *On Faith* 9.41, p. 508.25–28 Holl (*SVF* 1.538).
59 *Etymologicum magnum* 751.16–22, col. 2108 Gaisford (*SVF* 2.1008; *FDS* 650).
60 See Hermann Diels, *Philodemus: Über die Götter. Drittes Buch, Erläuterung des Textes* (Berlin: Akademie der Wissenschaften, 1917), 7, who dryly noted that he considered this as "etwas abenteuerlich."
61 Arius Didymus on his turn is quoted by Eusebius (c. 260–339), *Preparation for the Gospel* 15.15.5 (*SVF* 2.528; LS 67L).
62 See also Philo of Alexandria (first half of the first century CE), *On the Creation of the World* 142–43 (*SVF* 3.336, 337).
63 See Dirk Obbink and Paul A. Vander Waerdt, "Diogenes of Babylon: The Stoic Sage in the City of Fools," *Greek, Roman and Byzantine Studies* 32 (1991): 355–96; Schofield, *City*, 64–92; Brouwer, *Stoic Sage*, 90 n. 128.

automatically become a "world citizen" (*kosmopolitēs*), participating on the highest level of being. If more human beings will have achieved perfection, by virtue of their virtuous disposition they will be part of a community of sages, however far removed they may be from each other.

For ordinary human beings, who have not (yet) achieved that highest level, the interconnectedness of the world and their place within this whole are experienced in a way that can be formulated in terms of the modern sense of sympathy or common feeling. As we have seen, human beings are special, in the sense that unique among the living beings they have their rational faculties. However, as explained above, whereas the initial development of the rational faculties occurs naturally, human beings need to develop these rational faculties further in order to bring these to perfection. The Stoics were keen to describe these natural and self-induced developments in terms of what they called "appropriation" (*oikeiōsis*), a term they coined. Containing the root *oikeios*, belonging to one's "house" (*oikos*), appropriation is best described as the process of discovering or ensuring that something belongs to oneself or is one's own (hence English translations as appropriation or familiarization).[64] For human beings various phases in this process can be discerned: for a human being who has not yet developed reason, such as a child (and therefore by the Stoics put on a par with an animal), one of the first things "according to nature" that this animal will discover as its own is itself, that is the impulse (*hormē*, or *inclinatio* in Latin) to preserve itself. Once the child develops a rational faculty, the process of appropriation becomes more complicated. The impulses will still present themselves, but can no longer be processed automatically: human beings will have to use their rational faculties in order to decide what to do with them, that is—in Stoic terminology—to assent to them or not. Again, according to the Stoics, all human beings

---

64 The literature on the Stoic interpretation of appropriation is vast. See Ilaria Ramelli, ed., and David Konstan, trans., *Hierocles the Stoic: Elements of Ethics, Fragments, and Excerpts* (Atlanta: Society of Biblical Literature, 2009), xxxii n. 33, for an overview (to which can be added Christopher Gill, "The Stoic Theory of Ethical Development: In What Sense Is Nature a Norm?" in *Was ist das für den Menschen Gute?*, ed. Jan Szaif and Matthias Lutz-Bachmann [Berlin: De Gruyter 2004], 101-25).

should in the end assent to those impulses that are in line with the course of the active principle that governs the world. In doing so they will gradually discover that they belong to different groups. In a passage from his *How to Behave towards Relatives*, Hierocles, a Stoic who lived in the second century CE, used a nowadays familiar image.[65] According to him, each of us is encompassed by a set of concentric circles, of which the innermost circle represents the impulse to self-preservation. The next one stands for family, and subsequent circles for friends, the particular community one lives in, and so on. The outermost circle represents the whole human race. If one were to find a place for sympathy in the modern sense of common feeling, then it it has to be found in relation to these circles that represent family, friends, and political community. Appropriation can thus be related to sympathy in the modern sense, as the process in which human beings slowly discover their common feelings toward other rational beings.

5. Conclusion

I have discussed the naturalist origins of sympathy, with sympathy first used to connote the relation between the human body and soul. The Stoics appear to have expanded this body-and-soul relationship, giving sympathy its broadest possible scope, making it into a feature of the natural world. According to the Stoics, it is because of the world soul that pervades all matter that the world itself and everything in it are in a state of interconnectedness. Although the modern sense of sympathy as common feeling is not explicitly made in this context, even here the Stoics can be said to have prefigured the modern sense: their view that human beings familiarize themselves with the world through circles of "sympathy" would prove to be a source of inspiration for later thinkers.[66]

---

65 The passage from *How to Behave towards Relatives* is preserved by Stobaeus, at 4.671.2–3.11 (LS 57G). Interestingly, at 671.6 (not in LS) Hierocles uses *sumpaschein*, but only in the sense of how this particular text is connected with an earlier text.

66 I would like to thank Eric Schliesser for organizing the stimulating colloquium on sympathy, its participants for their helpful contributions, and Peter Struck, Brooke Holmes, and (again) Eric Schliesser for encouragement and written comments.

CHAPTER TWO

Plotinus on *sympatheia*

Eyjólfur K. Emilsson

Plotinus (204/5–70 AD) was the founder of the late ancient variety of Platonism that usually is called "Neoplatonism," the dominating philosophical movement in the Graeco-Roman world in late antiquity. Plotinus and the other late ancient Platonists did not see themselves as "Neo-" something but simply as followers and systematizers of Plato's thought. Plotinus's Platonic predecessors had actually started attempts at such a systematization.[1] Hence, it is in many ways misleading to suggest that something quite new starts with Plotinus. This does, however, not change the fact that he was a very significant philosopher both in terms of his influence and the depth of his thought. Arguably, he was the next greatest Platonist ever, after Plato, and if we do not count Aristotle as a Platonist.[2]

---

[1] There is an insightful account of the development of imperial Platonism in George Karamanolis, *Plato and Aristotle in Agreement? Platonists on Aristotle from Antiochus to Porphyry* (Oxford: Oxford University Press, 2006).

[2] The ancient philosophers, especially those who came after Plotinus, did count Aristotle so; the case for this has recently been made by Lloyd P. Gerson, "What Is Platonism?" *Journal of the History of*

These late ancient Platonists deeply influenced early Christian thinkers both in the West and the East, indeed eventually Muslim thinkers as well. Their own works, however, were largely absent in the West during the Middle Ages. In the latter half of the fifteenth century, however, when these and other Greek texts became available and were translated and published, Plato and his late ancient followers became extremely popular in Europe. There is no question that they left marks on early modern thinkers such as Descartes, Spinoza, and Leibniz.

We possess a fairly reliable account of Plotinus's life and writings by his student, friend, and editor, Porphyry. The latter composed a biography, *On the Life of Plotinus and the Order of His Books*, which prefaced Porphyry's posthumous edition of Plotinus's writings. Plotinus wrote in Greek, which may, however, not have been his mother tongue. At the age of twenty-eight he begins his philosophical studies in Alexandria under a certain Ammonius (often called Ammonius Saccas) and studied with him for eleven years. In an attempt to acquaint himself with the philosophy of Persia and India, he joined the emperor Gordian on a campaign against the Persians. Gordian was murdered on the way and Plotinus escaped with difficulty (see *Life of Plotinus* 3). He settled in Rome at the age of forty, where he established a school of philosophy. He stayed in Rome for the rest of his life except during his final illness, when he retired to Campania (*Life of Plotinus* 2).

The extant corpus of Plotinus's writings is one of the largest we have of any ancient philosopher and presumably we possess everything he wrote. His works are treatises that grew out of discussions in his school and they vary greatly in length and scope. Porphyry arranged the treatises according to subject matter into six sets of nine treatises, that is, six "enneads" (an "ennead" is a set of nine). In order to arrive at this division he had to split some treatises. Conventionally, references to the *Enneads* are often given only in numbers: "V.3. (49) 2, 14–16," for instance, means

---

Philosophy 43.3 (2005): 253–76, and *Aristotle and Other Platonists* (Ithaca, NY: Cornell University Press, 2005).

"5th *Ennead*, 3rd treatise (which is number forty-nine on Porphyry's chronological list of Plotinus's writings), chapter 2, lines 14 to 16.[3]

1. Plotinus's Precursors

Plotinus's notion of *sympatheia* is commonly plainly said to be a borrowing from the Stoics.[4] This may need some qualification. The fact is that much of the background of *sympatheia* as Plotinus conceives of it is to be found in Plato's *Timaeus*—one of the most important dialogues for the late ancient Platonists. In that work Plato emphasizes that the physical world is animated by a World-Soul that renders it a unified and unique living being (*Tim.* 30 B–C; 37 C–D) of which the ordinary animal species are somehow parts. Human souls are made of the same stuff as this World-Soul, although somewhat more diluted, and are thus akin to the World-Soul (*Tim.* 41 D); Plato notes, moreover, that in fashioning the world, the Demiurge, the world maker, made the number of souls equal to the number of stars and assigned each soul to a star (*Tim.* 41 D–E). Thereby he suggests a connection between different parts of the universe, though he does not specify the nature or consequences of this assignment. I believe now that Plotinus saw his notion of *sympatheia* as a part of the Platonic heritage, mainly from the *Timaeus*. As in some other cases where the Stoics seem to build on and develop views expressed by Plato,[5] Plotinus is liable to turn to the Stoics

---

[3] References to Plato, Cicero, Galen, and Plotinus are standard references that are given in all serious editions and translations of their works. A reference to Plotinus such as IV.5.4, 10 means: 4th *Ennead*, treatise 5, chapter 4, line 10.

[4] In my *Plotinus on Sense-Perception: A Philosophical Study* (Cambridge: Cambridge University Press, 1988), 47, I affirmed that Plotinus's notion of *sympatheia* is a Stoic borrowing; cf. e.g. Agnès Pigler, "La réception plotinienne de la notion stoïcienne de sympathie universelle," *Revue de philosophie ancienne* 19.1 (2001): 45–78; and Katerina Ierodiakonou, "The Greek Concept of Sympatheia and Its *Byzantine* Appropriation in Michael Psellos," in *The Occult Sciences in Byzantium*, ed. P. Magdalino and M. Mavroudi (Geneva: Pomme d'or, 2006): 97–117. The self-criticism here is mitigated by the fact that later in the work, 59–62, I actually recognize the relevance of the *Timaeus* for Plotinus's views on *sympatheia*.

[5] See Eyjólfur K. Emilsson, "Plotinus on Happiness and Time." *Oxford Studies in Ancient Philosophy* 40 (2011): 339–60, at 348, on Plotinus's use of Stoic ethical notions and tenets.

and use their insights to develop what by his lights is essentially a Platonic view. We shall see some of the details of this here below.

The Stoic notion of cosmic *sympatheia* is perhaps best elucidated as an inference from their belief that the cosmos is an organism.[6] Just as in the case of an ordinary organism different parts may be so connected that an affection in one place leads to an affection in another—a bad stomach may for instance be accompanied by a headache though the lungs and the other parts in between are left quite unaffected—so in the cosmic organism distant parts may be affected by one another. The Stoic theory of the soul provided an explanation of such phenomena. According to the Stoics, the soul is *pneuma*, fiery air, that permeates the body as a whole (*SVF* 2, 773–89). This *pneuma* is in a state of tension, as a result of which there is continuous wave-like motion back and forth in the organism (*SVF* 2, 448, 450–57). It appears that *sympatheia* is effected by means of such tensional motion.[7] By means of the tensional motion the organism is affected as a whole by an impact that hits only a part. It is worth remarking that the tensional motion is neither movement of physical particles from one place to another nor the kind of action-affection relation by which the quality of a thing is imparted on the things adjacent to it. Rather, it seems to be the transmission of a state through the *pneuma* as a vehicle; hence when a change occurs at a given place, this is reflected in the tensional motion and may cause a similar or different affection elsewhere in the organism according to the disposition of these other parts. *Sympatheia* is affection depending on the tension of the *pneuma* that permeates the organism.

The Stoics did not limit the principle of *sympatheia* to familiar organisms. They conceived of the whole cosmos as an organism unified by all-pervasive *pneuma* in a state of tension, and they put the principle of *sympatheia* to various uses on the cosmic scale. They used it, for example, to explain the connection between the moon and the tides, the

---

[6] For the Stoic notion, see chapter 1 in this volume.

[7] For this aspect of Stoic physics, see Samuel Sambursky, *Physics of the Stoics* (London: Routledge and Kegan Paul, 1959). For tension and tensional motion in Stoicism, see *SVF* 2. 389, 416, 439, 442, 447, 546, 716, and 911.

change of seasons, and the efficacy of so-called occult phenomena, such as divination (see *SVF* 2.441, 446, 475, 1013). *Sympatheia* as a cosmic principle thus exemplifies the tendency of ancient Greek thinkers to explain events in the physical world and the cosmos as a whole on the model of an organism.

The Stoic notion of *sympatheia* depends on their view of the unity of the soul. Each ordinary organism is of course animated by its particular soul. So is the whole cosmos. The individual souls enjoy a relative unity and coherence but ultimately they are just parts of the great World-Soul. So there is one continuous *pneuma* that pervades everything and it is on this that *sympatheia* depends. As in the case of the Stoics, *sympatheia* in Plotinus depends on the unity of the soul. There are, however, significant differences between Plotinus and the Stoic view on the soul that matter for their respective views on *sympatheia*.

2. Plotinus on *sympatheia*: Some General Remarks

First and most importantly, Plotinus the Platonist does not believe that the soul is any kind of physical stuff, not even the fine and clever *pneuma*. It follows from this that when invoking *sympatheia* he cannot appeal to any physical properties of the *pneuma* to explain how it works. Nor does he think he has to: the unity of soul suffices. We shall see more about that below.

Second, Plotinus's views on the taxonomy of souls differ from those of the Stoics. The latter believe that the world at large is a rational animal containing within itself both rational and nonrational animals. These are genuine parts of the whole that, however, mirror it as kinds of microcosms. Plotinus's views on that taxonomy of souls are complex and perhaps not quite consistent. It seems that there are basically three kinds of soul: the hypostasis soul, the World-Soul, and individual human souls.[8] In some sense that Plotinus has a somewhat hard time

---

8 See Henry J. Blumenthal, "World-Soul and Individual Soul in Plotinus," in *Le Néoplatonisme: Colloques internationaux du Centre de la recherche scientifique*. (Paris: CNRS, 1971), 55–63; and Wypkje

explaining these are supposed to be all identical, because they are all identical with the hypothesis soul (see especially IV.9). Matters become even more complicated by the fact that human beings are partly animated by the World-Soul: the latter is responsible for the rational orderly behavior of the cosmos; this includes the biological functions of animals, including man. In the human case the line between the functions of the World-Soul and individual human souls seems to be drawn in the middle of the process of sense perception: insofar as sense perception is a biological phenomenon, involving an affection of the organism by external objects it is a function of the World-Soul or something "we," that is, our bodies, have from the World-Soul; insofar as sense perception is a cognitive activity on our part it is an act performed by our individual soul; insofar as it is an affection it is the work of the soul we share with the cosmos (IV.9.3, 25–27).[9]

These distinctions matter for Plotinus's employment of the notion of *sympatheia*. Even if he insists that all souls are somehow one, it seems that *sympatheia* on the cosmic scale is based on the unity of the World-Soul alone. This means that if, say, a human being is sympathetically affected by something external and distant, this affection is a function of the unity of the World-Soul in which we, through the animation of our bodies, have a share. This is so because our "lower" soul is a part of or is derived from the World-Soul as noted above. This has the further consequence that for Plotinus the working of *sympatheia* and of phenomena that depend on it such as magical spells is limited: it is not the case, for instance, that we can, through incantations or the like, change the mind of the gods or that they deliberately affect us by the means of *sympatheia*—I shall return to this point shortly. Moreover, we as individual, primarily rational, souls are not directly affected by cosmic *sympatheia*. As individual rational souls we are in a sense raised above the natural

---

Helleman-Elgersma, *Soul-Sisters: A Commentary on* Enneads *IV 3 (27), 1–8 of Plotinus* (Amsterdam: Rodopi, 1980), especially 98–101.

9 See Emilsson, *Plotinus on Sense-Perception*, 23–25 with further references.

causal nexus of which *sympatheia* is a part. Despite this, thanks to the ultimate unity of all souls, *sympatheia* is possible between individual human souls as we shall see shortly.

So there can be *sympatheia* between different parts of the same organism and between souls IV.3.8, 1–3). It seems that any sort of causation and coordination of states and events that is not to be explained as affection through direct physical contact is the working of *sympatheia*. In general *sympatheia* can occur without affection of the parts that stand between those that are in the relation of *sympatheia*, whereas what is in between may reduce its effect, and similar things are particularly susceptible to sympathetic influence on one another (IV.4.32.).

Sympatheia turns up in a number of passages in the *Enneads*.[10] In many of these the mention is cursory and hard to make much of. but there are two extensive discussions, both in the long treatise "The Problems of Soul," *Ennead* IV, 3–5.[11] More precisely, we have in IV.4, chapters 31–45, a discussion of the influence of the stars, magic, and prayer in all of which *sympatheia* plays an essential role, and in IV.5, especially chapters 3 and 5, a discussion of visual and auditory transmission. In what follows, I shall primarily be concerned with these two extended passages. Before turning to these core passages, however, I would like to address one interesting passage that we find in the early treatise IV.9 (8), "If All Souls Are One." Here Plotinus writes:

> Indeed, the argument deriving from facts opposed [to the assumption of complete separation of souls] asserts that we do sympathize [*sympathein*] with one another when we suffer along [*synalgountas*] from seeing them suffer and when we rejoice [in their company] and

---

10 Just about all these passages are commented on by Gary Michael Gurtler, "Sympathy: Stoic Materialism and the Platonic Soul," in *Neoplatonism and Nature*, ed. Michael Frank Wagner, International Society for Neoplatonic Studies, vol. 8, Studies in Plotinus' *Enneads* (Albany, NY: SUNY Press, 2002), 241–76, and in chapter 3 of *Plotinus: the Experience of Unity* (New York: Peter Lang, 1988).

11 This treatise is one of a number of cases where Plotinus's editor, Porphyry, split a treatise, in this case into three known to us as *Ennead* IV, "The Problems of Soul" 3, 4, and 5.

are naturally drawn to love [*philein*] them; for else there could not be any love for this reason. (IV.9.3, 1–4)[12]

The final sentence here is extremely elliptical. I read it as saying: "for without the unity of souls there would not by any love for the reason of *sympatheia*." The context of the quote is Plotinus's notorious claim that all souls are but one soul. It would take us too far afield to address that thesis as such. My suspicion is that even if Plotinus's language often suggests strict identity between all souls, that is not quite what he means but some slightly weaker relation. I shall not speculate here what that relation may exactly amount to. He considers some obvious objections to this thesis, for example that if all souls were one, I should have your sensations and you mine and, in general, what is true of you should be true of me. Our quote is a part of his response to objections of this sort. He has in the previous chapter admitted that indeed we do not share each other's sense perceptions but argued that this does not refute his thesis. Our quote comes as an afterthought and addendum to this: indeed we can share in each other's experiences through *sympatheia* and this supports the claim about the unity of souls.

What makes the passage especially noteworthy is the fact that this is a rare case of *sympatheia* between persons. Moreover, the cases suggested seem to be of the following kind: person A notes that person B is suffering or that person B is rejoicing and A for that reason suffers or rejoices. This kind of *symthatheia* is not merely a biological function but involves A's judgment: A has to see and note that B suffers or is joyful in order to become similarly affected himself: Plotinus says that the sympathetic affect comes from *seeing* the other suffer. Needless to say, this is the sort of sympathy that Hume and Smith appealed to in their respective moral theories.[13]

---

12 This and other translations from the *Enneads* in this chapter are Arthur Hilary Armstrong's in *Plotinus* in Loeb Classical Library (Cambridge, MA: Harvard University Press, 1966–88), 7 vols. In some cases I have modified Armstrong's translation.

13 See chapter 7 in this volume.

3. *Sympatheia* in Astral Influence, Magic, and Prayer

Belief in occult phenomena such as astrology, divination, and magic were extremely widespread in antiquity, not least in the Hellenistic and imperial era.[14] Some intellectuals, such as Cicero, remained skeptical about such practices[15] but for instance most of the great Stoic school of thought seems to have accepted the occult phenomena as natural facts that should be given a natural explanation.[16] Plotinus simply follows suit here. He is indeed clearly concerned about doing just that: to provide natural explanations and put a limit to fantastical ideas that make the divine vulnerable to affection or present it as a mischievous agent. Of the occult phenomena he discusses, the influence of the heavenly bodies receives by far the most attention. This may have to do with the fact that astrology was a particularly ingrained part of Egyptian culture, in which Plotinus presumably grew up and surely received his education.[17]

The context of the discussion of astral influence, magic, and prayer in *Ennead* IV.4 is quite remarkable: Plotinus has discussed the psychological powers of the stars and the earth at considerable length. He admits that even if they do not have sense organs like ours they are capable of sense perception. This does, however, not necessarily mean

---

14 For a good overview, see M. Lawrence "Hellenistic Astrology," *The Internet Encyclopedia of Philosophy*. (2005), http://www.iep.utm.edu/a/astr-hel.htm; and Wendy Elgersma Helleman, "Plotinus as Magician," *International Journal of the Platonic Tradition* 4.2 (2010): 114–46.

15 See Cicero, *De divinatione* II, and especially 33 (*SVF* 2.1211).

16 See chapter 1 also for references.

17 See Helleman, "Plotinus as Magician." There is considerable literature (Philip Merlan, "Plotinus and Magic." *Isis* 44[1953]: 341–48; Arthur Hilary Armstrong, "Was Plotinus a Magician?," *Phronesis* 1[1955]: 73–79; and Helleman, "Plotinus as Magician" (with more references) on the question whether Plotinus practiced magic himself. The main ground for this allegation is an anecdote told by Porphyry in *Life of Plotinus* 10 relating about a certain Olympius of Alexandria, a self-proclaimed philosopher, "who adopted a superior attitude towards Plotinus out of rivalry. This man's attacks on him went to the point of trying to bring a star-stroke upon him by magic [*astrobolēsai auton mageusas*]. But when he found his attempt recoiling upon himself, he told his intimates that the soul of Plotinus had such great power as to be able to throw back attacks on him on those who were seeking to do him harm. Plotinus was aware of the attempt and said that his limbs on that occasion were squeezed together and his body contracted 'like a money-bag pulled tight'" (10, 3–13).

that they do perceive sensible objects because in order to do so "the soul must be so disposed as to incline towards sense-objects" (IV.4.25, 2–3). The soul of the cosmos and the heavenly bodies, however, is wholly concerned with the intelligible realm and they have no need for sense perception: there are no threats or variation in their surroundings that are of concern to them and, therefore, no need of sense perception. Plotinus emphatically denies that these souls have memories; they have no need for that facility (IV.4.6–12).

Given all this, how does prayer work? Must we not suppose that the heavenly souls hear our prayers? And if they hear them and postpone their fulfillment for some time, must they not remember them? Plotinus' response to such questions is that

> [t]heir awareness [*gnôsis*] of prayers is the result of a sort of linking [*hoion synapsis*] and a particular disposition of things fitted into the whole, and the same applies to their accomplishment of what we pray for; and in the art of the magicians everything is directed to this linking; this means that magic works by powers which follow on sympathetically. (IV.4.26, 1–4)

Shortly after this, Plotinus fully embarks on his account of the occult: the influence of the heavenly bodies and astral divination (IV.4.32–39) and magic and prayer (40–45). Having rejected bodily causes (*aitiai sômatikai*) and deliberate decisions (*proaireseis*) as general explanations of what "comes from the sky to us and the other living creatures," Plotinus raises the question what other explanation there may be. He sets the stage as follows:

> First of all we must posit that this All [the perceptible universe] is a "single living being which encompasses all the living beings that are within it."[18] It has one soul which extends to all the parts, insofar as each individual thing is a part of it; and each thing in the perceptible

---
18 Cf. Plato, *Timaeus* 30 D–31 A.

> All is a part of it, and completely a part of it as regards its body;...and those things which participate in the soul of the All alone are altogether parts, but all those which also participate in another soul [i.e., individual human soul] are in this way not altogether parts, but the less are affected by the other parts insofar as they have something of the All, and in a way corresponding to what they have. (IV.4.32, 4–14)

These lines affirm what I already have noted: the cosmos is animated by one soul that also animates us humans and other living beings; this makes us parts of this cosmos; insofar, however, as we also have another soul, that is, our individual soul, we are not merely parts of the cosmos but something more. Plotinus then continues:

> This one universe is all sympathetic [*sympathes dê pan touto to hen*] and is like one living creature, and that which is far is really near, just as, in one of the individual living things, a nail or horn or finger or one of the other limbs which is not contiguous: the intermediate part leaves a gap in the affection and is not affected, but that which is not near is affected. For the like parts are not situated next to each other, but are separated by others between, but they are sympathetic [*sympaschonta*] by their likeness, and it is necessary that something which is done by a part not situated beside it should reach the distant part; and it is a living thing and all belongs to a unity, nothing is so distant in space that it is not close enough to the nature of the one living thing to be sympathetic. (IV.4.32, 14–23)

This passage shows some crucial features of Plotinus's notion of *sympatheia*: (1) *sympatheia* is based on the unity of soul; (2) affections resulting from *sympatheia* are typically between nonadjacent parts of the organism—distance is no hindrance; (3) whether part B of an organism becomes sympathetically affected by part A is determined by similarity: if parts A and B are similar, a certain affect in A may give rise to a similar sympathetic affect in B. This explains why there may be no discernible affection in the intervening space. A further point to note about this similarity requirement is that this must primarily be a similarity of disposition or constitution, not of actual properties: in the most clear-cut cases, at least, *sympatheia* involves B's becoming F as a result of A's being or becoming F. This implies that B was not F before A became F. The claim is, however, that A and B are similar, and this must mean that they share some relevant properties. These are evidently not the properties that come to be as a result of *sympatheia*.

Plotinus's insistence on the similarity of disposition or constitution between things that enter into a sympathetic relation is indeed quite pronounced (IV.4.32, 19). In practice, however, it seems that the similarity both in the case of things that are potentially in a sympathetic relation and in the case of the property sympathetically brought about is not very strict: what is really similar in the ear and the sound to the sonorous body? The effects of the stars in humans need not be evidently similar to anything in the stars nor does Plotinus make it clear what is the similarity of constitution between them or their constellations and us. In short: he does not seem to follow up the similarity requirement very strictly in practice. In the majority of cases at least he does not spell out exactly in what the similarity is supposed to consist.

In his discussion of the causality of the heavenly bodies, Plotinus's primary objective is to avert some views on the nature of this causality that apparently were current at the time. One might even say that while admitting the efficacy of the occult phenomena, Plotinus's primary concern is to hold their scope and power in check. The heavenly bodies enjoyed the status of divine beings—Plotinus does not question this (see IV.4.30, 31). What he wishes to avoid, however, is to attribute to the heavenly bodies deliberate actions affecting us. His claim here concerns any action, good or bad, but what he particularly objects to is any view that renders the heavenly bodies deliberate agents of evil. His answer, quite in accordance with his general views on causation and on evil as lack of good,[19] is twofold: (1) the heavenly bodies do not delib-

---

19 See e.g. *Ennead* I. 8, "On What Are and Whence Come Evils."

erately act so as to have an effect on things on earth and (2) insofar as there are bad effects of the heavenly bodies on us, these are due to our incapacity to receive what in itself is good or to a kind of chance. Let us consider these answers a little more closely.

The heavenly bodies do not deliberate or plan things and events on earth. In general, the higher intelligible principles—the One, the universal Intellect, and Soul—do not deliberate about lower things such as the sensible world. The sensible world and its course of life is not the result of anybody's deliberation or planning, even if, as a matter of fact, it is ordered *as if* it was supremely well planned (see IV.4.16; V.8.6). In general, the higher principles contemplate only what is above them (except the first principle, the One, of course, which has nothing above it and doesn't contemplate anything). The lower strata in the Plotinian hierarchy of being are in general explained as side effects, a kind of irradiation or emanation, from the higher strata.[20] Plotinus explicitly applies this to the effects of the heavenly bodies on us. He says:

> If then the sun and the other heavenly bodies act in any way on the things here below, one must think that the sun—it is best to speak of one body only—remains looking above, but just as its warming of things on earth proceeds from it, so do any subsequent actions upon them, by a transmission [*diadosis*] of soul, as far as it is in its power, since there is plenty of the growth soul in it. And in the same way any other heavenly body, without choosing to do so, gives off a kind of irradiation [*ellampos dynamis*] from itself. (IV.4.35, 37–44)

Sympatheia is not explicitly mentioned here but, as we have seen, in the context of the same discussion Plotinus has ascribed the effects of the heavenly bodies to *sympatheia*. So we must suppose that what he says here about the "subsequent actions" of the sun that take place "by a transmission of soul" refers to sympathetic effects. This relates *sympatheia* to

---

20 For emanation in Plotinus see Eyjólfur K. Emilsson, *Plotinus on Intellect* (Oxford: Oxford University Press, 2007), ch. 1, which also contains further references.

the pattern of emanation and double activity that pervades his thought. So sympathetic effects of the heavenly bodies are nondeliberate effects of their internal activity; they are side effects, emanations, of the internal activity of the higher beings.

As regards bad things that occur as a result of sympathetic influence of the heavenly bodies, Plotinus notes that in general these are due to our incapacity for receiving effects, which so far as the agent is concerned are not bad at all, even good (IV.4.38). There is an elaboration of this point in the later treatise "Whether the Stars Are Causes," chapter 11. Here we see that an example of this is when the heavenly bodies inspire manliness (*andreia*) but on account of his incapacity, the recipient takes this in as violent temper and lack of spirit. The word *sympatheia* (or cognates) is not used here but from the other treatise, IV. 4, it is fairly clear that this is the sort of case where *sympatheia* gives bad results: the star intended no evil. On the contrary, its own affection was only such as to inspire a good sympathetic affect in the recipient. The recipient, however, was only able to receive some of this, and on account of his inability it was perverted to something less than good.

In the course of his discussion of the influence of the heavenly bodies, Plotinus raises the following questions:

> But since the heavenly bodies move according to reason and their relationships within the [universal] living being vary, and then here below these events occur in our own sphere in sympathy [*sympathes*] with those above, it is reasonable to enquire whether we should assert that these earthly occurrences follow on those above by correspondence [*synepesthai symphonounta*], or whether the figures [*schêmata*] have the powers which bring about what is done, and whether it is simply the figures or the figures made by particular heavenly bodies. (IV.4.34, 10–15)

To start with the last question: Plotinus asserts right after these lines that indeed both the figure as such and the particular heavenly body entering into the figure are relevant to what the effects are on things on earth (IV.4.34, 22–23). As to the question whether the combination of figures and particular heavenly bodies is a real causal agent or there is merely correspondence between astral and earthly phenomena, his response is that there may be both but in some cases there is only the power of signification (*sēmasia*). I take it that this is a different wording for "follow on by correspondence." The reference is no doubt to astrology: Plotinus is saying that there are cases where the stars and their figures signify or indicate certain earthly phenomena without being directly the causal agents of these phenomena.

Plotinus concludes this discussion in an interesting albeit somewhat enigmatic way:

> This argument, then, gives powers to the figures and powers to the bodies arranged: since with the dancers each hand has a distinct power and so the other limbs, but the figures also have great power, and then there is a third group of consequential things [*synepomena*], the parts of the limbs which are brought into the dance and their constituents, for instance the clenched fingers of the hand and the muscles and veins which are affected along [*sympathounta*; "sympathize"] with these. (IV.4.34, 26–34)

The reference to dance picks up an analogy or illustration Plotinus has used in the previous chapter to indicate the interconnectedness of everything in the cosmos. He is thinking of a pantomime dance where a soloist dancer enacts a whole myth through his dance. Just like in the case of the cosmos with its heavenly circuit, the dance consists of predetermined figures and moves. Moreover, from the pattern of the dance a great many details about the dancer's body follow: "as his body follows the pattern of the dance and bends with it, one of his limbs is pressed hard down, another relaxed, one works hard and painfully, another is given a rest as the figuring changes" (IV.5.33, 14–16). So in the subsequent chapter we have been considering Plotinus is saying that three phenomena are relevant: the figures, the particular members of the figures, and the consequentials. I take it in all cases it is a question of the effects of the dancer's body on itself: the head and the arms in a left-bending position have a certain effect on his legs. This is the combined result of the figure they form and of the power of each. Furthermore, as a sympathetic effect of a particular figure involving a clenched hand, the veins and sinews of the forearm will become visible. Plotinus does not say so explicitly but I surmise that phenomena of this last type are what makes astrology work: suppose we are the feet of the dancer and that these feet can see: we may see only the stretched sinew of the arm, which is an effect of the clenched hand which is a part of a figure; even if the stretched sinew may not have any particular effect on us, it is a sign of something else that may have such an effect.

Despite the fact that Plotinus goes on about these phenomena at considerable length, we do not really get an account of how *sympatheia* works, "the mechanics of *sympatheia*," so to speak. Presumably, the reason is that there is no such mechanics: Plotinus takes *sympatheia* as a basic fact, which is evident in the case of ordinary organisms animated by a single soul. Given the unity of soul within the cosmos and such observations as we have seen that similar things are particularly liable to sympathetic affections, *sympatheia* needs no further explanation.

4. Sympatheia *in Perceptual Transmission*

In IV.5 (which is the last part of what originally was a single treatise comprising *Ennead* IV.3–5) Plotinus discusses the nature of the transmission that evidently takes place in the distant senses, sight and hearing. As it turns out, however, most of what he has to say relates to sight. He thinks that the same account can be transferred to hearing. In both cases the transmission is explained by *sympatheia* (IV.5.5).

In order to appreciate this solution, we must consider the competitors. Given that vision is the perception of a distant object, somehow some sort of "contact" must be established between this object and the perceiver's eye. The question is how is happens. In chapters 2–4 of IV.5, Plotinus considers several theories that apparently had been proposed, even if he mentions no names of proponents and their identity remains not entirely certain in some cases.[21] He spends considerable effort at refuting a theory—this may be his reading of Aristotle's account—according to which the air is progressively affected by the object till the affection reaches the eye of the perceiver. He criticizes this theory for failing to explain how we can see the distant object *itself* (we ought to see merely the affection that has reached the eye) and for failing to explain how we can see large objects as a whole, for example a mountain (the affection made by the object on the air must be equal in size to the object whereas the pupil of eye, obviously, is many times smaller). He also attacks the Stoic theory according to which a certain pneumatic cone extends from the eye to the object. The Stoics held that in vision we use this cone like blind people use a stick. Obviously taking this analogy quite strictly, Plotinus criticizes this view for making vision indirect and inferential, something he thinks vision evidently is not.

We should expect that Plotinus's account in terms of *sympatheia* avoids the faults he finds in the other theories. Indeed, since his account does not presuppose a medium that is progressively affected, he at least avoids this reason for admitting that the eye never is in direct contact with the distant object itself, at best with a remote copy that is the affection of the air that meets the eye. We may further presume that he thinks that the "contact" with the object made by *sympatheia* is such as to ensure that vision is a direct apprehension of the object itself, though he does not explain in detail how this is so. As to the problem of how the whole large object gets to be seen, he has this to say:

> But as it is, the whole object is seen, and all those who are in the air see it, from the front and sideways, from far and near, and from the back, as long as their line of sight is not blocked; so that each part of

---

21 For a fuller discussion of these theories see Emilsson, *Plotinus on Sense-Perception*, 38–41.

the air contains the whole seen object, the face for instance; but this is not a bodily affection [*sômatos pathêma*], but is brought about by higher necessities of the soul belonging to a unitary sympathetic organism [*psychikas kai zôou henos sympathous*].

Even if Plotinus, unfortunately, does not give us details here, the passage makes an interesting connection: one might think that in sympathetic sensory transmission, nothing at all really passes from object to eye (or the other way). We know from many other passages, however, that Plotinus adopts a version of the Aristotelian view that in sense perception we receive the form of the perceived object (without the matter) and that this form somehow traverses the air.[22] We see here that this is not an alternative account to the *sympatheia* account. Rather, the *sympatheia* account contains the view that the form crosses the distance between object and eye and is, as a matter of fact, as whole at every point of the intermediate space. It is just not the case that this transmission is effected by means of any sort of bodily affection of the intermediate space.

Given what we have about *sympatheia* in connection with magic and the influence of the stars, a question that naturally arises about *sympatheia* in vision is why I only see things in front of my eyes? Why isn't there the relevant kind of *sympatheia* with the objects behind me? Well, Plotinus remarks that *sympatheia* is in general hindered or weakened by intermediate stuff between agent and patient (IV.5.2, 23–26). In the case of vision, this must mean that the transmission of the forms is obstructed by intermediate bodies—entirely obstructed by non-transparent solids, and less entirely by air, which explains why things seen at a great distance appear less clear than those close by (see II.8.1).

Why don't I see with my fingertips, why do they not enter into a sympathetical relation with the colors of things? As we have seen, *sympatheia* depends on similarity. Similar things are capable of sympathetic

---

22 See II.8, VI.4.12; and Emilsson, *Plotinus on Sense-Perception*, chapter 4.

relations to one another: "If it is in the nature of a given thing to be sympathetically affected [*paschein sympathôs*] by another thing because it has some resemblance to it, the medium is not affected, or at least not in the same way" (IV.5.1, 35–38). (He does not tell us, however, what the similarity is e.g. in the case of hearing.) The reason for this connection between *sympatheia* and similarity is not entirely clear. It has already been mentioned that *sympatheia* is also supposed to depend on the organic unity of the cosmos. In IV.5.8 Plotinus considers a hypothetical objection, which aims at showing that the similarity requirement for sympathetic relation is inconsistent with the requirement of organic unity. The objection goes like this: suppose you are placed at the edge of the cosmos you are a part of and look out toward another cosmos. Since this is another cosmos, it is by definition a different organism, and hence there cannot be organic unity between you and it. But let us assume that the part of this other cosmos in front of you is colored just like the things in this cosmos. It would be absurd to suppose that you did not see the color placed directly in front of your eyes.

Plotinus's response to the hypothetical objection is most obscure. The best I can make of it is that he wants to say that the hypothesis itself in inconsistent in that it supposes that things can be similar without belonging to the same organism. For the organ is supposed to be similar to what is perceived. But there is no way for two things to be similar unless they participate in the same form, bleak copies of which are transmitted to them by the same soul. In other words: similarity demands common origin. Hence, the supposition that we see a different cosmos must be rejected.[23] Though Plotinus does not say so explicitly here, the further justification for the claim that similar things must be made so by the same soul is no doubt the fact that any two similar things participate in the same intelligible Form by virtue of which they come to have the same quality. This being so, it is natural to conjecture

---

23 In the account given here of the notoriously difficult chapter IV.5.8, I am relying on Émile Bréhier's reconstruction in his "Notice" for IV.5 in *Plotin: Ennéades IV* (Paris: Les belles lettres, 1927).

that *sympatheia* holds between similar things somehow because they are linked through a common origin and are therefore in a sense "closer" to one another than dissimilar things. It would, however, be idle to speculate further about how exactly this is supposed to work. In any case, the statement that *sympatheia* is between similar things fits together with Plotinus's general teaching about the nature of the eye. Following Plato in *Timaeus* 45 B, he holds that there is ensouled light in the eyes.[24] This is the light we can see if we push on the eye with a finger (V.5.7, 28–29). And the proper object of vision is color (II.8.1, 13), which Plotinus regards as light-like in nature (II.4.5, 10–11).

The following considerations may help us see the crucial difference between Plotinus's theory and the one in terms of affection and medium. The directness of the object's action on the visual organ is secured by the fact that the object emits its color (form), which reaches the eye without any intermediaries. It is also evident from the last lines of IV.5.3 quoted above that Plotinus conceives of the presence of the form in the air not as the familiar local presence of a body in space or as the presence of a quality in matter. Thus, the red of the apple is not present in the intermediate space in the same way as it is present in the apple itself. The latter sort of presence presupposes an extended magnitude, a body, which is affected by the presence of the quality. This presumably explains why Plotinus thinks that within his own theory the question of seeing something in the air as opposed to in the object does not arise.

Without evidence to the contrary one would naturally assume that Plotinus the Platonist's doctrine of visual transmission is based on Plato and in particular the Plato of the *Timaeus*. Thus, it is perhaps surprising to find that as opposed to Plato's, Plotinus's theory is not of the projective type, holding that something goes out from the eyes to the object. However, let us note that in *Timaeus* 45 B–D Plato does not explicitly say that the light emitted through the eyes reaches all the way out to the object that is seen, though this may well be what he

---

24 See I.6.9, 31, II.4.5, 10, IV.5.7, 24, V.5.7, 22–30.

meant to imply. Plotinus, however, may not have understood him thus, and may not have thought that he was deviating from his master in denying that the eye's proper light goes all the way out to the object. However this may be, Plotinus surely deviates from the *Timaeus* doctrine in denying that the intermediate light of day has a function in vision. For according to the *Timaeus*, the emitted internal light fuses with the external light with the result that a continuous pencil of light extending from eye to object is formed. As Plotinus's refusal to assign a function to the intermediate light is quite clear, we are here presented with a case where Plotinus deviates from the Plato of the *Timaeus*.

Despite this I think that Plotinus's doctrine can be described as a modification of that of Plato, and that this is how he saw it himself. Let us consider how this may be. I have already pointed out that Plotinus holds that the eye contains some sort of light, that hence the eye is similar to the objects of vision, and that it is by virtue of this similarity that the eye can be affected by them. Even if Plotinus's views on *sympatheia* and its relation to organic unity may have undergone influence from Stoicism, this particular detail is without doubt based on the *Timaeus*: it is also Plato's view that vision depends on the similarity between the eye's internal fire and the light of day. So here we have a significant connection between Plotinus's doctrine and that of Plato. But there are other connections as well. Plato regarded the pencil of light that is formed by the merging of the internal light with the light of day as an extension of the percipient's body. But there are at least two different ways of conceiving of such an extension. On the one hand, we can conceive of the extension as an instrument that is attached to the body without belonging to the organism. The Stoic comparison with a stick used by the blind suggests this conception. On the other hand, one can conceive of the extension as a genuine part of the organism.[25] Galen is one who interprets the *Timaeus* doctrine in this way. Since there is a

---

25 Such is Alfred Edward Taylor's understanding of the *Timaeus* 45 B–C in "*A Commentary on Plato's* Timaeus" (Oxford: Oxford University Press, 1929).

strong affinity between Plotinus's view and Galen's views on visual transmission, let us consider the views of the latter. They are revealing of Plotinus's understanding of the *Timaeus* passage.

In Galen's opinion "it is impossible to perceive the sizes of the objects unless we see that which we look at at the place where it is."[26] And he attacks the Stoics, the Epicureans, and Aristotle and the Peripatetics for failing to give due notice to this fact in their respective theories of visual transmission. It is needless to point out that in this respect Galen's criticisms reveal exactly the same intuitions as we have seen in Plotinus about these matters. It is in fact plausible to conjecture that there is a historical connection between Plotinus's and Galen's views on this subject. Since they are dissatisfied with other people's theories for the same reasons, it seems not unlikely that their positive views have something in common.

Now, Galen's positive views, which can be described as an up-to-date version of the *Timaeus* account, are stated in terms of a visual ray theory.[27] As regards the visual ray, Galen's view is of course unacceptable to Plotinus. However, Galen evidently thinks of this visual ray theory as of a special sort, and different from that of the Stoics. What makes it special is his view of the relation between the outgoing visual ray, the sunlight, and the air. The main idea is this: the intermediate air becomes sensitive by virtue of the presence of the outgoing *pneuma* in the sunlight. To explain this, Galen refers to the relation between the brain and the nerves that lead from the sense organs to the brain: when the external light, the visual ray, and the air intermingle, the intermediate air has the same relation to the eye as the nerve leading from the eye has to the brain (VII.5, 32–33). He also says that vision works like touch, which operates through the nerves from the surface of the body

---

26 Galen, *De Plac. Hipp. et Plat.* VII 7, 9–10, cf. Plotinus, IV.6.1, 14–17.
27 See Galen, *De Plac. Hipp. et Plat.* 5.5–10, 7, 19. For accounts of Galen's views on sense perception, see Harold Cherniss, "Galen and Posidonius' Theory of Vision," *American Journal of Philology* 54 (1933): 154–61; and Phillip de Lacy's commentary in Galen, *On the Doctrines of Hippocrates and Plato*, ed. and trans. with commentary by Phillip De Lacy, 2nd ed. (Berlin: Akademie, 1984).

to the brain, the idea being that the sensitive air close to the colors seen is analogous to the nerve ends in our skin (VII.7, 18). In short, Galen is basically saying that the intermediate air functions as an extension of the nerves. Thus, one might say that in Galen's view the intermediate air becomes in vision an organic part of our bodies.

Now, I am going to suggest that Plotinus's *sympatheia* theory is conceptually kindred to Galen's theory, especially to the aspect of Galen's theory just related. We do know that in Plotinus's view we are parts of the cosmic organism, and the *sympatheia* on the cosmic scale depends on this organic unity. More specifically, we are in organic unity with the rest of the cosmos by virtue of the unity of our lower soul, which animates our bodies, with the soul, which animates the cosmos. Still more specifically, this means, in the case of vision, that our eyes are parts of the same organism as the objects of vision. Now, we can take the import of this organic unity to be that essentially the same conditions hold on Plotinus's view as on Galen's and Plato's as read by Galen: we should regard the distant objects as if they were a part of our own bodies. Apart from the role that Galen attributes to the intermediate air, which Plotinus rejects, the difference between their views comes down essentially to this: Galen does not take the organic unity of the percipient's eyes with the objects of vision and the intermediate space to be a permanent condition but rather something that is brought about by the visual *pneuma*, whereas Plotinus sees it as a permanent condition. This is why Plotinus has no need for visual rays: the state of affairs that the visual rays bring about on Galen's (and Plato's) theory is already there according to Plotinus.[28]

The idea, then, of the unity of the cosmic organism on which vision is supposed to depend is to be taken quite literally: vision is to be seen as analogous to internal sensation within an ordinary organism. This

---

28 Thus, it turns out that we can say, after all, that in substance Karl Reinhardt, *Kosmos und Sympathie: Neue Untersuchungen über Poseidonios* (Munich: Beck, 1926), 187–92, was right in pointing out the affinity between Galen's and Plotinus's views, although he went too far in identifying their theories.

idea is to some extent strengthened by a consideration of Plotinus's criticisms of the Stoic theory of internal perception, that is, perception of pain, itches, and the like. The Stoics speak of transmission (*diadosis*) from the affected part of the body to the principal part of the soul (IV.2.2, IV.7.7). Plotinus interprets this transmission as progressive affection of a medium in vision in IV.5.1–3: he claims that the ruling part of the soul could at most perceive the affection adjacent to itself. Now we learn from IV.3.23 that Plotinus assigns some function to the nerves in the sense of touch and it seems reasonable to suppose this to include perception of pain. And in the same passage, he says that the brain is the part of the body from which the activity of the perceptive soul has its origin. So one might speculate that he wants to assume some sort of psychic transmission from the aching part of the body through nerves to the brain, analogous to his account of visual transmission. Further, he implies that internal perception depends on something he calls *homopatheia*, and there are other passages that suggest that *homopatheia* can be synonymous with *sympatheia*.[29] So one might suppose that in Plotinus's view vision is exactly analogous to internal perception as it seems to be in Galen's theory.

However, it must be admitted that this idea does not work out in all details as an explanation of Plotinus's theory. First, in those passages where Plotinus criticizes the Stoic theory of internal perception, he does not, in his positive account, propose a theory of psychic transmission through the nerves to the brain. What he says instead is that the soul is present as a whole in every part of the body. There are certain common features, though: the presence of the soul as a whole at every point of the body inevitably brings to mind the doctrine that the form of the object is present as a whole at every point of the intermediate space. Indeed, the property of being as a whole in many is a general characteristic of the soul and the psychological as opposed to the corporeal, and as such, it indicates that both phenomena are psychological; but so far as I have

---

29 See IV.7.3, 2–5, where *sympathēs* and *sympatheia* replace *homopatheia*, and IV.9.2, 20–32.

been able to detect, it does not indicate anything special beyond that. This may explain why Plotinus does not explicitly bring up the analogy between vision and internal perception through the nerves.

On reflection, we should not really expect an exact parallelism between vision and internal perception: for there is nothing in the perception of pain that corresponds exactly to the role of the eye in vision. Even if Plotinus believed that perception of pain takes place somehow through the mediacy of the brain and the nerves, neither the brain nor the nerves seem to be affected in the way the eye is. The eye's sensing the colors of a distant object is a relation between two distinct bodily parts of the cosmic organism whereas the brain does not sense pain in the finger in the way the eye senses the colors: as introspection and the history of physiology teach us, it is not at all evident that the brain is in any way involved in the perception of pain. Plotinus suggests that the perception of pain is a relation between a bodily part and the soul as a whole (IV.4.19, 11–19); visual sensation, on the other hand, is a relation between the eye and some other part of the cosmic organism. If we were to have something exactly analogous within an ordinary organism, it would be something like the finger's sensation of what goes on in the toe. So my suggestion is, then, that we should understand the *sympatheia* between parts of the cosmic organism that makes vision possible as if it were such a sensation by part of a part. This analogy, though correct, is, however, not particularly illuminating, since there is no such thing as a sensation of what goes on in the toe by the finger—or if there is, it entirely escapes our consciousness.

In conclusion, then, Plotinus sees the idea of organic unity between the eye and the object of vision at work in the theory of the *Timaeus*. But whereas Plato and Galen arrive at this unity by presupposing temporary extensions of our own bodies, Plotinus takes it to be an instance of the more permanent unity of our own living bodies with the cosmic organism.

Reflection
GALEN'S SYMPATHY
Brooke Holmes

If we are to believe Galen, the origins of sympathy lie with medicine's founding father, Hippocrates. Time and again in his vast corpus of medical writings—nearly 10 percent of extant Greek literature before 400 CE—and in a range of contexts, Galen paraphrases a passage from the laconic Hippocratic treatise *On Nutriment*: "There is one confluence; there is one common breathing; all things are in sympathy."[1]

From our perspective, however, the "Hippocratic" provenance of the tag, and of sympathy itself, is less secure. *On Nutriment* is widely thought to be from the Hellenistic period—third century BCE or later (the classical Hippocratic texts date from the late fifth and early fourth centuries BCE)—in part because the passage on sympathy is so anomalous: most scholars think the author has been influenced by Stoic notions of cosmic sympathy. The texts at the core of the Corpus make no mention of sympathy.

Yet it would be a mistake to see Galen's sympathy as simply a Stoic concept masquerading as Hippocratic insight, a philosophical

---

1 See [Hippocrates], *On Nutriment* 23 (IX 106 Littré). For sources, see list of abbreviations at beginning of bibliography. Translations are my own. For Galen's citation of the passage, see, e.g., *Causes of Pulses* 1.12 (IX 88 Kühn), *On the Natural Faculties* 1.12 (II 29 Kühn = 122,6–9 Helmreich), *On the Usefulness of Parts* 1.8 (III 17 Kühn = 1:12,23–25 Helmreich).

idea appropriated wholesale by a physician.[2] Most important, we would be better off speaking of Galen's sympathies. There is the "Hippocratic" concept of a body in which everything suffers together (and breathes together and flows together) that Galen often invokes to defend his vision of nature and the living beings within nature as organized by a kind of immanent intelligence or logic.[3] But the noun "sympathy" (*sympatheia*) is overwhelmingly used by Galen to express what must have been an existing technical notion within the learned medical tradition, according to which diseases or, more properly, "affections" (*pathē*)—anything that the body or one of its parts suffers, almost always, in medical parlance, abnormally—are trafficked from one part of the body to another.

Of course, these are not unrelated ideas. Each insists on interconnectedness within a microcosm. Each, on different occasions, causes Galen to mention the magnet, the paradigm of sympathy in antiquity.[4] But they point to different ways of understanding sympathy within the context of a living—and, more specifically, a human—body. It is tempting to see these ideas as corresponding to different facets of Galen himself, the philosopher and the physician, respectively. That would be too simple, though. What is fascinating about sympathy in Galen's writings is the way in which it behaves in contexts where difficult questions about the nature of life and causal relations are enmeshed in the concreteness of a body intimately known through anatomy and closely observed in its dysfunctionality, as well as in contexts where the messy vascularity of that body is translated into a precisely coordinated network in order to make sense of symptoms. In short, in Galen's writings, the workings of sympathy manifest in a privileged and

---

2 On the Stoic notion of sympathy, see chapter 1 in this volume.

3 To the extent that Galen recognizes this as a Stoic idea, he makes the Stoics indebted to Hippocrates: see *Method of Medicine* 1.2 (X 16 Kühn).

4 See Galen, *Commentary on Hippocrates, Epidemics II* 2.103 (236,32–44 Pfaff); *On the Natural Faculties* 1.14 (II 44–52 Kühn=133,11–139,9 Helmreich). On the magnet in antiquity, see Richard Wallace, "'Amaze your Friends!': Lucretius on Magnets," *Greece and Rome* 43 (1996): 178–87.

unique way the logic of living bodies in their flourishing and in their suffering.

I look at several examples where the different aspects of sympathy come into focus with particular clarity. I start with *On the Natural Faculties*, where Galen elaborates the Hippocratic tag at some length in a polemic against corpuscular models of the body. I then turn to a discussion of some clinical cases of sympathy that illuminate Galen's model of the networked body, a model that is also for him a crucial causal map.

On the Natural Faculties takes up the nonconscious, vegetal stratum of human life: generation, development, and nutrition, all of which are governed by what Galen calls the "natural faculties." These faculties, in Galen's eyes, reveal nature to be the sort of thing that acts in a way that is both "technical"—that is, in strategic pursuit of particular ends, here the flourishing of the organism—and "right" or "just." Galen thinks that for nature to be this way substance has to be a continuum capable of qualitative change, a position he associates with one "sect" of natural philosophy headed, predictably, by Hippocrates (although he almost certainly also has Aristotle and the Stoics in mind). The other sect, by contrast, holds to a view that substance is itself unchangeable and parceled out into small bodies with void in between—in other words, atomism, although Galen's main target here is the late Hellenistic physician-theorist Asclepiades of Bithynia, whose corpuscular model of the physical body may or may not have been overtly atomist (his writings are lost). Those affiliated with the second sect scandalously reject the existence of anything like the natural faculties. Instead, they explain phenomena like growth or, in the example that Galen develops in baroque detail, the excretion of urine by purely mechanical principles, namely, the principle of *horror vacui*. In so doing, Galen alleges, they strip nature of all skill and purposefulness.

Galen does not deny the workings of something like *horror vacui* both inside and outside the body. He uses the example of the bellows to illustrate this kind of attraction. But he thinks this is insufficient to account for the complex, purpose-driven labor of living. In addition to the simple attraction of matter into a void, bodies work with faculties of attraction and, importantly, expulsion that recognize qualitative differences in matter; indeed, the natural faculties are largely defined through their capacity to attract and expel different kinds of substance based on the "appropriateness of quality."

But how do these faculties exercise such discernment? Galen is careful not to attribute reasoning or mind to the natural faculties. Instead, he likens the attraction and expulsion performed by the natural faculties to a range of phenomena observed in inanimate things: the capacity of emetics to attract specific humors from the body, of antidotes to draw out snake venom, or, most tellingly, of the lodestone to attract iron. These examples were all regularly explained in terms of sympathy in antiquity. By using them here, Galen implies that the entire physical world is organized by relationships of appropriateness and foreignness governed by nature rather than actively pursued by individual bodies.[5] (Elsewhere, however, Galen is uncomfortable putting the genesis, growth, and maintenance of living bodies on the same level as the behavior of drugs and stones.)

The larger context suggests, then, that when Galen invokes the "Hippocratic" idea of a body that is "in sympathy" with itself in his polemical denunciation of atomist models, it is likely he is not just imagining a body in which different parts suffer together. Rather, he seems to have in mind a more robust notion of sympathy, according to which different parts of the body relate to one another and the outside world in ways that enable the organism to perpetuate its life. So fundamental is the orchestration of life in

---

5 See further Brooke Holmes, "Galen on the Chances of Life," in *Probabilities, Hypotheticals, and Counterfactuals in Ancient Greek Thought*, ed. Victoria Wohl (Cambridge: Cambridge University Press, 2014), 230–50.

these terms that he can sum up the heresy of the corpuscular theorists as the denial of sympathy: for Asclepiades, "nothing is naturally in sympathy with anything else, all substance being divided and broken up into inharmonious elements and absurd 'molecules.'"[6] To deny sympathy is to deny not just the continuum of substance but also the coherence of nature.[7]

In *On the Natural Faculties*, Galen appears to be mobilizing a particularly rich concept of sympathy to build his case against Asclepiades and like-minded thinkers. The reference to two warring sects turns sympathy into a core philosophical commitment that no doubt held associations with the Stoics for Galen. But in his discussion of "appropriateness of quality," he also draws on notions of sympathy and antipathy that were common in pharmacology and natural history (books 20–32 of Pliny's *Natural History*, for example, are a gold mine of such beliefs).[8] All of this material is marshaled in support of a vision of human nature focused not on the higher capacities of thought or emotion but on the wondrous everyday labor of the plant-like body. Here, the bladder becomes the stage for an epic battle in which sympathy is central.

---

6 Galen, *On the Natural Faculties* 1.13 (II 39 Kühn = 129,7–9 Helmreich).

7 As Armelle Debru writes, "Galen's thought is shot through with the notion that the general intercommunication within and synergy of actions in the organism creates from it a unity, which accounts for our being able to speak of it as a 'system'" ("Physiology," in *The Cambridge Companion to Galen*, ed. R. J. Hankinson [Cambridge: Cambridge University Press, 2008], 275). While Galen tends to focus on the coherence of the human body, the examples he gives to show "attraction by quality" in *On the Natural Faculties* suggest that he sees sympathies and antipathies as distributed throughout the whole of nature. This would be keeping with his view of nature as exhibiting the intelligence of the Demiurge, a view more Platonic than Stoic. Yet how that intelligence is communicated is a topic that Galen has no firm opinion on (he rejects, for example, the Platonic notion of a "world soul"): see esp. *On the Formation of the Fetus* 6 (V 687–702 Kühn = 90,27–106,13 Nickel); and R. J. Hankinson, "Philosophy of Nature," in *The Cambridge Companion to Galen*, ed. R. J. Hankinson (Cambridge: Cambridge University Press, 2008), 233–36.

8 For sympathy in Pliny, see Françoise Gaide, "Aspects divers des principles de sympathie et d'antipathie dans les textes thérapeutiques latins," in *Rationnel et irrationnel dans la médecine ancienne et médiévale: Aspects historiques, scientifiques et culturels*, ed. Nicoletta Palmieri (Saint-Étienne: Publications de l'Université de Saint-Étienne, 2003), 129–44; Patricia Gaillard-Seux, "Sympathie et antipathie dans l'*Histoire Naturelle* de Pline l'Ancien," in *Rationnel et irrationnel dans la médecine ancienne et médiévale: Aspects historiques, scientifiques et culturels*, ed. Nicoletta Palmieri (Saint-Étienne: Publications de l'Université de Saint-Étienne, 2003), 113–28.

More often in Galen, however, sympathy designates the narrower idea that one part of the body may suffer affections generated in another part. Though the language of sympathy is not used in fifth- and fourth-century BCE medical texts, the belief that diseases can travel through passages within the body is a basic tenet of humoral pathology.[9] Moreover, these texts already evince a belief that certain parts of the body, such as the breasts and the uterus in the female body, are related and, as a result, share affections. Those relationships and the circulation of affections more generally are described by some postclassical authors, including Galen, in terms of sympathy.

Yet even in these more technical instances, sympathy provides an occasion to reflect on the complex organization of the human body. But whereas in *On the Natural Faculties* we are interested in the maintenance of life, Galen's references to sympathetic affections arise in cases where the interconnectivity of the body allows for damage to migrate from one part to another.[10]

These migrations occur along well-defined pathways in Galen. As we just saw, our earliest medical writings describe a body whose interior is crisscrossed with channels along which fluids and air are transported. These channels acquire a newfound specificity and more precise coordinates with the rise of systematic human dissection in third-century BCE Alexandria and the isolation of the veins, arteries, and nerves. Galen inherited a finely networked body in his anatomical training, and he spent much of his career honing his understanding of these networks and the vital functions they support. Indeed, Galen's

---

[9] Nearly all the fifth- and fourth-century treatises in the Hippocratic Corpus work with a model of the body oriented toward innate fluid stuffs in the body, sometimes called humors (*khymoi*), that circulate through generic vessels from one part to another. These stuffs and their number vary from author to author. The four-humor model that will become dominant in western medicine (thanks to Galen) appears only in one treatise, *On the Nature of a Human Being*.

[10] For an overview of the means by which these affections travel, see R. E. Siegel, *Galen's System of Physiology and Medicine: An Analysis of His Doctrines and Observations on Bloodflow, Respiration, Tumors, and Internal Diseases* (Basel: Karger, 1968), 360–82.

investment in anatomy as a resource for answering philosophical and clinical questions alike is a hallmark of his work.

The map of the body uncovered by anatomy is essential, in Galen's eyes, to understanding sympathetic affections. More specifically, that map enables the physician to grasp a complex causal scenario only hinted at—or not suggested at all—by observable symptoms. It is only because Galen has such a command of the nervous system that he understands, for example, why a patient who has suffered a fall loses command over his legs and his voice: whereas the other physicians apply treatment to the affected parts—legs and voice—Galen recognizes that a nerve in the spine has been damaged and directs his therapies there. It is not that other physicians do not accept affections "by sympathy" in principle. Yet they often fail to see how it works in practice because they lack adequate training in dissection. Galen mocks some colleagues, for example, for explaining a case of sympathetic affection in the Hippocratic text *Epidemics* II by means of a blood vessel that cannot be seen during dissection: they have seen it only "in their dreams."[11]

Galen himself is guilty of some dreaming here. For as we have seen, the language of sympathy does not appear in the classical-era texts of the Hippocratic Corpus. It is true that in the case just mentioned, the text presents a constellation of symptoms—an enlarged spleen, shoulder pain, a taut blood vessel at the elbow—as facets of a single affection. But in keeping with the style of the *Epidemics*, the text does not explain how these could be related. Galen steps in with an explanation that rests on his own map of the networked body, all the while insisting that he is simply making clear what is latent in the text. For Hippocrates himself, he claims,

---

11 Galen, *Commentary on Hippocrates, Epidemics II* 2.102 (236,22–23 Pfaff). For further discussion, see Brooke Holmes, "Sympathy between Hippocrates and Galen: The Case of Galen's *Commentary on Hippocrates 'Epidemics', Book Two*," in *Epidemics in Context: Greek Commentaries on Hippocrates in the Arabic Tradition*, ed. Peter E. Pormann (Berlin: De Gruyter, 2012), 49–70, at 65–68.

had dissected the human body. But as *Epidemics* II represents notes to himself, Galen argues, he does not spell out the underlying structure that connects the symptoms. Here, then, the identification of affections as sympathetic in the source text becomes an opportunity for Galen to supply his own anatomical model as the submerged causal map and, in so doing, to bolster his vision of Hippocrates as the father of anatomy.

In the case of affections "by sympathy," parts within the body are rendered vulnerable by the communication they have with other parts. Such a level of interconnectedness means that even the brain, which Galen sees as the command center for the entire body, can fall prey to affections originating elsewhere. In *On the Affected Parts*, the brain is especially vulnerable to disturbances in the gut, which travel upward as vapors or along a large nerve (the vagus nerve in modern terms). Galen elsewhere strongly rejects the incorporeality of the soul by arguing that mental functioning depends on the mixtures of the body. Here he offers a different model of how mind is implicated in bodily disturbance, namely by its participation in the networked body and its "proximity at a distance" to the gut.[12]

Interestingly, however, Galen never argues that the soul is in sympathy with the body. From one perspective, his reticence is unexpected. From Aristotle onward, philosophers had described what they saw as the soul's ability to transmit its suffering to the body and vice versa in terms of sympathy.[13] But from another perspective, Galen's silence is not surprising at all. Throughout his writings, he affirms time and again an agnosticism about the nature of the soul and its relationship to the body observed in dissection.

---

[12] For further discussion, see Brooke Holmes, "Disturbing Connections: Sympathetic Affections, Mental Disorder, and the Elusive Soul in Galen," in *Mental Disorders in the Classical World*, ed. W. V. Harris (Leiden: Brill, 2013), 147–76, at 163–75.

[13] See, e.g., Aristotle, *De anima* 403a16-19; [Aristotle], *Physiognomy* 805a5-6; Epicurus, *Letter to Herodotus* 64; Lucretius, *De rerum natura* 3.158–60; Nemesius, *On the Nature of Man* 2. See also Holmes, "Disturbing Connections," 155–63.

Galen's elusive soul, then, predictably escapes the web of sympathetic affections.

Yet for all that the anatomical body makes sense of sympathies observed on its surface, sympathy itself often remains an elusive phenomenon. In the example where Galen lacerates other commentators on the Hippocratic *Epidemics* II for dreaming up a blood vessel, he himself cannot identify a vein to draw together the scattered symptoms that appear not only in the source text but also, Galen says, to anyone who has observed a case of this kind. But that failure is not grounds to deny sympathy. Rather, the very fact that one observes the constellation of affections proves that sympathy must exist. The example that Galen supplies of a phenomenon that is easy to observe but hard to explain is the lodestone's attraction of iron.

In *On the Natural Faculties*, we can again observe, Galen stresses the apparently discerning attraction exercised by the bladder on urine or by certain drugs on specific humors. Yet we may wonder what allows unthinking bodies to exercise these powers of discernment. If Galen here refers those powers to an overarching concept of nature, he also struggled openly in other treatises with the question of how the Demiurge's intelligence becomes immanent in mindless bodies. He knows that sympathy, like the soul, exists. But he is not always clear on what the power is that governs its operations. The body in which everything is in sympathy mirrors the macrocosm. But the quandary of what allows the parts to work and to suffer together is one that Galen, despite all his empirical inquiries, struggled with to the end.

CHAPTER THREE

Sympathy in the Renaissance

Ann E. Moyer

As a word and concept with a distinctly ancient Greek pedigree, "sympathy" serves as a fascinating focus for tracing the revival, spread, and assimilation of ancient letters in the world of Renaissance Europe. Both word and concept appeared especially though not exclusively in the realms of natural philosophy and medicine, enhanced with the luster of ancient authorities and Greek sources. By the middle of the sixteenth century, it was in use in several related contexts: works in the traditions of later Platonic thought, particularly those related to magic, medical and Galenic writings, practical "books of secrets" literature in a Plinian tradition, and moral philosophy with a Stoic cast. The earliest appearances make apparent the authors' use of Greek sources, and are themselves written in Latin, the language of formal scholarship. Yet by the later sixteenth century, the word had also been adopted into several European vernaculars to identify the human responses and emotions of fellow-feeling that are familiar to modern usage. By the seventeenth century it was sufficiently prominent not only to figure in arguments about the nature of scientific explanations but also to focus attention on human fellow-feeling in ways increasingly of interest to moral philosophers and others.

Modern scholars have at times improvised narratives about the history of sympathy as a Renaissance term and concept, some but not all of which have borne up under closer scrutiny. Some of these associated sympathy with magic and a persistent, traditional mode of explanation of nature that dissipated with the rise of more rational and scientific approaches, a feature that premodern Europeans supposedly shared with other premodern societies.[1] Others associated it with magic by means of the era's revival of Platonic thought.

A closer look at the sources shows that sympathy as a term was reintroduced to Latin from Greek by scholars in the late fifteenth and early sixteenth centuries, especially but not exclusively in the context of natural philosophy. The term and concept were little used in preceding centuries; in Renaissance and early modern thought they did not represent a substratum of popular belief, but rather new and innovative humanistic scholarship. Some of these scholars identified themselves with Platonic thought. During the sixteenth century the term picked up currency; among new adopters were those who worked the medical traditions now labeled rather loosely as Paracelsian, though Galenists might take an interest in the subject as well. Yet natural philosophy was not sympathy's only context. Its increased presence in European vernaculars by the later sixteenth century does not seem due solely to this Latin scientific usage, though that was surely an important factor. It also arose from European readers' greater familiarity with ancient texts, often in translation, in which the word also referred to human emotions in the less technical ways that now constitute the word's more common usage.

---

[1] See for example Keith Thomas, *Religion and the Decline of Magic: Studies in Popular Beliefs in Sixteenth and Seventeenth Century England* (London: Weidenfeld & Nicolson; New York: Scribner's, 1971).

When the attention of many natural philosophers turned in the later sixteenth and seventeenth centuries to some particular sorts of action at a distance—especially the phenomenon of magnetism, but also of contagious diseases, gravity, and other natural forces—sympathy figured increasingly in efforts at explanation. Discussion and debate on those topics grew and continued in the seventeenth century. Detractors suggested that theories of sympathy smacked of old-fashioned superstition, a charge of which they were not actually guilty. These explanations were not old-fashioned, nor did they arise out of popular superstitions or superstitious attitudes, however one might define such a term. Nonetheless, some of the ways that advocates of sympathy used ancient texts and modern evidence, especially in the tradition of Pliny, helped to lend credence to such a claim made by those who attacked them.[2] These seventeenth-century polemics appear to have been the basis for the subsequent modern assertions that sympathy had been a pervasive traditional, folk, or prescientific mode of explanation in Renaissance thought and culture.

1. Early Usage: Philosophy, Natural and Moral

To follow the use in Latin thought of a term used by Greek scholars, it would seem reasonable to turn first to the figures who made those sources accessible by publishing them and translating them from Greek into Lain. Editions of Plotinus make a good starting point. His writings became accessible thanks to the Latin translations by Marsilio Ficino (1433–99) in the 1460s. Plotinus was already well known thanks to references to his writings in the works of other late Roman authors, and Ficino himself enjoyed a high profile among persons of letters both within Florence and beyond. The rise and rapid spread of print technology at the same time the project was under way helped to

---

2 Pedro Amaral, "Harmony in Descartes and the Medical Philosophers," *Philosophy Research Archives* 13 (1988): 499–556.

ensure their relatively broad and rapid distribution. Ficino himself had strong interests in religion, medicine, and magic, and he composed his own works in addition to translating ancient texts. He became an exponent of Platonic philosophy, and his own writings also saw numerous editions throughout the century after his own death. His translations of Plotinus were part of his ambitious project to translate the works of Plato and related authors, including the works of the Hermetic corpus, into Latin so as to make them available to western scholars. At times, his name has been associated with sympathetic magic. Yet in this case, access to the term and concept did not lead automatically to their use.

Ficino's Latin writings have enjoyed greater attention in recent decades thanks to new editions and translations. While scholars agree that Ficino developed theories of magic, they no longer emphasize the term "sympathy" in discussing his work or theories. For it would seem that while Ficino had the opportunity to employ and develop theories of sympathy in his discussions of magic and other effects at a distance, notably due to his familiarity with Plotinus, he chose instead different explanatory models that were more consistent with his thought as a whole. His case is especially useful for presenting some of the alternatives to sympathy as explanations for the kinds of action at a distance that were of interest in Renaissance magic.

Ficino published his translation of Plotinus's *Enneads* in 1492. The word *sympathia* appeared frequently in Plotinus's writings (over thirty times) and it figured importantly in his arguments at a number of points.[3] Yet Ficino did not single it out in his translation. As one might expect of a Renaissance scholar, he avoided borrowed words and neologisms in his Latin, so he did not simply use *sympathia* written in Latin letters. In a number of instances he used the Latin parallel term *compassio*,[4] but he was not entirely consistent. Sometimes he used

---

3 See chapter 2 in this volume.
4 Marsilio Ficino, *Three Books on Life*, ed. and trans. Carol V. Kaske, Medieval and Renaissance Texts and Studies (Binghamton, NY: Center for Medieval and Early Renaissance Studies, 1989), introduction, 40.

harmonia instead, and on other occasions the term simply disappeared into a longer phrase. The inconsistency suggests that he was not particularly focusing on sympathy as a concept to highlight in the translated text or to develop elsewhere.

More important is the evidence of his own writing. The relevant works are the *Three Books on Life* (*De triplici vita*) and the *Platonic Theology*, and in neither does he use the term "sympathy." Although a dislike of borrowed words might once again account for its absence, in fact *compassio* scarcely appears either, and it is not an important term in either work. Ficino definitely believed in the reality of forces acting at a distance that would fall under a general term "magic," and he developed arguments to explain that action. *Influentia*, or influence, is one He also discusses powers of attraction on the basis of similarities or correspondences. His notions of both influence and attraction develop from his arguments about emanations of power from the levels that are higher and closer to the divine to those that are lower and farther away. That is, the operator may invoke or call down these powers from higher levels, focusing and magnifying them. Or the operator may seek out points in which particular features are more concentrated; for example, to invoke solar influence, one might wear a ring containing a stone that concentrates solar power. Normally these powers move from the divine center downward (or outward) to the particular and the material; yet humans may also reach upward to invoke them. The operator has the capacity for learning about such powers and developing his or her volition in order to strengthen this power, in order to draw the operator back toward the divine. To improve that ability in himself and others was one of Ficino's major goals.

This language appears throughout his works. In book 3 of *De triplici vita* he discusses "[i]n what, according to Plotinus, the Power of Attracting Favor from the heavens consists." He notes: "But if he employs things which pertain to such and such a star and daemon, he undergoes the peculiar influence of this star and daemon...and he undergoes this influence not only through the rays of the star and the daemon themselves, but also through the very Soul of the World everywhere present."[5] Elsewhere he notes that doctors trained in astrology are able to produce powders or liquids with more efficacy than images "because powders, liquids, unguents, and electuaries, made at the right time, receive celestial influences more easily and quickly."[6] In other works he uses general terms such as "attraction," "affinity," and "love" to define magic, in a manner that recalls Pliny: "the work of magic is the attraction of one thing to another by some affinity of nature.... [F]rom the shared affinity arises a shared love, and from this love a common attraction."[7] Had he chosen to do so, he might have developed this point into a more general theory of sympathy; some subsequent scholars did so.

Ficino built up a complex medical system based on humoral physiology and "spirits," or very attenuated substances, that offer material, medical explanations for the workings of these powers. Ficino, then, hopes that his readers will learn to manipulate and concentrate these influences to their own medical benefit, but more importantly, for their religious and spiritual growth. These arguments have a number of points in common with theories of sympathy, but are consistently and distinctly different. As Carol Kaske has noted, his arguments about rays and the influence they wield owe a great deal to al-Kindi's ninth-century work *De radiis* (*On Rays*) as well as to the *Picatrix*, and not simply to Plotinus. Both works had been available since the thirteenth century; influence explained in terms of rays had been treated by scholars from Roger Bacon onward, particularly in works on astrology. Thus, while the new

---

5 "Adhibitis autem quae ad stellam talem pertinent atque daemonem, stellae daemonisque huius proprium subit influxum, [a]tque hunc non modo per ipsos stellae daemonisque radios, sed etiam per ipsam mundi animam ubique praesentem," Ficino, *Three Books of Life*, 244–45, lines 36–40.
6 "tum quia pulveres, liquores, unguenta, electuaria opportune confecta coelestes influxus facilius citiusque suscipiunt." Ficino, *Three Books of Life*, 306–7, lines 36–37.
7 "Magicae opus est, attractio rei unius ab alia ex quadam cognatione naturae...ex communi cognatione communis innascitur amor, ex amore communis attractio." Marsilio Ficino, "Commentarium," in *Omnia divini Platonis opera translatione Marsilii Ficini....* (Basel: Froben and Episcopius, 1532), 401. See Stephen Clucas, "John Dee's Annotations to Ficino's Translations of Plato," in *Laus Platonici Philosophi: Marsilio Ficino and His Influence*, by Stephen Clucas, Peter J. Forshaw, and Valery Rees, Brill's Studies in Intellectual History (Leiden; Boston: Brill, 2011), 227–47, at 245.

access to Greek sources increased the set of tools Ficino had at his disposal for building his theories, they did not simply displace older ones.

So too Ficino's younger colleague and friend Giovanni Pico della Mirandola (1463–94) added these and other new sources to his personal bibliography without abandoning those works long available to western scholars. Pico seems to have used the word "sympathy" only once, though in a passage that attracted more than its share of attention in the nineteenth and twentieth centuries. In the introduction to his nine hundred theses that came (already in the sixteenth century) to be known as his *Oration on the Dignity of Man*, Pico notes that some of these theses treat the subject of magic. He distinguishes an evil type from a worthy one; it is the second type, an investigation of the divine secrets of nature, that he proposes to discuss:

> The latter, in calling forth into the light as if from their hiding-places the powers scattered and sown in the world by the loving-kindness of God, does not so much work wonders as diligently serve a wonder-working nature. The latter, having more searchingly examined into the harmony of the universe, which the Greeks with greater significance call συμπάθεια, and having clearly perceived the reciprocal affinity of natures... brings forth into the open the miracles concealed in the recesses of the world.[8]

The reference is brief; the source seems to be Pliny 20.1 rather than Plotinus, as Eugenio Garin noted in his modern edition of the work.[9] Pico

---

8 Giovanni Pico della Mirandola, "Oration on the Dignity of Man," trans. Francesco Borghesi, Michael Papio, and Massimo Riva (Cambridge: Cambridge University Press, 2012), 244–47. The original reads: "Haec inter sparsas Dei beneficio, & inter seminatas mundo virtutes, quasi de latebris evocans in lucem. Non tam facit miranda quam facienti naturae sedula famulatur. Haec universi consensum, quem significantius Graece συμπάθειαν dicunt, introrsum perscrutatius rimata, & mutuam naturarum cognitionem habens perspectam, nativas adhibens unicuique rei & suas illecebras." Giovanni Pico della Mirandola, *Opera omnia* (Basel: Petrina, 1557), 328.

9 Giovanni Pico della Mirandola, *De hominis dignitate; Heptaplus; De ente et uno; e scritti vari*, ed. Eugenio Garin, Edizione nazionale dei classici del pensiero italiano 1 (Florence: Vallecchi, 1942), 152 n. 3. On Pico's manuscript of Pliny see Anthony Grafton, "Giovanni Pico della Mirandola: Trials

writes the word in Greek and does not incorporate it into his normal Latin prose. Related words also appear only rarely in his writings; while he uses the word *harmonia* on occasion, or *consensum* as in this instance, these do not figure large in his writings either. Terms related to love and desire are more frequent, especially in the *Commentary on a Canzone of Benivieni*, not surprising as the poem and commentary both focus on love.

Plotinus and Pliny were not the only sources available to Pico or Ficino in which the word "sympathy" appeared; they had both Cicero and Vitruvius as well. Pico used Cicero's *De divinatione* in his treatise against astrology, though he did not refer specifically to the passage on sympathy.[10] Both Pico and Ficino were surely aware of Vitruvius's treatise; Poggio Bracciolini had disseminated the text in Florence earlier in the century, and art and architectural theory enjoyed a relatively high profile in the learned culture of their generation. Both Ficino and Pico were voracious readers, and Pico in particular was a book lover and collector. Neither, however, mentioned the text or Vitruvius's use of the term. The fact that Pico used the term *sympathia* at all certainly suggests some amount of engagement with the subject, as for Ficino. Yet to neither of them does it appear to have been a major interest or a concept central to their thought such that it required comparison with influence or other similar concepts. Neither author, it would seem, can be credited with giving the term significant play at the end of the fifteenth century, though they helped inspire those who did. Pico's importance among later nineteenth-century scholars from Walter Pater onward (1873), and the availability in modern vernaculars of the *Oration* alone among his writings, probably were factors more relevant in identifying him so strongly with "sympathetic" magic.[11]

---

and Triumphs of an Omnivore," in *Commerce with the Classics: Ancient Books and Renaissance Readers* (Ann Arbor: University of Michigan Press, 1997), 104 n. 34.

10 Giovanni Pico della Mirandola, *Disputationes* 11; Cicero, *De divinatione* 2.97 (on the unreliability of Chaldean records). See Steven Vanden Broecke, *The Limits of Influence: Pico, Louvain, and the Crisis of Renaissance Astrology* (Leiden: Brill, 2003), 74.

11 For a discussion of Pico's fortunes among modern scholars, mainly in the twentieth century, see William G. Craven, *Giovanni Pico della Mirandola, Symbol of His Age: Modern Interpretations of a Renaissance Philosopher*, Travaux d'humanisme et Renaissance (Geneva: Droz, 1981).

Both Ficino and Pico emphasized the spiritual quest of the operator in their discussions of magic or of the harnessing of hidden powers. The operator exercises choice and volition to move closer to God and the divine, and away from the earthly and finite. Theories of influence emanating from above were consistent with these goals. Certainly Plotinus's theories of sympathy could also be made consistent with such spiritual ends, since Plotinus himself had found them so; and Ficino's interests extended into the world of everyday health in his *De triplici vita*. Nonetheless, it fell to Heinrich Cornelius Agrippa (1486–1535) to treat the unseen connections between and among parts of the world in terms of sympathy in the light of these recently available Platonic sources and with sufficient emphasis to move the concept closer to the center of attention. Agrippa's more sustained interest in magic offered a large conceptual space to develop notions of sympathy. "Magic" itself remained a somewhat elastic term throughout the era both for its proponents and its detractors. It referred in general to techniques intended to cause action over a distance by means of unseen forces. Such action need not require assistance of a conscious, nonphysical being; authors might refer to such instances of harnessing unseen but natural powers as natural magic.

Agrippa took a particular interest in these hidden or unseen powers. His engagement with the subject seems to have begun already in his student years; his university studies began at Cologne in 1499 and continued in Paris circa 1507. Many of his travels during these years are poorly documented, but it is clear that he completed his first version of his work on magic early in 1510, dedicating it to the monk Johannes Trithemius. Agrippa maintained his interests in Platonic thought and magic during an extended residence in Italy, 1511–17; in addition to the imperial service that seems to have taken him there, he lectured at Pavia on the *Pimander* in 1515.[12] His peripatetic career brought him

---

12 Charles Nauert, *Agrippa and the Crisis of Renaissance Thought* (Urbana: University of Illinois Press, 1965), 35–54. Ficino's translation of the *Pimander*, part of the Hermetic corpus, dates from the 1460s and had been available in print since 1493. See also Christopher I. Lehrich, *The Language of Demons and Angels: Cornelius Agrippa's Occult Philosophy* (Leiden: Brill, 2003).

back to Cologne at the time of the work's publication. Book 1 finally appeared in print in 1531 (Paris); after he had some difficulties with Dominican inquisitors, the full version was finally published in Cologne in 1533.[13]

The work displays Agrippa's admiration for the work of both Ficino and Pico. His continued reading and study after composing its first version can be seen in the references to Francesco Zorzi, Paolo Ricci, Ludovico Lazzarelli, and others with whom he spent time in Italy or whose own works were produced after 1510. The *De occulta philosophia* is reminiscent of Ficino's *De triplici vita* in its breadth, moving from physical topics to spiritual. Its emphasis on magic is lengthier and more explicit than Ficino's work. His discussion of causation combines the discussions of rays and influence used by Ficino, in which the forces flow from the higher powers downward, with the notions of sympathy presented by Pliny and Plotinus, according to which the connections are more multidirectional. The former relate more to celestial power, the latter to the earthly level.[14]

Agrippa uses Pliny's term *amicitia* for this relationship between entities; its opposite is *inamicitia* or *odium*. He devotes several chapters of book 1 to the subject, beginning with a passage clearly based on Pliny: "Now it should be considered how all things have among them friendship and enmity, and each thing has something it considers fearsome and dreadful, inimical and destructive; and on the contrary, something enjoyable, pleasurable, and helpful. So among the elements fire is set against water and air against earth, yet they get along themselves."[15] He continues to develop these themes, turning to particular cases as he

---

13 Heinrich Cornelius Agrippa von Nettesheim, *De occulta philosophia: Liber primus* (Paris: Wechilus, 1531), and *De occulta philosophia libri tres* (Cologne: Johannes Soter, 1533). See Agrippa, *De occulta philosophia libri tres*, ed. V. Perrone Compagni (Leiden: Brill, 1992), 8.

14 Agrippa, *De occulta philosophia libri tres* (1992), 22–27.

15 "Restat nunc videre quod omnes res habent inter se amicitiam et inimicitiam et omnis res habet aliquod temendum et horribile, inimicum et destrutivum; contra, aliquod exultans, laetificans et confortans. Sic in elementis ignis adversatur aquae et aer terrae, caeterum inter se convenient." Agrippa, *De occulta philosophia*, 117–18.

moves through the topics of book 1. Some of these relationships between things are based on the whole of the entity in question, others on a part. Some may persist after the death of a living object, others not. Some are caused by celestial influences. Although the causes of some connections are apparent to the observer, many are known only by experience. Agrippa's sources include not only Pliny but Ficino, Zorzi, the Albertine and pseudo-Albertine texts, and a range of other sources. Book 2 develops mathematical and astrological principles; book 3 turns to the study of the divine. V. Perrone Compagni, the work's modern editor, has argued that while Agrippa's cultural environment changed over the many years in which he continued to work on the book, his own goals remained reasonably consistent. He sought to refound magical studies on sure and ancient principles, and he combined theories of influence and sympathy into a reasonably consistent argument to support the practical information of his sources and experience.

The text of Pliny that Agrippa had at his disposal had improved considerably over several decades of humanistic editorial attention. By the time of his first draft, the available text was better still. New editions continued to appear over several decades. The *Natural History* had enjoyed early print circulation that began in 1469 and continued with fifteen incunabula editions. The commentary and critical tradition began at this point; it resulted largely from the problems encountered by the humanists charged with editing the text.[16] Ermolao Barbaro, Filippo Beroaldo Senior, Sabellicus, Niccolò Leoniceno, and Angelo Poliziano all weighed in with editions, emendations, or criticisms of the work of their colleagues; indeed, the strenuous disagreement between Leoniceno and Poliziano launched a significant debate about the usefulness of Pliny and the corrections of the text.[17] University lectures began to

---

16 Charles Nauert, "Humanists, Scientists, and Pliny: Changing Approaches to a Classical Author," *American Historical Review* 84.1 (1979): 72–85, at 76–77.
17 Nauert, "Humanists, Scientists", 76–83; Peter Wagner, "Renaissance Readings of the Corpus Aristotelicum—Not among the Herbalists," in *Renaissance Readings of the Corpus Aristotelicum: Proceedings from the Conference Held in Copenhagen 23–25 April 1998*, ed. Marianne Pade (Copenhagen: Eckhard 2001), 167–83, at 173–74.

include the work, and the editorial issues involved in justifying textual variants, empirical experience relating to content, and similar topics contributed to its recurring interest. Desiderius Erasmus produced an edition, with Froben in 1525.[18] His friend and younger colleague Beatus Rhenanus produced a set of *Annotationes* to the *Natural History* (1526) that presented both corrections and his best thoughts on the methods of editing classical texts.[19] By the middle decades of the century, this new and improved Renaissance Pliny was attracting considerably more attention among medical scholars, as well as other persons of learning, than the work had enjoyed a century earlier.

The *Natural History*'s great length and the vast number of topics covered meant that sympathy was only one issue among many that might draw the attention of readers.[20] Nonetheless, Erasmus himself produced an early example of interest in Pliny and sympathy in his *Colloquies*. These collections of short dialogues, written as exercises in Latin reading, enjoyed great popularity and went through many editions. In "De amicitia," written in the early 1530s, the interlocutors discuss the attractions and dislikes one person has for another. One of them relates an anecdote about Thomas More's pet monkey, who saved the family's rabbits when it saw a weasel try to invade their hutch. Discussion then turns to the ways in which animals and objects all exhibit innate attractions or repulsions, with a long list of specific examples taken largely from Pliny. The speakers note the terms for such attractions: "this type of sympathy and antipathy—for so Greeks call the natural feelings of friendship and hostility—is found even in things

---

18 Pliny, *Historia Mundi*, ed. Desiderius Erasmus (Basel: Froben, 1525).

19 John F. D'Amico, *Theory and Practice in Renaissance Textual Criticism: Beatus Rhenanus between Conjecture and History* (Berkeley: University of California Press, 1988), 72–101.

20 See, for example, B. S. Eastwood, "Plinian Astronomy in the Middle Ages and Renaissance," and R. K. French, "Pliny and Renaissance Medicine," both in *Science in the Early Roman Empire: Pliny the Elder, His Sources and Influence*, ed. R. K. French and Frank Greenaway (London: Croom Helm, 1986), 197–251, 252–81. On the illustration tradition see Lilian Armstrong, "The Illustrations of Pliny's *Historia naturalis* in Venetian Manuscripts and Early Printed Books," in *Manuscripts in the Fifty Years after the Invention of Printing: Some Papers Read at a Colloquium at the Warburg Institute on 12–13 March 1982*, ed. J. B. Trapp (London: Warburg Institute, University of London, 1983), 97–106.

lacking soul or sense."[21] The little dialogue ends by enjoining all to follow their natural propensities to friendships as to ways of life in general; in that way there would be genuine friendships in society.

That Erasmus would turn his editorial work on Pliny to advantage in another project is hardly surprising. Yet given Agrippa's contemporary association of sympathy with late-antique Platonic thought and theories of magic, Erasmus's approach stands out as distinctly different. He has taken his reading of Pliny in the direction of Stoic moral philosophy, and in so doing has returned the term "sympathy" to some of its earlier Greek contexts.[22] The colloquy hopes to inspire the reader to live more according to nature; it was aimed not at philosophers but general readers. The great popularity and frequent reprinting of the *Colloquies*, as well as their appearance in vernacular translations, helped give both terms and concepts much wider circulation in this less technical, more conversational usage, though one based nonetheless on Greek traditions.

Just over a decade later there appeared in print the first work devoted explicitly to the subject of sympathy and antipathy. It added a significantly different set of sources and contexts to the Renaissance concept. Girolamo Fracastoro (1478–1553) brought back the medical uses of the term, and in doing so developed a more general, atomist theory of nature as well as a theory of disease. A student at Padua of Pietro Pomponazzi, Fracastoro's distinguished career included serving as physician at the Council of Trent and authoring an epic poem on syphilis. Fracastoro published his *De sympathia et antipathia rerum* together with a work on contagion and contagious disease.[23] In the dedication to Cardinal Alessandro Farnese, Fracastoro emphasizes the latter. The work on sym-

---

21 Desiderius Erasmus, *Colloquies*, trans. Craig R. Thompson, vol. 2 of *Collected Works of Erasmus*, 2 vols. (Toronto: University of Toronto Press, 1997), 707. The original is: "Verum mihi videtur mirabilius hac genus sympathias et antipathias, sic enim Graeci vocant amicitiae et inamicitiae naturales affectus, etiam in rebus anima aut certe sensu carentibus deprehendi." Desiderius Erasmus, *Opera omnia*, vol. 1.3 (Amsterdam: North-Holland, 1969), 1043.

22 See chapter 1 in this volume.

23 Girolamo Fracastoro, *De sympathia et antipathia rerum liber unus. De contagione et contagiosis morbis et curatione libri iii* (Venice: Heredes Lucaeantonii Juntae Florentini, 1546).

pathy is a necessary prerequisite to it: "to it I have added a little work on a subject the lack of which is no less pressing, on the accord and disaccord of things, otherwise defined "sympathy" and "antipathy," without which I do not see how one could conduct proper study and present an orderly exposition on the nature of contagion."[24] He begins the "little book" with a list of sympathies and antipathies from Pliny. He also echoes the language of the medieval handbook attributed to Albertus Magnus, *De mirabilibus mundi* (*The Marvels of the World*), in print since 1472, in referring to the phenomena as marvelous. Among these phenomena, he notes, is the nature of contagion. The next step in his argument recalls the *De mirabilibus mundi* in asserting that in the physical world, like favors like; heavy objects all tend to fall, light ones to rise. But Fracastoro moves immediately into greater detail and depth than the medieval handbooks, with their emphasis on the practical. The cause of these tendencies that pertain to heavy or light objects is the end of avoiding a vacuum. Objects tend to conserve themselves and to place themselves in the natural locations of the elements of which they are composed. There is, further, an accord between the parts and the whole of a body such that if one part is struck—Fracastoro uses sound production in the air as an example—the density (a quality of the body) will alter throughout that body, as the wavelike motion of a sound moves through the air. He builds these features into his explanations of motion, and of the alterations in quality that bodies may undergo.

The attraction of one body for another, as for example a magnet, calls for a more complex explanation. Action requires contact, and yet initially the objects are not in contact. In order to identify the necessary contact, Fracastoro invokes the notion of atoms or particles, a concept advanced by Democritus, Epicurus, and Lucretius. Though

---

24 "Magna quidem materia et admirationis non parvae plena, cui et commentarium adieci non minus (ut arbitror) desideratum de consensu et dissensu rerum, quam sympathiam et antipathiam vocant, sine quo natura contagionum plane perquiri et monstrari posse non videbatur." Girolamo Fracastoro, *De sympathia et antipathia rerum*, ed. Concetta Pennuto, Studi e testi del Rinascimento europeo 31 (Rome: Edizioni di storia e letteratura, 2008), 6.

these authors had been incorrect in the details and had been attacked by Galen and Alexander of Aphrodisias, he notes, their basic idea was correct.[25] Objects, composed as they are of atoms, give off effluvia composed of atoms. It is these atoms, having drifted away from their main body, that encounter other atoms in the air; just as they are attracted to or repelled by these other atoms, so they either draw or repel the object of which they are a part in relation to the other object in question. Not only elements have effluvia; so too do qualities. Qualities have a particular physical existence as spiritus, and that spiritus can also move through the air (which condenses and rarefies again as objects move through it). Fracastoro works out this discussion in more detail, and then uses it to develop his theories of contagion in the subsequent book on disease. Such natural movements of attraction and repulsion, accompanied by theories of perception and imagination, also explain emotional responses in humans. Appetite, for example, occurs when the anima perceives a good but does not possess it; the heart accordingly expands so that the good may be used in all relevant parts.

In this little work, then, Fracastoro articulates a general theory of nature that explains the behavior of inanimate objects as well as human responses, including emotions, in entirely material terms. That allows him in turn to discuss his theories about contagious diseases in the work that follows. In the process, he has taken up the Greek terms "sympathy" and "antipathy," words known to Renaissance writers at this point but still in restricted use, and given them a relatively precise, scientific definition. The mechanisms of sympathetic and antipathetic motion and attraction are not visible and hence may appear to the casual observer to be mysterious powers, but in fact they can be explained entirely in physical and material terms using current principles of natural philosophy in the Aristotelian tradition.

---

25 Fracastoro, *De sympathia* (Pennuto ed.), ch. 5, and see Pennuto's introduction, 32–33.

Fracastoro had a number of sources with which to work that employed the terms he used, though he preferred in this treatise simply to present his own argument without discussing explicitly his points of similarity or difference with other authors. Clearly, the long-accessible Pliny was one source. So were the Albertine books of secrets, though some of them used *amicitia*, a term Fracastoro avoided. He had access to both the writings and the translations of Ficino, including Plotinus, as well as Agrippa's text.[26] As a physician trained at sixteenth-century Italian universities, he was familiar with a significant and growing body of Greek authors in medicine and natural philosophy. Among them were several who had written on sympathy in a medical context, including Galen.[27] Although many Galenic texts had long been available in Latin thanks to medieval translations, others had appeared only recently through the efforts of Thomas Linacre and others, and they were having an enormous impact on medical education.[28] Fracastoro also had Alexander of Aphrodisias's commentaries on Aristotle; indeed, he cited both Galen and Alexander early on as critics of the theory of atoms.[29] Some of Alexander's works had been published in Venice in 1495–98, and the *De fato* as well as the *De anima* (which uses the term "sympathy") appeared in 1534. Fracastoro's professor, Pomponazzi, was a noted proponent of Alexander. Fracastoro, then, was very much a participant in what is often called the medical Renaissance or medical humanist scholarship, recovering previously inaccessible ancient texts and working to apply them in the modern world.

Fracastoro's work found readers across Europe for over a century. Concetta Pennuto, who has produced a critical edition and translation

---

26 Pennuto's edition includes references and parallels to a wide range of sources and notes points at which Fracastoro seems to be countering the published opinions of other authors. See for example his differences with Ficino on the causes of magnetism in Fracastoro, *De sympathia* (Pennuto ed.), 167–303.

27 See Holmes's Reflection on "Galen's Sympathy" in this volume.

28 For a general discussion, see Andrew Wear, "Galen in the Renaissance," in *Health and Healing in Early Modern England: Studies in Social and Intellectual History* (Aldershot, UK.: Ashgate, 1998), I.

29 Eckhard Kessler, "Metaphysics or Empirical Science?" in *Renaissance Readings of the Corpus Aristotelicum: Proceedings from the Conference held in Copenhagen 23–25 April 1998*, ed. Marianne Pade (Copenhagen: Museum Tusculanum, 2001), 79–101, at 95. Kessler notes particularly the contrast with contemporaries writing in Platonic traditions.

of the treatise, identified a total of twenty-one editions, most with surviving exemplars, twelve of which she was able to examine and describe. Either they combine *De sympathia et antipathia rerum* with *De contagione*, or they are reprintings of his *Opera omnia*. Thirteen editions appeared before 1600; the last was in 1671, in a Geneva *Opera omnia*.[30] His theories of contagion found widespread interest and debate throughout those years.[31]

The physician known as Paracelsus (Philippus Aureolus Theophrastus Bombastus von Hohenheim, 1493–1541) and his followers pursued a different path to new medicine that nonetheless also relied on sympathy as a concept. Paracelsus was a university-educated son of a physician, and also grew up with mining experience. He became convinced that traditional descriptions of the composition of physical compounds, that is, chemistry, were deficient, as were the Galenic principles that underlay medicine. He turned instead to the cosmological arguments of Platonists. The stars were certain; earthly creation, having emanated from the celestial, carried the signs of the connections that linked parts of the world together. A careful observer could learn to see these signs; other observers might also pass on information about them, observers who may well not have been men of learning or of antiquity, but everyday people past or present.[32] Paracelsus advocated not only the careful study of nature but also thoughtful attention to trade and craft practices and even to popular beliefs as sources of information.

A strongly spiritual and religious sensibility colored the thought of Paracelsus and many Paracelsians.[33] For many, the rejection of standard, classical medical authorities such as Galen ran parallel with a desire to understand divine will via biblical revelation; conversely, the ability to

---

30 Fracastoro, *De sympathia et antipathia rerum*, xxxv–xlvii.
31 Vivian Nutton, "The Reception of Fracastoro's Theory of Contagion: The Seed That Fell among Thorns?," *Osiris*, 2nd series 6, *Renaissance Medical Learning: Evolution of a Tradition* (1990): 196–234.
32 Allen G. Debus, *The Chemical Philosophy: Paracelsian Science and Medicine in the Sixteenth and Seventeenth Centuries*, 2 vols. (New York: Science History Publications, 1977), 1.45–61.
33 Debus, *Chemical Philosophy*, 1.103–5.

read a similar revelation in the book of nature gave a religious gravity to the study of medicine. Allen Debus has thus associated many followers of Paracelsus with religious dissent and Protestant thought in the religious Reformation. Although these physicians disagreed often and strenuously with their predecessors and with one another, they agreed with Agrippa that theories of divine and celestial emanation could be consistent with theories of sympathetic connection in the sublunary realm. Those connections left signs of their presence that could be read by the operator so that the connections could be marshaled to the tasks desired, such as curing disease. Debates over Paracelsian approaches developed in the second half of the century with writings by Peter Severinus, Joseph Duchesne, and others.[34]

Thus by the middle of the sixteenth century, the term *sympathia* itself, as along with the specialized usage of related Latin words such as *amicitia*, had been well introduced to Latin writing; it appeared in several contexts. One was Late-Platonic in philosophical outlook and focused on magic, though not all writings on magic in Platonic learned traditions employed the concept. The Paracelsians might be included here. Another was medical and decidedly materialist, with roots in Galen and others; Fracastoro would be the most noted example. A third might be referred to as the "book of secrets" tradition that arose as part of the use of Pliny; this tradition was deliberately practical and often avoided any attempt at explaining the phenomena it described, emphasizing instead the value of observation and experience. A fourth employed the term as part of a Stoic approach to moral philosophy. All these uses would continue for another century, though these categories overlapped frequently in combinations that varied from one scholar to another.

Nonetheless, they did share some general features. Most of these writers continued to address a learned readership and generally wrote in Latin, though increasingly at least some of these works acquired

---

34 Debus, *Chemical Philosophy*, 1.127–204, and "The Chemical Philosophers: Chemical Medicine from Paracelsus to Van Helmont," in *Chemistry, Alchemy and the New Philosophy, 1550–1700: Studies in the History of Science and Medicine* (London: Variorum Reprints, 1987), III.

vernacular translations. Despite this audience, the authors and their texts were not necessarily fully situated in university culture. Many authors were practicing physicians rather than professors. Paracelsians often set themselves rhetorically as well as professionally against the mainstream of Galenic medicine. Sympathy served most of the writers as an explanatory label for phenomena that attracted their attention for which they found only inadequate explanations in more standard accounts of natural philosophy. Yet they differed greatly in what one might call the theoretical standing of sympathy in their work. For Fracastoro, "sympathy" was a term that denoted a phenomenon whose cause was not intuitively obvious, but which he understood and undertook to explain to his readers. The concept was essential to his theory of contagion. For others, sympathy served more as a placeholder, something of a way station on the road to an explanation. They were obliged to stop there because the limits of their knowledge allowed them to go no further, though they might believe that the road itself continued on and would perhaps be followed by others. Many such authors, like their medieval predecessors, emphasized empirical observation and description rather than causation.

And even among these latter authors, the means by which the operator might discover such connections differed, as did the implications of the discovery. Some emphasized the Platonic arguments that both the hidden links and the signs they left on objects had their origins in the divine mind; the signs were thus left deliberately, and reading them had religious implications. Others emphasized the connections as a part of nature; these links exemplified the need for close observation and empirical collection of data, both so that one might benefit from the practical application and so that one might investigate the hidden causes.

2. More Sympathies, More Contexts

During the later sixteenth century and the first years of the seventeenth, the use of sympathy as word and concept multiplied quickly. A cluster of

Italian writers continued to build on the "book of secrets" tradition, especially in the realm of popular and popularizing publishing. The medieval texts disappeared from print, replaced by these new ones. They described medical cures, natural phenomena, and curiosities. The writings of Giambattista Della Porta (1535–1615) are perhaps the most significant. They share some features with both Agrippa and Paracelsus, but like the book of secrets tradition itself, they lack a religious tone.[35] Born into a noble Neapolitan family, Della Porta had the means to dedicate himself to the study of natural philosophy, and attained a significant reputation; he was an early member of the Accademia dei Lincei in Rome. The first edition of his *Magia naturalis* (1558), his first published work, covered topics that continued to hold his interest throughout his life.

Della Porta organized his own group in Naples, the Accademia dei Secreti, to which he referred in the second edition of his *Magia naturalis* (1589). His books discuss causation from the outset and carry the themes throughout. Della Porta begins in book 1 by presenting basic theories. Chapter 7, devoted to sympathy and antipathy, is strongly reminiscent of Pliny. The sympathies and antipathies, he says, show us the otherwise hidden virtues in the world. Things receive their particular powers or virtues from the heavens, which leave a mark that can be discovered, though one not obvious to the casual observer. It is the discovery and use of these sympathetic connections that constitute natural magic: "the attractions or fetching out of one thing from another, by a certain affinity of Nature."[36] Like Pliny, he also uses the terms "friendship" (*amicitia*) and "enmity." Sympathy explains for Della Porta matters both great and small, from the workings of the lodestone to the ability of nuts and onions to do well together in storage or rue to grow well next to a fig tree. Likewise it accounts for the host of hidden associations revealed in Pliny, in the earlier books

---

35 On Della Porta, including the work's connections with the Venetian Accademia Segreta, see William Eamon, *Science and the Secrets of Nature: Books of Secrets in Medieval and Early Modern Culture* (Princeton, NJ: Princeton University Press, 1994), 194–233.
36 Giambattista Della Porta, *Natural Magick* (London: Thomas Young and Samuel Speed, 1658), 1.9, 13.

of secrets, and in similar works. Della Porta's text saw numerous editions in Latin. An Italian translation appeared just two years after the original publication, followed within a few more by Dutch, German, and French versions. His second expanded edition of 1589 was also quickly translated into Italian and then into German. All versions continued to appear in numerous editions into the early eighteenth century.

Paracelsus and his followers may have developed their theories as a reaction against Galen; yet Galen himself had used the term "sympathy" often, and so its appearance in medical and medical-related writing was not restricted to Paracelsians or other anti-Galenists.[37] A number of works appeared in the late sixteenth and early seventeenth centuries that used the concept in ways that recall both Pliny and Galen, often explicitly. Lynn Thorndike identified a number of them in his multivolume *History of Magic and Experimental Science*.[38] Some focused on natural magic as had Della Porta. The physician and mathematician Girolamo Cardano discussed it in his *De rerum varietate*.[39] Caspar Peucer explained natural divination with it.[40] Walther Hermann Rhyff published an entire commentary on Pliny's book 30, itself devoted to the subject of natural magic (1548).[41] Francesco Patrizi da Cherso discussed similar issues in essays that accompanied a 1593 edition of the Chaldean oracles, the *Pimander*, and other texts in a volume entitled *Magia philosophica*.[42]

---

37 See Holmes, "Galen's Sympathy."
38 Lynn Thorndike, *A History of Magic and Experimental Science*, 8 vols. (New York: Columbia University Press, 1934), esp. vols. 5 and 6.
39 Girolamo Cardano, *De rerum varietate libri XVII* (Lyon: Apud Stephanum Michaelum, 1556); see Thorndike, *A History of Magic and Experimental Science*, 5.571–76.
40 Caspar Peucer, *Commentarius de praecipuis divinationum generibus, in quo a prophetiis divina autoritate traditis, et physicis praedictionibus, separantur diabolicae fraudes et superstitiosae observationes, et explicantur fontes accausae physicarum praedictionum, diabolicae et superstitiosae confutatae damnantur, ea serie, quam tabula indicis vice praefixa ostendit* (Wittenberg: J. Crato, 1553); see Thorndike, *A History of Magic and Experimental Science*, 6.493–501.
41 Walther Hermann Ryff, *In Caii Plinii Secundi Naturalis historiae argutissimi scriptoris I. & II. cap. libri XXX. commentarius*.... (Würzburg: Mylius, 1548); see Thorndike, *A History of Magic and Experimental Science*, 5.560–62.
42 Francesco Patrizi, *Magia philosophica hoc est Francesci Patricii summi philosophici Zoroaster. & ejus 320. Oracula chaldaica. Asclepii dialogus. & Philosophia magna. Hermetis Trismegisti Pomoander... & alia*

Others focused on the production of medicines, whether simples or compounds, as well as poisons and antidotes in terms of sympathies and antipathies, following Pliny and Galen. Albertus Schegelius claimed on his title page that his work was based on lectures by his former professor Girolamo Mercuriale, who offered and explained antidotes by these principles.[43] Anselm de Boot also discussed the sympathetic action of antidotes in his work on gems and stones.[44] Andreas Vesalius, in his surgical treatise *Chirurgia magna*, referred to Galen's principles of sympathy underlying his presentation of simples.[45] The Brescian physician Giovanni Francesco Olmo published a *De occultis in re medico proprietatibus* (Brescia, 1597), in which he presented a set of medical cures and treatments.[46] Francis Bacon included a number of sympathetic cures in his posthumously published *Sylva Sylvarum*, along with other associations more like Pliny.[47] Andreas Libavius, a physician and educator at Jena and Coburg who engaged in a number of education-related controversies, weighed in on such issues in a publication of 1594.[48] He argued against the claims made for sympathetic weapon salve recently being made by some Paracelsian practitioners, but suggested a murdered corpse would indeed bleed anew in the presence of the murderer. In this instance he drew on arguments from both

---

miscellanea. Jam nunc primum ex bibliotheca Ranzoviana è tenebris eruta & latine reddita (Hamburg: Jakob Wolff, 1593); see Thorndike, *A History of Magic and Experimental Science*, 6.460.

43 Albertus Schegelius, *De venenis et morbis venenosis tractatus locupletissimi variaque doctrina referti non solum medicis, verum etiam philosophis magnopere utiles Ex voce...Hieronymi Mercurialis... excepti, atque in Libros duos digesti* (Venice: Paolo Meietti, 1584), see Thorndike, *A History of Magic and Experimental Science*, 5.479–81.

44 Anselmus de Boot, *Gemmarum et lapidum historia: qua non solum ortus, natura, vis et precium, sed etiam modus quo ex iis, olea, salia, tincturae, essentiae, arcana et magisteria arte chymica confici possint, ostenditur* (Hanau, 1609); see Thorndike, *A History of Magic and Experimental Science*, 6.318–23.

45 Andreas Vesalius, *Chirurgia magna in septem libros digesta* (Venice: Officina Valgrisiana, 1568); see Thorndike, *A History of Magic and Experimental Science*, 5.527.

46 Thorndike, *A History of Magic and Experimental Science*, 6.230–32.

47 Francis Bacon, *Sylua Syluarum; or, A Naturall Historie in Ten Centuries...Published after the authors death, by VVilliam Rawley Doctor of Diuinitie, late his Lordships chaplaine* (London: John Haviland and Augustine Mathewes for William Lee, 1626). See esp. century 1.95, devoted to sympathy and antipathy.

48 Andreas Libavius, *Tractatus duo physici; prior de impostoria vulnerum per unguentum armarium sanatione paracelsicis usitata commendataque; posterior de cruentatione cadaverum in justa caede factorum praesente, qui occidisse creditur* (Frankfurt: Joannes Saur, 1593).

Pliny and Fracastoro.[49] Francis Bacon concurred on the bleeding corpse, and the principle was invoked in English practice.[50]

Many other authors on natural philosophy included discussions reminiscent of Pliny as well as their own contemporaries in discussing sympathies in nature. Nicolo Contareni (Venice, 1576), Antoine Mizauld (Paris, 1571), Johannes Thomas Freige (1579), Gulielmus Adolphus Scriborius (1583), Cesare Evoli, Matthias Mairhofer, and many others all included such theories.[51] A number of Ulisse Adrovandi's posthumously published works include passages in which the famous Bolognese physician and naturalist had noted hidden affinities in the tradition of Pliny.[52] Indeed, a considerable amount of Aldrovandi's work continued a practice very like Pliny's of collecting data on many topics from all possible sources and presenting them without evaluation, as a guide to ongoing scholarship. His emphasis on the importance to natural philosophy of reporting all observations, past as well as present, was a feature shared by many of these writers who brought Pliny and Galen into their modern world.

Nearly all the early uses of the word *sympathia* through the first half of the sixteenth century were in Latin, the language of formal learning, philosophy, and medicine. By the middle of the sixteenth century and continuing thereafter, the use of vernacular languages continued to expand across much of Europe to include a broader range of subjects, including more and more that had previously been written about primarily in Latin. During these years the word began to appear in vernacular usage as well, arriving by slightly different routes in each language. Some of the Paracelsians had rejected Latin in favor of vernaculars for their medical writings just as they rejected the classical authorities of established medical learning. Rather than establishing a vernacular equivalent term, they simply moved the Latin (originally, of course, Greek) term in as a loan

---

49 Thorndike, *A History of Magic and Experimental Science*, 6.238–44.
50 Thomas, *Religion and the Decline of Magic*, 220.
51 Thorndike, *A History of Magic and Experimental Science*, 6.349–51 (Contareni), 6.127–28 (Mizauld), 6.186–87 (Freige), 6.351–55 (Scriborius), 6.414 (Evoli), 6.414–18 (Mairhofer).
52 Thorndike, *A History of Magic and Experimental Science*, 6.280–97.

word; for them, then, the word retained the context it had for them in Latin, as a medical and natural philosophical term. In other cases, however, the work's subject was far less technical. Nonetheless, written transmission and Latin texts were of primary importance.

English may serve as an exemplary case; the relatively thorough coverage of Early English Books Online offers a solid, though not yet quite exhaustive, survey of written vernacular usage. The earliest attested appearance of the word "sympathy" in English is 1567. By the end of the century the word had appeared in something over 140 sources. Many of these texts had not been originally composed in English, but rather were translations of works that had been published previously in French or Italian. The most common usages are general medical or humoral references appearing in texts that are not themselves technical in nature. Nonetheless, the earliest appearances of the word relate to human feelings and emotions, whether referring to a single individual such as body and soul or to connections between people, particularly in romantic love. This usage remained the most common through the end of the century.

The *Oxford English Dictionary*'s first reference is a work whose full text has yet to be included in Early English Books Online: Geoffrey Fenlon's translation of Matteo Bandello's *Certaine Tragicall Discourses*.[53] The word appears four times in borrowed form as *sympathia* or *simpathia*, referring to an accord of feeling between two persons.[54] All instances describe romantic love. Thomas Paynell used the word in the same way (1572) in his translation from French of the *Treasury* of Amadis.[55] Words such as "amity" and "friendship" appear with it; this usage recalls the usage of Erasmus with its Stoic sensibility.

Others are Galenic. A translation of André Thevet's description of New World discoveries (1568) cites Galen as the authority for the

---

53 Matteo Bandello, *Certaine Tragicall Discourses Written out of Frenche and Latin....*, trans. Geoffrey Fenton (London: Thomas Marshe, 1567).
54 Matteo Bandello, *Certain Tragical Discourses of Bandello*, ed. Robert Langton Douglas, 2 vols, Tudor Translations (London: D. Nutt, 1898), 1.142, 197, 2.186, 247, 312.
55 Thomas Paynell, *The Treasurie of Amadis of Fraunce Conteyning Eloquente Orations, pythie epistles, learned letters, and feruent complayntes, seruing for sundrie purposes* (London: Henry Bynneman for Thomas Hacket, 1572), 260.

"Simpathie" that connects a location and its climate with the manners of the region's inhabitants.[56] Richard Cavendish enlists such a concept in discussing the soul's connection with the body in a work with a much more Christian focus, *The Image of Nature and Grace* (1571): "And euen naturall Philosophy teacheth this, that betwéene the soule and the body, there is a certaine sympathy or knitting of affection: for who seeth not that in melancholy bodyes the mynde is heauy and solitary, in sanguine bodies mery and lyght, &c."[57] Richard Huloet's dictionary, intended to provide French and Latin terms for English ones, associates sympathy in French and Latin forms with the English "combination."[58] Thomas Newton's translation of the Dutch physician Levinus Lemnius's *Touchstone of Complexion* (1576) uses "sympathy" to describe the connection between inner complexion or balance of humors and outward appearance.[59] Newton also translated Lemnius's *Herbal for the Bible* (1587), in which a claim about the power of saffron might recall Pliny as well as Galen: "But it is so comfortable for the hart, that if it be tied to the ring finger of the left hand, it presently pearceth and sendeth his vertue to the hart. The agreement and sympathie betweene it and the hart is so great, that being either taken inwardly, or applied outwardly, it foorthward worketh by the Arteries, and ceaseth not till it get accesse vnto it."[60] In a few cases the word appears in a translation of a classical text that had itself used it, for example the Thomas North version of

---

56 André Thevet, *The New Found Worlde; or, Antarctike Wherin is Contained Wonderful and Strange Things.*...(London: Henrie Bynneman for Thomas Hacket, 1568), fol. 4v.

57 Richard Cavendish, *The Image of Nature and Grace Conteynyng the Whole Course, and Condition of Mans Estate* (London: John Daye, 1571), 15.

58 Richard Huloet, *Huloets Dictionarie Newelye Corrected, Amended, Set in Order and Enlarged...by vvhich you may finde the Latin or Frenche, of anye English woorde you will*, ed. John Higgins (London: Thomas Marsh, 1572), n.p.: "*Combination, or mutuall and naturall operation of thinges according to their kyndes, as water doth participate with ayre in moystnes, with the earth in coldnes. & c.* Sympathia, ae. foe. g. *Conueniance, Sympathie. S.*"

59 Levinus Lemnius, *The Touchstone of Complexions Generallye Appliable, Expedient and Profitable for all Such, as be Desirous & Carefull of their Bodylye Health*, ed. and trans. Thomas Newton (London: Thomas Marsh, 1576), fol. 36v.

60 Levinus Lemnius, *An Herbal for the Bible. Containing a Plaine and Familiar Exposition of such similitudes, parables, and metaphors, both in the olde Testament and the newe*...., trans. Thomas Newton (London: Edmund Bollifant, 1587), 192.

Plutarch's *Lives* (itself based on a French translation and not the original Greek); the word appears as part of the explanation of naphtha in the "Life of Alexander," likened to the material used by Medea.[61] But the usage in Pliny found its way into English only later; the earliest English publications (1566, 1585, 1587) included only the first sixteen books, in which the term did not appear. A full version appeared only in 1601.

The English example, then, points to earlier vernacular usage in Italian and French that then moved into English when these texts were translated for an English market. They employed sympathy as a way of offering a brief, medical or natural-philosophical explanation for a particular feature being described in the work. Those features might be the habits of foreigners as a function of climate in a description of travels and discoveries; or they might involve the phenomenon of romantic love as it sprang up and grew between two people. Some of these texts had moved directly into English from Latin, for example those of Levinus Lemnius. Those that were translated quickly into English were his less technical works; others of Lemnius were translated only a century later. So the word moved into English along with other features of cultivated leisure reading from the Continent. It exemplifies the ways educated writers might dot their prose with allusions to natural philosophy, all with a classical pedigree.

For most of these authors, the word remained at the periphery of their interest. Most English authors who used the word "sympathy" used it only once or perhaps twice in a given publication, so that is difficult to know whether the word held a precise, philosophical meaning for them. This pattern is a far cry from an author like Fracastoro, with a whole book devoted to the subject and a theory of disease that relied on it. Over the course of the seventeenth century, when English natural philosophers and other scholars began to compose professional works

---

61 Plutarch, *The Lives of the Noble Grecians and Romanes Compared Together by That Graue Learned Philosopher and Historiographer, Plutarke of Chaeronea; translated out of Greeke into French by Iames Amyot . . . ; and out of French into Englishe, by Thomas North* (London: Thomas Vautroullier and John Wight, 1579), 742.

increasingly in English, the word picked up more such technical usage. At the same time, its use in nontechnical, more ordinary language continued to spread. These different kinds of usage also continued to overlap, especially due to tendencies in natural philosophy. Paracelsians, "professors of secrets," and many others deliberately invoked a rhetoric and a practice of seeking observations of nature from whatever source. That included observations recorded in writing by others, in ancient times or modern, in sources philosophical or literary, or observations that circulated orally. Pliny and Galen both served as models and as sources of particular observations, but hardly as exclusive sources.

3. Attacks on Sympathy

Natural philosophy, like any scholarly field, inhabited a world of debate and disputation. The various ways in which "sympathy" figured in descriptions and explanations were no exception. Further, the sixteenth century was full of religious controversy, often accompanied by legal, political, and other coercive implications. The term was not associated with a single definition, usage, philosophical school, or method, but it appeared in a number of controversial environments. Given this varied usage, it is not surprising that those who attacked concepts of sympathy were not always aiming at the same target; nor were they participants in a single set of disputes. Yet most criticisms fall into a few main groups. One was the widespread and multifaceted assault on magic, witchcraft, and related activities that spread in both Protestant and Catholic regions. That wave gained force over the course of the century. This was just the era in which the Plinian and "book of secrets" traditions were themselves growing.

Nothing about natural magic required or even involved a belief in the existence of conscious nonphysical beings—demons—whose assistance might be invoked by operators; quite the contrary. Yet the use of term "magic" itself was inflammatory to persons who sought to defend access to divine power. Those authors who claimed to see the creator's hand at work as they read nature's hidden signs were not the only ones subject to attack on religious grounds; those who wrote without mention of matters divine at all fared little better. Church officials of whatever confessional stripe, Catholic or Protestant, labeled such efforts to invoke hidden powers "superstition." They tended to presume the possibility of demonic role in the positions of those they attacked, even evoking the early church's battles with paganism. And in fact some of the authors of works on natural magic did confirm their opponents' worst fears by examining and considering seriously the possibility that nonphysical beings or demons might exist and be brought into service. The attacks on their writings, therefore, were not always entirely unfounded. Eamon observes that Della Porta developed an interest in the possibility of such demons and wrote about them in his unpublished *Criptologia*, though even here his claims were far from those advanced by the persecutors of witches or supposed demon worshippers as the objects of their investigations.[62]

Within natural philosophy, some major changes in thinking about the nature of causes and explanations of causes chipped away at the uses of "sympathy" more or less as soon as they appeared. As Keith Hutchison has shown, opinion gradually shifted during the seventeenth century in how hidden or occult qualities were understood, and in how they served in a search for causes.[63] For many scholars of earlier generations, the ability to identify an object as possessing a given quality served as an acceptable level of explanation about the properties in question. By the later sixteenth and early seventeenth centuries, more and more scholars found such use of the old Aristotelian classification "quality" to be inadequate, particularly as a source of explanation rather than just description. Perhaps even more significant was the decreased usefulness seen in distinguishing between the sensible and the hidden qualities or causes. Natural philosophers found far greater utility in proceeding from the

---

62 Eamon, *Science and the Secrets of Nature*, 206–10.
63 Keith Hutchison, "What Happened to Occult Qualities in the Scientific Revolution?," *Isis* 73.2 (1982): 233–53.

outset as if a given quality of an object was something that required investigation and explanation; and further, as if any quality, whether hidden or manifest to human senses, called for an equal level of explanation. That is, all qualities were coming to be treated as hidden or occult qualities had once been treated, so the distinction lost its meaning.[64]

Such a view was consistent with an attitude seen in many works that could be identified with books of secrets or Plinian traditions. "Sympathy" was used by many as a label or placeholder for an unseen and otherwise unknown connection between an observed cause and effect. It left open the possibility that an understandable cause might be discovered. In such a scenario, "sympathy" would simply retreat gradually as it was replaced by these more specific explanations. Descartes asserted confidently that natural explanations would eventually be produced for all phenomena: "there are no qualities which are so occult, no effects of sympathy or antipathy so marvelous or so strange, nor any other thing so rare in nature (granted that it is produced by purely material causes destitute of thought and free will), that its reason cannot be given by [the principles of the mechanical philosophy.]"[65] Most of these practical texts had concerned themselves so little with the particulars of causal explanation that no explicit attack on "sympathy" was necessary. Indeed, identifying a previously unknown cause for observed phenomena might be seen as consistent with some, at least, of the goals of the compilers. Bacon had, after all, included some in his lists of proposed experiments in the *Sylva sylvarum*.

Many such authors—or compilers—had taken the rhetorical stance that they merely recorded observations of nature whatever their source, however inexplicable the observation might be or how humble the observer. That claim left them vulnerable to attacks when some, at least, of those observations were tested and found wanting. Brian Copenhaver

---

64 Hutchison, "What Happened to Occult Qualities," 244.
65 René Descartes, *Principia philosophiae*, pt. IV, par. 187 (in *Oeuvres,* ed. Charles Adam and Paul Tannery [Paris: Vrin/CNRS, 1964], 9.309), quoted in Hutchison, "What Happened to Occult Qualities," 242.

has detailed the efforts to explain the purported ship-stopping power of the echeneis fish that were coupled with the search for the fish itself; those efforts gradually led to assertions that Pliny had offered his readers not a genuine observation, but a mere fable.[66] The label "superstition" was not the sole property of churchmen. It had its own distinguished pedigree as a classical term of disapprobation for irrational credulity and adherence to practices that lacked rational justification. The Paracelsians had made a point of taking their observations where they found them, whether from the learned or the unlettered; many of the agricultural associations from books of secrets seemed redolent of peasant lore; Pliny's lists looked increasingly suspect as more failed one test or another. It had become standard practice for such writers to recite, Pliny-like, a long list of apparently bizarre associations to emphasize the hidden nature of the connections; even Fracastoro had done so. The lists became an easy target for those who wished to attack arguments about sympathy or natural magic in general, or an author in particular, as a mere survival of old superstitions.

Superstition had been a matter of increasing concern for many in later medieval Europe, a concern that may have shifted focus but did not decline in the sixteenth century. Michael Bailey has argued that while superstition never achieved a consistent definition, attacks on superstition tended in two different directions. One, taking its cue from early authorities such as Augustine, addressed learned studies that claimed or seemed to relate to magic or to predictive sciences such as astrology. The other strove to define and direct popular devotion and hence took issue with practices of the unlearned.[67] Sympathy had the misfortune to fall into both categories at once, attacked by some as part of a condemnation of magical arts, by others as a feature of the untrustworthy observations and rustic practices of the uneducated.

---

66 Brian P. Copenhaver, "A Tale of Two Fishes: Magical Objects in Natural History from Antiquity through the Scientific Revolution," *Journal of the History of Ideas* 52.3 (1991): 373–98.
67 Michael David Bailey, *Fearful Spirits, Reasoned Follies: The Boundaries of Superstition in Late Medieval Europe* (Ithaca, NY: Cornell University Press, 2013), 228–29.

The weapon salve controversy gave these disagreements a particularly high profile. Rudolph Goclenius's 1608 treatise, in which he discussed an ointment or powder purported to cure wounds by sympathetic action when applied to the weapon that had caused the injury, produced strong supporters, equally strong detractors, and an extended set of publications and debates.[68] Magnetism and theories of magnetic action were invoked; the arguments, the scholarship, and even the honor and religion of opponents were impugned. Sir Kenelm Digby also weighed in with a treatise on the salve, which went through numerous reprintings.[69] The controversies that swirled around Goclenius's text did not serve to strengthen the cause.[70] Nor did the efforts by opponents to associate the cure with witchcraft, either in the eyes of those who saw witchcraft as a threat or of those who saw it as foolishness. Thus the Pliny-type argument—a type that developed in the sixteenth century as very modern, using evidence both from the most recently available classical sources and the observation of nature—could be dismissed by various detractors as the outdated survivals of popular superstition. Such attacks were too easily taken at face value by later scholars predisposed to such a narrative.

Renaissance theories of sympathy thus did not develop continuously from medieval foundations, and certainly not as a traditional cast of mind that was finally rejected in a general move toward rationality. Their proponents occupied an intellectual environment that included greater access to a fuller range of classical sources, a broader learned community that reached beyond the universities to include practicing

---

68 Rudolph Goclenius, *De Vita proroganda, hoc est animi corporisque vigore conservando salubriterque producendo tractatus* (Mainz: J. Albinus, 1608).

69 Sir Kenelm Digby, *A Late Discourse . . . Touching the Cure of Wounds by the Powder of Sympathy: With Instructions How to Make the Said Powder*, trans. R. White (London: Lownes and Davies, 1658).

70 The literature on the powder of sympathy or weapon salve controversy is extensive. Among others, see Debus, *Chemical Philosophy*, 1.279–90, 2.303–6, and "Robert Fludd and the Use of Gilbert's *De Magnete* in the Weapon-Salve Controversy," in *Chemistry, Alchemy and the New Philosophy, 1550–1700: Studies in the History of Science and Medicine* (London: Variorum, 1987), XII; Ernest B. Gilman, "The Arts of Sympathy: Dr. Harvey, Sir Kenelm Digby, and the Arundel Circle," in *Opening the Borders: Inclusivity in Early Modern Studies: Essays in Honor of James V. Mirollo*, ed. Peter C. Herman (Newark: University of Delaware Press; London: Associated University Presses, 1999), 265–97.

physicians and other educated people, and a print industry sufficiently developed to support the circulation of a wide range of works. They saw themselves as innovators in one way or another. This scholarly use of the term in natural philosophy originated in Latin and moved only gradually to vernaculars with the linguistic transition of scholarly writing.

By that time, "sympathy" had moved into European vernaculars in other less technical contexts, as a word with medical or learned connotations that might be used to describe human character and the relations between people and their environment, or between one another. The vernacular word recalls any of a range of ancient contexts, including Stoicism, Galenic medicine, and Christian moral philosophy, but without a clear allegiance to any of them. The rapid introduction of this word, and the cluster of concepts that it expressed, into European languages allowed writers to use it in a number of different ways from the seventeenth century onward.

Reflection
MUSIC AND SYMPATHY
Giuseppe Gerbino

Already in antiquity musicians observed that the strings of an instrument can vibrate without being touched. For example, if two strings are tuned at the unison and we pluck one of them, the second string will respond to the vibration, producing the same sound. The phenomenon is known as sympathetic resonance or sympathetic vibration. What causes the second string to resonate with the first, with no direct physical connection between the two, is the transmission of energy carried by sound waves traveling in the air. However, the term "sympathetic resonance" reveals a different worldview, one that postulated the existence of a hidden force, sympathy, operating throughout nature and binding the universe in all its parts. In such a world, the two strings respond to each other's motion because of a mysterious affinity that can be conceived by the mind but cannot be directly perceived by the senses. Thus, the notion of sympathy, especially in the Ficinian-Platonic version, provided an explanation for an otherwise incomprehensible wonder of nature, while sympathetic resonance in its turn provided evidence of the existence of universal sympathy.[1] This was a

---

[1] One of the most comprehensive investigations into the phenomenon of sympathy in the early modern period is Girolamo Fracastoro, *De sympathia et antipathia rerum liber unus. De contagione et contagiosis morbis et curatione libri iii* (Venice: Heredes Lucaeantonii Iuntae Florentini, 1546), on

powerful conceptual alliance. Its influence extended well beyond the investigation of the acoustic properties of sound to the problem of how to understand the very nature of music and its relation to a hierarchically ordered and sympathetically interconnected universe.

Historically, practical applications of sympathetic resonance are usually found in instruments with sympathetic strings, in part because the successful reproduction of this phenomenon depends on systems that can generate sustained and high-energy vibrations like those produced by bowing. There is a reference to such an instrument in Francis Bacon's 1627 *Sylva Sylvarum; or, A Natural History in Ten Centuries*: "It was devised, that a viol should have a lay of wire-strings below, as close to the belly as a lute; and then the strings of guts mounted upon a bridge, as in ordinary viols; to the end that by this means the upper strings strucken should make the lower resound by sympathy, and so make the music the better; which, if it be to purpose, then sympathy worketh as well by report of sound, as by motion."[2] Although skeptical about the actual functionality of such a device, Bacon is probably describing a precursor of the viola d'amore, a type of unfretted viola with a flat back and sloping shoulders that became popular between the end of the seventeenth century and the beginning of the eighteenth. Two versions of the same instrument are known, with or without sympathetic strings. In the latter case, the viola d'amore usually has six or seven bowed strings running along the fingerboard, as in a regular viola, and six or seven resonating strings running beneath the fingerboard and through holes in the bridge. The resonating strings prolong the sound's decay time,

---

which see Concetta Pennuto, *Simpatia, fantasia e contagio: Il pensiero medico e il pensiero filosofico di Girolamo Fracastoro* (Rome: Edizioni di storia e letteratura, 2008). Further examples of the enduring influence of and interest in sympathetic resonance may be found in Penelope Gouk, "Music in Francis Bacon's Natural Philosophy," in *Number to Sound: The Musical Way to the Scientific Revolution*, ed. Paolo Gozza (Dordrecht: Kluwer Academic, 2000), 135–52; and Claude Palisca, "Moving the Affections through Music: Pre-Cartesian Psycho-Physiological Theories," in *Number to Sound: The Musical Way to the Scientific Revolution*, ed. Paolo Gozza (Dordrecht: Kluwer Academic, 2000), 289–308.

2 Francis Bacon, "Sylva Sylvarum," in *Works*, ed. James Spedding, Robert Leslie Ellis, and Douglas Denon Heath, 15 vols. (New York: Hurd and Houghton, 1869–72), century 3, 4.294–95.

producing a silvery and soft halo. Leopold Mozart famously remarks that the instrument sounds "especially lovely in the stillness of the evening."[3] Antonio Vivaldi wrote extensively for the viola d'amore, especially for the female music ensembles of the Ospedale della Pietà in Venice, including a particularly evocative concerto for lute, viola d'amore, and muted strings (RV 540). He himself played a six-string version of the instrument. In the autograph manuscripts of two of his concertos (RV 393 and RV 397) the name is spelled *viola d'AMore*, probably an homage to his best pupil and virtuoso player at the Pietà, Anna Maria. As late as 1904, in Giacomo Puccini's *Madama Butterfly*, in the middle of the night, as Cio-Cio-San, her son, and her maid Suzuki await the return of Lieutenant Pinkerton, the viola d'amore accompanies the wordless voices of an invisible chorus, as if to invoke the resonance between souls at an incommensurable distance.[4]

The origin of the term "viola d'amore" (literally "viol of love") is uncertain. But the body of the instrument, with its ordered arrangement of sympathetically vibrating strings, inhabits a metaphor that is at the same time visual and auditory. Its pegbox is often decorated with a carved head in the form of a blindfolded Cupid or a woman with eyes closed. It suggests a worldview in which love and sympathy are still understood as intimately related principles of an occult bond, evoking the image of a sympathetically coherent and unified cosmos in which the affinity or force of attraction between the parts and the whole is experienced as love. Or perhaps the blindfolded Cupid, looking down the instrument's strings like a tutelary deity, pushes the musical metaphor of love and sympathy further. One of the

---

[3] Leopold Mozart, *The Art of the Violin*, trans. Elisabeth Kaplan, ed. Matthias Michael Beckmann, ([Salzburg]: Kunstverlag Polzer, 2008), 40.

[4] Act 2, last scene (Humming Chorus). Puccini had a viola d'amore built by Leandro Bisiach for the premiere of the opera at La Scala. The instrument is housed in the Museo degli Strumenti Musicali in Milan. See Andrea Gatti, ed., *Museo degli strumenti musicali* (Milan: Electa, 1998), 50–51.

characteristics of sympathetic vibration is that, if the two strings share sufficient harmonic likeness, its effect is inescapable. Like love, sympathetic response is not an act of volition but an irresistible and blind force. It is not a subjective participation in someone else's emotions, but an objective property of being. Moreover, as I mentioned, sympathetic vibration only happens if the right conditions are present. The two vibrating bodies have to be somewhat alike, their form or mode of being somehow congruent. Modern acoustics has explained the nature of such congruence by demonstrating that sympathetic resonance occurs when the natural oscillatory periods of sonorous vibrators are harmonically related and the vibrations are isochronous, thus demystifying the enigmatic properties of musical sympathy.[5] But in a world in which an adequate physical understanding of such a phenomenon was not yet available, the symbolism of the viola d'amore allowed ideas of ontological similitude, love, and sympathy to coalesce into a cohesive object and a sensory experience.

The stratification of meanings discernible in the viola d'amore rested on the long-standing authority of philosophers who turned to sound phenomena to explain the evanescent notion of sympathy. And they probably did so because the behavior of strings in musical instruments had one fundamental advantage: it allowed them to demonstrate, in an easily observable fashion, that in the chain of beings action exerted on an object can affect another object, and that therefore the two objects must be somehow connected by a principle of concordance or similitude. Discussing the influence of heavenly bodies and the efficacy of prayer, Plotinus writes:

---

[5] On the development of musical acoustics in the early modern period, including the important contributions of Galileo Galilei and Christian Huygens, see Hendrik Floris Cohen, *Quantifying Music: The Science of Music at the First Stage of the Scientific Revolution, 1580–1650* (Dordrecht: D. Reidel, 1984).

But the sun, or another heavenly body, does not hear his prayer. And that which he prays for comes about because one part is in sympathetic connection with another, just as in one tense string; for if the string is plucked at the lower end, it has a vibration at the upper. But often, too, when one string is plucked, another has a kind of sense of this by its concord and the fact that it is tuned to the same scale. But if the vibration can even pass from one lyre to another in so far as a sympathy exists, then there is also one single harmony in the All, even if it is composed of opposites; and it is in fact composed of parts which are alike and all akin, even when they are opposite.[6]

In Marsilio Ficino's hands, this musical conception of the correspondence between beings and things, coupled with the medical theory of the time, was further developed into an explanatory model for the power that music wields over the human soul. For Ficino sound and spirit—the thin vapor produced in the heart by mixing air and blood and the bond between body and soul—are linked by a special affinity. They both owe their almost imperceptible materiality to their likeness to air. Therefore, music, which as movement of the air uses air as its medium, excites the spirit into the same motion, and through the spirit the soul, with a force that has no equivalent in human physiology.[7] For centuries the power of music to affect human emotions thrived on the memory of this sympathetic resonance, long after its philosophical underpinnings had waned. Caught in the resonance of its own *spiritus*, the whole human being becomes music. Or in T. S. Eliot's words, "music heard so deeply that it is not heard at all, but you are the music while the music lasts."

---

[6] Plotinus, "On the Problems of Soul," *Ennead* IV.4.41, trans. A. H. Armstrong, Loeb Classical Library 443 (Cambridge, MA: Harvard University Press, 1984), 265. This passage is discussed at length in chapter 2 in this volume.
[7] On Ficino's music-spirit theory see D. P. Walker, *Spiritual and Demonic Magic from Ficino to Campanella* (1958; University Park: Pennsylvania State University Press, 2000), 3–11; and Gary Tomlinson, *Music in Renaissance Magic* (Chicago: University of Chicago Press, 1993), 101–44.

CHAPTER FOUR

Seventeenth-Century Universal Sympathy

STOICISM, PLATONISM, LEIBNIZ, AND CONWAY

Christia Mercer

The concept of sympathy plays an increasingly important role in philosophy over the course of the seventeenth century. In this chapter, I explore some of the most prominent debates about the concept in the middle decades of the century and then use this material to display its significance in the metaphysical systems of G. W. Leibniz and Anne Conway. Both philosophers are committed to universal sympathy, according to which all creatures correspond sympathetically to all the others. Although this is primarily a metaphysical claim, it has moral implications.[1]

Section 1 offers an overview of the notion of sympathy in the seventeenth century. At the beginning of the century, sympathy is an "occult

---

[1] Eric Schliesser has been enormously helpful in designing the arc of this volume and making fine comments on my chapter. The other contributors have helped me think more clearly about sympathy. I would also like to thank the Herzog August Bibliothek and the American Academy in Rome for support during the time I was working on this project.

power" treated mostly by thinkers on the periphery of philosophy. During the second half of the century, it becomes a central component of mainstream philosophical systems. Section 2 discusses Stoic ideas about sympathy extant in the period and displays how three seventeenth-century thinkers use them. Section 3 turns to Platonist doctrines that constitute some of the raw materials for thinking about sympathy and articulates two kinds of relations: sympathy and enhanced sympathy. Section 4 displays the important role sympathy plays in the thought of G. W. Leibniz (1646–1716). Leibniz transforms the traditional notion into a central doctrine in one of the most significant metaphysical systems in the history of philosophy. Section 5 turns to the thought of the English Platonist Anne Conway (1631–79). Conway uses enhanced sympathy to create a metaphysics of striking originality. She goes beyond Leibniz to affix a moral aspect to universal sympathy. Finally, section 6 offers some concluding remarks about the concept's arc in the century.

1. Understanding the Occult

In 1600, Giordano Bruno was burned at the stake in the Campo de' Fiori in Rome. The public execution of a prominent philosopher and cosmologist exemplifies the struggles and passions that philosophical ideas in the period provoked. By 1600, the Protestant reformers had splintered into warring factions and the counter-reformation was well under way. Europe was embroiled in political instability, religious chaos, and random acts of violence. Passionate disagreements extended to debates about the interconnections among the parts of the world. Many philosophers and students of nature assumed that worldly parts shared a sympathetic connection, although there were diverse ways of referring to, describing, and explaining these interconnections. In chapter 3 of this volume, Ann Moyer notes the history of the word *sympathia* and its cognates in the Renaissance, and displays the wide range of views about the "sympathetic" or "friendly" powers of nature. The common assumption underlying these diverse views is that there is, in the words of one prominent thinker, "a certain affinity of Nature."[2] The disagreements arose in attempting to describe and explain this affinity.

By 1700, Leibniz's philosophy of preestablished harmony was known throughout Europe and Isaac Newton's *Mathematical Principles of Natural Philosophy* of 1687 was changing the course of science. Seventeenth-century views about sympathy influenced this groundbreaking work.[3] The path from Renaissance notions of sympathy as a mysterious and magical power to something that could be rendered with logical and mathematical precision is more complicated than can be given here, but some of the most prominent steps along the way are as follows.

The sixteenth century was full of thoughtful people who believed in various forms of sympathetic magic and hidden forces.[4] As Moyer shows, a wide array of medical doctors and natural philosophers took there to be phenomena whose explanations demanded a "sympathy," "friendship," or "affinity" among parts of the world. Important fifteenth-century thinkers like Marsilio Ficino and Giovanni Pico della Mirandola promote the idea that bodies can be manipulated to "influence" one another "at a distance." Although some considered the manipulation of the hidden or occult powers of nature to be demonic, many assumed that a thorough familiarity with such powers was a means to benefit humankind and discover, in Pico's words, the "miracles concealed in the recesses of the world."[5]

Debates about sympathy as an "occult power" persist through the seventeenth century and continue to include questions about magic and the

---

2 Giambattista della Porta, *Natural Magick* (London: Thomas Young and Samuel Speed, 1658), 1.9, 13; quoted in chapter 3.
3 This is a controversial claim for which I will not argue here.
4 See Giuseppe Gerbino's Reflection in this volume, which discusses the fascinating case of "sympathetic resonance" as evidence of "a hidden force, sympathy, operating throughout nature and binding the universe in all its parts." Particularly relevant here is the association assumed between love and sympathy.
5 Giovanni Pico della Mirandola, "Oration on the Dignity of Man," trans. Elizabeth Livermore Forbes, in *The Renaissance Philosophy of Man*, ed. Ernst Cassirer, Paul Oskar Kristeller, and John Herman Randall (Chicago: University of Chicago Press, 1948), 248–49. Moyer discusses Pico's views and a longer version of this passage.

dangers of manipulating such hidden forces. Many consider it important to distinguish natural from supernatural powers and to identify the kind of magic involved in their manipulations.[6] For some, because sympathetic powers are supernatural, they defy understanding and even proper description. For others, because they are natural, their effects allow for study and careful description, even though their underlying cause might lie beyond what is "intelligible." A widely used philosophical lexicon published in 1613 distinguishes between "natural magic," which marks the "perfection" of philosophy, and "superstitious magic," which involves "incantations and impure spirits" and is "diabolical."[7] The same lexicon defines the occult as what is "hidden or concealed from either sense or intellect or both."[8] Given our concerns, the most important sense of the term "occult" in the period is to designate natural powers that, with the right training, humans can learn to manipulate for their benefit. Leibniz, in his typical clear-headed fashion, distinguishes between an occult power whose cause is unknown and one whose "effect...can never become intelligible." The latter must be avoided in serious philosophy.[9] In short, well into the seventeenth century, there is widespread disagreement about whether sympathetic powers afford careful exploration and articulation or defy understanding altogether.

Beginning in the early seventeenth century and lasting for several decades, the most prominent site for such debates about these issues is a medical phenomenon, "the power of sympathy," on which hundreds of pages were written by learned experimenters and thoughtful physicians. It was widely agreed that an effective way to treat a wound was to apply a salve or powder (usually made out of copper sulfate) to an object that

---

[6] As the *Oxford English Dictionary* entry on magic notes, to study and manipulate natural powers in the period were often considered "legitimate and necessary fields of enquiry." But some manipulation, especially of "supernatural" powers, was considered dangerous or "demonic." See *OED* (Oxford University Press, 2013, http://www.oed.com).

[7] See Rudolph Goclenius, *Lexicon Philosophicum* (Frankfurt, 1613; repr. Hildesheim: Georg Olms, 1980), 657. Goclenius has a lengthy discussion of the term "magic" and its sources.

[8] Goclenius, *Lexicon Philosophicum*, 273.

[9] Leibniz, *Die philosophischen Schriften von Gottfried Wilhelm Leibniz*, ed. C. I. Gerhardt, 7 vols. (Leipzig: Lorentz, 1879; repr. Hildesheim: Georg Olms, 1978), 3.519, hereafter Gerhardt.

contained blood from the wound (say, the sword that caused the wound or a bandage that had bound it). Well-respected medical doctors confirmed the healing powers of the treatment and then debated how best to describe the "sympathetic bond" between the wound and the blood to which the salve was applied. Rudolph Goclenius (1572–1628), a prominent Protestant professor of Marburg, promoted the use of the treatment, which he described as "natural magic," operating through sympathy.[10] In response, a Jesuit and professor of Würzburg and Mainz, Jean Roberti (1569–1651), warned against using any form of magic since it involved the "deceitful work" of the devil with whom practitioners were clearly in cahoots.[11]

Jan Baptiste van Helmont (1580–1644), an influential Flemish physician and "chemist," helps to shift the discussion in 1621 with the publication of *On the Magnetic Curing of Wounds*, in which he insists that the debate between Goclenius and thinkers like Roberti, "who would involve demons," could be easily resolved: all that was needed was to explain thoroughly the salve's healing powers and make them "open to understanding."[12] Van Helmont offers a neat account of the debate and its history. According to him, the well-known physician and cosmologist Paracelsus (1493–1541) showed "sympathy to be natural" and so paved the way for a fully naturalistic account of this feature of the world.[13] Anyone who wants "to explain sympathy and antipathy" in terms of demonic powers has simply misunderstood what it means to be natural. When doctors "manipulate" these "vitalities," they are merely using their understanding of powers in God's world. Because the effects of these vital forces sometimes seem "paradoxical," they are often attributed to the devil. In fact, they result from a vitality that "has scattered itself

---

10 Goclenius wrote a number of popular books, including the *Lexicon Philosophicum* of 1613.
11 For more on this debate, see Walter Pagel, *Joan Baptista Van Helmont: Reformer of Science and Medicine* (Cambridge: Cambridge University Press, 1982), 8–9.
12 Jan Baptiste van Helmont, *De magnetica vulnerum curatione*, in *Opera omnia* (Frankfurt: Johann Justus Erythropilus, 1632), §105–6.
13 For more on Paracelus, the name given to Philippus Aureolus Theophrastus Bombastus von Hohenheim, see chapter 3, 86–90.

around" so that "all things" mutually "feel, move, are related, etc."[14] I will say more about Van Helmont's views about vitality, power, and sympathy in the next section. The main point now is that he represents a shift in the seventeenth century to an attempt to offer an account of sympathetic powers that is thoroughgoing enough to be understood by all.

The "powder of sympathy" as a medical treatment and philosophical conundrum persisted at least through the 1660s. One of the most widely known English philosophers of the seventeenth century, Kenelm Digby, gave an account of the treatment in terms consistent with the new mechanical philosophy.[15] According to the physical model offered by philosophers like Descartes, Hobbes, Gassendi, and Digby, all the features of the corporeal world could be explained in terms of corporeal components and their motions.[16] In his *Two Treatises* of 1644, Digby offers an eclectic metaphysics based on a radical reinterpretation of Aristotle's theory of elements and an atomistic account of nature.[17] Having studied medicine and experimented with the healing powers of "the

---

14 Van Helmont, *De magnetica vulnerum curatione*, §142–43. Also see Pagel, *Joan Baptista Van Helmont*, 10–12.

15 Kenelm Digby was an early member of the Royal Society and correspondent with prominent figures like Hobbes, Descartes, and Marin Mersenne. Digby wrote and lectured on this phenomenon in the 1650s. His book *A Late Discourse… Ttouching the Cure of Wounds by the Powder of Sympathy: With Instructions How to Make the Said Powder*, trans. R. White (London: Lownes and Davies, 1658), was originally published in French in 1658; it went through many editions and was translated into numerous languages. For a helpful account of Digby as situated in the complications of English religious politics and some secondary literature, see John Henry, "Sir Kenelm Digby, Recusant Philosopher," in *Insiders and Outsiders in Seventeenth-Century Philosophy* ed. G. A. J. Rogers, Tom Sorrell, and Jill Kraye (London: Routledge, 2010), 43–75. This context is important, but so is the "reformed philosophy" movement of which Digby was part. On this, see my *Leibniz's Metaphysics: Its Origins and Development* (Cambridge: Cambridge University Press, 2001), ch. 3. Also see my "Kenelm Digby," in *Routledge Encyclopedia of Philosophy*, ed. E. Craig (London: Routledge), 1998; e-book, http://www.rep.routledge.com/article/DA028SECT3.

16 The young Leibniz places Digby alongside Galileo, Gassendi, Descartes, and Hobbes as a prominent "new philosopher." References to Leibniz's work in this chapter are mostly to *Sämtliche Schriften und Briefe* (Darmstadt: Berlin Academy, 1923–), cited by series, volume, and page number; hereafter "A." A standard English edition is *Philosophical Papers and Letters*, trans. Leroy E. Loemker, 2nd ed. (Dordrecht: Reidel, 1970); hereafter "L." The reference here is to A VI 1.489–90; L 110.

17 Kenelm Digby, *Two Treatises: In the one of which, the Nature of Bodies, in the other, the Nature of Mans Soule; Is Looked into; In the Way of Discovery, of the Immortality of Reasonable Soules* (Paris: Gilles Blaizot), 1644. For a discussion of Digby and some of his views, see my *Leibniz's Metaphysics*, 105–7, 109–11.

powder of sympathy," Digby became known throughout Europe for his atomistic explanation of sympathy. According to his account, because "the atoms of blood" on the object treated with the powder will seek their "proper source and original root" and because the powder "cannot choose but make the same voyage together with the atoms of blood," the power will find "the proper source and original root whence they [the atoms of blood] issue" and "will joyntly be imbibed together within all the corners, fibres, and orifices of the Veins which lye open about the wound" so that the wound "must of necessity be refresht, and in fine imperceptibly cured."[18] Digby insists that instead of resigning ourselves to a "hidden Secret of Nature" or "some occult property," it is possible to "examine the business, as it ought to be, observing all that is done."[19] If we are properly careful in our observations, then "we need not have recourse to a Demon or Angel,"[20] but rather can grasp the "profound and hidden mysteries of Nature." To discern the workings of sympathy, we need only "take the pains to discover them."[21]

The main conclusion to draw from this section is that the middle decades of the seventeenth century witness a shift in discussions about the "sympathetic" or "friendly" powers in nature. Although accounts involving occult forces and demons persist, physicians and philosophers increasingly seek a detailed account of the cause and nature of these powers. They begin, in other words, to attempt to offer a metaphysical grounding for phenomena traditionally associated with occult sympathetic forces.

2. Universal Sympathy: Early Modern Stoicism

The primary goal of this section is to display the significance of Stoicism as a source of ideas for those seventeenth-century thinkers attempting to

---

18 Digby, *Powder*, 191–93. Digby's proposals were taken very seriously and even applied to the so-called "longitude problem." See Dava Sobel, *Longitude* (New York: Walker, 1995), 41–42.
19 Digby, *Powder*, 191–93.
20 Digby, *Powder*, 205.
21 Digby, *Powder*, 167.

create a systematic account of universal sympathy. Before turning to Stoicism, however, it will be helpful to note briefly one of the main philosophical difficulties that Stoic notions of sympathy were supposed to help solve. With the dismantling of the Ptolemaic universe and the promotion of new conceptions of the cosmos, as suggested by Johannes Kepler (1571–1630) and others, the need to rethink the forces in God's world seemed increasingly obvious.[22] The slow demise of Aristotelian physics coupled with the failure of the mechanical philosophers to ground their new physics in a satisfactory metaphysics encouraged many in the second half of the century to rethink the vital powers in nature.[23] The 1650s and 1660s saw an explosion of creative ways of describing and explaining natural activity. The need to reconsider the activity and interrelations among natural things partly motivates the thought of prominent thinkers like Spinoza, Leibniz, and Newton as well as a long list of lesser known philosophers, including Henry More, Margaret Cavendish, Erhard Weigel, Nicolas Malebranche, and Anne Conway. Some of these thinkers found inspiration in the notion of sympathy, and many turned to Stoicism as a source for ideas about sympathetic powers.

In discussing early modern Stoicism, it is important to distinguish between Stoic ideas inherited from medieval Christianity and those introduced in the Renaissance. As one scholar puts it, ancient Stoicism was "absorbed into the complex amalgam of Judaic and Greek teaching that became Christian theology and ethics.... Of all the ancient philosophies, Stoicism has probably had the most diffused but also the least explicit and adequately acknowledged influence on western thought."[24]

---

22 For example, Kepler uses the Platonic solids as a means to understand the movement of the planets. For a fine introduction to Kepler's thought, see Daniel A. Di Liscia, "Johannes Kepler," in *The Stanford Encyclopedia of Philosophy* (Summer 2011 ed.), ed. Edward N. Zalta, http://plato.stanford.edu/archives/sum2011/entries/kepler/.

23 For an account of some of the problems facing the first mechanists and the role of Platonism in solving those problems, see my "Platonism in Early Modern Natural Philosophy: The Case of Leibniz and Conway," in *Neoplatonic Natural Philosophy*, ed. Christoph Horn and James Wilberding (Oxford: Oxford University Press, 2012), 103–26.

24 A. A. Long, "Stoicism in the Philosophical Tradition: Spinoza, Lipsius, Butler," in *Cambridge Companion to the Stoics*, ed. Brad Inwood (Cambridge: Cambridge University Press, 2003), 365–92, at

Stoic ideas were part of the intellectual materials that early modern Europe inherited from medieval theism. When the term "sympathy" and its cognates gained common currency in the fifteenth and sixteenth centuries, they could comfortably apply to long familiar ideas.

The history of Stoic metaphysics in the first half of the seventeenth century has yet to be written, but two things are clear. With the rediscovery of Stoic writings in the Renaissance, new raw materials were available and a careful inventory of Stoic metaphysical views became possible for the first time in hundreds of years. The late sixteenth and early seventeenth centuries witnessed an increasing fascination with Stoicism as a philosophical source set against Aristotelianism and Platonism. Originally this interest focused on the moral philosophy of thinkers like Seneca and Epictetus. But in 1604, Justus Lipsius (1547–1606), the most prominent early modern promoter of Stoicism, published what one scholar has called "the first systematic attempt to gather together the fragments of the Stoics."[25] The result of Lipsius's scholarly work led to a much better understanding of Stoic metaphysics and a clearer sense that, as Lipsius noted, Stoic ethics and metaphysics are inseparable. The effects of this important publication, however, were probably not what its author intended: Stoic metaphysical doctrines were so clearly unorthodox that there was a rising tide of disapproval.[26] By the 1670s, condemnations became international and vitriolic.[27] For example, the English Platonist Ralph Cudworth and the important German Aristotelian Jakob Thomasius are willing to list the dangers of

---

365–67. Also, as Eyjólfur Emilsson suggests in chapter 2 of this volume, Platonists often employed Stoic ideas. It follows then that Christian thinkers used this amalgamation to construct their Platonist Christianity.

25 John Sellers, "Is God a Mindless Vegetable? Cudworth on Stoic Theology," *Intellectual History Review* 212. (2011): 121–33, at 121–22.

26 See Justus Lipsius, *Manuductionis ad Physiologiae Stoicorum libri tres, L. Annaeo Senecae, aliisque scriptoribus illustrandis* (Antwerp: J. Moretus, 1604). For a helpful overview of Lipsius, see Jan Papy, "Justus Lipsius," in *The Stanford Encyclopedia of Philosophy* (Fall 2011 ed.), ed. Edward N. Zalta, http://plato.stanford.edu/archives/fall2011/entries/justus-lipsius/.

27 As protests increased about the dangers of Spinoza's thought, Spinoza was increasingly branded a Stoic so that, in Sellers's words, "the fate of Stoicism became intertwined" with the fate of Spinozism. See Sellers, "Is God a Mindless Vegetable?," 124.

Stoic metaphysics. In his *True Intellectual System of the Universe* of 1678, Cudworth offers a sustained critique of Stoic philosophy.[28] In a lengthy book published in 1676 on the dangers of Stoic philosophy, Leibniz's mentor, Thomasius, presents a detailed comparison of the views of Aristotelians, Platonists, and Stoics on a number of points, emphasizing the false and dangerous views of the Stoics.[29] Unsurprisingly, Leibniz is thoroughly familiar with Stoic ethics and metaphysics. Although he applauds some of their ideas, he rejects their claims that "God is the soul of the world or, if you wish, the primary power of the world" resulting in "a blind necessity" that "determines him to act."[30] In other words, as Stoic metaphysical views became increasingly understood in the seventeenth century, more and more thinkers rejected their views as too heterodox. Few philosophers explicitly align themselves with Stoic metaphysics after the middle part of the period, although many combine Stoic ideas with those of other schools to explain the sympathetic powers of nature.[31] It is virtually impossible to identify specific Stoic doctrines that directly influenced the development of seventeenth-century treatments of sympathy because, as we will see, they are so often combined with ideas from Platonism. In the remainder of this section, I survey the thought of three seventeenth-century philosophers who are particularly interested in sympathy, frequently refer to the Stoics, and propose ideas that seem indebted to Stoicism.

Jan Baptiste Van Helmont wrote a series of treatises in the first half of the seventeenth century that range from mystical to medical and

---

28 See Sellers, "Is God a Mindless Vegetable?." But it is important to acknowledge that, as Sarah Hutton points out, Cudworth employed Stoic terminology and was sympathetic to some Stoic ideas. Also, according to Hutton, Cudworth's "Stoicism is blended with Platonism." See her introduction to *Ralph Cudworth: A Treatise concerning Eternal and Immutable Morality with a Treatise of Freewill* (Cambridge: Cambridge University Press, 1996), ix–xx.
29 See Jakob Thomasius, *Exercitatio de Stoica Mundi Exustione* (Leipzig: Lanckisius, 1676).
30 Leibniz, A VI 4[B].1384–85. Find the English in *Philosophical Essays*, ed. and trans. Roger Ariew and Daniel Garber (Indianapolis: Hackett, 1989), 282, hereafter, AG. Leibniz refers to Stoic views frequently. See, for example, A VI 4[B].1313, 1320, 1480, 1482.
31 See Long, "Stoicism in the Philosophical Tradition," 385–92.

explicitly draw on ideas from Paracelsus, the Stoics, and Platonist authors.[32] There is insufficient space here to give an overview of Van Helmont's thought or even to list his various concerns. Instead, I give a rough summary of those metaphysical claims that form the context for the thought of Leibniz and Conway. According to Van Helmont, God is responsible for a spirit that permeates the "whole universe" and "preserves concord" among all things.[33] In chapter 1 of our volume, Brouwer discusses the Stoic notion of fire or "pneuma" that fills and enlivens the world. Van Helmont sometimes describes God as full of light and fire, insisting that the "flame" of God fills all things and constitutes their essence. Because this spirit, fire, or vital "power has scattered itself around," there is "a connection among things as active spirits"[34] and hence a mutual "sensing and common attraction" among them.[35] That is, the activity of all things seems to entail that they "feel, move, [and] are related" to one another and hence form a tightly "unified and interrelated whole."[36] Van Helmont sometimes asserts that God shares the "simple essence" of vitality and spirit so that "all things are unified" and thereby form a perfect "unity among substances."[37] Regardless of how inactive some earthly bodies may appear, everything stands in sympathetic attraction and concord with everything else and so is active.[38] Because all things are active and all active things "sense" and "feel," it follows that all things sense and feel all the others. As far as I know, Van Helmont does not explicate his views about perception and feeling in any detail, although he acknowledges an "ineffable intellectual light"

---

32 See Jan Baptiste Van Helmont, *Opera omnia* (Frankfurt: Johann Justus Erythropilus, 1632). The references to Paracelsus and the Stoics are scattered throughout his works. There are significantly fewer explicit references to Plato and Platonists. See 254, 273, 290, 654, 811.
33 Jan Baptiste van Helmont, *De magnetica vulnerum curatione*, in *Opera omnia*, §151.
34 Van Helmont, *De magnetica*, §131.
35 Van Helmont, *De magnetica*, §142–43.
36 Van Helmont, *De magnetica*, §108.
37 Jan Baptiste Van Helmont, *Imago Dei*, in *Opera omnia*, 666–68.
38 Van Helmont, *De magnetica*, §151. Leibniz famously talks about the "mirroring" of substances or monads. As we will see, the mirroring among creatures is an important feature of his account of universal sympathy.

filling the world,[39] which motivates humans to recognize "the Goodness, Power, infinity, Glory, and Truth" of God. This light is a "mirror" of the divinity.[40] To summarize the most important points for us: the spirit and vitality of God permeates the world and each creature; each creature is an active and perceiving thing; each perceiving thing senses and feels all other creatures; the result of the shared vitality and the mutual perception is a "perfect harmony" among creatures.

Sylvester Rattray, a Scottish physician, published a book in 1658 entitled *New Approach to Recently Discovered Occult Causes of Sympathy and Antipathy: Brought to Light through the Principles of Natural Philosophy*.[41] According to Rattray, his contemporaries attempt to explain the causes of sympathy and antipathy using the theories of Aristotle and Galen. Instead of engaging in the errors of these and "other Ancients," it is time to offer an account based on new experiments. Rattray describes the various means by which he has studied the causal relations among plants, animals, and minerals. By submitting their "elements" to the fire and carefully studying the results, he is able to describe their sympathetic interactions.[42] He summarizes the views of the Aristotelians and the Epicurean atomists and finds each insufficient as an explanation of the medical phenomena. The Aristotelians fall short because "substantial forms" are "not useful" and cannot be understood.[43] The atomists fail because their two principles, "the Atoms and the void," do not "explain in what way matter is active in itself."[44] They neither offer a sufficient explanation of the "constancy of essences" nor do their explanations allow real understanding of "how things are formed." In the end, Rattray prefers the account of Van Helmont because it offers

---

39 Jan Baptiste Van Helmont, *Venatio scientiarum* in *Opera omnia*, §17.
40 Van Helmont, *Venatio scientiarum*, §46–48.
41 Leibniz is familiar with Rattray. See Leibniz, A VI 4[A].682.
42 Silvester Rattray, *Aditus Novus ad Occultas Sympathiae et Antipathiae Causas Inveniendas: Per Principia Philosophiae Naturalis, ex Fermentorum Artificiosa Anatomia hausta Patefactus* (Glasgow: Andreas Anderson, 1658). See "To the Reader."
43 Rattray, *Aditus Novus*, 84–86.
44 Rattray, *Aditus Novus*, 90–94.

better explanations of natural activity, the "diverse grades of things," and their interconnections. Rattray's work includes a very long list of the powers of plants, vegetables, and minerals, including the way they ferment and interact. Although Rattray's articulation of Van Helmont's metaphysical views is somewhat cursory, his main concern is to describe the healing powers "of Sympathy" in the world.[45]

In 1669, a young German philosopher, Jacob Heinrich Gangloff, published his university dissertation, *On Sympathy*.[46] The fifty-page work explores the current metaphysical and physical debates about sympathy. One of its main concerns is to show that sympathetic "effects" are not the result of "occult powers"; another goal is to use the Aristotelian notion of substantial form to help explain sympathy. Gangloff avers that when phenomena occur "concerning humans, animals, and other natural things" whose causes "are not able to be seen," people turn immediately to "occult qualities," which are "as a whole called SYMPATHY" and of which they have "a feeble understanding."[47] In an attempt to define the term in a way that "unifies" its various senses, Gangloff proposes in chapter 1 that sympathy is "a mutual natural harmony among natural things, arising from a particular hidden affinity on account of which these things, by a friendly affect or secret love, are mutually drawn to each other."[48] He gives a brief history of the notion, citing a wide range of philosophers. He mentions the ancient Aristotelian Alexander Aphrodisias, who explained "natural affinity and loving concord" in terms of a similarity "whether of origin, or nature or temperament," and refers to the ancient Sicilian philosopher Empedocles (ca. 495–435 BCE), whom

---

45 Rattray, *Aditus Novus*, 135–36.
46 The major claims in seventeenth-century dissertations are very often those of the presiding professor, the equivalent of a dissertation adviser. The presiding professor here is Johann Michael Schwimmer, a professor at the university in Jena, who wrote on related topics.
47 Jacob Heinrich Gangloff, *Disputatio physica de sympathia* (Jena: Samuel Adophus Müller, 1669), A 2r.
48 Gangloff, *De sympathia*, A 2r. The Latin is: "SYMPATHIA est *conspiratio* mutua naturalis inter res physicas, orta ex peculiari occulta cognatione, ob quam istae res amico affectu, seu occulto amore, ad se invicem trahuntur." The word *cognatio* here appears frequently in the second half of the seventeenth century in explications of sympathy. In Stephanus Chauvin's *Lexicon*, for example, we find that sympathy is "affectionum cognatio [an affinity of affections]." See Chauvin, *Lexicon Philosophicum*, 2nd ed. (Leeuwarden, repr. Düsseldorf, 1713), 647.

he quotes as claiming that sympathy is "mutual love, friendship of things, harmony of things, agreement of natural things."[49] He also cites the sixteenth-century Dutch scholar Joseph Justus Scaliger (1540–1609).[50]

Gangloff distinguishes in chapter 1 between "natural" and "moral" sympathy. The former concerns "the harmony of natural bodies." Moral sympathy, on the other hand, concerns "jointly commiserating or mutual benefit." Gangloff intends to explicate the notion in terms of substantial forms. Because there is a substantial form "in every individual," which constitutes its "principle of individuation" and the cause of its distinctive "temperament," one can turn to the form of a thing to explain its sympathy.[51] God, the "author of nature," has constructed natural things to be drawn to one another, although the amount of "mutual harmony [*conspiratuo*]" among them differs. After presenting the definition and brief history of sympathy in chapter 1, Gangloff turns his attention in chapter 2 to describing its effects, insisting that we can "know sympathy by its effects." Relying on the work of Galen, Avicenna, and especially Rattray, he lists various natural phenomena and then avers: "the only reasonable cause is *Sympathia*."[52] Finally, in chapter 3, Gangloff turns to various accounts of sympathy. He moves through the views of a diverse group of thinkers (including Aquinas and Francisco Suárez) to take up the proposal of Jan Baptiste van Helmont and the idea that there is "a universal form and soul of the world" and that this "universal form...permeates all things." It is this form or "soul of the world" that is the cause of the "gentle sympathy" of all things. In the end, therefore, it is this "spirit of God" that "animates the world."[53] The implication is that this divine animating spirit constitutes the forms of things. Gangloff endorses the Aristotelian notion that the individual substantial

---

49 Gangloff, *De sympathia*, A 2v. The Latin is: "amor mutuus, amicitia rerum, rerum concordia, rerum naturalium convenientia."
50 Gangloff, *De sympathia*, A 2r.
51 Gangloff, *De sympathia*, §6.
52 Gangloff, *De sympathia*, §22–23.
53 Gangloff, *De sympathia*, §47–49.

form of a substance constitutes its principle of activity. But he also makes each form the source of "affinity" and "love." The amount of sympathy is partly a function of the similarity among creatures (for example, horses are more sympathetic to horses) and partly due to proximity in space and time.

Van Helmont, Rattray, and Gangloff offer impressively detailed descriptions of the effects of sympathy. Despite their different concerns, they are strikingly similar in their fundamental claims. They are all willing to mix Stoic ideas with those of Paracelsus and other sources, both ancient and modern, to explain sympathy. They agree that the greater the similitude among creatures, the greater the affinity. And they agree that the ultimate cause of sympathy is a divinely produced spirit that is shared among creatures so that each has an affinity for all the others. Although the details of their explanations differ, they concur that sympathy is a divinely produced power or, in Gangloff's words, "a hidden affinity" that draws things together.

3. Universal Sympathy: Platonism

By the fifth century, Christianity had absorbed Platonist assumptions. Although few works by the historic Plato were extant in the Latin west, the Platonist ideas promulgated by Plotinus (204/5–70 CE) and Proclus (412–85 CE) informed much of medieval philosophy.[54] When Aristotelianism was imported from the Arab world in the thirteenth century, it too was full of Platonism. Scholasticism resulted from the blending of this Platonized Aristotelianism and medieval Christianity.[55] European Platonism changed radically in the fifteenth century, when the great

---

54 For a helpful account of Platonist views about causation between the fourth and twelfth centuries, see Ian Wilks, "Efficient Causation in Late Antiquity and the Earlier Medieval Period," in *Efficient Causation: A History*, ed. Tad Schmaltz (New York: Oxford University Press, 2014).

55 Brian Copenhaver and Charles Schmitt have written: "Given the quantity of Platonic material transmitted" through Arabic authorities "or generally in the air in medieval universities, it is not surprising that parts of Thomist metaphysics owe more to Augustine, Proclus, or Plotinus than to Aristotle." See Brian P. Copenhaver and Charles B. Schmitt, *Renaissance Philosophy* (Oxford: Oxford University Press, 1992), 133.

Florentine humanist Marsilio Ficino (1433–99) produced an edition and translation of all of Plato's dialogues.[56] The awkward truth about Ficino's Platonism, however, is that it owes almost as much to the thought of Plotinus and Proclus as to Plato himself.[57] By the middle of the seventeenth century, many philosophers had rejected Ficino's interpretations and were keen to distinguish between the "mystical things" he says about Plato and "the teaching of...the great man."[58] But the die had been cast: Ficino's editions and commentaries would continue to define future discussions. Another major source of early modern Platonism is the Augustinianism endorsed by both Protestants and Catholics. Luther himself emphasized the importance and profundity of Augustine's thought[59] and counter-reformation theologians praised the "divine Augustine."[60] Seventeenth-century discussions of sympathy are informed by many forms of Platonisms. Unsurprisingly, the designation "Platonism" is frustratingly vague although various strands and loosely connected doctrines can be associated with the term.[61] In the remainder of this section, I explicate metaphysical commitments that reveal Platonist sources and that constitute the raw materials out of which seventeenth-century thinkers

---

56 Ficino's edition and translations were circulated widely and remained prominent well into the eighteenth century.

57 Ficino also edited and translated Plotinus's *Enneads*. Much has been written about Ficino, his thought, and his influence. A fine place to begin an exploration of these topics is Michael J. B. Allen, Valery Rees, and Martin Davies, *Marsilio Ficino: His Theology, His Philosophy, His Legacy* (Leiden: Brill, 2002).

58 Leibniz, Gerhardt, 7.147. Leibniz's mentor, Thomasius, complains that Ficino's account of Plato is more "poetic" than philosophical. See *Exercitatio*, 184.

59 Albrecht Beutel writes that Augustine was "of utmost importance to Luther" and a major source of his "reformational renewal." See Albrecht Beutel, "Life," in *The Cambridge Companion to Martin Luther*, ed. Donald K. Mckim (Cambridge: Cambridge University Press, 2003), 3–19, at 5.

60 For the importance of Augustinianism in seventeenth-century France and for other examples of major figures proclaiming the importance of the "divine Augustine," see Stephen Menn, *Descartes and Augustine* (New York: Cambridge University Press, 1998), esp. 21–25.

61 It is an awkward truth about prominent Platonists that they put forward elaborate theories that are sometimes only remotely connected to the texts of the Athenian philosopher himself. On the heterogeneity of early modern Platonism, see Paul O. Kristeller and Michael Mooney, eds., *Renaissance Thought and Its Sources* (New York: Columbia University Press, 1979); and my "Platonism and Philosophical Humanism on the Continent," in *A Companion to Early Modern Philosophy*, ed. Steven Nadler (Oxford: Blackwell, 2002), 25–44. For a recent discussion of Platonism, see Lloyd P. Gerson, "What Is Platonism?," *Journal of the History of Philosophy* 43.3 (2005): 253–76.

like Leibniz and Conway build their metaphysics of universal sympathy. They are as follows.

Supreme being assumption: For many ancient thinkers, ontological priority was to be explained mainly in terms of self-sufficiency. As one scholar makes the point, "that which stands in need of nothing for being what it is is ontologically primary."[62] For many Platonists, there was a hierarchy of self-sufficiency and being such that each of the lower strata in the hierarchy was supposed to depend on and be caused by the higher. Many Christian and non-Christian Platonists assumed that there is a supremely perfect, wholly simple, and unified being on which all else depends. Only the highest being was wholly perfect, self-sufficient, simple, and real. The beings in the lower strata had diminishing degrees of these features. Modern philosophers have tended to think of being as an all or nothing affair, but there is a long line of Platonists who endorse a hierarchy of being. The assumption is that the strata in the hierarchy differ according to their unity, self-sufficiency, and perfection. What is more self-sufficient is more unified and therefore more fully what it is. What has less self-sufficiency and unity is less independent and therefore less fully what it is.[63] For many in this tradition, self-sufficiency required activity and awareness. Van Helmont, Rattray, and Gangloff endorse main parts of the supreme being assumption: they all seem to believe that the supreme being shares its self-sufficient vitality with its creatures so that the latter have a lesser kind of self-sufficiency. Each creature is itself relatively unified and each contributes to the unity of the whole. For Van Helmont and Gangloff, the unity of the world is grounded in the fact that each active thing has a degree of "feeling" and "relatedness" with all the others.

---

62 Eyjólfur K. Emilsson, "Cognition and Its Object," in *The Cambridge Companion to Plotinus*, ed. Lloyd Gerson (Cambridge: Cambridge University Press, 1996), 217–49, at 245.

63 Needless to say, this is a thorny topic. The hierarchy of being is often described in terms of ontological and causal dependency, but not always. For a good introduction to the issues, see Dominic J. O'Meara, "The Hierarchical Ordering of Reality in Plotinus"; and Kevin Corrigan, "Essence and Existence in the *Enneads*," both in *The Cambridge Companion to Plotinus*, ed. Lloyd Gerson (Cambridge: Cambridge University Press, 1996), 66–81, 105–29. For more recent discussions of these topics, see Lloyd P. Gerson, *The Cambridge History of Philosophy in Late Antiquity* (Cambridge: Cambridge University Press, 2010), 638–48.

Emanative causation: There are two closely related kinds of emanative causation. By far the more significant in the history of philosophy is hierarchical emanation, where the cause is taken to be more perfect than its effect. The assumption here is that, for a being A that is more perfect than a being B, A emanates its attribute f-ness to B in such a way that neither A nor A's f-ness is depleted in any way, with the result that B has f-ness, though in a manner inferior to the way it exists in A. The emanative process is continual so that B will have f-ness if and only if A emanates f-ness to it.[64] For many theists, for example, God conceives triangularity or has it as "an idea," which is the emanative cause for created triangles. The divine idea is perfect; its effect is not. The latter is often said "to participate in" or be an "image of" the former. For theists, one of the great benefits of hierarchical emanation is that it allows God to be both transcendent from and immanent in creatures. In his *Philosophical Lexicon* of 1613, Goclenius says he is following Plato and Augustine in claiming that God "contains all things" in the best and "most excellent way" while creatures contain them with "a certain limitation." Although "creatures are not the being [esse] of God himself, nonetheless they are in him…[because] whatever is in creatures proceeds from God."[65] For those philosophers who endorse more than one stratum in a hierarchy of being, each of the strata has its attributes independently of its emanated effect and yet those attributes are immanent in the effect. As Conway puts it, God is "in a real sense an essence or substance distinct from his creatures" and yet "is not divided or separate from them but present in everything most closely and intimately in the highest degree." God "gives to them form and figure but also essence, life, body, and whatever good they have."[66]

---

64 The history of the causal theory of emanation is rich and complicated. For more on the views in early modern philosophy discussed here, see my *Leibniz's Metaphysics,* especially 178–95. In the seventeenth century, there were a number of different accounts of emanation. The account I offer here covers the most important of those. For a recent helpful survey, see Eric Schliesser, "Newtonian Emanation, Spinozism, Measurement and the Baconian Origins of the Laws of Nature," *Foundations of Science* 10.3 (2012): 1–18.

65 Goclenius, *Lexicon Philosophicum,* 694.

66 Anne Conway, *The Principles of the Most Ancient and Modern Philosophy,* trans. Alison Coudert and Taylor Corse (Cambridge: Cambridge University Press, 1996), I §3, 9. References to this edition include book, section, and page number. So the citation here is book I, section 3, p. 9.

The nonhierarchical sense of emanative causation is modeled on the hierarchical, but does not require that the effect be inferior to its cause. As the fifth-century Platonist Proclus writes in his influential *The Elements of Theology*: "Every productive cause produces... while itself remaining steadfast. For if it imitates the One, and if the One brings its consequents into existence without movement, then every productive cause has a like law of production."[67] For us, the important point is that certain sorts of active things produce their effect without being diminished. Like the hierarchical notion, the f-ness of B is assumed to be coexistent with the emanative activity of A.[68] And like the hierarchical notion, the effect is often understood to follow with necessity in the sense that A's action constitutes the necessary and sufficient conditions of B.[69] In the *Immortality of the Soul* of 1659, the English philosopher Henry More writes: "An Emanative Effect is coexistent with the very substance of that which is said to be the Cause thereof. This must needs be true, because that very Substance which is said to be the Cause, is the adequate and immediate Cause, and wants nothing to be adjoined to its bare essence for the production of the Effect."[70]

Plenitude: In order to understand the role of sympathy in early modern philosophy, we need to be clear about what was supposed to follow from God's nature. The principle of plenitude assumes that God fills the world with as many beings as possible. For Plotinus, the supreme being emanates the fullness of its being continually so that every possibility exists. He writes: "it is not possible for anything else to come into being; all things have come into being and there is nothing

---

67 Proclus, *The Elements of Theology*, ed. and trans. E. R. Dodd (Oxford: Oxford University Press, 1964), prop. 26.
68 My account of nonhierarchical emanation owes a good deal to Eileen O'Neill, "Influxus Physicus," in *Causation in Early Modern Philosophy*, ed. Steven Nadler (University Park: Pennsylvania State University Press, 1993), 27–55; and to Schliesser, "Newtonian Emanation."
69 See O'Neill, "Influxus Physicus," for a thorough discussion of the nonhierarchical notion in early modern natural philosophy.
70 Henry More, *Immortality of the Soul, so farre forth as it is demonstrable from the Knowledge of Nature and the Light of Reason* (London: Flesher, 1654), book 1, ch. 6, 2. Leibniz took notes on More's book during the years 1677–78, and he compares More's views about the "common sense" to those of Van Helmont. See Leibniz, A VI 4[B].1678–80.

left."[71] The common assumption is that God's nature implies not only that the world is filled with creatures but also that they stand in harmony with one another. As the influential Jewish Platonist Philo of Alexandria (c. 20 BCE–50 CE) makes the point: "And being superior to, and being also external to the world that he has made, he nevertheless fills the whole world with himself; for, having by his own power extended it to its utmost limits, *he has connected every portion with another portion according to the principles of harmony*."[72] Generations of theists insist that divine goodness and unity apply to the organization of created things and that God adds to the goodness of the world by making the world appropriately harmonious. As Thomas Aquinas (c. 1225–1274) succinctly makes the point about order: "each thing in its nature is good, but all things together are *very good*, by reason of the order of the universe, which is the ultimate and noblest perfection in things."[73] Philosophers in the Platonist tradition take universal sympathy to add significantly to the goodness of worldly order.

Universal sympathy: The conjunction of the supreme being assumption, emanative causation, and plentitude implies a good deal about the order of the world. It was common in the seventeenth century to relate vitality or self-sufficiency to perception or sense and affinity. As we have seen, Van Helmont assumes that active things have active spirits and that active spirits feel and sense one another. Gangloff describes the harmony formed by mutually sympathetic creatures as one of "friendly affect or secret love." The underlying assumption for such thinkers is that God causes creatures to have vitality, from which it is supposed to follow that each creature responds sympathetically to the states of all the others. For the purposes of this chapter, it will be helpful to think of the sympathetic relation as follows: two creatures bear a

---

71 Plotinus, *Enneads*, V.5.12.46–47.
72 Philo, *The Works of Philo*, trans. C. D. Yonge (Peabody, MA: Hendrickson, 1952), 5.14, my emphasis.
73 Thomas Aquinas, *Summa Contra Gentiles*, trans. and ed. James F. Anderson (Notre Dame, IN: University of Notre Dame Press, 1975), 2.45 [10].

sympathetic relation to one another when each perceives and responds to each of the states of the other. When every created thing bears a sympathetic relation to every other, there is universal sympathy. For thinkers like Conway, the sympathetic relation helps explain antipathy in that a creature cannot be repelled by another (or otherwise antipathetic to it) unless it bears a sympathetic relation to it.

Enhanced universal sympathy: As we have seen, many philosophers took the divine nature to entail an order among creatures and many conceived that order in terms of universal sympathy. For those interested in theological questions about divine justice and the problem of evil, universal sympathy was taken to contribute significantly to the goodness of the world. The sympathetic relation among creatures not only seemed to constitute an additional good, it was also believed to increase worldly goodness over time because creatures could enhance one another's progress. As an introduction to the metaphysics of Leibniz and Conway, it will be helpful to explicate what I will call enhanced universal sympathy. When two creatures bear a sympathetic relation to one another, each responds to the other. When two creatures bear an enhanced sympathetic relation to one another, an increase in the goodness of one will cause an increase in the goodness of another, although the relation is nonreciprocal (that is, the increase in the second will not then promote an increase in the first).[74] Since enhanced sympathy means that an increase in the goodness of one creature will promote an increase in the goodness of those creatures with which it has this enhanced relation, it follows that an increase in the goodness of any creature will cause an increase in the goodness of every other. In a world in which enhanced sympathy holds among all creatures, each is capable of contributing much more to the goodness of the world than merely its present state of goodness: with every increase in its goodness, it contributes to the goodness of every other creature with which bears the relation.

---

74 For a fuller account of these notions in the period, see my, *Leibniz's Metaphysics*, ch. 6, and "Platonism in Early Modern Natural Philosophy," especially 111–13.

There is enhanced universal sympathy when all creatures bear an enhanced sympathetic relation with all others. The supreme being assumption can be taken to suggest that an increase in goodness involves an increase in vitality or self-sufficiency, which itself is related to moral perfection. As we will see, Leibniz seems to think that human beings bear an enhanced sympathetic relation to one another. Although he is not committed to enhanced universal sympathy, Conway is.

4. Gottfried Wilhelm Leibniz

Leibniz is one of the most significant figures in the history of philosophy, mathematics, logic, and physics. He is famous for his metaphysics of preestablished harmony, according to which created substances do not causally interact, but stand in perfect harmony with one another, each expressing God and all other substances from its own unique point of view. Like so many other early modern thinkers, he grounds his metaphysics in the belief that God shares divine self-sufficiency with created things, whose mutual affinity creates a tightly unified whole. But unlike his predecessors, Leibniz transforms this idea into a metaphysics of astonishing originality: each of an infinity of substances corresponds perfectly with all the others and each expresses God, the world, and every other substance. Preestablished harmony is universal sympathetic harmony pushed to its limits.[75]

From the very beginning of his philosophical career, Leibniz conceives the relation between God and the world in emanative terms and the relation among creatures as a tightly unified harmony among substances. Consistent with the supreme being assumption and with hierarchical causal emanation, Leibniz insists that God is a supremely perfect, self-sufficient, and unified being that emanates its attributes to

---

[75] I have argued elsewhere that these constitute the materials out of which Leibniz developed his famous doctrine of preestablished harmony. For that account, see *Leibniz's Metaphysics*, esp. chs. 6, 8, and 10 (sect. 3).

an infinity of creatures. Every substance contains all the attributes of God, although in a manner inferior to their divine source. In a very early essay, he acknowledges that his account of the relation between God and creatures owes a good deal to Platonism and Stoicism. As he explains in 1668–69, he agrees with the Stoics and "Plato in the Timaeus about the world soul" in understanding God to be "diffused through everything."[76] Like Van Helmont and Gangloff, Leibniz takes God to share divine self-sufficiency and vitality with every creature. Like Gangloff, he describes the vital nature of each substance as having a form. *On the Origin of Things from Forms* of 1676 claims that God "contains the absolute affirmative form that is ascribed in a limited way to other things."[77] In a related essay, he adds: "all things are in a way contained in all things. But they are contained in a quite different way in God from that in which they are contained in things."[78] All creatures contain all things and sympathetic harmony relates them all to one another.

Before turning to Leibniz's account of universal sympathy, it is important to acknowledge that he does not use the term *sympathia* or its cognates very often. When he does use the term, it is usually in the context of analyzing bodies, their "coherence" and motions.[79] As we have seen, Leibniz's early modern predecessors disagree in what sense sympathetic powers are occult and whether they resist understanding. Even for thinkers like Van Helmont and Gangloff who struggle to make the "affinity" and "love" among natural things "understandable," sympathy remains a somewhat mysterious power binding the parts of the universe. Leibniz famously complains that Isaac Newton's account

---

76 Leibniz, A VI 1.510. He also mentions Aristotle's agent intellect in this context.
77 A VI 3.520. For an edition and translation of some of these important papers, see *De Summa Rerum: Metaphysical Papers, 1675–76*, ed. and trans., G. H. R. Parkinson (New Haven, CT: Yale University Press, 1992), Hereafter "Pk." Pk 79–81.
78 Leibniz, A VI 3.523: Pk 85. Also see A VI 1.485.
79 In his early works, the term is restricted to discussions of bodies. For example, see Leibniz, A VI 2.190, 240, 245, 257, 325, and 498. But he also acknowledges the role of "sympathy and antipathy" in "vulgar" science. See A VI 4[A].457, 638, 639. In the notes of 1672–76, he often writes that bodies of the world are in sympathy among themselves. See A VI 3.79, 85, 87, 91.

of gravity as "action at a distance" is itself occult.[80] In a letter to Christian Huygens of 1693, Leibniz goes so far as to compare Newton's views to that of sympathy a kind of "inexplicable quality."[81] It seems likely that Leibniz chose to coin new terms in order to avoid misunderstanding about his reinterpretation of universal sympathy. By such means he could sidestep pejorative associations with *sympathia* and use untainted terminology. Whatever his reasons to refer to sympathetic harmony by other means, it is clear that his views about the interrelations among substances have roots in the tradition described above. While Leibniz is developing the details of his elaborate metaphysical system, he often acknowledges that his conception of creaturely relations is a form of sympathetic harmony.[82] In the late 1670s and 1680s, he echoes philosophers like Van Helmont when he associates sympathy and perceptions. He argues, for example, that because there is a "universal sympathy of things,"[83] they "all perceive together [comperceptibilia]."[84] In short, Leibniz was perfectly familiar with the debates about sympathy and chose not to use the term in presenting his views about preestablished harmony.

In the remainder of this section, I display the roles that universal sympathy and enhanced sympathy play in Leibniz's philosophy. There is insufficient space to give a detailed presentation of Leibniz's thought, but even a brief account reveals his debt to these relations.

Leibniz's preestablished harmony is constituted of (at least) three closely related claims. As a group, they constitute a reinvention of universal sympathy. The first claim, which is sometimes called "spontaneity,"

---

80 As noted in section 2, Leibniz distinguishes between a sense of "occult" as something whose cause is unknown and as "an effect that can never become intelligible." He suggests that Newton's account of gravity falls in the latter category. See Leibniz, Gerhardt 3.519. For a recent account of Leibniz's disagreement with Newton and Newton's response, see Andrew Janiak, *Newton as Philosopher* (Cambridge: Cambridge University Press, 2008), ch. 3.
81 A II 2.520–21. Thanks to Eric Schliesser for helping track down this passage.
82 A VI 4[B].1011.
83 A VI 4[A].308. See also A VI 4[B].1613.
84 A VI 4[A].669.

is the view that the nature of a substance contains the cause or source of all of its features or states. In 1686, Leibniz writes in *Discourse on Metaphysics* 8: "the nature of an individual substance or of a complete being is to have a notion so complete that it is sufficient to contain and to allow us to deduce from it all the predicates of the subject to which this notion is attributed."[85] Roughly speaking, all the perceptions and states of every creature arise from the substance's substantial form or inner nature, which God has given it. Not only do the perceptions and features of every substance arise "spontaneously" from its nature, its perceptions contain those of every other substance and, in that sense, "expresses" every other. Leibniz writes in a somewhat later work, entitled *First Truths*: "*Every individual substance contains in its perfect notion the entire universe* and everything that exists in it, past, present, and future.... Indeed, *all created substances are different expressions of the same universe* and different expressions of the same universal cause, namely, God."[86] So each substance expresses not just its own states but also those of all other substances. In other words, each of the infinity of substances bears a sympathetic relation to all the others.

The second main constituent of preestablished harmony, which is sometimes called the "world-apart thesis," maintains that no feature or state of any created substance has as a real cause some feature or state of another substance. Substances do not directly interact; there is no intersubstantial causation. As Leibniz puts it in *Discourse on Metaphysics* 14, "each substance is like a world apart, independent of all other things, except for God.... God alone (from whom all individuals emanate continually and who sees the universe not only as they see it but also entirely differently from all of them) is the cause of this correspondence of their phenomena." The perceptions of every substance correspond perfectly with those of every other because God has guaranteed that they do so. Each substance is in perfect sympathetic harmony with every

---

85 A VI 4[B].1646: AG 41.
86 A VI 4[B].1646: AG 32.

other because God has created each to "contain" all the others. Leibniz continues: "one particular substance never acts upon another particular substance nor is acted upon by it," but "what happens to each is solely a consequence of its complete idea or notion alone, since this idea already contains all its predicates or events and expresses the whole universe."[87]

The third main doctrine of preestablished harmony, what is sometimes called "parallelism," owes the most direct debt to universal sympathy. It claims that the perceptions or states of a substance correspond perfectly with those of every other substance at any given time. *Discourse on Metaphysics* 14 asserts: "God produces various substances according to the different views he has of the universe and through God's intervention the proper nature of each substance brings it about that what happens to one corresponds with what happens to all the others, without their acting upon one another directly."[88] Leibniz's doctrine of parallelism has the benefits of universal sympathy while avoiding its problems. It insists that all created substances correspond perfectly but sidesteps the need to explain how exactly the sympathetic force between creatures is transmitted. For Leibniz, God constructs each substance so that it bears a sympathetic bond to every other and yet nothing is transmitted between them. As he summarizes the point in *Discourse on Metaphysics* 9, "each singular substance expresses the whole universe in its own way.... Moreover, every substance is like a complete world and like a mirror of God or of the whole universe, which each one expresses in its own way."[89] Toward the end of the *Discourse on Metaphysics*, he makes the point that "everything that happens to the soul and to each substance follows from its notion, and therefore the very idea or essence of the soul carries with it the fact that all its appearances or perceptions must arise spontaneously from its own nature and precisely in such a way that they correspond by themselves to what happens in the whole

---

87 A VI 4[B].1550–51: AG 47.
88 A VI 4[B].1549: AG 46.
89 A VI 4[B].1541–42: AG 41–42.

universe."⁹⁰ Then, using a cognate of *sympathia* to refer to the correspondence among bodies, he explains that each "body receives the impression of all other bodies, since all the bodies of the universe are in sympathy, and, even though our senses are related to everything, it is impossible for our soul to attend to everything in particular; that is why our confused sensations are the result of a truly infinite variety of perceptions."⁹¹ Each of the infinity of substances perceives all the others with more or less confusion in perfect preestablished harmony.⁹²

If universal sympathy is the glue that binds the parts of preestablished harmony, then enhanced sympathy contributes to its aesthetic and moral luster. The comparison of creatures to mirrors is a prominent fixture in Leibniz's philosophy and a vivid means to enhance sympathetic harmony. His earliest use of the comparison, in a note of 1669–70, is striking:

> If God did not have rational Creatures in the world, he would have the same harmony, but barely and devoid of Echo, the same beauty, but barely and devoid of reflection and refraction or multiplication. On this account, the wisdom of God required [*exigebat*] rational Creatures, in which things might multiply themselves. In this way one mind might be a kind of world in a mirror, or a diopter, or some kind of point collecting visual rays.⁹³

Leibniz assumes that rational creatures bear a sympathetic relation to one another. Consistent with the principle of plenitude, the correspondence

---

90 A VI 4[B].1582: AG 65.
91 A VI 4[B].1582.19: AG 65.
92 I am ignoring the many debates among scholars about how to articulate Leibniz's doctrines. For a helpful general account of Leibniz's philosophy, see Brandon C. Look, "Gottfried Wilhelm Leibniz," *The Stanford Encyclopedia of Philosophy* (Spring 2013 ed.), ed. Edward N. Zalta http://plato.stanford.edu/archives/spr2013/entries/leibniz/.
93 A VI 1.438. Leibniz is not innovative in comparing creatures to mirrors. We have seen the comparison in Van Helmont. And in his *Platonic Theology* of 1482, Ficino describes each soul as a "mirror of the divine." See Marsilio Ficino, *Platonic Theology*, 6 vols., trans. Michael J. B. Allen, ed. James Hankins and William Bowen (Cambridge, MA: Harvard University Press, 2001–06), 3. ch. 2.

among these creatures is itself beautiful and good, but such beauty and goodness are greatly increased when they also mirror one another. That is, when two creatures mirror one another, each enhances the good of the other. Leibniz is even more explicit about the benefits of enhancement in a related note:

> But as a double reflection can occur in vision, once in the lens of the eye and once in the lens of a tube, the latter magnifying the former, so there is a double reflection in thinking: for since every mind is like a mirror, there will be one mirror in our mind, another in other minds. Thus, if there are many mirrors, that is, many minds recognizing our goods, there will be a greater light, the mirrors blending the light not only in the [individual] eye but also among each other. The gathered splendor produces glory.[94]

Juxtaposing modern scientific images (of lenses and magnification) and ancient ones (of shadows and light), Leibniz creates a vivid picture of the effects of enhanced sympathy among rational minds. Throughout his long philosophical career, he thinks of enhanced sympathy as a significant addition to the world. Consistent with plenitude, it adds to worldly goodness and makes it easier for rational beings to recognize the order and beauty of the world and hence the divinity itself. When Leibniz talks about the "glory" that results from mirroring, he means to emphasize the insight into the divinity that mirroring makes possible. In his most important publication, *Essays on Theodicy* of 1710, Leibniz summarizes the point:

> The perfections of God are those of our souls, but he possesses them in boundless measure; he is an Ocean, whereof to us only drops have been granted; there is in us some power, some knowledge, some goodness, but in God they are all in their entirety. Order, proportions, harmony

---

94 A VI 1.485. Also see A VI 1.479.

delight us; painting and music are samples of these: God is all order; he always keeps truth of proportions, he makes universal harmony; all beauty is an effusion of his rays.[95]

In short, according to Leibniz, enhanced sympathy among rational creatures encourages them to discern the order, beauty, and goodness in the world. In the end, they will begin to understand God and, as he argues in the *Essays on Theodicy*, become "familiar with virtue."[96]

5. ANNE CONWAY

Anne Conway is an English philosopher whose only work, *The Principles of the Most Ancient and Modern Philosophy*, was published posthumously in 1690. Although many of her contemporaries offered the work high praise,[97] like the works of so many women, her book was left out of the history of philosophy by later thinkers.[98] Conway's vitalist philosophy exemplifies the power of enhanced universal sympathy to solve a number of philosophical problems extant in the early modern

---

95 Gerhardt, 6.27. The standard translation of the *Theodicy* remains *Theodicy*, trans. E. M. Huggard (LaSalle, IL: Open Court, 1985), 51. The French here is: "Les perfections de Dieu sont celles de nos ames, mais il les possede sans bornes: il est un Ocean, dont nous n'avons receu que des gouttes: il y a en nous quelque puissance, quelque connoissance, quelque bonté, mais elles sont toutes entieres en Dieu. L'ordre, les proportions, l'harmonie nous enchantent, la peinture et la musique en sont des echantillons; Dieu est tout ordre, il garde tousjours la justesse des proportions, il fait l'harmonie universelle: toute la beauté est un épanchement de ses rayons."

96 Gerhardt, 6.25.

97 Leibniz developed his metaphysics independently of Conway, but he did think very well of her ideas. In his *New Essays on Human Understanding*, for example, he mentions her as the "best" among the vitalist philosophers. See *New Essays on Human Understanding*, ed. and trans. Peter Remnant and Johathan Bennett (Cambridge: Cambridge University Press, 1981), 72. For the range of significant figures with whom she corresponded and who referred approvingly of her work, see Anne Conway, *The Conway Letters: The Correspondence of Anne Viscountess Conway, Henry Moore, and Their Friends (1642–1684)*, ed. Marjorie Hope Nicholson and Sarah Hutton (New York: Oxford University Press, 1992); for Leibniz's various comments, see 454–57.

98 For the classic article on this phenomenon, see Eileen O'Neill, "Disappearing Ink: Early Modern Women Philosophers and Their Fate in History," in *Philosophy in a Feminist Voice: Critiques and Reconstructions*, ed. Janet Kournay (Princeton, NJ: Princeton University Press, 1998), 17–62. For the most important study of Conway's intellectual life and the history of the publication, see Sarah Hutton, *Anne Conway: A Woman Philosopher* (Cambridge: Cambridge University Press, 2004). For a thorough account of the state of Conway's writings, see Hutton's introduction.

period. Her metaphysics is not only the most prominent example of the impact of universal sympathy on mainstream philosophy, it is important for what it reveals about the relationship between metaphysical and moral sympathy at the end of the seventeenth century.

Conway argues that there are three distinct substances: God, Logos, and the created world. *Perfectly exemplifying hierarchical emanation*, God, the first substance, emanates the second, which then emanates the world. As the middle substance between God and world, Logos is the metaphysical conduit and mediator between God and creatures.[99] The created world is a single, infinitely complex vital substance, whose various modes constitute individual creatures. Like Leibniz, Conway maintains that the world contains an infinity of creatures. Like him, she takes their vitality to result from God's emanation. And like him, she thinks that all vital things perceive and correspond to all others.[100] But whereas Leibniz considers each creature to be substantially distinct from every other, Conway insists that all creatures are constituted of the same vital "substance or essence" although they differ radically in their degree of vitality.[101] Her commitment to the supreme being assumption, hierarchical emanation, and plenitude leads her to insist that the created world is constantly bettering itself so that all creatures eventually become conscious moral beings and attain the "excellent attributes" of "spirit and light."[102] Each creature shares in God's goodness and therefore has a capacity to perceive, understand, and love all things: "God is infinitely good and communicates his goodness to all his creatures in infinite ways" so that "there is no creature which does not receive something of his

---

[99] Conway refers to this second substance as "Christ," which suggests a more thorough commitment to Christianity than she in fact has. For a summary of Conway's metaphysics and her non-Christian use of "Christ," see my "Anne Conway's Metaphysics of Sympathy," in *Feminist History of Philosophy: Recovery and Evaluation of Women's Philosophical Thought*, ed. Eileen O'Neill and Marcy Lascano (New York: Springer, 2015).

[100] Conway wrote her *Principles* in the 1670s, at the same time that Leibniz was developing the details of his own system. Because she developed her views entirely independently of his, their similarities are all the more striking.

[101] Conway, *Principles*, VI §4, 29–30.

[102] *Principles* IX §6, 66.

goodness." This "goodness of God is a living goodness, which possesses life, knowledge, love, and power, which he communicates to his creatures."[103] It follows that every created thing is capable of "every kind of feeling, perception, or knowledge, even love," although the "transmutations" required to achieve those capacities will occur over a very long time. For example, as a mode of vitality, the slug can be transmuted to that of a horse and eventually to that of a conscious human being. God has so arranged things because he "sees that it is more fitting for all things…to attain, through their own efforts, ever greater perfection as instruments of divine wisdom, goodness, and power, which operate in them and with them."[104] Given our concerns, it is particularly important that the perfection of creatures is the direct result of enhanced universal sympathy. One of the most basic features of the third substance is that every creature has an enhanced sympathetic relation with every other: "God has implanted a certain universal sympathy and mutual love into his creatures so that they are all members of one body and all, so to speak, brothers, for whom there is one common father."[105]

There is insufficient space here to discuss the details of Conway's views about the development of consciousness and moral improvement. The underlying point is that an increase in the vitality of one creature contributes, if only slightly, to the goodness of others. A succession of increases in vitality will lead to moral improvements until every creature becomes sufficiently vital to *be conscious*. Once conscious, creatures move slowly to moral perfection. She writes: "the more spiritual [vital] a certain creature becomes…the closer it comes to God,…the highest spirit."[106] The enhanced sympathetic harmony among the individual modes or creatures guarantees that they will progress toward ever-increasing perfection "to infinity."[107] So the third substance constantly improves,

---

103 *Principles* VII §7, 44–45.
104 *Principles* IX §6, 66.
105 *Principles* VI §4, 31.
106 *Principles* VII §1, 41–42.
107 *Principles* VI §1, 42.

although its "progression and ascension cannot reach God…whose nature infinitely surpasses every creature, even one brought to the highest level."[108] Because of enhanced sympathy, "a creature is capable of a further and more perfect degree of life, ever greater and greater to infinity, but it can never attain equality with God. For his infinity is always more perfect than a creature in its highest elevation."[109] In the end, like Leibniz, Conway believes that enhanced sympathy allows all human beings to discern the "excellent order" and "splendor" of the world.[110] Like him, she takes enhanced sympathy to help them find virtue. But she differs from Leibniz in allowing all creatures the benefit of enhancement. For her, universal enhanced sympathy guarantees that all creatures will become virtually divine.

6. Conclusion

The seventeenth century begins with debates about "occult" sympathetic powers in nature. Physicians, natural philosophers, and theologians disagree about the intelligibility of such powers and worry about their demonic associations. Then, often using Stoic and Platonist ideas, philosophers begin to rethink and sometimes to clarify the description and explanation of those powers. Over the century, universal sympathy is increasingly rendered more precisely until it becomes a key ingredient in prominent metaphysical systems. In the philosophical proposals of Leibniz and Conway, it is the main unifying force among an infinity of creatures in God's world. Worldly sympathy acquires a moral aspect that adds significantly to the goodness of the world and to the ethical development of rational beings. By the end of the century, sympathy is a moral force to be reckoned with. In Conway's words, it encourages "love, all power and virtue, joy and fruition."[111]

---

108 *Principles* IX §5, 65.
109 *Principles* IX §7, 67.
110 *Principles* VI §5, 31–32.
111 *Principles* IX §6, 66.

Reflection

"TAKE PHYSIC, POMP": KING LEAR LEARNS SYMPATHY

Sarah Skwire

In act 3 of Shakespeare's *King Lear*, Lear, who was been cast out into a brutal storm and stripped of his retainers by his grasping daughters Regan and Goneril, begins his process of transformation. The self-centered autocrat of the play's opening scenes is forced, in this scene, to begin to move out of his self-pity through his encounters with Kent, who is disguised as a peasant, and with Edgar, who is disguised as the mad beggar Poor Tom. Offered hospitality in a poor hovel, Lear realizes as he suffers and is offered relief that he has failed to sympathize with his subjects' suffering because he has been so wrapped in self-regard.

> Poor naked wretches, whereso'er you are,
> That bide the pelting of this pitiless storm,
> How shall your houseless heads and unfed sides,
> Your loop'd and window'd raggedness, defend you
> From seasons such as these? O, I have ta'en
> Too little care of this! Take physic, pomp;
> Expose thyself to feel what wretches feel,
> That thou mayst shake the superflux to them,
> And show the heavens more just.
>
> (3.4.27–36)

That Lear calls for "physic" as the remedy for his lack of sympathy reminds all of us that the process in which he must engage—in which we all much engage—in order to "show the heavens more just" is not a pleasant one.

Medicine in the age of Shakespeare—and for quite a long time after—was famously uncomfortable. As the father-in-law of John Hall, a physician in Stratford-on-Avon, Shakespeare would have had the opportunity to see and hear a great deal about medical practice from an expert. In fact, Hall treated patients for eye trouble with various herbs combined with egg white,[1] which is precisely the treatment used in *King Lear* by Gloucester's sympathetic servant after Gloucester is blinded: "I'll fetch some flax and whites of eggs / To apply to his bleeding face" (3.7.105–6). That may not sound so uncomfortable, but flax and egg whites were a treatment for external wounds.

For internal ailments, of the kind to which Lear's "pomp" is analogized and for which the expression "take physic" would have been used, treatment was quite different. Based on the theory that the best way to treat an illness was to balance a patient's humors by "getting the bad stuff out," bleeding, emetics, and purgatives—alone or in combination—would have been the most commonly prescribed courses of physic. And the general assumption was that

---

[1] John Hall, "Counsel 11: Hurt in the Eye," in *Select observations on English bodies of eminent persons in desperate diseases first written in Latin by Mr. John Hall…; after Englished by James Cook…; to which is now added, an hundred like counsels and advices, for several honourable persons, by the same author; in the close is added, Directions for drinking of the bath-water, and Ars cosmetica, or beautifying art, by H. Stubbs….* (London: Benjamin Shirley, 1679). The treatment reads thus: "The Honourable, Mr. *Algernoon Grevil,* being hurt with a Foil in the Eye, was cured by Dr. *Bates's* direction, which was as followeth: The Foil being run into his left Eye, it presently swell'd, and he bled at the Nose, and was troubled all the afternoon with vomiting. There was immediatly applied to it a Plaster of *Conserve of Roses.* At night Dr. Bates being sent for, he pre|scribed what follows: He took a Clyster of *a pint of new Milk, and six spoonfuls of Sugar.* As soon as it had done working, he bled from the *Cephalic* on the same side. After was applied this: *Take green Wormwood* M ss. *Carduus* M iss. *red Roses* ʒii Mij. *boyl them in Milk and Water to a Pultess, being taken from the Fire, there was added the Yolks and Whites of three Eggs well beaten, and after all well mixed.*" Hall also applied egg whites for other eye trouble, as recorded in observation 4 from his first century of observations: "Upon the Eyes were applied *Whites of Eggs well beaten with Rosewater and Womans milk.*"

the more violently a medicine acted on the patient, the better it worked. This led early modern medical advertisers to tout the effectiveness of their cures by emphasizing the thoroughness with which they will "work" on the patient's system. For example, George Jones's broadside advertisement for his "Friendly Pills" promises that the pills will "bring away almost a Chamber-pot full the first Stool, and one, two, or three stools of corruption afterwards."[2] Similarly, Samuel Pepys mentions, on January 16, 1659/60, that "I slept late, and then in the morning took physic, and so staid within all day."[3] The reasons for his confinement to the house are presumably obvious. Mercury was thought to be an excellent medicine for all types of severe ailments because of its ability to provoke sweating and vomiting. With courses of physic like this, it is little wonder that John Donne and other early moderns tended to be somewhat fascinated by the biblical curse in Ecclesiasticus 38:15: "He that sinneth before his maker, let him fall into the hand of the physician."

Equally significant in early modern medicine was the medical-magical concept of healing by sympathy and the "doctrine of signatures." Keith Thomas explains: "every herb was stamped with a more or less clear sign of its uses; so that, for example, a yellow blossom indicated a likely cure for jaundice, or a root shaped like a foot became a remedy for gout."[4] Thomas further explains that the "like cures like" philosophy of sympathetic cures lay behind such early modern oddities as the weapon salve, a preparation that was smeared on an edged weapon in order to "assist the vital spirits of the congealed blood to reunite with the victim's body, and thus heal

---

[2] George Jones of London, Student in the Art of Physick and Chyrurgery....," Wellcome Institute broadside collection, London, c. 1675.

[3] Samuel Pepys, *Diary*, 16 January 1659/60, http://www.pepysdiary.com/diary/1660/01/15/, accessed September 10, 2013.

[4] Keith Thomas, *Religion and the Decline of Magic: Studies in Popular Beliefs in Sixteenth and Seventeenth Century England* (London: Weidenfeld & Nicolson; New York: Scribner's, 1971), 190.

the wound even at a distance of thirty miles."[5] The prevalence of belief in such sympathetic cures in Shakespeare's time—based in a theory that likenesses attract—suggests that one part of Lear's course of physic may well be the application to himself of some of the sufferings he has caused others. (See chapter 4 and Holmes's reflection in this volume.)

If King Lear's process of learning to sympathize, to take more "care of this," is going to require a metaphorical course of physic, we should assume that the process will be unpleasant in the extreme, and that it will require the purgation and the exposure of the foul matter of self-regard that has infected him. And this is precisely what happens when Lear is forced to "[e]xpose [himself] to feel what wretches feel."

There is no need to rehearse the plot of *King Lear*. But it is worth pointing out a few of these moments during which Lear's sufferings force him, fairly literally, into the place of various people who have suffered from his carelessness. First, of course, there is Lear's banishment of Cordelia. Told to let her "truth be then thy dower" (1.1.109), Cordelia is turned out with Lear's promise that, henceforth, he shall:

> disclaime all my paternal care,
> Propinquity and property of blood,
> And as a stranger to my heart and me,
> Hold thee from this for ever. The barbarous Scythian,
> Or he that makes his generation messes
> To gorge his appetite, shall to my bosom
> Be as well neighboured, pitied and relieved,
> As thou my sometime daughter.
>   (1.1.114–21)

Lear turns Cordelia out and turns her into a stranger. This forswearing of the familial bond is duplicated in the next act as

---
[5] Thomas, *Religion and the Decline of Magic*, 190–91.

Goneril and Regan each turn Lear out of their homes and seek to strip him of his retainers, just as he banishes Cordelia and strips her of her only support.

In a pathetic echo of his banishment of Cordelia, the banished Lear tells Goneril:

> I will not trouble thee, my child. Farewell:
> We'll no more meet, no more see one another.
> But yet thou are my flesh, my blood, my daughter,
> Or rather a disease that's in my flesh,
> Which I must needs call mine. Thou art a boil,
> A plague sore, or embossed carbuncle
> In my corrupted blood.
>
> (2.2.406–14)

Here, the banished Lear stands in Cordelia's place. Like Cordelia, who never ceases to refer to him as "father" no matter how often he abjures their relationship, Lear repeatedly refers to his connection with Goneril. No matter how corrupt their blood tie is, he insists, it is still a tie. The irony of this reversal is not lost on the audience, but Lear does not see it yet.

We should note, as well, the medical language that Lear uses here. In a play where pomp must "take physic," Lear's analogizing of Goneril to "a boil / a plague sore, or embossed carbuncle / In my corrupted blood" is not an accident. Lear's ungrateful daughters are the outward and visible signs of his inward and invisible corruption and illness. They are not the sickness itself, but in the medical terminology of the time, they are the "tokens" thereof.

Lear's turning out of Cordelia rebounds on him again in this same scene as Goneril and Regan wrangle with him over the number of retainers he should be allowed to keep. While, when accepting their portions of Lear's kingdom, they had agreed he could bring one hundred retainers with him when he came to stay with them, they rapidly begin to bargain their way down from that number—from fifty, to twenty-five, to ten, to five, to none. While nothing is explicitly said, this wrangling must be intended to make the audience think of Cordelia's comment that "I love your majesty / According to my bond, no more nor less" (1.1.92–93). When Lear is forced into the same banished and unsupported state to which he has condemned Cordelia, what initially seems an "untender" comment is revealed as a quietly firm assertion of a love worth valuing more highly.

Similar moments of exposure to the suffering experienced by other wretches occur for Lear when Kent—whom he has banished—becomes Lear's protector and guide during his madness. And Lear's madness is itself a forced opportunity for Lear to experience not only the madness and deprivation of the poorest of his subjects, but the fear and instability that runs wild in the mad world he has created by the "unkinging" of his kingdom.

I have written in other contexts[6] of the challenging nature of learning to practice sympathy as described by the eighteenth-century moral philosopher Adam Smith. Smith acknowledges that the practice of sympathy can be quite difficult, as overcoming these "selfish and original passions" is enormously effortful and unpleasant.

> In the same manner, to the selfish and original passions of human nature, the loss or gain of a very small interest of our own, appears to be of vastly more importance, excites a much more passionate joy or sorrow, a much more ardent desire or aversion, than the greatest concern of another with whom we have no particular connexion. His interests, as long as they are surveyed from this station, can never be put into the balance with our own, can never restrain us

---

6 Sarah Skwire, "Reading Each Other," *The Freeman,* June 27, 2012, http://fee.org/the_freeman/detail/reading-each-other.

from doing whatever may tend to promote our own, how ruinous soever to him. Before we can make any proper comparison of those opposite interests, we must change our position. (3.3.3)

While Smith suggests that the necessary "change in position" is a shift to the position of neutrality that he connects with the impartial spectator (see chapter 7 in this volume), Shakespeare's *King Lear* suggests that what is needed in order for some individuals to learn to sympathize is a radical course of "physic" in the form of directly experiencing the sufferings of others for oneself. For Lear, the practice of sympathy is such a difficult exercise that only the loss of everything—kingdom, family, servants, and wealth—can force him to learn it.

But what are Lear's rewards? It's possible to look at the stage littered with bodies at the end of the final act of *King Lear* and argue that nothing of significance has been achieved since Lear's epiphany in the storm. But Lear has changed. At the end of act 4 he expresses a newly perfect and instinctive understanding of the suffering of others when he notes, "I should even die with pity to see another thus" (4.7.53–54). His transformation is not enough to save him or to save Cordelia, but it may be enough to allow us to hope that, with sympathy, we can restore some kind of order to the "gored state" of the play.

CHAPTER FIVE

Spinoza's Parallelism Doctrine and Metaphysical Sympathy

Karolina Hübner

> By what natural connection and as it were harmony and mutual agreement, which the Greeks call sympathy, can there be coordination between the fissure in a liver and my small fortune, or between my small profit and heaven, the earth, and the nature of things?
> (CICERO, *On Divination* 2.34)

1. INTRODUCTION

There are many different ways one can think about the notion of cosmic "sympathy."[1] In this chapter I want to approach this idea as a thesis of a fundamental connectedness of all things—a *connexio rerum*—and show how this ancient idea is rehabilitated in the metaphysics of an early modern thinker, Baruch Spinoza (1632–77). More precisely, I want to show that the ancient idea of cosmic "sympathy," reinterpreted in accordance with Spinoza's demand for universal intelligibility, illuminates key doctrines of his metaphysics, and in particular his conceptions of identity and of the relation between thought and being.[2]

---

1 Thanks to the volume editors and to the participants of the "Sympathy" conference at the University of Richmond, especially Eric Schliesser, for invaluable comments on an earlier version of this essay.
2 For an account of how Spinoza understands sympathy in his ethics, see chapter 6 in this volume.

Admittedly, one may be surprised to find Spinoza and "sympathy" as bedfellows. For one might have expected that the advent of mechanism as the dominant explanatory paradigm in the early modern period had rendered the idea of cosmic sympathy "occult," and hence philosophically illegitimate, for most thinkers. Prima facie sympathetic relations between things seem irreducible to explanations in terms of size, shape, and motion alone, as mechanism demands. Likewise, sympathetic action at a distance seems to evade the basic mechanistic requirement that there be contact between bodies for action to occur.

In fact, however, many early moderns did not reject the notion of "sympathy" tout court. Instead, they undertook to better explain the phenomena that had been deemed "sympathetic" by their predecessors, and to reduce allegedly sympathetic relations to mechanistic ones.[3] And so for example Descartes—arguably Spinoza's most important intellectual precursor—writes,

> I have deduced the causes—which I believe to be quite evident—of these and many other phenomena from principles which are known to all and admitted by all, namely the shape, size, position and motion of particles of matter. And anyone who considers all this will readily be convinced that there are no powers in stones and plants that are so mysterious, and no marvels attributed to sympathetic and antipathetic influences that are so astonishing, that they cannot be explained in this way.[4]

---

[3] For an example of early modern resistance to such mechanistic reduction of sympathetic phenomena see Henry More, *Immortality of the Soul*, ed. A. Jacob (Dordrecht: Martinus Nijhoff, 1987), 3.5.1.

[4] René Descartes, *Principles of Philosophy*, in *The Philosophical Writings of Descartes*, ed. and trans. John Cottingham, Robert Stoothoff, and Dugald Murdoch (Cambridge: Cambridge University Press, 1985), vol. 1, 4.187, AT 8A.314. Cf. "The sciences, however abstruse [*occultae*], are to be deduced only from matters which are easy and highly accessible, and not from those which are grand and obscure.... To inquire whether a natural power can travel instantaneously to a distant place...I shall not immediately turn my attention to the magnetic force, or the influence of the stars.... I shall, rather, reflect upon the local motions of bodies...readily perceivable.... [N]or shall I prattle on about the moon's warming things by its light and cooling them by means of some occult quality. Rather, I shall observe a pair of scales" (Descartes, *Rules for the Direction of the Mind*, in *Philosophical Writings*, vol. 1, rule 9, AT 10.402).

In similar spirit, Hobbes (another major influence on Spinoza) tries to explain magnetism—the sympathetic phenomenon par excellence—by reference to infinitesimal motions of bodies: "the attractive power of the loadstone is nothing else but some motion of the smallest particles thereof"; hence appealing to "sympathy" is "to no purpose."[5]

This kind of deflationary attempt to integrate elements of ancient thought within a modern framework is also, as is well known, one of the hallmarks of Spinoza's thought. Spinoza systematically reinterprets received doctrines—what, as he puts it, others saw but only "as if through a cloud"—in accordance with the demands of what he takes to be truly "adequate" thought: timelessly true descriptions of the essences and properties of things.[6] In Spinoza's system, the newfangled mechanistic physics is thus made to coexist with a Platonic, emanative metaphysics, as well as, as is often emphasized, with a neo-Stoic ethics.[7]

---

[5] Thomas Hobbes, *De Corpore* 4.26, 30.

Leibniz's notion of a "pre-established harmony" among the perceptions of causally isolated substances can also be seen as an attempt to rehabilitate the idea of a sympathetic connectedness of all things. See e.g. his claim that "pre-established harmony...between all the monads or simple substances...takes the place of that untenable influence of the one on the others" (Gottfried Wilhelm Leibniz, *New Essays on Human Understanding,* ed. and trans. Peter Remnant and Jonathan Bennett [Cambridge: Cambridge University Press, 1996], 296). See also "Discourse on Metaphysics," 33 (*Philosophical Essays,* ed. and trans. Roger Ariew and Daniel Garber [Indianapolis: Hackett, 1989]). See also David Hume's invocation of physical sympathy in *A Treatise of Human Nature,* ed. David Fate Norton and Mary J. Norton (New York: Oxford University Press, 2000), 3.3.1.7.

On Leibniz and sympathy, see Christia Mercer, *Leibniz's Metaphysics: Its Origins and Development* (Cambridge: Cambridge University Press, 2001), 193–94, 354–55, and chapter 4 in this volume. For a general overview, see Brian Copenhaver, "The Occultist Tradition and Its Critics," in *The Cambridge History of Seventeenth-Century Philosophy,* ed. Daniel Garber and Michael Ayers (Cambridge: Cambridge University Press, 1998), 1.455–512.

[6] Baruch Spinoza, *The Ethics,* in *The Collected Works of Spinoza,* ed. and trans. Edwin Curley (Princeton, NJ: Princeton University Press, 1984), 2p7s; 1app (II/79); 2p44c2. In citing from Curley's translation of Spinoza's *Ethics,* I use the following standard abbreviations: ax = axiom, def = definition, p = proposition, d = demonstration, s = scholium, c = corollary, app = appendix, pref = preface. "NS" refers to the posthumous 1677 Dutch edition of Spinoza's writings, *De Nagelate Schriften van B.D.S.*

Cf. Leibniz's comments about "restoring" and "rehabilitating" the Aristotelian "substantial forms" "in a way that would render them intelligible, and separate the use one should make of them from the abuse that has been made of them" ("New System of Nature," in *Philosophical Essays,* 139).

[7] *Ethics* II/97–103; 1p17s[1] (II/62); 4app32 (II/276). On Spinoza's emanationist framework see e.g. Martial Gueroult, *Spinoza* (Paris: Aubier-Montaigne, 1968), 1.246–97; and Valtteri Viljanen, "Spinoza's Essentialist Model of Causation," *Inquiry* 51.4 (2008): 412–37. On Spinoza's Stoic influences see e.g. Susan James, "Spinoza the Stoic," in *The Rise of Early Modern Philosophy: The Tension between the*

Although this is not usually noted, Spinoza was familiar also with the ancient concept of cosmic "sympathy." The term appears in his writings as a label for relations and processes in nature that appear to us as less than fully intelligible, insofar as we cannot fathom their underlying causes. Thus Spinoza writes, for example, "it can happen that we love or hate some things *without any cause known to us*, but only (as they say) from Sympathy or Antipathy [*sympathia...et antipathia*]."[8] In other words, from Spinoza's point of view, to see sympathy as a force operative in nature is just to fail to grasp the causes of things.

Spinoza famously describes this kind of knowledge of effects alone as a knowledge of "conclusions without premises."[9] For him, as for most ancient and early modern philosophers, causes are the key to intelligibility: things are what they are, and have the properties they do, because of their causes. So to adequately know any thing we must know the causes that necessitate its existence and properties.[10]

Spinoza's fundamental commitment to universal intelligibility is today often referred to by scholars as his commitment to the Principle of Sufficient Reason (PSR), and I will adopt this shorthand in what

---

New and the Traditional Philosophies from Machiavelli to Leibniz, ed. Tom Sorrell (Oxford: Oxford University Press, 1993), 289–316.

8 *Ethics* 3p15s (II/152), emphasis added. Spinoza also mentions metaphysical "sympathy" in his early manual on Descartes's philosophy, when he notes that Descartes's commitment to a "real distinction" between parts of matter shows that "Sympathy and Antipathy are to be rejected as false" (*Descartes' Principles of Philosophy*, in *Collected Works*, 2p8s; I/197). Of course in his own philosophy Spinoza rejects the Cartesian thesis that parts of matter are really (as opposed to merely modally) distinct from one another—as well as the idea that real distinction corresponds to a numerical distinction between substances (cf. *Ethics* 1p10s).

9 *Ethics* 2p28d.

10 Cf. "The knowledge of an effect depends on, and involves, the knowledge of its cause" (*Ethics* 1ax4). There is much controversy about whether 1ax4 applies to adequate knowledge only. In this essay I assume that the axiom applies at least to adequate knowledge, such that to know a thing adequately (or, equivalently, to make it fully intelligible) we need to grasp its causal dependencies. On the problem of the axiom's scope see e.g. Margaret Wilson, "Spinoza's Causal Axiom (*Ethics* I, Axiom 4)," in *Ideas and Mechanism: Essays on Early Modern Philosophy*, by Wilson (Princeton, NJ: Princeton University Press, 1999), 141–65.

Such perfect causal knowledge of things is not only Spinoza's epistemic ideal; it is also something he believes to be already given in nature, insofar as all things are eternally adequately conceived by God's "infinite intellect." See *Ethics* 2p3, 2p7c.

follows.[11] This commitment to the PSR means that Spinoza's metaphysics will be thoroughly hostile to any phenomenon or law of nature that would in principle be inexplicable.[12] The commitment also means that natural phenomena that once may have been deemed "sympathetic"—that is, phenomena that, on Spinoza's diagnosis of "sympathy," are known to us only through their effects—have to be either simply eliminated from metaphysics or made fully intelligible. That is, a Spinozist must either uncover the causes on which purportedly "sympathetic" effects depend (thus making the influences in question intelligible) or show that it is metaphysically impossible for a causal relation to hold in a particular case. (For example, one of Spinoza's basic metaphysical principles is that relations of causal dependence are possible only within the boundaries of the same kind of being.[13] That means, for instance, that only bodies can enter into causal relations with bodies, and only minds can enter into causal relations with minds. As a result, for Spinoza, any putative "sympathetic" influence that crosses from the mental realm to the corporeal realm, or vice versa, will turn out to have been illusory.)[14]

---

11 *Ethics* 1ax2, 1p11altd1. For a discussion of the role of PSR in Spinoza's philosophy see Michael Della Rocca, *Spinoza* (London: Routledge, 2008), and "Rationalist Manifesto: Spinoza and the Principle of Sufficient Reason," *Philosophical Topics* 31.1–2 (2003): 75–94.

12 This is so even though Spinoza allows both that it is not within the powers of finite human minds to grasp the entire series of finite causes leading up to any particular phenomenon and that there are entire realms of nature—those that are neither mental nor physical—that are in principle excluded from being known by human minds. See Spinoza, *Treatise on the Emendation of the Intellect*, in *Collected Works*, [100], *Ethics* 2ax5, and *The Letters*, trans. Samuel Shirley, ed. Steven Barbone, Jonathan Adler, and Lee Rice (Indianapolis: Hackett, 1995), letter 66. For discussion of the letter see Yitzhak Melamed, "Spinoza's Metaphysics of Thought: Parallelisms and the Multifaceted Structure of Ideas," *Philosophy and Phenomenological Research* 86.3 (2012): 636–83.

13 *Ethics* 1p3, 1p10, 2p5–6.

14 As we have seen, Spinoza identifies purportedly "sympathetic" relations with misconstrued *causal* relations. But could some *non*causal relation be responsible for the purported sympathetic influence crossing from one realm of being to another? In addition to causal relations, in his metaphysics Spinoza recognizes also conceptual relations, relations of inherence (see e.g. *Ethics* 1def3,5), relations of intentionality and ontological dependence (2p11, 13), and, finally, relations of numerical identity (2p7s). Let's take these one by one. Inherence relations are coextensive with, and perhaps even identical to, causal relations. Hence ruling out the possibility of causal relations in a particular case also rules out the possibility of inherence relations. Conceptual relations are, like causal relations, subject to the principle of closure of kinds of being, such that only mental things can help us cognize other mental things. Hence they also could not be responsible for cross-realm influence.

Spinoza thinks that an adequate understanding of nature will show it to be a genuine unity, grounded in a single, thoroughly deterministic causal power.[15] But, he also thinks, for the most part we fail to understand this: we fail to understand not only the causal mechanisms at work around us but equally the fact that every one of our own actions and appetites depends on an infinite series of prior causes. This failure, Spinoza proposes, is precisely what's behind our long-standing, but erroneous, belief in "free will" where "freedom" is understood as the absence of determination.[16] More generally, our ignorance of the nature of causal relations leads us to see nature as a realm of merely "sympathetic" influences between discrete beings, each one a "conclusion" detached from its "premises."

In one sense then, thinking of nature in terms of "sympathetic" relations is from Spinoza's point of view simply an error, analogous to thinking of ourselves as endowed with free (undetermined) will. But Spinoza's vision of the fundamental unity of nature, and in particular his belief that all finite things are just modifications of one fundamental entity, also makes him particularly well suited to the task of *rehabilitating* the notion of cosmic "sympathy." That is, my suggestion is that in a Spinozistic context "sympathy" does not have to be understood merely pejoratively, as a symptom of our causal ignorance. This, to be sure, is how Spinoza himself uses the term. But in addition to this explicit and negative discussion of sympathy, in Spinoza's writings there is also— and more importantly in my view—an implicit rehabilitation of the idea of cosmic sympathy. In Spinoza's version, the doctrine of sympathy is a metaphysical doctrine of the fundamental relatedness and unity of all beings, a fully intelligible (according to Spinoza's standards

---

However, it seems possible in principle that a particular allegedly "sympathetic" relation may have been a way of confusedly recognizing that a given mind and a given body are in fact numerically *identical* (as Spinoza holds [*Ethics*, 2p7s]), or perhaps that minds ontologically *depend* on bodies they represent (2p11, 13).

15 *Ethics* 1p16, 1p26, 1p28–29, 1p34. Indeed, more precisely, Spinoza is not just a determinist but a necessitarian.

16 See *Ethics* 1p28, 1app (II/78–79), 2p48, 3p7d, 3p9s, 4pref (II/207), 4def7.

of intelligibility) *connexio rerum* ultimately rooted in Spinoza's conviction that in metaphysical rigor there exists only one thing.[17] This point—that Spinoza makes the doctrine of cosmic sympathy a part of his monistic metaphysics—is the first main claim I want to make in this chapter.

Spinoza discusses the idea of a fundamental connection of all beings at length in one of the most important, and controversial, passages in his magnum opus, the *Ethics*: in 2p7, its corollary and scholium. As we shall see in what follows, these passages bear not just on the relation between distinct entities but also on the relation between being and thought more generally. The doctrine put forth in these passages is usually referred to as Spinoza's "parallelism" doctrine. However, I will avoid this terminology here, for the following reason. As has often been noted, "parallelism" is not a term Spinoza himself employs, and in my view it is at best unhelpfully vague, and at worst outright misleading. The word "parallelism" suggests mere correspondence, or some sort of isomorphism.[18] In fact, however, as we shall see, the fundamental relations at stake in the passages in question—in 2p7, its corollary, and scholium—are relations of *identity and unity*. (Other scholars have argued that the term "parallelism" is misleading because it suggests the presence of a single doctrine while in fact 2p7 and its scholium advance two distinct doctrines, one concerned with representation, and the other with identity: a blind or ontological parallelism to be distinguished from a representational or epistemological

---

17 However, Spinoza would, to be sure, be wary of describing nature as "harmonious," as some advocates of cosmic sympathy do. According to Spinoza such predicates as "harmonious" tell us nothing about things as they are in themselves, only about how they happen to affect us at a particular time or place (see *Ethics* 1app; II/78). Given his well-known criticisms of cosmic teleology (1app; 4pref, 3p7d, 4def7), Spinoza would be equally wary of thinking of sympathetic relations among things as if these served some cosmic *end* nature as a whole could have, as Plotinus for example does.

18 Unfortunately, all too often scholars merely gloss "parallelism," rather vaguely, as "mirroring," "correspondence," "isomorphism," "structural similarity," "mapping," "correlation," and "matching," without going into the precise nature of the relation. Melamed is an exception, writing, "I take parallelism to be a relation of isomorphism in the strict sense of the term, i.e., *one-to-one* and *onto* mapping. This relation preserves the causal structure among the relata" ("Metaphysics of Thought," 637 n 3).

parallelism.[19] There are reasons to resist this kind of reading too, as we shall see later.)

This then is the second main claim I will make in what follows: that Spinoza's positive reconception of cosmic "sympathy" as a thesis of a fundamental connectedness of things revolves around relations of identity and unity, especially as understood in terms of the real unity of the single substance.

However, before I can argue for these points in more detail, I need to provide the necessary background: a brief outline of the basic building blocks of Spinoza's metaphysics. This will be the task of the next section. (Readers familiar with Spinoza's metaphysics should feel free to skip directly to section 3.)

2. Background

The pillar of Spinoza's ontology is his substance monism, or the doctrine that there is only one fundamental entity. This entity, which Spinoza calls the "absolutely infinite substance" or "God," is defined by its existential and conceptual self-sufficiency.[20] Everything else that exists—and according to Spinoza there necessarily exists an "infinity" of things—is merely a dependent property and modification of this fundamental entity.[21] This sole possible substance and its modifications ("modes") exhaust Spinoza's ontological inventory: they are the only two metaphysically possible kinds of entities.[22]

---

19 For this reading see e.g. Gilles Deleuze, *Expressionism in Philosophy: Spinoza*, trans. M. Joughin (London: Zone Books); 113–14; Michael Della Rocca, *Representation and the Mind-Body Problem* (Oxford: Oxford University Press, 1996), 19, and *Spinoza*, 90; Alan Donagan, *Spinoza* (Chicago: University of Chicago Press, 1988), 180; Melamed, "Metaphysics of Thought"; Steven Nadler, *Spinoza's Ethics: An Introduction* (Cambridge: Cambridge University Press, 2006), 124.

20 *Ethics* 1def3, 1def6.

21 *Ethics* 1d5, 1p14–16, 1p18.

22 *Ethics* 1p4d.

Spinoza's conception of substance is perhaps most unorthodox in that Spinoza does not take substance to have a single essential nature.[23] Substance—and, derivatively, its modifications—possesses multiple, qualitatively heterogeneous essential natures.[24] Following Descartes, Spinoza calls these natures substance's "attributes."[25] The diversity of attributes are does not contravene the ontological unity of Spinozistic substance: this substance is equally essentially a thinking thing and an extended thing (and every other kind of thing, if there are other kinds of being, inaccessible to human minds). The same is true, derivatively, of all its finite properties: each is at least a mind and a body.

Spinoza identifies each of substance's attributes by means of one principal concept: "thought," "extension," and so on. Each of these concepts represents the property that all things of this particular kind, and only of this kind, presuppose for their explanation.[26] (For example, explanation of any particular idea, volition, or doubt presupposes our use of the concept of "thought," but not that of "extension" for instance; all explanation of bodies, movements or rests presupposes the use of the concept "extension" but not "thought.") As a consequence, different attributes by definition have no common conceptual denominator in any relevant sense.[27] Given Spinoza's commitment to universal intelligibility, entities under different attributes—for example, a particular body and a particular mind—thus cannot enter into causal relations.[28] This is because, in the absence of a shared conceptual sphere, such an event would be in principle inexplicable. For this reason, in Spinoza's eyes such an event is therefore also metaphysically

---

23 See in contrast Descartes, *Principles*, 1, 53.
24 *Ethics* 1def6, 2p1–2.
25 See Descartes, *Principles*, 1, 53.
26 Cf. Descartes, *Principles*, 1, 53.
27 It would be more accurate to say that what different attributes do have in common they have in common in the *wrong way:* abstractly of course all attributes have that in common that they can be classed together under universals like "attribute" or "expression." (For a fuller account of abstraction and universals in Spinoza's metaphysics see Karolina Hübner, "Spinoza on Essences, Universals and Beings of Reason," *Pacific Philosophical Quarterly*, forthcoming.)
28 *Ethics* 1p3, 1p10, 2p5–6.

impossible. All causal connections have to be underwritten by conceptual connections.

3. CONNEXIO RERUM

With this sketch of Spinoza's basic metaphysical framework in place, let me now turn to what I want to claim is his reinterpretation of the sympathetic *connexio rerum* in terms of fully intelligible relations of unity and identity.

Spinoza's key pronouncement on the subject of the connectedness of things in nature can be found, as noted earlier, in 2p7 and associated passages. It begins as follows:

> The order and connection of ideas is the same as the order and connection of things [*Ordo et connexio idearum idem est ac ordo et connexio rerum*].
>
> *Dem.*: This is clear from 1ax4. For the idea of each thing caused depends on the knowledge of the cause of which it is the effect. (2p7)

Spinoza manages to compress many ideas into these few short sentences. Let me take them one by one, starting with the notion of an "order and connection" of *things*.[29]

The demonstration to 2p7 makes clear that the "connection of things" described in the proposition is supposed to be understood as a connection of things qua *causes*. That is, the *connexio rerum* at stake here is a connection of things standing in relations of causal dependence. Now, if we draw on what Spinoza says elsewhere in the *Ethics*, we can characterize the nature of this causal *connectio rerum* a bit more precisely, and thus also understand why for Spinoza a connection of "things" is equivalent to a causal connection.

---

29 Since for Spinoza there seems to be no significant difference between the notions of "order" and "connection"—in 2p7s (II/90) and 3p2s (II/141), for example, Spinoza suggests their synonymity— I will use them interchangeably in what follows.

We should thus recall, first, that in Spinoza's view all things (including substance) *have* causes (more precisely, all things, including substance itself, are causally dependent on substance insofar as they are the necessary consequences or implications of its essence).[30] In particular, each *finite* thing depends on prior members of an infinite series of finite causes.[31] (In other words, a finite thing's causal dependence on substance is mediated by its dependence on other finite things.)

Second, for Spinoza every "thing" also *is* a cause (as he puts it, "Nothing exists from whose nature some effect does not follow").[32] So modes are not merely substance's effects; more precisely, they are effects by means of which substance brings about still further effects.

Now, to assert that all "things" both are and have causes is tantamount to saying that only what can enter into causal relations has being or metaphysical "reality."[33] Hence, for Spinoza, a comprehensive characterization of causal relations in nature will include in its scope all entities: the "causal order of nature" is extensionally the same as the "connection of things."

I suggest that this causal sense of *connexio rerum* is the first sense in which all things in nature are fundamentally connected in Spinoza's view—the first sense in which there is something like cosmic metaphysical sympathy.[34] The in-principle intelligibility of this *connexio rerum* is guaranteed simply by the existence of the things' causes. In the case of finite things, their dependence on an infinite series of prior causes also means that no finite thing can be truly known apart from other finite things. In this sense for Spinoza, as for many earlier advocates of cosmic

---

30 *Ethics* 1def1, 1p16, 1ax3, 1p25, 1p28. Substance can be described as causally dependent on itself in the sense that its existence follows necessarily from its essence.

31 *Ethics* 1p28. It is only this whole infinite series that is an immediate consequence of substance's essential nature; cf. Charles McCracken, "Knowledge of the Soul," in *The Cambridge History of Seventeenth-Century Philosophy*, ed. Daniel Garber and Michael Ayers (Cambridge: Cambridge University Press, 1998), 796–832, at 816.

32 *Ethics* 1p36.

33 See *Ethics* 2def6.

34 Contrast this with Leibniz's *non*causal rehabilitation of sympathy as preestablished harmony (see footnote 5 above).

sympathy, things that prima facie appear distinct and distant can be shown to be in metaphysical rigor causally and explanatorily related.

4. CONNEXIO IDEARUM

So much for how Spinoza understands the "connection of things" in nature. But 2p7 also bears on the connection of *ideas*. More precisely, the proposition describes the connection of ideas as the "same" as the connection of things. This raises at least two questions: (1) How are we to understand the notion of a *connexio idearum*? And (2), in what sense exactly is this *connexio idearum* the "same" as the *connexio rerum*?

To begin finding answers to these questions, we should note first of all that Spinoza understands the nature of "ideas" ("thoughts," "concepts," "cognitions"—all equivalent terms in his view) quite differently from what we today might understand by these terms. In part this is because Spinoza regards thought as a universally predicable property: all natural things—pebbles, dragonflies, trees—are in his view "minded" or "animate" (even if the "thinking" in which all these disparate "minds" engage is characterized by very different degrees of complexity and autonomy).[35] As a consequence, from Spinoza's point of view, what we today may associate with "thinking" is not the whole of thinking, nor the essence of thinking, but instead only our experience of the degree of thinking proper to finite human minds—the sorts of ideas that we can be determined to produce. The properly Spinozistic vantage point requires us to see thinking as an activity, a causal process, that belongs first and foremost to substance.[36] All other ideas, including those that constitute human minds, are for Spinoza merely more or less fragmented

---

35 *Ethics* 2p13s. This thesis of universal mindedness follows from Spinoza's controversial identification of a thing's "mind" with God's idea of this thing. With this identification in place, universal mindedness follows straightforwardly from Spinoza's entirely orthodox commitment to divine omniscience (2p3). For further discussion, see Margaret Wilson, "Objects, Ideas and 'Minds': Comments on Spinoza's Theory of Mind," in *Ideas and Mechanism: Essays on Early Modern Philosophy*, by Wilson (Princeton, NJ: Princeton University Press, 1999), 126–40.
36 Cf. Melamed, "Metaphysics of Thought," 678.

and incomplete "parts" of the necessarily true idea formed by this unlimited, cosmic thinking subject.[37] Whatever metaphysical "connections of ideas" are possible will thus be determined by the order of ideas proper to substance's "infinite idea," veridically representing all that is (namely, substantial essence and all its implications).

The way Spinoza demonstrates 2p7 suggests that the "sameness" of the orders of things and ideas follows immediately from the causal requirement on knowledge, set down in 1ax4. The general line of thought here seems clear enough:[38] if to know a thing requires us to know its causes, then an infallible intellect must represent in its ideas the causal order of things that in fact obtains in nature. So far so good. However, this might lead us to conclude further that when Spinoza asserts that ideas depend on one another in the "same" way that things do, he is saying that substance as a perfect knower *reproduces or mirrors* in the relations among its ideas the relations of causal dependence that obtain among things in nature.[39] That is, we could read Spinoza's claims as an implicit endorsement of some version of the correspondence theory of truth.

It is tempting, furthermore, to add here that Spinoza must have had in mind here a *purely logical* order of ideas, constituted by relations of entailment or inference among propositions. On this kind of reading, 2p7 would assert the existence of some sort of isomorphism or correspondence of the causal order of things with a purely logical order of ideas.

---

37 *Ethics* 2p11c, 2p33, 2p35.

38 If little more than the general line of thought: the brevity and purported self-evidence of this demonstration have caused much consternation among scholars. For discussion see e.g. Jonathan Bennett, *A Study of Spinoza's Ethics* (Indianapolis: Hackett, 1984), 127; Della Rocca, *Representation*, 22; Wilson, "Causal Axiom," 153. As has often been noted, for the demonstration of 2p7 to go through, we must arguably assume also 2p3, i.e., the existence of ideas of all things. See e.g. Edwin Curley, *Behind the Geometrical Method: A Reading of Spinoza's* Ethics (Princeton, NJ: Princeton University Press, 1988), 64; Deleuze, *Expressionism*, 114–15; Della Rocca, *Representation*, 22–23; Wilson, "Causal Axiom," 154.

39 Note the added complication that Spinoza seems to hold that God's infinite idea is simple. It's not clear in what way a simple idea could reflect the causal order among things in nature.

This is in fact a very common reading of Spinoza.[40] But there are good reasons to demur.[41] The biggest problem with such interpretations of the Spinozistic *connexio* has to do with the "sameness" of the causal order of things and the order of ideas, asserted in 2p7. Let's assume, as most scholars do, that this "sameness" of the two orders amounts to some sort of isomorphism, "mirroring," or "correspondence" of causal dependence relations in nature and entailment relations between propositions. The problem is that classical models of inference fail to mirror in the desired way the relations of causal dependence that Spinoza regards as metaphysically possible.[42] That is, if we assume that in Spinozistic nature effects "follow" from their causes along the lines of either material or strict implication, we end up attributing to Spinoza causal views he cannot hold. Take, for example, the proposition "God exists." For Spinoza this is a necessarily true proposition. As a true proposition, it is materially implied by any proposition; as a necessary proposition, it is strictly implied by any proposition. So if either of these models of inference mirrored Spinozistic relations of causal dependence, Spinoza would have to be committed to the view that God's existence is caused by the existence of *any* thing. But it is a fundamental tenet of Spinoza's system that God is *causa sui*: his existence follows from his essence alone.[43]

---

40 See e.g. Bennett's claim that for Spinoza "a cause relates to its effect as a premiss does to a conclusion which follows from it" (*Study*, §8.3); cf. Edwin Curley: "Spinoza assimilates the relation of causality to the relation of logical implication" (*Spinoza's Metaphysics: An Essay in Interpretation* [Cambridge, MA: Harvard University Press, 1969], 45–46).
This paragraph and next are developed more fully in Karolina Hübner, "On the Significance of Formal Causes in Spinoza's Metaphysics," *Archiv für Geschichte der Philosophie*, 2015.

41 One rudimentary difficulty for this sort of reading is that Spinoza does not seem very interested in logic, and has nothing to say about the nature of inference in particular (cf. Donagan, *Spinoza*, 74–75). The little he does say on related topics suggests that like many other seventeenth-century thinkers, he thought of logic as a normative and therapeutic "art" akin to medicine (see *Ethics* 5Pref [II/277], CM 1 [I/233]). That is, he does not belong to that philosophical tradition for which logic is concerned with being qua known. So logical relations would be a rather poor candidate for constituting an order capable of being the "same" as the causal order of *things*. See Spinoza, *Treatise on the Emendation of the Intellect* [91].

42 To my knowledge Don Garrett was the first to point out this difficulty; his own solution to the problem is to appeal to relevance logic ("Spinoza's Necessitarianism," in *God and Nature: Spinoza's Metaphysics*, ed. Yirmiyahu Yovel [Leiden: Brill, 1991], 97–118, at 194). See also Della Rocca, "Manifesto," 81, 92 n. 12.

43 *Ethics* 1def1.

In short, there are reasons to hesitate before identifying the Spinozistic "connection of ideas" simply with stand-alone entailment or inference relations among propositions, at least as classically understood. Minimally, we would have to restrict in some way the set of relevant entailment relations, so as to prevent inferences to what for Spinoza are metaphysically impossible causal dependencies. One plausible solution here is to introduce a prior metaphysical constraint restricting the set of the conceptual relations under consideration to entailment relations between (the definitions of) things' essences and the properties implied by those essences. This, I suggest, supplies the missing metaphysical constraint on which relations of conceptual dependence, among all those possible on classical models of inference, can genuinely be the "same" as causal relations obtaining in Spinoza's nature: namely, only those that hold between the substantial essence and the properties its definition analytically contains, and between the essences of those properties and their properties. (To return to the case we were considering above, this prior metaphysical constraint rules out for example the possibility of deriving substantial existence from truths about modes.)

We have then the beginnings of an answer to the question of how to interpret the notion of a "connection of ideas" within Spinoza's metaphysical framework: the ideas being "ordered" or "connected" are, in the first place, ideas produced by substance as a thinking thing; and, second, the "order" or "connection" in question is, at least on one plausible reading, the logical order of entailments from the essences of things to their properties.

Do we want to endorse the further claim that the *connexio rerum* and the *connexio idearum* are the "same" in the sense that they "correspond" to or "mirror" one another? Again, there are reasons to hesitate. For merely to assert the existence of some sort of a correspondence hardly sheds more light on the problem. In what sense could such two, prima facie entirely heterogeneous, sorts of relations—relations of causal dependence on the one hand and conceptual relations of essential implication on the other—be judged to have one and the same order?⁴⁴ Should we opt here for an *idealist* reading, on which the *connexio rerum* and the *connexio idearum* are the "same" just in the sense that there is really only *one* order, that of ideas? On such a reading, to be a "thing" would be reducible to being conceived. Unfortunately, this kind of reading seems inconsistent with Spinoza's explicit commitment to multiple kinds of beings, including an "extended" nature conceivable "through itself," and thus, it would seem, precisely *not* in terms of thought.⁴⁵

Another, more plausible, interpretative possibility here is to opt for a reductive reading of the "sameness" of the two orders that operates in the opposite direction, so to speak. On this reading, the order of causes and the order of ideas would be the same just in the sense that relations of ideas would reduce to *causal* relations between things:⁴⁶ the "connection" of ideas is given by the order of their causal dependence on one another as things. This interpretation is encouraged by the fact that for Spinoza "thing" is a perfectly general ontological category, and as such includes ideas in its extension.⁴⁷ It also has the explanatory

---

44 Margaret Wilson for instance glosses the "sameness" in terms of a single "relation of necessary determination" that obtains between "physical things" and "*cognitiones*" alike; but she confesses that this doesn't tell us much about the nature of this relation ("Causal Axiom," 155). Della Rocca suggests that the sameness in question boils down to a "structural similarity," such as having the same "number of immediate effects" (*Representation*, 18). An Aristotelian would presumably interpret this "sameness" as the *adequatio*, or formal identity, of the object being known and of the intellect that receives the intelligible form of the object. See also footnote 18 above.

The corollary to 2p6 states that nonmental "things" are generated according to a principle independent from thought. This means that the order of things cannot be the "same" as the order of ideas because things depend on ideas (as in theologies according to which God models the world on preexisting ideas in his intellect).

45 *Ethics* 1def8, 2p2, 1p10. For further criticisms of idealist readings of Spinoza's metaphysics, as advanced by Della Rocca, see Mogens Laerke, "Spinoza's Cosmological Argument in the *Ethics*," *Journal of the History of Philosophy* 49.4 (2011): 439–62; and Samuel Newlands, "Thinking, Conceiving, and Idealism in Spinoza," *Archiv für Geschichte der Philosophie* 94 (2012): 31–52.

46 This seems to be the view in Melamed, "Metaphysics of Thought," 640.

47 This reading is also suggested by a passage in which Spinoza seems to infer from the "sameness" of the two orders that ideas are subject to the causal order proper to things: "the order and connection of ideas (by [2]p7) is the same as the order and connection of causes. *Therefore, the cause of one singular idea is another idea*, or God, insofar as he is considered to be affected by another idea; and of this also [God is the cause], insofar as he is affected by another, and so on, to infinity" (*Ethics* 2p9d; emphasis added).

advantage that it makes self-evident why, and in what sense, relations between ideas must be the same as relations between things: the necessity of this "sameness" follows from the fact that an idea is just a certain kind of "thing." Unlike the correspondence reading, this account is thus not vulnerable to the charge of failing to illuminate the precise sense in which the two orders are the same. For the only limit on our precision in specifying the properties of this shared order is the limit of our understanding of Spinozistic causality more generally.[48]

5. Connexio rerum as identity

We can shed still more light on the alleged "sameness" of the order of ideas and the order of things in Spinoza's metaphysics if we draw on a different source—namely, on the Scholastic and Cartesian distinction between "formal" and "objective" reality. Consider the corollary that Spinoza appends to 2p7, immediately following the demonstration: "From this it follows that God's [NS: actual] power of thinking is equal to his actual power of acting. i.e., whatever follows formally from God's infinite nature follows objectively in God from his idea in the same order and with the same connection. [*quicquid ex infinita Dei natura sequitur formaliter, id omne ex Dei idea eodem ordine eademque connexione sequitur in Deo objective*]."[49] Let me first clarify the terminology used in the passage. The "formal reality" of a thing picks out what this thing is in its intrinsic nature—for example, as an extended thing, or a thinking one. The "objec-

---

[48] One might object that Spinoza's habit of modeling causal relations on relations of ideas—in particular, modeling substantial causality on relations of inference of properties from the essences of geometrical figures (see e.g. *Ethics* 1p17s)—counts against this second reductive reading, insofar as it suggests that the order of ideas constitutes an independent standard by which we can determine how things in nature depend on each other causally. But in fact the most passages like 1p17s entitle us to conclude is that this is how in Spinoza's view *we* can grasp the nature of causal relations. This is a matter of the order of knowing, and perhaps even solely of Spinoza's pedagogical strategy.

On the import of Spinoza's geometric analogies for Spinoza's causal picture see e.g. Bennett, *Study*, §8.3; John Carriero, "Spinoza's Views on Necessity in Historical Perspective," *Philosophical Topics* 19.1 (1991): 47–96; Curley, *Spinoza's Metaphysics*, 45–46; Gueroult, *Spinoza*, 246–97; Viljanen, "Essentialist Model"; Hübner, "Formal Causes."

[49] *Ethics* 2p7c.

tive reality" of a thing refers in turn to what this thing is insofar as it is represented in thought. For example, the sun as a thing existing in nature possesses certain physical properties, a certain mass and size among them. These belong to its formal reality. But the sun exists not only in nature, as a particular, formally real body, but also, whenever some intellect represents it, in thought. This objectively real sun also has a certain reality, one proper to intentional objects. To quote Descartes,

> if the question is about what the idea of the sun is...we answer that it is the thing which is thought of, in so far as it has objective being in the intellect.... 'Objective being in the intellect'...will signify the object's being in the intellect in the way in which its objects are normally there. By this I mean that the idea of the sun is the sun itself existing in the intellect...in the way in which objects normally are in the intellect.[50]

Spinoza makes this dual conception of metaphysical reality or being part of his system. (Presumably he sees objective reality simply as part of the nature of thought as such—that is, as part of the self-explanatory essence of substance as a thinking thing.)[51] The twist Spinoza puts on this inherited framework is that Spinozistic formal reality comes in infinite, or all possible, kinds, rather than only the two—extension and thought—acknowledged by Descartes. And the corollary Spinoza appends to 2p7 clarifies the nature of the relation between this infinitely varied formal reality (i.e., substance and its modes under all the attributes as things in nature) and the objective reality of substance's "infinite idea" (i.e., the objective reality of substance's perfect representation of its own essence and all its implications). As a perfect knower, substance adequately represents every formally real effect it gives rise to. So whatever has formal reality in Spinozistic nature also has objective reality in substance's idea or representation of this nature. In other

---
50 Descartes, *Author's Replies to the First Set of Objections*, in *Philosophical Writings*, AT 7.103.
51 Hence Spinoza regards as something "known through itself" that truth amounts to "what is contained objectively in the intellect" being "necessarily...in nature" (*Ethics* 1p30d).

words, for Spinoza, whatever has any reality at all has at the same time both formal and objective reality.

This is the sense in which substance's two fundamental causal "powers"—the power to think or to produce representations, and the power to "act," or to produce formally real things—are, as Spinoza puts it in the corollary, "equal": the order of ideas (what is represented by substance as an omniscient knower) and the order of things (what is produced by this substance as the universal cause) are "equal" in their respective degrees of reality.[52] It is a matter of two different, but equal, ways of having being.

The corollary to 2p7 thus suggests that if we want to think of Spinoza's substance-monistic metaphysics as nonetheless also a kind of dualism, we can draw the dividing line in at least two different places: not just between being and thought, as has been proposed before,[53] but equally between formal and objective reality. (These two dualisms are orthogonal to one another, since "thought" includes both the objective reality of the ideas' representational content, and the formal reality specific to thought as a causal power proper to substance.)

The corollary also helps us flesh out further the sense of Spinoza's claim in the proposition that the order of ideas is the "same" as the order of things. I proposed above that the two orders can be regarded as the "same" insofar as ideas, like all "things," are causally ordered. The corollary suggests that, in addition, understanding the "sameness" of the orders of ideas and things also involves grasping that everything exists with two kinds of reality: in nature and in the infinite intellect. In this case, the "sameness" of the order of things and the order of ideas amounts to an *identity*: the identity of every thing, whether substance or mode, as it is in nature, with this thing as it is in the infinite

---

52 Note that in asserting this equality Spinoza departs from Descartes, who treats objective reality as a "mode of being...much less perfect than that possessed by things which exist outside the intellect" (*First Replies*, AT 7.103).
53 See Melamed, "Metaphysics of Thought," 677–78.

intellect.[54] We can thus conclude that, in Spinoza's framework, certain relations of identity (of formal with objective realities) must obtain if ideas are to be causally so ordered as to veridically represent the order of things. (And, conversely, ideas must have a certain causal order for those relations of identity to obtain.)

For Spinoza the "sameness" of the orders of being and thought, of the *connexio rerum* and the *connexio idearum*, is thus not a matter of a mere correspondence or an isomorphism or a "mapping" of one order onto the other. Likewise, it seems inaccurate to say that the corollary to 2p7 is concerned solely with a "representational parallelism," or with epistemological relations, *as opposed to* identity, which (it is alleged) Spinoza raises as a concern only in the scholium that follows.[55] As we have seen, for Spinoza issues of representation are inseparable from matters of ontology: being represented just *is* having a certain kind of being. To be sure, as has been pointed out before, in the corollary to 2p7 there can be no question of the identity of the relata as *formally* real, since the whole of formal reality—which includes the "absolutely infinite" substance—cannot be numerically identical with a mere idea representing this substance's essence and its consequences; like any idea, this idea is only a mode.[56] Nonetheless, the corollary does assert the identity of the formal reality of all that is with the *objective* reality of the substance's idea: it is one and the same absolutely infinite object taken first in its formal reality and then in its objective reality.

To conclude this discussion of the corollary, let me underscore a more general point. This is that the corollary offers us a unique vantage point onto Spinoza's metaphysics as a whole. Typically this metaphysics gets introduced—as I have done earlier in this chapter—by asserting that there are three fundamental building blocks to this metaphysics

---

54 Cf. Deleuze, *Expressionism*, 117. Although the corollary asserts this sameness of order only of the objective reality of ideas (rather than of ideas tout court), I think this is an insignificant difference from the proposition, since in the corollary the order of objective realities is also supposed to be a gloss on substance's "power of thinking" as a whole.
55 For such readings see my footnote 19 above.
56 See Melamed, "Metaphysics of Thought," 641.

(substance, modes, attributes), defined so and so, and relating to each other in specific ways. This approach to understanding Spinoza's metaphysics is certainly correct, as far as it goes, and it is encouraged by Spinoza's own manner of presentation in the *Ethics*, which opens with definitions of such terms. But to consider Spinoza's metaphysics from this perspective is to consider it (to borrow a Heideggerian term) merely "ontically," that is, in terms of what this metaphysics says about *entities*.[57] But there is another, equally valid but relatively neglected, approach possible to the foundations of Spinoza's metaphysics: one that defines them not in terms of the kinds of entities it allows but rather in terms of the *kinds of being or reality* it posits and how it relates them. And seen from this point of view, the crux of Spinoza's metaphysical framework as a whole is the claim that the fundamental "structure" (for lack of a better word) of all that is is given by the fundamental distinctness, but also the unity or inseparability, of formal and objective reality. The corollary to 2p7 is one place in which this metaphysical picture emerges with particular clarity.

6. Attributes and Monism

In conclusion, let me turn to the last passage under scrutiny, the scholium to 2p7. Here is the crucial section:

> *we must recall here what we showed [NS: in the First Part], viz. that whatever can be perceived by an infinite intellect as constituting an essence of substance pertains to one substance only*, and consequently that the thinking substance and the extended substance are one and the same [*una eademque*] substance, which is now comprehended under this attribute, now under that. *So also* a mode of extension and the idea of that mode are one and the same thing, but expressed in two

---

57 See Martin Heidegger, *Being and Time*, trans. John Macquarrie and Edward Robinson (1927; San Francisco: SCM Press, 1962).

ways [*una eademque est res sed duobus modis expressa*].... For example, a circle existing in nature and the idea of the existing circle, which is also in God, are one and the same thing, which is explained through different attributes. Therefore, whether we conceive nature under the attribute of Extension, or under the attribute of Thought, or under any other attribute, we shall find one and the same order, *or one and the same connection of causes*, i.e., that the same things follow one another [*unum eundemque ordinem sive unam eandemque causarum connexionem hoc est easdem res invicem sequi*].[58]

As a rule, the point of the scholium is taken to be the *numerical identity* of entities differing in attribute (that is, in the essential properties of the *kind* to which these entities belong). On this reading, the lesson of the scholium is that every mind is, rather paradoxically, numerically identical to some body, and vice versa.[59]

I read the scholium slightly differently. For it seems to me that one of its principal points is to remind the reader, in the wake of a discussion of how things are *represented* in the corollary and the proposition, of Spinoza's fundamental commitment to substance monism, and thus to the fundamental unity of all things that this monism entails. It is substance monism that determines the sense in which there is, as Spinoza writes above, only one "connection of causes": this is the connection proper to substance, the order of things that follows necessarily from its essence. To put the point slightly differently, the scholium is meant to remind us that whatever can be conceived in the various, attribute-specific ways (as thinking substance, as extended substance, as minds, as bodies, and so on) nonetheless constitutes just a single order of things—a single connection of causes.

In other words, in the scholium Spinoza is cautioning us about what conclusions about the order of formal reality we are entitled to draw

---

58 *Ethics* 2p7s, emphases added.
59 See footnote 19 above. Gueroult claims that this identity of entities under different attributes is already asserted in 1p16d (*Spinoza*, 1.339); cf. Melamed, "Metaphysics of Thought."

on the basis of how ideas are ordered, and the ways they can and cannot connect with one another. More precisely, he is cautioning us that the diverse objective realities of various ideas are *not* sufficient grounds to conclude that these ideas refer to a numerical plurality of formally real things that would be "really distinct" from one another, as substances are.[60] For even if we represent thinking things and extended things with the aid of concepts that have nothing in common with one another in the relevant sense, we also must refer all these representations to one and the same formally real entity in nature.[61]

This helps clarify in what sense Spinoza can assert in the scholium that every mind is numerically identical to some body, and vice versa. That is, I do not think that he is putting forth solely a thesis about identity relations *directly between modes*. Instead, I suggest that when he writes that a mind and a body, or a circle and an idea of that circle, are "one and the same thing," he is reminding us first that they are *both identical to the one substance*, as its modifications. Every mind and every body, and every circle and idea of a circle, all "pertain to one substance only," just as infinite extension and infinite thought do. Spinoza's point throughout the passage remains the same: don't forget that there is only substance.

This helps us give sense to a relation of numerical identity that would hold between modes of distinct attributes. As has been pointed out before, there is a very rudimentary problem for this interpretation of 2p7s. The problem is that for any attribute-specific predicates F and G, we *cannot* infer from the fact that a given mind is essentially F, or causes some idea to be G, that the body with which this mind is purportedly numerically identical either is F or causes another body to be G. What sense can we then give to the claim that the mind and body in

---

60 Indeed, Spinoza reduced "real distinction" to the distinction between the various attributes of the one substance (1p10s), such that this distinction no longer aligns with a numerical distinction between substances.

61 Hence I also don't think that we should see 2p7s as the "more general" formulation of parallelism, as suggested e.g. by Della Rocca (*Spinoza*, 91).

question are "identical," if they fail to share such basic properties?[62] I suggest that we not take the scholium to make claims simply about the numerical identity of modes with one another, but instead more fundamentally take it to assert the real identity of modes *with substance* (where "real identity" just means the absence of real distinction).

Let me close with the following more general remark. As I noted above, it is often claimed that the scholium to 2p7 is concerned with a different set of problems than the proposition, demonstration, and corollary (in opposition to those who see all these passages as expressing some single and uniform doctrine of "parallelism"). The claim is that the scholium deals with the relation of numerical identity and introduces the subject of the attributes, while the proposition, demonstration, and corollary are silent on all these topics and instead concern themselves solely with representational or epistemological relations.[63] I have already raised doubts about the wisdom of separating epistemological and ontological matters in this way within Spinoza's framework. To this criticism I now want to add that those who favor this kind of a "disjunctive" reading of the passages rarely (to my knowledge at least) attempt to explain *why* Spinoza would append the scholium to the corollary if, ex hypothesi, the two make such distinct claims.

It seems to me that there are two complementary explanations for the existence and placement of the scholium. First of all, as already noted, the scholium functions as a reminder to the reader of how to interpret the import of what our ideas represent within a substance monistic framework. Second, *all* the passages under consideration, from the proposition all the way to the scholium, are thematically unified around a single metaphysical problem (though it is not the problem of interattribute relations, as Spinoza's "parallelism doctrine"

---

62 Della Rocca suggests that Spinoza treats causal contexts as referentially opaque, as well as that pairs of identical modes share attribute-neutral properties, such as having the same number of effects (*Representation*, ch. 7). He also proposes that there is pressure toward the identity of body and mind pairs given their same causal relationships, and a lack of a possible explanation for their *non*identity (*Spinoza*, 100–101).

63 See my footnote 19 above.

is also often glossed). Namely, the thematic unity of all these passages is furnished, as the wording of the proposition itself suggests, by the metaphysical problem of the connection of things in nature—that is, the problem of cosmic sympathy—whether we understand this problem as one of the relation of the two kinds of being, or as the problem of the "real" unity of all things in nature, despite the intellect's apprehension of conceptual gulfs and chasms.

CHAPTER SIX

The Eighteenth-Century Context of Sympathy from Spinoza to Kant

Ryan Patrick Hanley

1. THE AGE OF SYMPATHY

That the eighteenth century was the age of sympathy is well appreciated today. Literary theorists have insisted on this for some time, political theorists are now more than ever emphasizing it, and versions of it are today commonplace even among economists.[1] Taken together,

---

Earlier versions of this essay were presented to the "Workshop in Political Theory and Policy Analysis" at Indiana University (February 2012) and at the conference for this volume held at the University of Richmond (June 2012). For many helpful comments and suggestions, I am grateful to the audiences on both occasions, and especially Aurelian Craiutu, Kate Abramson, Mark Yellin, Geoff Sayre-McCord, Remy Debes, Karolina Hübner, René Brouwer, Christia Mercer, and Eric Schliesser. I am also grateful to the Earhart Foundation for a research grant that facilitated the completion of this essay.

[1] For a helpful introduction to the way in which scholars of literature and the theater have conceived of sympathy in the eighteenth century, see e.g. David Marshall, *The Surprising Effects of Sympathy: Marivaux, Diderot, Rousseau, and Mary Shelley* (Chicago: University of Chicago Press, 1988), 1–8. On eighteenth-century sympathy from the perspective of political theory, see e.g. Michael Frazer, *The Enlightenment of Sympathy: Justice and the Moral Sentiments in the Eighteenth Century and Today* (Oxford: Oxford University Press, 2010). In experimental economics, see esp. the work of Vernon Smith, e.g. *Rationality in Economics: Constructivist and Ecological Forms* (Cambridge: Cambridge University Press, 2007), 15–16. In this volume, see also on eighteenth-century sympathy esp. chapter 7 and Hayes's reflection.

such efforts ought to be welcomed, as they have done much to lead us to rethink convenient but sadly oversimplified associations of the Enlightenment with the "age of reason," and have also done much to remind us of the eighteenth-century foundations of a great deal of contemporary ethics. But for all this a key issue remains unexplained. Even amid our general agreement *that* the eighteenth century was the age of sympathy, less well understood is *why* this was so. Exactly what then explains the remarkable ubiquity of the concept of sympathy in the eighteenth century?

This, I will be the first to admit, is a staggeringly difficult question—which perhaps explains why so little work has been done to answer it. Part of the difficulty concerns the plasticity of the concept. Thus Marc André Bernier, in one of the best recent surveys of eighteenth-century sympathy, calls our attention to "l'incroyable vitalité et la surprenante hétérogénéité qui caractérisent la notion de sympathie au cours de la période."[2] Yet the concept was hardly up for grabs, as three meanings are particularly common in eighteenth-century philosophy. These include sympathy as "mechanical communication of feelings and passions," as a "process of imagination, or of reason, by which we substitute ourselves for others," and as our "delight in the happiness and sorrow in the misery of other people."[3] Each definition points in a different direction and has a distinct heritage, as explored in several contributions to this volume; sympathy as mechanical communication of course hearkens back to understandings of sympathy as *contagio*; sympathy as substituting self for others hearkens back to traditions of common sense, or *sensus communis*; and sympathy as passionate concern for

---

[2] Marc André Bernier, "Les Métamorphoses de la sympathie au siècle des Lumières," in *Les lettres sur la sympathie (1798) de Sophie de Grouchy: Philosophie morale et réforme sociale*, ed. Bernier and Deidre Dawson (Oxford: Voltaire Foundation, 2010), 1–17 at 4. For similar statements of the heterogeneity of the eighteenth-century concept, see e.g. Jonathan Lamb, *The Evolution of Sympathy in the Long Eighteenth Century* (London: Pickering and Chatto, 2009), 18; and Evelyn Forget, "Evocations of Sympathy: Sympathetic Imagery in Eighteenth-Century Social Theory and Physiology," *History of Political Economy* 35 (2003): 282–308, esp. 284–89.

[3] These helpful definitions are given in Luigi Turco, "Sympathy and Moral Sense, 1725–1740," *British Journal for the History of Philosophy* 7 (1999): 79–101, at 79.

others hearkens back to traditions of other-directedness like compassion, pity, and charity. Clearly then, eighteenth-century sympathy was plural in both its meanings and origins. But it was also plural in its contexts, for sympathy was hardly an idea exclusive to philosophers but also key to chemists and physicists who invoked it to describe principles of affinity, astronomers and physicians who used it to describe interactions and attractions of material and corporeal parts and functions, novelists and playwrights who used it to describe the interactions of characters and readers and actors and audiences, and moral and political theorists who used it to describe the nature and extent of our obligations to distant others.

We are left then with a truly dizzying array of substantive definitions as well as historical and methodological contexts. Untangling these alone would be more than the work of a day. Even so, there remains our other task of explaining just why sympathy, in all its forms, became so ubiquitous in the eighteenth century—and it is to this task that this effort is dedicated. And thus the thesis this chapter aims to defend. Sympathy's eighteenth-century explosion, it will argue, is best traced to its unique status as a sophisticated philosophical response to a pressing practical challenge. This practical challenge concerned the disorientation consequent to the seismic shift in the forms of social organization experienced over the course of the eighteenth century. Most simply, the eighteenth century (especially but not only in Britain and France) witnessed a shift from traditional and more intimate forms of community to new forms of social organization; now societies of strangers emerged alongside more traditional and familiar communities of intimates. But what holds a society of strangers together? Some of course posited that self-interest alone could maintain a social structure, but it seems fair to say that this was a minority opinion then and now. Others continued to defend traditional Christian ideas of charity, but here too it seems fair to say that secularizing and skeptical tendencies in eighteenth-century epistemology and ethics made this remedy increasingly less viable. Where then to turn? It is here that sympathy emerged and then flourished, specifically as a new and creative philosophical response to the practical political problem of human connectedness in an increasingly disorienting world. Sympathy, that is, emerged as an other-directed sentiment capable of sustaining the minimal social bonds needed to realize the new social order and indeed one capable of so doing without requiring acceptance of the theistic foundations of Christian conceptions of neighbor love. In this sense, the eighteenth-century theorists of sympathy not only cemented its shift or translation from the domain of the physical to the domain of the ethical—that is, from a principle primarily dedicated to explaining connections between substances to a principle dedicated to explaining connections between human individuals—but in so doing also gave birth to a novel concept that, we might say with only a minimal amount of hyperbole, was intended to serve as a substitute for love.

2. Spinoza's Conception of Sympathy

Such in any case is our thesis—now to the demonstration. We begin with Spinoza, who more than any other single thinker would inaugurate the eighteenth-century tradition of thinking about sympathy. As Karolina Hübner's contribution to this volume demonstrates, Spinoza was an active participant in a debate over "the metaphysical doctrine of sympathy" that looked back to antiquity.[4] Yet Spinoza was also a key figure in the emergence of the ethical concept of sympathy, and his categories would shape later debate in this vein. In particular, his theory introduces three discrete elements of the concept that would prove central to later eighteenth-century theorists of sympathy: its foundations in epistemic associationism, its role as an action-motivating sentiment, and its relationship to self-interest and self-love.

Spinoza's idea of sympathy is itself a direct product of and key contribution to his broader ethical outlook. As is well known, this ethical

---

4 Chapter 5, 1–2.

outlook is founded in large part on the proposition that the primary motivating concern of human beings is the preservation of their material substance—the notion that "each thing, in so far as it is in itself, endeavors to persist in its own being."[5] Spinoza of course would go on to reinterpret all ethical phenomena through this specifically egocentric lens, but most important for our purposes is how this lens leads him to rethink love. Love, Spinoza notoriously explains, is "merely 'pleasure accompanied by the idea of an external cause'" and hatred "merely 'pain accompanied by the idea of an external cause.'"[6] To say only the very least, this is a pronounced shift away from traditional theological definitions of love in the context of the divine or transcendent toward an understanding of love grounded in the perspective of the self. And it is this perspective that frames Spinoza's ethical theory of sympathy. For not only do we love or hate those things that immediately affect us, he asserts, but so too we "love or hate some things without any cause known to us, but merely from sympathy and antipathy."[7] Spinoza is clearly fighting battles on several fronts here; in continuing he explicitly distances his sympathy from conceptions that associated it with occult qualities.[8] But he also makes also another fundamental move here. Sympathy, in his theory, connects us to distant phenomena that might not seem to be immediately related to the self in any obvious sense, but which in fact shape its pleasures and pains.

Spinoza develops this claim as part 3 of the *Ethics* progresses. Gradually he reveals that sympathy is best regarded as a type of association: "as soon as we think of an object that we have seen in conjunction with others, we immediately recall the others as well and thus from regarding

---

[5] Spinoza, *Ethics* pr.6,III; cf. pr.7,III and sch.pr.44,III. Quotations from the *Ethics* are from the translation by Samuel Shirley (Indianapolis: Hackett, 1992). For an extremely helpful introduction to the way in which Spinoza's ethics derives from his understanding of the conatus, see Don Garrett, "Spinoza's Ethical Theory," in *The Cambridge Companion to Spinoza* (Cambridge: Cambridge University Press, 1995), esp. 271–74 and 302–5.

[6] *Ethics* sch.pr.13,III.

[7] *Ethics* sch.pr.15,III.

[8] Cf. e.g. among others Thomas Hobbes, *Leviathan*, ed. Richard Tuck (Cambridge: Cambridge University Press, 1996), 468; on sympathy and occult qualities see also chapters 5 and 3 in this volume.

the one we immediately pass on to regarding another."[9] This is especially true of our ideas of other people; indeed "from the fact that we imagine a thing like ourselves, towards which we have felt no emotion, to be affected by an emotion, we are thereby affected by a similar emotion," and thus "if we imagine someone like ourselves to be affected by an emotion, this thought will express an affection of our own body similar to that emotion. So from the fact that we imagine a thing like ourselves to be affected by an emotion, we are affected by a similar emotion along with it."[10] And herein lies both the import of sympathy as an epistemic concept of association and as a normative ethical concept. Our experience of the emotions felt by others not only conveys their feelings to us but also leads us to feel certain pains and pleasures that themselves prompt specific behaviors. For Spinoza, sympathy is thus crucially action motivating, and indeed action motivating in a socially salutary manner: "that which affects with pain a thing that we pity affects us too with similar pain, and so we shall endeavor to devise whatever annuls the existence of the former or destroys it: that is, we shall seek to destroy it; i.e. we shall be determined to destroy it. So we shall endeavor to free from its distress the thing we pity."[11]

Herein lies the key point. Sympathy leads us to relieve the distress of others; in this sense it serves other-directed purposes. At the same time, the motive behind our so doing is self-interest; we seek to relieve the pain of others because of the pain that we feel as a consequence of their distress. Spinoza like many after him does not explicitly entertain the possibility that sympathetic pains might lead their possessor to flee such scenes rather than to alleviate them. It may be that this would simply muddy the waters to such an extent that his central claim would be obscured: that pity prompts a form of practically beneficial

---

9 *Ethics* pr.52,III.
10 *Ethics* pr.27,III.
11 *Ethics* cor.3, pr.27,III. Spinoza's explicit focus here is pity (*commiserato*), defined earlier (and importantly for the eighteenth-century debate) as "pain arising from another's hurt" (*Ethics* pr.22,III), and which he explicitly equates with compassion (*misericordia*).

other-directed ethical activity consistent with his egocentric commitments. This is not to say that he fails to see the limitations of such a conception; indeed, Spinoza explicitly notes that "from the same property of human nature from which it follows that men are compassionate, it likewise follows that they are prone to envy and ambition."[12] But for now the crucial point is that Spinoza largely inaugurates the eighteenth-century tradition of theorizing about sympathy by articulating several discrete elements of the concept as it would come to be used, including especially the claim that sympathy concerns identification of one individual with another via an associative process founded on resemblance, the claim that sympathy is action motivating and leads its possessor to seek to relieve the distress of others, and the claim that the grounds for such action is not an altruistic concern for others but principally a concern for the self and its pleasures and pains.

3. Sympathy, Self-Interest, and Others

What follows takes up each of these themes in order to show how these three discrete strands of Spinoza's theory of sympathy came to be much more thoroughly developed by later eighteenth-century theorists. We begin with the most common way in which sympathy was discussed in the eighteenth century: namely as an action-motivating sentiment capable of serving to establish social bonds between individuals. Interestingly, this side of sympathy tends to receive the least attention from scholars today. This may be because contemporary scholarship on sympathy emerged in part out of the battles over "Das Adam Smith Problem" that had occupied earlier scholars. As an influential generation of revisionists demonstrated, the notorious "Problem" (which concerns the ostensible tension between the supposedly self-interested moral psychology of Smith's *Wealth of Nations* and the other-directed moral psychology described in his *Theory of Moral Sentiments*) is in fact predicated

---

12 *Ethics* sch.pr.32,III.

on a false dichotomy between self-interest and sympathy.[13] Much good came out of these revisionist efforts, including not only a more sophisticated understanding of Smith but also a greater appreciation of the role of moral sentiments in judgment more generally.[14] At the same time, the counterreaction to the simplifications on which "Das Problem" was founded had the effect of leading scholars to distance sympathy from related other-directed sentiments like compassion and pity and charity, and to emphasize instead its role as a mechanism of epistemic transfer for the purposes of conveying passions. One result of this has been a lack of emphasis on sympathy as an action-motivating sentiment capable of encouraging reciprocal care—a key element of the eighteenth-century definition.

Joseph Butler sounded one of the first keynotes for much of the eighteenth-century debate on this point. In his influential discussion of compassion in his *Sermons*, he argued that human beings, as "imperfect creatures," necessarily always "depend upon each other."[15] This state of perpetual interdependence is furthered by specific passions natural to human beings that lead them to be reticent to become the agents of another's harm. Thus compassion, according to Butler, may not lead its possessor always to promote the happiness of others, yet it will "prevent him from doing evil" and at least sometimes "incline him to relieve the distressed."[16] Compassion thus provides a necessary and salutary check on self-interest, in the absence of which "men would certainly be much more wanting in the offices of charity they owe to

---

[13] For an excellent history of this debate, see esp. Leonidas Montes, "Das Adam Smith Problem: Its Origins, the Stage of the Current Debate, and One Implication for Our Understanding of Sympathy," *Journal of the History of Economic Thought* 35 (2003): 63–90. Montes's article also does much to reestablish the centrality of Smith's own insistence on the action-motivating aspects of sympathy. I treat the specific implications of this debate for Smith scholarship in my "Adam Smith: From Love to Sympathy," *Revue internationale de philosophie*, 68 (2014): 251–73.

[14] For helpful recent developments, see Frazer, *Enlightenment of Sympathy*, esp. 3–10; and esp. Sharon Krause, *Civil Passions: Moral Sentiment and Democratic Deliberation* (Princeton, NJ: Princeton University Press, 2008), and chapter 7 in this volume.

[15] Joseph Butler, "Upon Compassion" (sermon 5), in *Fifteen Sermons*, in *The Works of Joseph Butler* (London: William Tegg, 1867; reprint, Adamant Media, 2006), 45–56 at 49.

[16] Butler, "Upon Compassion" (sermon 6), in *Fifteen Sermons*, 56–65 at 58.

each other, and likewise more cruel and injurious, than they are at present."[17] Other eighteenth-century thinkers would make related claims. Foremost among them is Rousseau, whose second *Discours* presents *pitié* as one of the two passions natural to men, and itself valuable not because it leads us to do positive good but because it compels us to be reticent to do harm by "moderating in every individual the activity of self-love": a check that Rousseau of course claims has been wholly and tragically overcome by civilization.[18] Rousseau would extend this claim in *Emile*, in arguing that *pitié* has a specific role to play not just in the life of the savage but also in the life of civilized man, insofar as a more cognitively developed pity is responsible for regulating *amour-propre*, the particular form of self-love endemic to developed human beings.[19]

Butler and Rousseau, together with Bernard Mandeville, who did much to stimulate Rousseau's thinking on pity in this sense, thus stand at the head of eighteenth-century traditions of thinking about the normative implications of other-directed passions such as pity and compassion as checks on self-interest. In time later thinkers would come to regard sympathy itself through this lens. Citing Butler's account of compassion, the influential Aberdeen philosopher David Fordyce observed that sympathy stands as a "security" devised by God for the public well-being, one that "draws us out of ourselves to bear a part of the misfortunes of others, powerfully solicits us in their favor, melts us at a sight of their distress, and makes us in some degree unhappy until

---

17 Butler, "Upon Compassion" (sermon 5), 45–56, at 52–53.
18 Jean-Jacques Rousseau, *Discourse on the Origins of Inequality*, in *Discourses and Other Early Political Writings*, ed. Victor Gourevitch (Cambridge: Cambridge University Press, 1997), at 154.
19 See Jean-Jacques Rousseau, *Emile*, trans. Allan Bloom, in *The Collected Works of Rousseau*, ed. Christopher Kelly and Roger D. Masters (Hanover, NH: University Press of New England, 2009), 13.373–75. In a similar vein, see e.g. Louis-Sébastien Mercier, who would wonder what heart could be so cruel never to have felt "cette Sympathie tendre qui le lie aux autres êtres" and could be drawn to agree with a cynical moralist who has "tout vu dans l'amour-propre & rien dans cette impression vive du sentiment qui l'entraîne & le maitrise" (*La Sympathie, histoire morale* [Amsterdam, 1767], 7–8). I develop this side of Rousseau's own theory of pity at greater length in my essay "Pitié développée: Aspects éthiques et épistémiques," in *Philosophie de Rousseau*, ed. B. Bachofen, B. Bernardi, A. Charrak, and F. Guénard (Paris: Classiques Garnier, 2014), 305–18.

they are relieved from it." Sympathetic compassion is thus "particularly well adapted to the condition of human life" insofar as it provides "an admirable restraint upon the more selfish passions, or those violent impulses that carry us to the hurt of others."[20] Thus the evidence that "men are formed for society and the delightful interchange of friendly sentiments and duties" lies precisely in that "instantaneous sympathy" by which "the impulses of pleasure or pain, joy or sorrow, made on one mind" are "communicated in some degree to all."[21]

This aspect of sympathy would receive further important expressions from a diverse range of thinkers crossing several traditions—including, among others, such prominent thinkers as Edmund Burke; Henry Home, Lord Kames; Immanuel Kant; and Sophie de Grouchy. Thus Burke, in his account of sympathy in his *Philosophical Enquiry*, notes:

> as our Creator has designed that we should be united by the bond of sympathy, he has strengthened that bond by a proportionable delight; and there most where our sympathy is most wanted, in the distresses of others. . . . The delight we have in such things, hinders us from shunning scenes of misery; and the pain we feel, prompts us to relieve ourselves in relieving those who suffer; and all this antecedent to any reasoning, by an instinct that works us to its own purposes, without our concurrence.[22]

Burke's statement attests to his belief that the particular pains and pleasures that we have been taught to feel by nature strongly incline (if not compel) us to come to the assistance of suffering others, as the pleasure derived from so doing outruns the mere relief of pain we could expect to experience were we to simply flee such scenes and try

---

20 David Fordyce, *The Elements of Moral Philosophy*, ed. Thomas Kennedy (Indianapolis: Liberty Fund, 2003), 44–45.
21 Fordyce, *Elements*, 91.
22 Edmund Burke, *A Philosophical Enquiry into the Origin of Our Ideas of the Sublime and Beautiful*, ed. Adam Phillips (Oxford: Oxford University Press, 2008), 42–43.

to forget about them. A related position is developed by Hume, who calls humanity—itself a proxy for sympathy in his later ethics—the only passion that can alone "be the foundation of any general system and established theory of blame or approbation," and more pointedly by Kames, who calls sympathy the "cement of human society" as it "attaches us to an object in distress so powerfully as even to overbalance self-love, which would make us fly from it."[23] For Kames, sympathy stands as the passion "to which human society is indebted for its greatest blessing, that of providing relief for the distressed."[24] Indeed society could hardly be imagined without it:

> as no state is exempt from misfortunes, mutual sympathy must greatly promote the security and happiness of mankind. That the prosperity and preservation of each individual should be the care of many, tends more to happiness in general, than that each man, as the single inhabitant of a desert island, should be left to stand or fall by himself, without prospect of regard or assistance from others.[25]

This perspective can even be found in the precritical Kant, for whom "sympathy and complaisance are grounds for beautiful actions that would perhaps all be suffocated by the preponderance of a cruder self-interest," though even in his precritical stage Kant took care to note that sympathy "is nevertheless weak and is always blind," and "not enough to drive indolent human nature to actions for the common weal."[26] In his most prominent comments on sympathy Kant quite

---

23 David Hume, *Enquiry concerning the Principles of Morals*, ed. L. A. Selby-Bigge and P. H. Nidditch (1751; Oxford: Oxford University Press, 1975), 9.5 (see Ryan P. Hanley, "David Hume and 'the Politics of Humanity,'" *Political Theory* 39 (2011): 205–33); Henry Home, Lord Kames, *Essays on the Principles of Morality and Natural Religion*, ed. Mary Catherine Moran (Indianapolis: Liberty Fund, 2005), 19–20.
24 Henry Home, Lord Kames, *Elements of Criticism*, ed. Peter Jones (Indianapolis: Liberty Fund, 2005), 308.
25 Kames, *Essays*, 17.
26 Immanuel Kant, *Observations on the Feeling of the Beautiful and Sublime*, in *Anthropology, History, and Education*, ed. Günter Zöller and Robert Louden (Cambridge: Cambridge University Press, 2007), 18–62, at 29–32 (Ak. 2:215–18).

notoriously suggests that even if actions done out of sympathy might "conform with duty" they should not be mistaken for actions done "*from duty*."[27] Yet this claim should itself be read against his claim in the *Metaphysics of Morals* that even though we indeed are under no duty to "share the sufferings of others," we yet indeed have "a duty to sympathize actively in their fate," and thus have an "indirect duty" to cultivate our benevolent affections insofar as they can help to spur us to our genuine duty. Thus Kant too insists that it is "a duty not to avoid the places where the poor who lack the most basic necessities are to be found but rather to seek them out," and indeed ultimately counts sympathy as among "the impulses nature has implanted in us to do what the representations of duty alone might not accomplish."[28]

Perhaps no eighteenth-century thinker emphasized this side of sympathy quite so strongly as Sophie de Grouchy. In her influential writings on sympathy de Grouchy calls special attention to those "new bonds of sympathy that unite us with other men" and constitute "an indissoluble tie between ourselves and our fellow men."[29] Herein indeed lies the chief import of sympathy on her definition:

> sympathy is the first cause of the feeling of humanity, the effects of which are so precious. It compensates for a portion of the evils issuing from personal interests in large societies, and it struggles against the coercive force that we encounter everywhere we go and that centuries of Enlightenment alone can destroy by attacking the vices that

---

27 Immanuel Kant, *Groundwork of the Metaphysics of Morals*, in *Practical Reason*, ed. Mary Gregor (Cambridge: Cambridge University Press, 1996), 37–108, at 53–54 (Ak. 4:398–99).

28 Immanuel Kant, *Metaphysics of Morals*, in *Practical Reason*, ed. Mary Gregor (Cambridge: Cambridge University Press, 1996), 353–604, at 575–76 (Ak. 6:457). For accounts of these passages, see esp. Paul Guyer, "Moral Feelings in the *Metaphysics of Morals*," in *Kant's Metaphysics of Morals: A Critical Guide*, ed. Lara Denis (Cambridge: Cambridge University Press, 2010), 130–51, at 145–49; and Frazer's helpful discussion of how "Kant's objection to treating sympathetic inclinations as the determining ground of one's moral choices is not a moral objection to sympathetic inclinations as such" (*Enlightenment of Sympathy*, 118).

29 Sophie de Grouchy, *Letters on Sympathy: A Critical Edition*, ed. Karin Brown (Philadelphia: American Philosophical Society, 2008), 132, 149.

have produced it! Amid the shock of so many passions that oppress the weak or marginalize the unfortunate, from the bottom of its heart humanity secretly pleads the cause of sympathy and avenges it from the injustice of fate by arousing the sentiment of natural equality.[30]

In all these discussions two elements are particularly noteworthy. The first is the claim that the value of sympathy lies in its capacity to check the pernicious effects of self-interest. The second is the claim that sympathy leads us to assist others. This is worth emphasizing because it not only testifies to the ubiquity of the eighteenth-century conception of sympathy as action motivating, but also suggests one possible answer to our larger question concerning why sympathy came to have such broad and deep appeal for eighteenth-century thinkers. In brief: the insistence on sympathy's capacity to check self-interest and to prompt other-regarding ethical action may owe at least in part to a general fear that self-interest was on the rise and benevolence on the wane. Tracing the causes of this fear would go well beyond the scope of this chapter, but it seems at least possible that the root of this concern lies in some familiar eighteenth-century phenomena. From the urbanization that brought more strangers together as neighbors than ever before to the commercialization that brought traders into ever more contact with distant others and expanded the public sphere at home, to the imperialism and colonization that pushed Europeans across the globe: all of these phenomena can be understood to have contributed in their own

---

30 De Grouchy, *Letters on Sympathy*, 113; see also, in this volume, Hayes's reflection, esp. 4–5. For a (slightly) more poetic rendering of the same thought, see Samuel Jackson Pratt's *Sympathy: A Poem*, 5th ed. (London, 1781):

 In cities thus, though trade's tumultuous train
Spurn at the homely maxims of the plain,
Not all the pride of rank, the trick of art,
Can chase the generous passion from the heart:
Nay more, a larger circle it must take,
Where men embodying, larger int'rests make,
And each perforce round each more closely twine,
Where countless thousands form the social line.
   (bk 2, lines 35–42)

different ways to the liberation of self-interest and thereby to a challenging of traditional concepts of neighbor love. These concerns, it thus seems reasonable to suggest, likely contributed to the eighteenth century's embrace of sympathy as a partial remedy for the negative externalities associated with these simultaneously progressive and dislocating phenomena.

4. Sympathy and Physiology

To this point my primary aim has been to demonstrate that the eighteenth-century concept of sympathy had a normative purpose. Yet to say that sympathy was principally conceived as a response to a practical problem begs another more fundamental question: why was *sympathy* per se the answer to this problem? Put differently, even if sympathy is indeed best regarded as an answer to the problem of human association, exactly why did its eighteenth-century theorists think it—and not some other concept or category—the best answer to this problem?

The reasons for this would seem to be twofold. The first is that the principal extant alternative to sympathy was increasingly coming to be regarded as less viable as a solution. Love, that is, conceived as the charity that bound neighbors together, required epistemic commitments that eighteenth-century thinkers became increasingly less willing to make. The reasons for such are easily enough seen. The Gospel commandment to love thy neighbor was of course one of two commands, the first being to love God with all one's heart and all one's strength. Only after this first command was fulfilled was it possible to pursue the second. This decisively shaped the nature and function of *caritas*, as love for one's self and for one's neighbor came to be mediated and informed by the love of the divine; indeed the very reason why it is good to love self and neighbor alike and equally is the belief that both are created in God's image.[31] This view was hardly absent in

---

[31] For a helpful recent statement of the foundations of this position in the Torah, see e.g. Simon May, *Love: A History* (New Haven, CT: Yale University Press, 2011), 17–18.

eighteenth-century debate; indeed the English philosopher David Hartley—himself a prominent contributor to debates over the nature and function of epistemic associationism—insisted in the course of his demonstration that goodwill and benevolence grow ever "weaker and weaker" as they are "extended more and more":

> Yet still the common blessings and calamities, which fall upon whole nations and communities; the general resemblance of the circumstances of all mankind to each other, in their passage through life; their common relation to God as their creator, governor, and father; their common concern in a future life, and in the religion of Christ, &c.; are capable of raising strong sympathetic actions towards all mankind, and the several larger divisions of it, in persons of religious dispositions, who duly attend to these things.[32]

Yet on the whole, eighteenth-century epistemology tended to separate sympathy from theism, and indeed to present sympathy as a substitute for a *caritas* whose theistic foundations were increasingly regarded as epistemically unavailable; in this sense, sympathy sought to take us straight to neighbor love without becoming waylaid by the necessity of a lexically prior love of God.[33] It is for this reason, one suspects, that a number of the most striking and prominent explicit invocations in eighteenth-century philosophy of the biblical command to love one's neighbor as one's self—including those of Smith and Rousseau and Kant—are silent on the first command.[34] But there is also a second

---

32 David Hartley, *Observations on Man* (London, 1749), 485.
33 Some scholars have emphasized the "Christian underpinnings" of sympathy and other forms of "sentimental humanitarianism"; see e.g. Norman Fiering, "Irresistible Compassion: An Aspect of Eighteenth-Century Sympathy and Humanitarianism," *Journal of the History of Ideas* 37 (1976): 195–218, at 214. And indeed one can find multiple eighteenth-century sermons that make this claim; see e.g. John Doughty, *Christian Sympathy* (London, 1752); and Peter Thatcher, *The Nature and Effects of Christian Sympathy* (Boston, 1794). But with regard to the philosophical literature it seems fair to say that sympathy was largely conceived as a nontheistic alternative to Christian concepts. For a helpful development of this claim, see esp. Frazer, *Enlightenment of Sympathy*, 11, 16, 30, 39.
34 Compare Mark 12:28–31, Matthew 22:36–40, and Luke 10:25–28 to Adam Smith, *The Theory of Moral Sentiments*, ed. D. D. Raphael and A. L. Macfie (Indianapolis: Liberty Fund, 1984), 1.1.5.5

epistemic reason for sympathy's ascendency. Even as eighteenth-century thinkers grew more skeptical toward the transcendent, they came ever more to embrace the immanent, and thus challenges to theism arose simultaneously with renewed interest in the nature of both human physiology and physical matter.

In physiology, the particularly important point concerned not corporeality merely, but a particular aspect of corporeality: sensation. The study of sensation stood at the forefront of several of the fields of inquiry focused on sympathy in the eighteenth century, including especially the medical and physiological researches that flourished in Edinburgh in its middle decades, and the epistemological studies being conducted in Paris during the same period. As has been noted with regard to the former, Scottish physicians regarded sympathy as "an extension of sensibility," which enabled them to generate fruitful associations of the "action of sensation, the coordination of organs in the body, and the 'social principle' that allows 'fellow-feeling' to emerge in a society."[35] So too in France, where the *Encyclopédistes* and their allies recognized in sympathy a type of social bond that comported well with their emphasis on the primacy of sensation in epistemic functioning. In this vein, the *Encyclopédie* itself included two substantial entries for *sympathie*, with the first (by Jean d'Alembert) dedicated to "the predilection that certain bodies have to unite or join as a result of a certain resemblance," and the second (by Louis de Jaucourt) dedicated to "communication that the parts of the body have with each other, and

---

(though cf. 3.6.1); Rousseau, *Emile*, 389n (which calls the second command the "summation of all morality" and also insists that it "has no true foundation other than justice and sentiment"); and Kant, *Metaphysics of Morals*, 570–71 (Ak. 6:450–52), and *Groundwork*, 54–55 (Ak. 4:399).

35 Forget, "Evocations of Sympathy," 291–92; see also Forget's helpful discussion at 286–88 of the explicit connections between the concept of sympathy as used by the Scottish social theorists and that employed by the Edinburgh physicians. Yet some caution here is needed; clearly for some of the Scottish physicians, the concept was still associated with the occult and was a placeholder for a failure to provide a fuller and more scientific explanation: a concept that may be employed "as long as we have no idea" what connects certain phenomena, but will be "no longer proper" once "we can find out its foundation, and the means of communication" (William Cullen, *Clinical Lectures, Delivered in the Years 1765 and 1766* [London, 1795], 28–29).

which holds them in a mutual dependence," and "transports to one part the pains and maladies which afflict another."[36] In both treatments, sympathy served to replace a need for recourse to theistic foundationalism with a more immediate set of empirical criteria available to all sensing beings.

This line of thinking would be particularly developed in France in discussions of *sociabilité*, which, as Hans Aarsleff has noted, commonly played a role in French-language debates similar to that played by sympathy in English-language debates.[37] In this vein Claude Helvétius might proclaim, in one of his chapter headings in *De l'homme*, that "la sensibilité physique est la cause unique de nos actions, de nos pensées, de nos passions, et de notre sociabilité" and argue that it is precisely this physical sensibility that gives rise to our affective interpersonal bonds.[38] This claim perhaps receives its fullest development in the work of the physiologist Pierre Cabanis, who not only offers one of the century's best developed accounts of the relationship between sympathy and immediate physical sensation but also goes on to suggest that the proper education and cultivation of such might in time engender a specifically "moral sympathy" of a type that he explicitly

---

36 See *Encyclopédie*, 15.735–36, available online via the ARTFL Project; see also Bernier, "Les métamorphoses de la sympathie," 14; Forget, "Evocations of Sympathy," 286–87; and Hayes's reflection, 1. Jaucourt's definition only briefly calls attention to that "rare and delicious" sympathy that promotes attachment between individuals, quickly dropping this line of inquiry and examining sympathy as a material principle. All eighteenth-century editions of the *Dictionnaire de l'Académie française* likewise focus exclusively on sympathy as a corporeal principle or as a means of describing the relationships of "humors and inclinations," only adding in the sixth edition (1835) an expanded entry on sympathy as enabling participation in pains and pleasures of others: see the definition in the sixth edition of the *Dictionnaire*, as available at http://artflsrv02.uchicago.edu/cgi-bin/dicos/pubdico1look.pl?strippedhw=sympathie. Cf. however Patrick Dandey, "Entre *medicinalia* et *moralia*: La Double Ascendance de la 'Sympathie,'" in *Les Discours de la sympathie: Enquête sur une notion de l'âge classique à la modernité*, ed. Thierry Belleguic, Eric Van der Schueren, and Sabrina Vervacke (Quebec: Les Presses de l'Université Laval, 2007), 3–23, esp. 3–4, 13.

37 See Aarsleff's introduction and editorial notes to his edition of Etienne Bonnot de Condillac, *Essay on the Origin of Human Knowledge* (Cambridge: Cambridge University Press, 2001), xxi–xxiii and n. and 37n. In a similar vein Marshall helpfully calls attention to the ways in which English and French discussions of sympathy overlapped with those of sentiment, sensation, and sensibility; see *Surprising Effects of Sympathy*, 3.

38 Claude Adrien Helvétius, *De l'homme* (Paris: Fayard, 1989), 171–86, at 171.

associates with both Francis Hutcheson and Smith and his sister-in-law de Grouchy.[39] And it is in de Grouchy's work that we find one of the best-developed versions of this line of thinking. For de Grouchy, sympathy is "the disposition we have to feel as others do" ("la disposition que nous avons à sentir d'une manière semblable à celle d'autrui"). In large part this took the form of feeling their pains via an extension of our sensibility through the imagination; hence de Grouchy's explicit claim that "reproduction of the general impression of pain on our organs depends on sensibility and above all on the imagination."[40] This would be a familiar claim by the time it was published in 1798, yet de Grouchy gave it an important turn that served to connect the normative elements of sympathy to its sensationalist origins: "Of what great importance it is, therefore, to train the sensibility of children so that it may develop to its fullest capacity in them. Their sensibility needs to reach that point where it can no longer be dulled by things that in the course of life tend to lead it astray, to carry us far from nature and from ourselves, and to concentrate our sensibility in all the passions of egoism or vanity."[41] De Grouchy, like other eighteenth-century sympathy theorists, would have resisted our familiar distinction today between the empirical and the normative. Owing in part to their conception of sensation, for eighteenth-century theorists, "sympathy is empirical truth of the first water."[42] At the same time, they regarded the cultivation of sympathy as a necessary duty if bonds of fellow feeling were to be sustained in a world in which such bonds often seemed besieged. And for this, natural sentiment alone without cultivation was simply too weak; representative in this vein is Mary Wollstonecraft,

---

39 Pierre Jean George Cabanis, *On the Relations between the Physical and Moral Aspects of Man*, trans Margaret Saidi (Baltimore: Johns Hopkins University Press, 1981), 589–601, at 598.

40 De Grouchy, *Letters on Sympathy*, 108–9; for the original see *Lettres sur la sympathie*, 31. On de Grouchy's debts to and differences from Adam Smith's account of sympathy with which she extensively engaged, see esp. Eric Schliesser, "Sophie de Grouchy, Marquise de Condorcet: Wisdom and Reform between Reason and Feeling," in *Feminist History of Philosophy*, ed. Eileen O'Neill and Marcy P. Lascano (Dordrecht: Springer, 2014).

41 De Grouchy, *Letters on Sympathy*, 111–12.

42 Lamb, *Evolution of Sympathy*, 6.

who argued in her discussion of the family that "natural affection, as it is termed, I believe to be a very weak tie, affections must grow out of the habitual exercise of a mutual sympathy."[43] In making such claims, both Wollstonecraft and de Grouchy reveal the influence of their careful engagements with Rousseau, who gave in his *Emile* perhaps the eighteenth century's best and fullest account of how natural sensation might be cultivated in a manner that best promotes the spread of "the joyfulness of loving humanity and serving it."[44]

Sympathy thus not only offered a normative response to a pressing problem but did so in a manner congenial to and commensurate with certain movements in eighteenth-century natural philosophy and epistemology. In an age obsessed with the investigation of the connections that bound together seemingly discrete entities sympathy struck a chord insofar as it presented the connections between discrete human individuals in a manner analogous to and already familiar from numerous prominent accounts of attractions between nonhuman entities across the natural and physical sciences. Bishop George Berkeley in this vein thus describes "that sympathy in our nature whereby we feel the pains and joys of our fellow-creatures" precisely by means of such an analogy:

> As the attractive power in bodies is the most universal principle which produceth innumerable effects, and is the key to explain the various phenomena of nature; so the corresponding social appetite

---

[43] Mary Wollstonecraft, *A Vindication of the Rights of Woman*, ed. Deidre Shauna Lynch, 3rd ed. (New York: Norton, 2009), 161. A helpful treatment of the significance of natural affection as developed in this passage in Wollstonecraft's political theory is provided in Eileen Hunt Botting, *Family Feuds: Wollstonecraft, Burke and Rousseau on the Transformation of the Family* (Albany: SUNY Press, 2006), 203–9; for the ways in which Wollstonecraft sought to distance herself from Burke on this front, see Daniel I. O'Neill, *The Burke-Wollstonecraft Debate: Savagery, Civilization, and Democracy* (University Park: Pennsylvania State University Press, 2007), 164–65.

[44] De Grouchy, *Letters on Sympathy*, 112. For a very helpful account of the stages of this education in de Grouchy, see Daniel Dumouchel, "Une Education sentimentale: Sympathie et construction de la morale dans les *Lettres sur la sympathie* de Sophie de Grouchy," in de Grouchy, *Lettres sur la sympathie*, 139–50. I explore the stages of Rousseau's moral-epistemic education at length in "Rousseau's Virtue Epistemology," *Journal of the History of Philosophy* 50 (2012): 239–63.

in human souls is the great spring and source of moral actions. This it is that inclines each individual to an intercourse with his species, and models everyone to that behavior which best suits with common well-being.[45]

So too the great Aberdeen philosopher George Turnbull:

> A careful examiner will find, that all our affections and passions are not only well-suited to our external circumstances; but that they themselves, and all the laws or methods of exercising them, with their different consequences, have a very exact correspondence with, and analogy to the sensible world, and its laws. Is there not an obvious similarity between the principle of gravitation toward a common center, and universal benevolence, in their operation? . . . Homogeneous bodies more easily coalesce than others: and so is it with minds. For is not friendship a particular sympathy of minds analogous to that particular tendency we may observe in certain bodies to run together and mix or adhere? Compassion, or a disposition to relieve the distressed, is it not similar to that tendency we observe in nutritious particles of several kinds, to run to the supply of wants in bodies which they are respectively proper to supply.[46]

Sympathy, conceived as the moral connection that binds one individual to another founded on the recognition of their mutual sameness, was thus deeply indebted for its rise to the ubiquitous discourse on attraction and action at a distance that dominated eighteenth-century

---

45 Bishop George Berkeley, *Guardian* 49, as quoted in Fiering, "Irresistible Compassion," 203–4. I am grateful to Eric Schliesser for calling to my attention Berkeley's specific claim that "God is a pure spirit, disengaged from all such sympathy or natural ties," which he rightly notes further suggests a conscious secularizing or distancing of sympathy from theological foundations; see Berkeley, "Three Dialogues," in *Philosophical Writings*, ed. Desmond Clarke (Cambridge: Cambridge University Press, 2008), 221.

46 George Turnbull, *The Principles of Moral and Christian Philosophy*, ed. Alexander Broadie (Indianapolis: Liberty Fund, 2005), 654.

philosophy across several branches—ranging from treatments of both planetary movement and gravitation in astronomy to discussions of electricity, magnetism, and elective affinities in physics and chemistry, to discussions of process coordination in the body in medicine and physiology, to discussions of the association of ideas in epistemology.[47] And very often these discussions took place in a genuinely interdisciplinary fashion; thus Goethe, in his celebrated novel *Die Wahlverwandtschaften*, used the laws of chemical elective affinities to describe the process of human romantic coupling, and the well-regarded American physician and statesman Benjamin Rush used the laws of corporeal sympathy to argue for the system of international free trade.[48] In these and many other cases, eighteenth-century ideas of human sympathy represented the extension into the moral realm of a principle already central to several other branches of philosophy.[49]

5. The End and the Means

Thus far we have seen that eighteenth-century sympathy was developed as a normative philosophical response to a pressing practical problem and that this response took the particular form it did in the eighteenth century because of certain movements and tendencies on the rise in several branches of contemporary philosophy. Yet for all

---

47 In addition to Forget's above-cited study, see, e.g., the discussion of the ways in which English and Scottish discourses on sympathy intertwined with discussions of magnetism and animal magnetism (and even mesmerism) in Patricia Fara, *Sympathetic Attractions: Magnetic Practices, Beliefs, and Symbolism in Eighteenth-Century England* (Princeton, NJ: Princeton University Press, 1996), 147–51, 189–91, 199, 208; on elective affinity in eighteenth-century Scottish chemistry, see A. L. Donovan, *Philosophical Chemistry in the Scottish Enlightenment* (Edinburgh: Edinburgh University Press, 1975), 129–31, 155–56.

48 For helpful illuminations of these connections, see esp. Monique Moser-Verrey, "Le Discours de la sympathie dans *Les affinités électives*," in *Les discours de la sympathie: Enquête sur une notion de l'âge classique à la modernité*, ed. Thierry Belleguic, Eric Van der Schueren, and Sabrina Vervacke (Quebec: Les Presses de l'Université Laval, 2007), 343–55; and Sari Altschuler, "From Blood Vessels to Global Networks of Exchange: The Physiology of Benjamin Rush's Early Republic," *Journal of the Early Republic* 32 (2012): 207–31.

49 On this point, see especially the useful development of this claim in Bernier, "Les Métamorphoses de la sympathie," 2.

this, a third question remain unanswered: namely, granting that sympathy offered a fitting answer to a specific question, and indeed a timely answer to this question, to what degree ought it be regarded as a *good* answer? In particular, was sympathy in fact capable of providing the check on self-interest and concomitant encouragement of other-directed feeling that it promised?

This question brings us to what might be regarded as a tension between the end of sympathy and the means of sympathy. The first section of the chapter argues that the primary aim of sympathy was to check the potentially pernicious effects of self-interest. The subsequent section goes on to argue that the sympathy theorists of the eighteenth century envisioned a means toward this end not simply equivalent to positing the sort of selfless other-directedness we today associate with altruism. On the contrary, sympathy's eighteenth-century appeal lay in the fact that far from requiring transcendence of all concern for the self, its means of sensitizing its possessor to the pains and pleasures of others was precisely the pleasures and pains experienced by the self. Yet this move may lead us to wonder whether in fact a system predicated on such a mechanism is likely to (so to speak) get us where it wants to go.

This tension between ends and means seems particularly pronounced in those theorists most concerned to defend sympathy as a counter to familiar forms of psychological and ethical egoism. This project was of course a central component of eighteenth-century ethics, especially in Britain, with partisans of natural human sociability and the existence of a genuine capacity for benevolent concern for others ranged against those who reduced all ethical action to manifestations of self-interest or self-love.[50] In the former camp were figures such as the Earl of Shaftesbury and Hutcheson, who saw themselves as the vanguard of an offensive against the egoism of the latter camp. Hobbes and Mandeville in particular had done much to spur the defenders of other-directedness

---

50 For an excellent introduction to eighteenth-century British moral philosophy and the centrality of the "Human Nature Question" to it, see Michael Gill, *The British Moralists on Human Nature and the Birth of Secular Ethics* (Cambridge: Cambridge University Press, 2006).

to action, specifically by insisting that even the most engaging of the other-directed passions has self-interest at its core; thus Hobbes equated pity with "compassion" and "fellow-feeling," and notoriously argued that "grief, for the calamity of another, is pity; and ariseth from the imagination that the like calamity may befall himself."[51] Mandeville, in a similar vein, reduced charity to a means of mitigating anxiety: "Thus thousands give money to beggars from the same motive as they pay their corn-cutter, to walk easy."[52] Writ large in both Hobbes and Mandeville is thus the psychological egoism that we saw in Spinoza. And it was of course precisely this that the defenders of other-directedness sought to counter in developing their idea of sympathy. But exactly how successful were they?

In truth the defenders of sympathy conceded a remarkable amount of ground to their opponents, and these concessions nearly proved fatal to their project. Their principal concession to the egoists came in the form of their acceptance of the claim that the proper frame for evaluating and defending sympathy is in fact the self and its pleasures and pains. Indeed it was this claim more than any other that bound the defenders of other-directedness to partisans of the selfish system. This is evident in their accounts of the relationship of sympathy to happiness. The indispensability of sympathy to genuine individual happiness is one of the keynotes of these accounts; thus Shaftesbury claims that "to have the natural affections (such as are founded in love, complacency, good-will, and in a sympathy with the kind or species) is to have the chief means and power of self-enjoyment," and indeed "to want them is certain misery and ill."[53] Here and in what follows it is difficult not to be struck by the claim that sympathy ought to be placed among man's "mental enjoyments," which prove to be "the only means which

---

51 Hobbes, *Leviathan*, 43.
52 Bernard Mandeville, "An Essay on Charity, and Charity-Schools," in *Fable of the Bees*, ed. F. B. Kaye (Indianapolis: Liberty Fund, 1988), 1.259.
53 Anthony Ashley Cooper, third Earl of Shaftesbury, "An Inquiry Concerning Virtue and Merit," in *Characteristicks*, ed. Douglas J. Den Uyl (Indianapolis: Liberty Fund, 2001), 2.57.

can procure him a certain and solid happiness."[54] Now in saying this, it is of course hardly Shaftesbury's intention to encourage egoism; the entire *Inquiry* is at its core a critique of such. But the particular route it takes to this end—a defense of sympathy as happiness promoting—poses a potential challenge, for even if it should be true that "exerting whatever we have of social affection, and human sympathy, is of the highest delight" and that with regard to "the pleasures of sympathy" there "is hardly such a thing as satisfaction or contentment, of which they make not an essential part," by insisting that sympathy is indispensable to the happiness of the individual, Shaftesbury takes an important step away from the traditional understanding of love's value, which privileged the well-being of the beloved over that of the lover, toward an other-directedness that privileges the subjective well-being of the self.[55]

Shaftesbury, moreover, was hardly alone on this front. Hutcheson likewise rejected the claim that sympathy is to be accounted for by a mere "conjunction of interest" where "the happiness of others becomes the means of private pleasure to the observer; and for this reason, or with a view to this private pleasure, he desires the happiness of another."[56] Hutcheson thought this far too reductionist. Yet when he came to speak in his own name, he articulated a position that comes close to this, insisting that "our sympathy or social feelings with others, by which we derive joys or sorrows from their prosperity or adversity," constitute an important "source of happiness or misery": "While there's any life or vigour in the natural affections of the social kind, scarce any thing can more affect our happiness and misery than the fortunes of others. What powerful relief under our own misfortunes arises from seeing the prosperity of such as are dear to us! And how is all our enjoyment of life destroyed and beat to pieces by seeing their

---

54 Shaftesbury, "Inquiry Concerning Virtue," 58.
55 Shaftesbury, "Inquiry Concerning Virtue," 62.
56 Francis Hutcheson, *An Essay on the Nature and Conduct of the Passions and Affections, with Illustrations on the Moral Sense*, ed. Aaron Garrett (1742; Indianapolis: Liberty Fund, 2002), 23.

misery!"[57] It is not a far step from here to the claim, urged by the egoists, that our beneficence is the fruit of a solicitude for our individual pleasures.[58] This would be particularly urged by Butler, who in arguing against Hobbes's definition of pity, insists that the self is the proper sphere of reference: "When we rejoice in the prosperity of others, and compassionate their distresses, we, as it were, substitute them for ourselves, their interest for our own; and have the same kind of pleasure in their prosperity, and sorrow in their distress, as we have from reflection upon our own."[59] And so too Fordyce: "a man of an enlarged benevolent mind, who thinks, feels, and acts for others, is not subject to half the disquietudes of the contracted selfish soul; finds a thousand alleviations to soften his disappointments, which the other wants; and has a fair chance for double his enjoyments."[60] As in the previous cases, Fordyce takes an explicitly eudaemonistic perspective, but one that raises the question of whether and how it can be distanced from the reductionism of his antagonists. The original line of demarcation separating the two camps was clearly defined. Where Hobbes and Spinoza insisted that good and bad were to be judged by the standard afforded by the passions, their opponents, such as the Cambridge Platonist Henry More, argued that "no man's private inclinations are the measures of good and evil," for "the inclinations themselves are to be circumscribed by some principle which is superior to them."[61] Yet it is not clear that this can be achieved if eudaemonism is substituted for theism. Put differently, we might wonder on such grounds whether the broader tradition of eighteenth-century sympathy might not be susceptible to the

---

[57] Francis Hutcheson, *Short Introduction to Moral Philosophy*, ed. Luigi Turco (Indianapolis: Liberty Fund, 2007), 60.
[58] As Turco has helpfully demonstrated, precisely this charge was levied against Hutcheson by John Clarke of Hull and Archibald Campbell, who "used the doctrine of sympathy to criticize his doctrines from an hedonistic point of view" ("Sympathy and Moral Sense, 1725–1740," 100–101).
[59] Butler, "Upon Compassion" (sermon #5), 45.
[60] Fordyce, *Elements*, 137, and see also 138–39.
[61] Henry More, *An Account of Virtue* (London, 1690), 81; cf. Hobbes, *Leviathan*, 39; Spinoza, *Ethics*, sch.pr.9,III.

challenge that Thomas Reid raised with particular reference to the sympathy theory of Adam Smith: namely that it was "only a refinement of the selfish system."[62] Whether Reid's critique of Smith is a fair one would require a separate study. At the same time, it helps to clarify that much of the issue hinges on how one ought to read the "necessary" in Smith's striking opening of *The Theory of Moral Sentiments*, which announces that "how selfish soever man may be supposed, there are evidently some principles in his nature, which interest him in the fortune of others, and render their happiness necessary to him."[63]

6. The Legacy of Sympathy

The foregoing account has covered a great deal of ground: too much perhaps for one brief survey, but not nearly enough, it must be said, to do justice to the full complexity of eighteenth-century sympathy. In particular, next to nothing has been said about one of its most important contexts, namely that of the literary and visual and performing arts. Indeed doing full justice would require detailed investigation of how the philosophical treatment of sympathy traced here maps onto the ways in which sympathy was conceived of and operationalized in sources as diverse as the novels of Henry Fielding, the engravings of William Hogarth, and the dramatic works of Rousseau—to say nothing of its central place in the erotic literature of the eighteenth century, and the role of sympathy on the French stage more generally.[64] So too almost nothing has been said about how this story maps on to the two greatest eighteenth-century theories of sympathy, those of David Hume and Adam Smith, which are the specific focus of Geoffrey

---

62 Thomas Reid to Lord Kames, 30 October 1778, in John Reeder, ed., *On Moral Sentiments* (London: Thommes, 1997), 66.
63 Smith, *Theory of Moral Sentiments*, I.I.I.I.
64 On these last fronts, see esp. Gaëtan Brulotte, "La Sympathie et la littérature érotique dans la France du XVIIIe siècle," in *Les Discours de la sympathie: Enquête sur une notion de l'âge classique à la modernité*, ed. Thierry Belleguic, Eric Van der Schueren, and Sabrina Vervacke (Quebec: Les Presses de l'Université Laval, 2007), 199–218; and Hayes's reflection in this volume.

Sayre-McCord's contribution to this volume. Readers of our pieces wishing to pursue this connection might do well to begin by considering what implications might follow from appreciation of the eighteenth-century context described here for our understanding of Hume's and Smith's theories. In particular, one might ask what implications there might be for the received understanding of Hume's and Smith's conceptions of sympathy as primarily valuable as elements of a phenomenological project to account for the mechanisms of judgment rather than as elements of a normative account of the sources of moral motivation.[65] Clearly there are grounds for such; that Hume and Smith thought sympathy central to judgment is beyond dispute and has been well demonstrated.[66] Yet in continuing to investigate the way in which Hume's and Smith's theories of sympathy undergird and illuminate their (and our) conceptions of judgment, we should take care to remind ourselves of the breadth and depth of those theories, and particularly their embrace of a vision of sympathy in ethical action. Attending to the contextual history of sympathy in the eighteenth century thus may prove especially valuable for the light that it can shed on Hume's and Smith's self-conscious participation in a long tradition of seeing sympathy as a principle (indeed a central principle) of agent motivation.[67]

Yet independent of Smith and Hume, the eighteenth-century understanding of sympathy remains of crucial import in its own right. The transition of sympathy into the human sphere made possible a new way of conceiving human relations. As several contributions to this

---

65 Sayre-McCord helpfully calls attention to both of these senses of sympathy in Hume and Smith, though he primarily focuses on the latter; see chapter 7.

66 See e.g. D. D. Raphael, *The Impartial Spectator: Adam Smith's Moral Philosophy* (Oxford: Oxford University Press, 2007), 116–17 (which likewise calls attention to sympathy's significance as a "motive"); and Fonna Forman-Barzilai, *Adam Smith and the Circles of Sympathy* (Cambridge: Cambridge University Press, 2010), 152–60.

67 For the beginnings of this debate, see esp. Leonidas Montes, "Das Adam Smith Problem," 82–85, and *Adam Smith in Context* (London: Palgrave Macmillan, 2004), 45–55 (which offer the clearest and most important statements of this position to date); Eric Schliesser's review of Montes and Raphael in *Ethics* 118 (2008): 569–75; and the responses to be found in Raphael, *Impartial Spectator*, 119–20; and in Ian S. Ross, *The Life of Adam Smith*, 2nd ed. (Oxford: Oxford University Press, 2010), 478 n.

volume have demonstrated, sympathy provided many premodern thinkers with a means of accounting for the affinity between seemingly distant and unrelated bodies. The insight of the eighteenth-century theorists was not merely to translate this principle into the moral sphere, but indeed to recognize the ways in which the particular moral sphere into which their principle was being translated resembled the very conditions of the physical world in which the earliest theories of sympathy had been forged. For just as the premodern theorists sought to account for connections between the different and diverse, so too the eighteenth-century theorists of sympathy sought to employ the concept to account for the sorts of connections necessary to maintain bonds between individuals in an increasingly less homogenized and more fluid world of diversity and differences. In this sense, sympathy provided eighteenth-century social theorists with a means of accounting for the minimal level of fellow-feeling needed to sustain their emerging pluralistic social order. This is of course not to say that sympathy provided an instant panacea; as many have noted, even amidst its many public campaigns against racism and the subordination of women, prominent vestiges of such persisted in the Enlightenment and indeed were sometimes given voice by such prominent theorists of sympathy as Hume and Kant. Clearly the work sympathy needed to do was both greater than a single day and greater than a single individual. At the same time, in articulating an account not only of how like and like might be combined but more crucially how like and unlike might establish that minimal degree of commonality necessary to sustain peaceful and harmonious coexistence—and perhaps even establish some degree of mutual recognition and respect—the eighteenth-century theorists of sympathy took a crucial step toward defining the key task of sympathy in the modern world.

Reflection

THE FRENCH THEATER OF SYMPATHY

Julie Candler Hayes

"Sympathy," *sympathie*, emerges in French from medical discourse during the early modern period. While the word participates as widely in the discourses of the "new affectivity" as its cognate "compassion," it retains the freight of its original context, suggesting physiological rootedness. In the article "Sympathie" of the *Encyclopédie*, Jean Le Rond d'Alembert's primary definition is medical: "the aptitude of certain bodies to unite or incorporate one another"; even the secondary definition by Louis de Jaucourt roots the emotional ("the lively understanding [*intelligence*] between hearts") in the physiological ("the communication that parts of the body have with one another").[1] It thus shares the semantic ambiguity of "sentiment," "sensibility," and "feeling": emotions grounded in corporeal experience. In eighteenth-century French writings, sympathy lives at the crossroads of medical, psychological, and moral discourses.[2]

Many commentators have examined the sea change in the late seventeenth- and eighteenth-century understanding of personal

---

1 Denis Diderot and Jean d'Alembert, eds., *Encyclopédie ou dictionnaire raisonné des sciences, des arts et des métiers* (Paris, 1747–65).
2 Patrick Dandrey, "Entre *medicinalia* et *moralia*: La Double Ascendance de la 'Sympathie,'" in *Les Discours de la sympathie: Enquête sur une notion de l'âge classique à la modernité*, ed. Thierry Belleguic, Eric Van Der Schuren, and Sabrina Vervacke (Laval: Presses de l'université Laval, 2007), 3–23.

identity, affectivity, and interpersonal relations.[3] What William Reddy dubbed the "sentimental revolution" manifested itself in a wide range of social and discursive practices, among them salon conversation, letter writing, and the reading and writing of novels, to name only some of the most prominent. In France, one of the most striking loci for the new affectivity was the theater, both in the stage action and in the behavior of the spectators.

From Pierre Corneille to Prosper Jolyot de Crébillon, French classical drama had long made use of "the call of blood" as a plot device enabling long-lost parents, children, and siblings to recognize one another through deeply rooted stirrings of affection.[4] The *cri du sang* by definition implies a physiological anchor to feeling, stimulated by apparently metaphysical means. In the eighteenth century, "sympathy" would extend such physical and emotional ties beyond the family.

> J'ai rencontré l'objet que je devois aimer.
> Un mutuel amour a su nous enflammer.
> C'est une sympathie invincible, absolue,
> Que j'ai d'abord sentie à la première vûe.
>
> I have met the man that I was meant to love.
> Mutual love enflamed us both.
> It's an absolute, invincible sympathy
> That I immediately sensed at first sight.
>   Pierre-Claude La Chaussée,
>   *La Fausse antipathie* (1733), act 2, scene 9[5]

---

[3] William Reddy, *The Navigation of Feeling: A Framework for the History of the Emotions* (Cambridge: Cambridge University Press, 2001); Jerrold Siegel, *The Idea of the Self: Thought and Experience in Western Europe Since the Seventeenth Century* (Cambridge: Cambridge University Press, 2005); Dror Wahrman, *The Making of the Modern Self: Identity and Culture in Eighteenth-Century England* (New Haven, CT: Yale University Press, 2006).

[4] For a thorough review of the *cri du sang* topos, see Clifton Cherpack, *The Call of Blood in French Classical Tragedy* (Baltimore: Johns Hopkins University Press, 1958).

[5] Pierre-Claude La Chaussée, *La Fausse antipathie*, in *Oeuvres*, 5 vols. (Paris, 1777; Geneva: Slatkine Reprints, 1970), vol. 1.

The "tearful comedies" (*comédies larmoyantes*) of Pierre-Claude Nivelle de la Chaussée (1692–1754) changed French dramaturgy forever by bringing the new affectivity to the stage, uniting the high emotions traditionally associated with tragedy with the marriage plot of comedy. Ironically, the "invincible sympathy" felt by the heroine of *La Fausse antipathie*, his first play, is for a man that she has failed to recognize as her long-lost, much hated spouse. Furthermore, her sympathy is "sensed": profoundly felt in a manner that suggests both physical sensation and cognition. As the play's title makes clear, the couple's "sympathy" is true, whereas their earlier antipathy was the product of circumstances that included an arranged marriage and a (presumably) veiled bride. (The groom vanished as soon as the ceremony was completed.) *La Fausse antipathie*, like La Chaussée's later plays, turns on characters' ability or inability to "see themselves" in one another's situations: "Put yourself in my place." "Je me mets à sa place" and "Mettez-vous à ma place" become the refrains by which they demonstrate their sensitivity to others and their desire for communication.[6] Typically, once all the "places" are fully elucidated, the misunderstanding that fuels the plot is resolved and the play ends happily.

"Feeling" infuses the cogito of the new era: "Plus je sens vivement, plus je sens que je suis" (The more intensely I feel, the more I feel that I am) (La Chaussée, *Mélanide*, 1741).[7] La Chaussée's innovations offered a new path to playwrights struggling with the burden of the legacy of Molière, Jean Racine, and Corneille. The mixture of genres remained controversial among critics, however, even after—and to a great extent because—the "mixed genre" was

---

[6] According to Bonar's catalog, Adam Smith owned a copy of La Chaussée's collected works; see James Bonar, *A Catalogue of the Library of Adam Smith* (London: Macmillan & Co., 1894). (I thank Eric Schliesser for pointing this out.)

[7] Pierre-Claude La Chaussée, *Mélanide*, in *Oeuvres*. (Paris, 1777; Geneva: Slatkine Reprints, 1970), vol. 2, p. 90.

taken up and theorized by Diderot and the parti philosophique.[8] In its variants *drame bourgeois, genre sérieux, comédie sentimental,* and *tragédie domestique,* the new dramaturgy overcame the class differences reified on the classical stage. Spectators were moved by the emotional struggles of commoners, a social group once thought worthy only of comic treatment (figure 6.1).

Earlier in the century, the abbé Du Bos had published his influential *Réflexions critiques sur la poésie et la peinture* (1719) analyzing the aesthetic experience as an act of sympathetic

FIGURE 6.1. Recognitions in La Chaussée's plays may come about through either the "call of blood" or emotionally-based sympathy.

---

8 I discuss these issues further in Julie Candler Hayes, *Identity and Ideology: Diderot, Sade, and the Serious Genre* (Amsterdam: John Benjamins, 1991), especially ch. 3, "The Equivocal Genre," 81–103.

spectatorship in which we enter into ourselves by means of artistic representation. For Du Bos, we are moved by scenes of suffering, but are able to take pleasure in the representation of such scenes through the mitigating and distancing effects of art. Extending this idea in his *Entretiens sur le Fils naturel* (1757), Diderot saw the spectator's imaginative participation in the action on the stage as a conduit for self-understanding and communitarian engagement: "He who does not feel his emotion increase from the large number of those who share it has some secret vice; there is something solitary in his character that displeases me."[9] As is well known, Rousseau took the opposite view of the role of the theater in public life, arguing in his *Lettre à d'Alembert* that theatrical artifice produced only a simulacrum of emotion that alienated spectators from themselves and from one another. And yet the public festivals that he held up as the ideal situation in order that "each see himself and love himself through others"[10] achieve a goal analogous to the philosophical *drames* of Diderot, Michel-Jean Sedaine, Louis-Sébastien Mercier, and Pierre-Augustin Caron de Beaumarchais: a community united by sympathetic bonds.

Given the key place that the theater represented in cultural life—a place that the novel struggled to attain over the course of the century—and given the very explicit role of sympathetic understanding not only in the plays themselves but in audience behavior, it is not surprising that theoretical discussions of sympathy are profoundly "theatrical," complexly bound up with the dynamics of spectatorship. For Adam Smith, the conditions of sympathy are inextricably linked to the problems of spectatorship and representation. Since, he tells us, we can never feel what others feel, we form an idea of another's suffering through an act of the

---

9 Denis Diderot, *Entretiens sur le Fils naturel*, in *Oeuvres esthétiques*, ed. P. Vernière (1757; Paris: Garnier, 1968), 122.

10 Jean-Jacques Rousseau, *Oeuvres complètes*, ed. Bernard Gagnebin and Marcel Raymond, 5 vols. (Paris: Gallimard, 1959–95), 5.125.

imagination and "become in some measure the same person with him."[11] Sympathy is produced when we "place ourselves" in another's situation and "conceive ourselves" undergoing the other's experience. As David Marshall has observed, Smith's acts of sympathy "depend on people's ability to represent themselves as tableaux, spectacles, and texts before others."[12] The sympathetic self is a spectator, not only of another being but of oneself observing the other being.

As commentators have pointed out, the *Lettres sur la sympathie* (1798) of Smith's late eighteenth-century translator Sophie de Grouchy, marquise de Condorcet, offers a critique of Smith with ties to French materialism and the revolutionary politics of the 1790s.[13] For de Grouchy, the theater of sympathy takes place deep within the self, almost at the cellular level, yet provides the key to social solidarity and progress.

De Grouchy initially couches her discussion of sympathy as an extension of Smith. The *Lettres sur la sympathie* are a material extension, as she published the work as an epilogue to her translation of Smith's *The Theory of Moral Sentiments*. They are also a conceptual extension: observing that Smith did not explore the "first cause" of sympathy, she proposes to rectify the omission. The first cause is complex, both physiological and psychological, pivoting between sensation and reflection. Thus her discussion of the *sentiment de l'humanité*: "The sentiment of humanity is a sort

---

[11] Adam Smith, "Of Sympathy," in *The Theory of Moral Sentiments*, ed. D. D. Raphael and A. L. MacFie (1759; Oxford: Clarendon Press, 1976), 9.

[12] David Marshall, *The Surprising Effects of Sympathy: Marivaux, Diderot, Rousseau, and Mary Shelley* (Chicago: University of Chicago Press, 1988), 5.

[13] Marc André Bernier, "Eloquence du corps et sympathie: Les 'Tableaux de sensations' de Sophie de Condorcet," in *Les Discours de la sympathie: Enquête sur une notion de l'âge classique à la modernité*, ed. Thierry Belleguic, Eric Van Der Schuren, and Sabrina Vervacke (Laval: Presses de l'université Laval, 2007), 171–81. For comparisons of Smith and de Grouchy, see also the scholarly essays included in a recent critical edition of her work: *Les Lettres sur la sympathie (1798) de Sophie de Grouchy: Philosophie morale et réforme sociale*, ed. Marc André Bernier and Deidre Dawson (Oxford: Voltaire Foundation, 2010), in particular the essays by Bernier, Daniel Dumouchel, and Michel Malherbe. All page references to de Grouchy are from this edition.

of seed planted in the depths of the heart that reflection will make fertile and develop" (39). Omissions accumulate, however, and she eventually sharpens her criticism to accuse Smith of relying on an undefinable *sens intime*, an ultimately fictitious entity redolent of the *esprit de systèmes* rejected by the philosophes (84). De Grouchy embarks on the subject of sympathy by evoking the interplay between self-observation and the observation of others, both the pleasure of introspection and the pleasure of the other achieved in the act of translation. Translation, which both mirrors the other and prompts new thoughts within oneself, thus serves as the springboard for her own reflections. For her, the imagination plays a role in the production of sympathy, but memory is primary. Memory provides the "présence morale" of one's own past pain, enabling us to relate to the pain of others through our own corporeal experience. De Grouchy's conjunction of memory, imagination, and sensibility offers a significant revision of traditional faculty psychology's trio of memory, understanding, and will, already recast in the *Encyclopédie* as memory, understanding, and imagination. For de Grouchy, then, the representational capacity of imagination conjoins the private world of memory with the felt materiality of sensibility.

The degree to which sensibility "ingrains" sympathy within us explains de Grouchy's insistence on moral education in childhood. Such exposure defeats *égoïsme* and lays the groundwork for social progress and *égalité naturelle*. De Grouchy credits her mother with having inculcated sympathy within her through the spectacle of her own virtuous example: "It was by seeing your hands bring comfort to those affected by misery and sickness; it was by seeing the pauper's suffering gaze turn to you and tearfully bless you, that I felt the depths of my heart" (36). Sympathy is thus born in a highly theatricalized scene in which the young Sophie experiences a double identification: both with the pauper, who like her is looking at her mother, and with her mother, the object of the pauper's emotional gaze, whom she desires to emulate. Over the course of the *Lettres*, sympathy is cast as a physical need (*besoin*), along with a range of similar emotions. From the primal scene of maternal charity, de Grouchy puts sympathy at the foundation both of the self and the social world. Following Rousseau, she argues that our fundamental "need to be good" is denatured by *institutions vicieuses* and unnatural laws.

De Grouchy takes up the question posed by Du Bos and others, of how we are able to feel sympathy and pleasure in the representation of pain on the stage or in a novel: "those painful emotions that we seek out" (45). Like Du Bos, she agrees that the aesthetic experience plays a role in our pleasure, but we also have a profound "need" for emotional activity and take pleasure in "feeling moved in a hitherto unknown manner." Later, she rejects Smith's claim that we are less moved by the representation of physical pain than that of emotional pain, arguing that, in general, sympathy for physical pain is more immediate, but observing that the dramatic illusion of physical pain is more difficult to sustain and more complex in its action on the spectator (57–58). The search for *émotions pénibles* is counterbalanced by the pleasures of art and enhanced experience of the self.

The curtain falls, curiously, on an evocation of social inequality and a portrait of an unhappy, unjust man. Do not be surprised, she tells the friend to whom the *Lettres* are addressed: we all carry some of these traits within us, the fruits of our imperfect society. Her rhetorically powerful conclusion denies human perfection, yet holds it out as a goal to be sought:

Where is he who, faithful to reason and nature, prefers the true pleasures of peace and homely virtues to the seductive pleasures of self-love, which over time make us lose not only the need, but the pleasure of fellow feeling?... Where is he who retains a corner of his soul to enjoy himself, to taste the feelings of nature with the ease and reflection that gives them their sweetness and their power? (103).

The series of questions, followed by a warning to those who neglect the quiet pleasures of peace and virtue, show that however deep our understanding of the roots of human goodness, the fully enlightened society remains an unfinished project.

CHAPTER SEVEN

Hume and Smith on Sympathy, Approbation, and Moral Judgment

Geoffrey Sayre-McCord

1. Introduction

David Hume and Adam Smith are usually, and understandably, seen as developing very similar sentimentalist accounts of moral thought and practice.[1] Hume's views are better known, not least because Smith's work on moral sentiments fell in the shadow of his tremendously influential

---

[1] This essay has benefited considerably from discussion at the "Sympathy" conference organized by Eric Schliesser at the University of Richmond and at the Adam Smith Society session at the Central Division Meetings of the American Philosophical Association Meeting in New Orleans. I am especially grateful for detailed comments from Houston Smit and John McHugh and helpful conversations with Remy Debes and Michael Gill.
  In what follows, in-text citations are to Hume's *A Treatise of Human Nature*, ed. L. A. Selby-Bigge and P. H. Nidditch (1738–39; Oxford: Oxford University Press, 1978), referenced as *Treatise*; Hume's *Enquiries concerning Human Understanding and the Principles of Morals*, ed. L. A. Selby-Bigge and P. H. Nidditch (1751; Oxford: Oxford University Press, 1975), referenced as *Enquiry*; and Smith's *The Theory of Moral Sentiments*, ed. D. D. Raphael and A. L. Macfie (1759: Oxford: Clarendon Press, 1976), referenced as *TMS*.

Wealth of Nations.[2] This shadowing is unfortunate, both because Smith's work on moral sentiments is deeply insightful and because it provides a crucial moral context for understanding his economic theory.

As similar as Hume's and Smith's accounts of moral thought are, they differ in telling ways. This essay is an attempt primarily to get clear on the important differences. They are worth identifying and exploring, in part, because of the great extent to which Hume and Smith share not just an overall approach to moral theory but also a conception of the key components of an adequate account of moral thought. In the process, I hope to bring out the extent to which they both worked to make sense of the fact that we do not merely have affective *reactions* but also, importantly, make moral *judgments*.

2. The Common Framework

As a first step, it is worth taking stock of just how similar Hume's and Smith's views are. To start where they do, Hume and Smith both take sentiments to be fundamental to moral thought and practice. They hold that whatever role reason and the understanding might have in explaining moral thought, an appeal to reason alone, unaided by sentiment, is insufficient. Absent sentiment, they hold, the deliverances of reason concerning, for instance, what causes, and what frustrates, human happiness, what generates gratitude or resentment, and what conforms to, and what violates, certain principles, will leave undiscovered a distinction favoring any of these facts over the others.[3] And they hold that, in particular, our capacity to sympathize with the sentiments of others is crucial. If that capacity for sympathy were entirely absent, they hold, so too would be moral thought and practice.

---

[2] *An Inquiry into the Nature and Causes of the Wealth of Nations*, ed. R. H. Campbell and A. S. Skinner (1776; Indianapolis: Liberty Fund, 1981).

[3] Hume argues extensively for the importance of sentiment in understanding moral thought; Smith does so much more briefly, but on the basis of the same general considerations. See *Treatise*, 456–76; and *TMS*, 318–21.

It is worth noting that, on their shared view, sympathy plays two different roles. First, sympathy with the plight of others engages our concern and prompts our actions in ways that are, they hold, morally important, crucial for constituting and sustaining a community, and more generally mutually advantageous. Second, sympathy is essential, as they see it, to our capacity to *approve* (or disapprove) of actions, motives, and characters as moral or not and, because of that, to our capacity to *judge* actions, motives, and characters as moral or not.

Thus, without sympathy we would not have a morally decent community, if we had a community at all (that is sympathy's first role), nor would we be able to judge communities (or anything else) as morally decent or not (that is sympathy's second role). Presumably, even with sympathy, we might enjoy a decent community without also making moral judgments. Yet as Hume and Smith see things, our capacity to make moral judgments plays a vital role in strengthening and supporting the bonds of community that sympathy makes possible.[4]

Moreover, they both are careful to distinguish between what, as it happens, garners moral approval or disapproval, on the one hand, and what merits approval and disapproval, on the other. That is, they distinguish being approved (or disapproved) from being approvable (or disapprovable). In funding this distinction, they move from an account of moral approbation to an account of moral judgment, an account that makes sense of the difference between someone thinking that something is moral and that person being right in her judgment. Finally, in developing their accounts of moral judgment they both appeal to a privileged point of view that sets the standard for our judgments. According to both of them, what would be approved of, from the appropriate point of view, is what is approvable. And to judge, for instance,

---

4 They were also aware of the many ways that moral judgment can reify differences, generate conflicts, and often wreck havoc, though they were generally optimistic, it seems, concerning the contributions of moral thought. As Eric Schliesser has pointed out to me, Smith's discussion of faction, in section 6 of the *Theory of Moral Sentiments*, which was added to the last edition, suggests that Smith's concerns over the negative effects of moral judgment may well have increased over time.

that some trait is a virtue is to make a judgment that is correct if, but only if, the trait would secure approval from the appropriate point of view.

To share this much is, clearly, to share a great deal. So it is not surprising that Hume and Smith are regularly grouped together as advancing very similar accounts of moral thought. Their allegiance to sentimentalism, their focus on sympathy, their emphasis on sympathetically engendered approbation, and their reliance on a privileged point of view as setting the standard for moral judgment, are distinctive and striking features of their shared view that rightly attract attention and comment.

Yet as similar as their views are, there are a number of interesting and instructive differences, especially in their accounts of sympathy's role in producing approbation and in their understanding of approbation. These differences have reverberations in their understandings of which sentiments matter and why, of how sympathy needs to work, and of the substance of the moral judgments that end up being vindicated by their proposed privileged points of view. In what follows, I concentrate first on the different accounts of sympathy's role in producing approbation and of the nature of approbation, and then from there turn briefly to the reverberations of these differences.

3. Sympathy

In identifying sympathy, Hume notes that "[a] cheerful countenance infuses a sensible complacency and serenity into my mind; as an angry or sorrowful one throws a sudden damp upon me" (*Treatise*, 317). Smith takes up the same examples, writing, "[a] smiling face is, to everybody who sees it, a cheerful object; as a sorrowful countenance, on the other hand, is a melancholy one" (*TMS*, 11).

They make a point of allowing all cases of fellow-feeling, whether the feelings shared are positive or negative. Sympathy operates, they both hold, not only when the person with whom one is sympathizing is suffering or in some other way badly off.[5] Drawing a contrast with pity and compassion, which are "appropriated to signify our fellow-feeling with the sorrow of others" Smith suggests that "sympathy," "though its meaning was, perhaps, originally the same, may now, however, without much impropriety, be made use of to denote our fellow-feeling with any passion whatever."[6] In adopting this broad use Smith was simply doing as Hume had done before him. For both of them, the idea that sympathy engages us with the positive, no less than the negative, feelings of others is important to its role in explaining the nature of moral judgment.

In general, Hume and Smith treat as standard cases of sympathy any occasion when one person feels *as* another does, *because* the other feels that way. Sympathy is, in these cases, fellow-feeling with a specific etiology. Yet in talking about sympathy, Hume and Smith sometimes have in mind just the process by which we, in the standard cases, come to feel as others do and sometimes have in mind just the product, the fellow-feeling, without regard to how it came about. So they each end up allowing that we might sympathize with another despite not actually feeling as the other person does (as when we imagine his feeling a certain way, though he does not) and that we might be in sympathy with others, that is, feel as they do, though not as a result of having been engaged by (the normal process of) sympathy. For Hume and Smith alike, what is important to their accounts of approbation and moral judgment is our capacity to be engaged by the process they identify with sympathy.

3.1. Hume

When it comes to approbation and moral judgment, the key element of Hume's account of sympathy is the idea that, when sympathy is in

---

[5] "Neither is it those circumstances only, which create pain or sorrow, that call forth our fellow-feeling. Whatever is the passion that arises from any object in the person principally concerned, an analogous emotion springs up, at the thought of his situation, in the breast of every attentive spectator" (*TMS*, 10).
[6] *TMS*, 10.

play, our *idea* of another person's pain or pleasure results in our having a painful or pleasant feeling. Yet it is worth noting, if only in passing, that Hume offers a detailed and elaborate account of how and why our ideas of other's feelings have this effect. On this account, the effect is achieved because the idea (of another's feeling) is itself transformed into the corresponding feeling.

> When any affection is infus'd by sympathy, it is at first known only by its effects, and by those external signs in the countenance and conversation, which convey an idea of it. This idea is presently converted into an impression, and acquires such a degree of force and vivacity, as to become the very passion itself, and produce an equal emotion, as any original affection. (*Treatise*, 317)

Hume explains this transformation by appeal to two distinctive aspects of his general theory of mind. The first is the (implausible) view that the difference between the idea of an experience and the experience of which it is an idea is simply one of relative vivacity, with the idea being, in effect, just a less vivid version of the experience. The second is that, under certain circumstances, ideas can be revivified to a point that they become the experiences (or at least the kinds of experiences) of which they are ideas, thanks to certain associations. With these two views in place, Hume suggests that in sympathizing with another we are imagining ourselves in that person's situation, or seeing ourselves as in some other way related to that person, and argues that the vivacity of our ever-present impression of our self (which is brought to the fore in sympathizing with others) is transferred to the idea of the feeling and thus transforms it into the feeling:[7] "The stronger the relation is betwixt

---

7 There is an important difference between sympathy—which transforms an idea into an impression—and merely being caused, by an idea, to have an impression. No sympathy is at work when the thought that someone is angry leads to the thought that he will be difficult to deal with and then in turn to a headache or anxiety; yet the idea of someone's anger is causing a pain. No part of that effect involves putting oneself in another's place.

ourselves and any object [including other people and their feelings], the more easily does the imagination make the transition, and convey to the related idea the vivacity of conception, with which we always form the idea of our own person" (*Treatise*, 318). Hume uses this general account of sympathy to explain some intriguing vagaries in our patterns of sympathy. To take one example, he notes that competing with pressures to identify with others (which are in play when we sympathize) there are also pressures to compare ourselves with others (which pull in the opposite direction). Indeed,

> We judge more of objects by comparison, than by their intrinsic worth and value; and regard everything as mean, when set in opposition to what is superior of the same kind. But no comparison is more obvious than that with ourselves; and hence it is that on all occasions it takes place, and mixes with most of our passions. This kind of comparison is directly contrary to sympathy in its operation. (*Treatise*, 593)

This explains why, on noticing that someone is happy, our first and natural sympathetic reaction may be to feel pleasure. Yet if we notice as well that we are sad, that comparison will work to increase our sadness: "*The direct survey of another's pleasure naturally gives us pleasure; and therefore produces pain, when compar'd with our own [assuming we are not as pleased]. His pain, consider'd in itself, is painful; but augments the idea of our own happiness [assuming we are not in as much pain], and gives us pleasure*" (*Treatise*, 594). Whether sympathy or comparison wins out, Hume holds, depends on how vivid our idea is of the other person's pleasure or pain. The more vivid the idea, the more likely, Hume thinks, we will sympathize with, rather than compare ourselves to, the other person. While our character and temper will influence the vividness of our ideas of others' pleasures and pains, Hume emphasizes specifically the extent to which the vividness of our ideas will depend on how close the relation is, in our thought, between ourselves and the other (*Treatise*, 594). The closer the relation, the stronger the sympathy; the further the relation, the weaker the sympathy. (The relations Hume has in mind are resemblance, contiguity, and cause and effect. So the more we see ourselves as resembling, or being near, or being causally connected to, the other person, the stronger will be the effects of sympathy.)[8]

Hume offers a thought experiment as some confirmation of his view. He has us consider first that we are safely on land and would welcome taking some pleasure from this fact. We would succeed, he suggests, if we just imagine the plight of those at sea in a storm. Comparing our situation to theirs, he thinks, will heighten the pleasure we take in being safe on land. Up to a point, he suggests, our pleasure would increase as the idea of the alternative becomes more vivid, say if we actually "saw a ship at a distance, tost by a tempest, and in danger every moment of perishing on a rock or sand-bank." But only up to a point. If the ship is brought near enough that we can "perceive distinctly the horror, painted on the countenance of the seamen and passengers, hear their lamentable cries, see the dearest friends give their last adieu, or embrace with a resolution to perish in each other's arms: No man has so savage a heart as to reap any pleasure from such a spectacle, or withstand the motions of the tenderest compassion and sympathy" (*Treatise*, 594). The lesson Hume draws is that "if the idea be too faint, it has no influence by comparison; and on the other hand, if it be too strong, it operates on us entirely by sympathy, which is the contrary to comparison" (*Treatise*, 289).

The forces of sympathy and comparison explain as well, Hume holds, the causes of respect, humility, pride, envy, and hatred. All of these, he maintains, are dependent on how we are affected by thoughts of others, and specifically by the degrees to which we either sympathize with, or compare ourselves to, them.

---

8 "Resemblance and contiguity are relations not to be neglected. . . . For besides the relation of cause and effect, by which we are convinc'd of the reality of the passion, with which we sympathize; beside this, I say, we must be assisted by the relations of resemblance and contiguity, in order to feel the sympathy in its full perfection" (*Treatise*, 320).

But, to the extent that our interest is in understanding Hume's account of approbation, these are details we can set to one side. All we need is the idea that when sympathy (as opposed to comparison) is in play, it works to transform the idea of an impression (of, say, a pleasure or a pain) into a corresponding impression.

Incidentally, Hume is not committed to holding that the transformation will, or even can, be effected with any and all ideas of feelings (let alone ideas of impressions more generally). For all he argues, there may be some feelings the idea of which cannot be turned into the feelings themselves. (It might be, for instance, that the idea of feeling rough sandpaper can never be changed into the feeling itself, nor the idea of someone being jealous into jealousy.) What is crucial, for his theories of approbation and moral judgment, is just that regularly the transformation does happen and, specifically, that ideas of pleasant and painful feelings can be transformed into pleasures and pains. Moreover, Hume does not need to hold that, when sympathy is at work, each idea of a specific kind of pleasure or pain is transformed into the very same kind of pleasure or pain; it is enough if the idea of a specific kind of pleasure is converted into a pleasant feeling and the idea of a specific kind of pain into a painful feeling.[9] Still, it is striking the extent to which sympathy does effectively turn the idea of someone's grief or fear into grief or fear and the idea of someone's cheerfulness or excitement into cheerfulness or excitement.[10]

3.2. Smith

Smith, as I have said, shares Hume's view that sympathy, in the standard cases, involves feeling *as* another does, *because* she feels that way. At

---

[9] Hume does sometimes write as if the effect of sympathy is the creation of "the very passion itself" of which one has formed the idea (*Treatise*, 317). Yet no part of his accounts of approbation and moral judgment depend on this.

[10] Movies seem especially effective in inducing sympathetic feeling and they seem to do so, often at least, by managing to make vivid our ideas of the experiences of others.

work in these standard cases is, Smith holds, our capacity to imagine ourselves (more or less successfully) in the other's place.

Of course, there are importantly different ways one might be imagining oneself in another's place. In particular, exactly how much of oneself and one's character is carried over might completely shift how one feels as a result.

In some cases, in order to sympathize with another, Smith notes that we do not simply imagine ourselves in that person's situation, we take up (in our imagination) that person's character and commitments: "When I condole with you for the loss of your only son, in order to enter into your grief I do not consider what I, a person of such a character and profession, should suffer, if I had a son, and if that son were unfortunately to die: but I consider what I should suffer, if I was really you, and I do not only change circumstances with you, but I change persons and characters" (*TMS*, 323). In other cases, though, we are sympathizing not with how people actually feel, nor even with how we imagine they feel, but with how we would feel, with certain of our capacities in place, were we (perhaps *per impossibile*) in their place. For example, considering someone who has lost all reason and so is incapable of appreciating his own miserable condition, Smith notes that

> [t]he anguish which humanity feels ... at the sight of such an object, cannot be the reflection of any sentiment of the sufferer. The compassions of the spectator must arise altogether from the consideration of what he himself would feel if he were reduced to the same unhappy situation, and, what perhaps is impossible, was at the same time able to regard it with his present reason and judgment. (*TMS*, 262)

Breaking significantly from Hume, Smith ends up holding that our conception of the circumstances matters significantly more than our idea of the passion itself. Sympathy "does not arise so much from the view of the passion, as from that of the situation which excites it. We sometimes feel for another, a passion of which he himself seems to be altogether incapable; because, when we put ourselves in his case, that passion arises in our breast from the imagination, though it does not in his from reality" (*TMS*, 12). This carries us so far as even to sympathize with the dead, though we know that they feel nothing (*TMS*, 12–13).[11]

Smith notes that some passions immediately engage sympathy: "Grief and joy, for example, strongly expressed in the look and gestures of any one, at once affect the spectator with some degree of a like painful or agreeable emotion" (*TMS*, 11). Yet other passions elicit sympathetic responses, if at all, only when the circumstances in which they are being felt are considered. "There are some passions," Smith observes, "of which the expressions excite no sort of sympathy, but before we are acquainted with what gave occasion to them, serve rather to disgust and provoke us against them. The furious behavior of an angry man is more likely to exasperate us against himself than against his enemies" (*TMS*, 11). That is, unless and until we learn what "gave occasion to" the furious behavior, in which case we might come to sympathize with the man's anger.

Smith explains the different sympathetic effects of these different passions by appeal to what their appearances bring naturally to the mind of a spectator: "If the very appearances of grief and joy inspire us with some degree of the like emotions, it is because they suggest to us the general idea of some good or bad fortune that has befallen the person in whom we observe them" (*TMS*, 11). Whereas in the case of anger, "we plainly see what is the situation of those with whom he is angry, and to what violence they may be exposed from so enraged an adversary. We readily, therefore, sympathize with their fear or resentment, and are immediately disposed to take part against the man from whom they appear to be in so much danger" (*TMS*, 11).

In order to sympathize with someone's anger, rather than with the fear or resentment of those at whom he is angry, we need to become

---

11 Needless to say, these examples of sympathy differ significantly from the standard cases of feeling *as* someone else does *because* she or he feels that way, since, in the examples, the person sympathized with most decidedly does not feel the same way.

aware of, and focus on, the grounds for his anger. If we find that we too would be angry in his place, sympathy with him can take hold and weigh against the sympathy we naturally would have with the targets of his anger. If, however, we find we would not be angry in his place, we will not sympathize with his anger.[12]

Smith ends up offering a wonderfully subtle catalog of the strange dynamics of our capacity for sympathy. But, unlike Hume, he shies away from offering general principles meant to explain the workings of sympathy. Smith is content to register the existence of sympathy (along with its intriguing complexities) and to use it to explain the nature of approbation and moral judgment.

An interesting question, though, is whether, or to what extent, Hume's theory might fit with, and explain, Smith's observations. This would require that the affective effects of imagining ourselves in another's place, which Smith highlights, are mediated by *thoughts* of the pleasures or pains we would be feeling under those circumstances. Smith clearly holds that we do often have such thoughts, and that they make a difference to whether we can sympathize with someone else. Yet it seems as if vividly imagining ourselves in the other person's circumstances might cause the feelings straight away, unmediated by thoughts of the feelings, just as actually being in the circumstances would. And it looks too as if sometimes, not having to imagine ourselves in different circumstances, we find ourselves sympathizing, as if by contagion, with the feelings of others.

Indeed, Hume and Smith both remark on how being in the company of those who are cheerful can lift one's mood and they both treat this as an example of sympathy at work. Hume offers an analogy: "As in strings equally wound up, the motion of one communicates itself to

---

[12] One of the real pleasures of Smith's discussion of sympathy is his perceptive descriptions of the peculiarities of sympathy. He notes, for instance, the asymmetric impact of positive and negative feelings and the ways in which we are able to sympathize more readily with emotional pains (which are more accessible to the imagination) than with physical pains. He appeals to the latter to explain why tragedies consistently revolve around emotional, rather than physical, loss (*TMS*, 29).

the rest; so all the affections pass readily from one person to another, and beget correspondent movements in every human creature" (*Treatise*, 575). Is this always thanks to our *thinking* of their cheerfulness, or of the cheerfulness we would feel if we were they? Hume could claim that the communication of affections is always via ideas of the affections, but he does not. And insisting that it is seems to press his theory substantially beyond the evidence.

So it is worth noting that Hume can allow that fellow-feeling might well be engendered in ways not covered by his theory. At least when it comes to approbation and moral judgment, Hume's account requires only the claim that our ideas of another's pleasures and pains can cause corresponding pleasures and pains. His account does not even require the claim that the effect is achieved via a transformation of the idea into an impression.[13]

4. Approbation

Hume and Smith see the workings of sympathy as crucial to understanding the nature of moral approbation, though their views of approbation differ dramatically. Just how different their views are will take a little time to bring out, not least because Hume's theory of approbation is quite complex (and largely ignored, perhaps for that reason).

4.1. Hume

According to Hume, approbation and disapprobation are "nothing but a fainter and more imperceptible love or hatred" (*Treatise*, 624). So the place to look for his theory of approbation and disapprobation is his discussion of love and hatred, which are given extensive attention at the beginning of book 2 of the *Treatise*. There Hume distinguishes

---

[13] Samuel Fleischacker offers a subtle discussion of the differences between Hume and Smith's accounts of sympathy in "Sympathy in Hume and Smith: A Contrast, Critique, and Reconstruction," in *Intersubjectivity and Objectivity in Adam Smith and Edmund Husserl*, ed. Dagfinn Føllesdal and Christel Fricke (Frankfurt: Ontos, 2012), 273–311.

impressions that are original from those that are secondary (or reflective), where the original impressions are those that arise "without any antecedent perception" while the secondary or reflective impressions "proceed from some of these original ones, either immediately or by the interposition of its idea" (*Treatise*, 275). Thus, when someone feels a pain, on barking her shin, she experiences an original impression (of pain), while the regret she later feels will be a secondary impression that arises thanks to the interposition of the idea of her earlier pain.

Hume goes on quickly to add two further distinctions among the secondary impressions, between those that are *calm* and those that are *violent*, and between those that are *direct* and those that are *indirect*. Hume grants right away that the distinction between the calm and the violent impressions is "far from exact" and notes that many impressions that are usually quite calm (his example is aesthetic appreciation) might "rise to the greatest heights," and that normally violent impressions "may decay into so soft an emotion, as to become, in a manner, imperceptible" (*Treatise*, 276). The sorting is at best rough and ready. But it is what Hume has in mind in saying approbation and disapprobation are simply "a fainter and more imperceptible love or hatred." He thinks approbation and disapprobation, like aesthetic appreciation, are usually relatively calm, whereas love and hatred are usually quite violent.

Yet approbation and disapprobation are, crucially, exactly like love and hatred (and pride and humility) in being *indirect*. Hume's initial description of what being indirect involves is fairly opaque. He mentions "desire, aversion, grief, joy, hope, fear, despair, and security" as examples of direct secondary impressions and "pride, humility, ambition, vanity, love, hatred, envy, pity, malice, generosity, with their dependents" as examples of indirect secondary impressions (*Treatise*, 276–77). Both arise, according to Hume, thanks to the presence of some other pleasant or painful feeling, but indirect secondary impressions depend as well on the presence of "the conjunction of other qualities" (*Treatise*, 276). Figuring out what those "other qualities" are is central to understanding Hume's account of approbation. Fortunately, it becomes clear as Hume's discussion of pride and humility and love and hate develops.

In setting out Hume's theory of indirect passions, it is useful to follow him in considering the four passions of pride, humility, love, and hatred together (keeping in mind that love and hatred are the models for approbation and disapprobation, respectively). Having the four together is helpful because they admit of two relevant pairings. First, pride and humility are paired together because they are both attitudes we have toward ourselves, whereas (as Hume is using the terms) love and hatred are attitudes directed at others. Hume describes this difference by saying that the *object* of pride and humility is ourselves, while the *object* of love and hatred is someone other than ourselves. Second, pride and love are paired together because they are both pleasant, whereas humility and hatred are paired together because they are both painful. Hume describes this difference by saying that the *sensation* of pride and love is pleasant, while the *sensation* of humility and hatred is unpleasant.

What explains when and why we feel attitudes directed at ourselves, rather than others, and when and why we feel the pleasant attitudes, rather than the painful ones? To provide an answer, Hume turns to what *causes* these attitudes and distinguishes, in the cause, between the *subject* and its *qualities*. He then argues that which indirect passion we feel, if any, depends on whether and how the subject, and its qualities, are related to the object and the sensation of the passion in question.

As an example, consider a person who is proud of his house (or a house he has built or designed). The pride is a pleasant feeling directed at himself. What in the cause explains this pride? Two aspects of it, Hume thinks. First, that the subject of the pride, the house, is *his* (or in some other way related to him); recognizing that fact naturally turns his attention to himself. Second, that the quality of the house, its beauty, is such that the idea of it gives him *pleasure*; feeling this naturally turns his attitudes positive. It is by this double relation—to the object of pride and to pride's pleasant feeling—that the cause prompts the pride.

According to Hume, if either relation were lacking—if the house were not his (or in some other salient way related to him), or were not a source of pleasure—it would prompt no pride. And if either relation (to the object or to the sensation of the passion) were changed appropriately, one of the other indirect passions would take pride's place. So, for instance, if the house was his, but it was a source of pain, the thought of it would cause humility; if, instead, the house was a source of pleasure, but belonged to another, the thought of it would cause love; or if it was another's and was a source of pain, the thought of it would cause hatred. The crucial relations, importantly, are among the person's thoughts and feelings. What matters for pride, in the case of the house, is that the person thinks of it as her own, or in some other way as related to her, not that it actually is. Similarly, if she thinks that the house is a source of pleasure, as long as that thought then causes her pleasure, enough will be in place for pride, even if, as a matter of fact, the house itself gives no one else pleasure.

Hume concludes that a double relation must be present for any of the indirect passions to arise, and, when present, the nature of each of the relations determines which of the passions will arise. The relations in play are (1) between the *idea* of the cause of the passion (in this case, of the beautiful house) and the *idea* of the object of the passion (self or others) and (2) between the *feeling* (of pleasure or pain) produced by the cause of the passion and the *feeling* of the passion.[14]

As Hume recognizes, not just any relation between a possible cause and oneself, or another, will be sufficient to produce pride or love, no matter how great the pleasure produced. At the same time, it is amazing just how tenuous a connection sometimes proves sufficient. (Simply having been in the room with someone famous can, it seems, generate

---

14 "That cause, which excites the passion, is related to the object, which nature has attributed to the passion; the sensation, which the cause separately produces, is related to the sensation of the passion: From this double relation of ideas and impressions, the passion is deriv'd" (*Treatise*, 286).

pride.) Similarly, not just any pleasure caused by something to which one is related will cause pride, no matter how close the relation.

Moreover, what might originally be a source of pride can easily lose its power when, for instance, the effects of comparison come into play. Thus, one might be proud of some accomplishment until one discovers how easily others manage to do so much better; at this point one's pride might well give way either to admiration and love—to the extent that one's attention is shifted to the more accomplished—or to humility—to the extent that one continues to consider what one has done, but now in a context where a comparison with others brings a painful realization of one's inadequacy. Or, of course, one's attention might well just shift away leaving all four of the passions unengaged.

In thinking about things with an approving (or disapproving) eye, just which qualities, and whose pleasures (or pains), will be taken into account turns on a number of factors, not least the person's conception of the nature and point of what she is considering. So, for instance, in considering a home as a place for one to live, attention is naturally turned to its comfort, function, and affordability; when one is considering it more as a work of art or an investment than a place for one to live, however, different aspects come into view and are given more significance. More generally, just what we end up approving or disapproving of is influenced by whatever factors make certain features of the object of our attention salient, including cultural practices and individual personalities. Significantly, these things too may come in for attention, with, say, cultural practices and particular personalities themselves becoming objects of disapproval.

It is important to keep in mind, especially when we turn to *moral* approbation, that the crucial feeling of pleasure produced by the cause, which then bears a relation to the feeling of the indirect passion (approbation, love, or pride), may be itself immediate or not. Thus, the pleasure caused by the beautiful house may result immediately on seeing it or it may arise, thanks to sympathy, on considering the pleasure others take in seeing the house, or a combination of the two.[15] This matters, in the case of moral approbation, because, on Hume's account, all moral approbation arises from a pleasure that is itself the result (thanks to sympathy) of considering, "in general, without reference to our particular interest," the pleasures a person's character brings to the person herself or to others (*Treatise*, 472). Moral approval is the approval prompted by the more or less durable traits of mind and character that are "*useful* or *agreeable* to the *person himself* or to others" (*Enquiry*, 268).[16] And these traits secure moral approval because the idea of the pleasure caused by what is useful or agreeable is transformed, thanks to sympathy, into a pleasant feeling, which then gives rise to the pleasant feeling of approval. (A similar story goes for moral disapproval, where ideas of painful feelings give rise, thanks to sympathy, to a painful feeling, which then, through the workings of the double relation, prompts the painful feeling of disapproval of the person for his character.)[17]

The indirect passions may themselves generate higher order attitudes of approval or disapproval, to the extent that one turns one's attention to them. So a person might disapprove of her own pride, or approve of the disapproval of others. What is important, in order to kick in the indirect passions, is the presence of both a suitable relation between the cause of the passion and the passion's object and a resemblance in sensation between the independent pleasure or pain that results from the cause (specifically, the qualities of the subject) and the sensation of the passion.

On Hume's account, moral approbation is distinctive because of two aspects of its cause: (1) the relevant pleasures are restricted to those that result from sympathy (you might approve of someone in light of

---

15 Comparison too might come into play, so that even a home that is not beautiful and would not give rise to pleasure in others might nonetheless be a source of pleasure, and so pride, when the owner realizes it is not nearly so bad as others.

16 Hume's focus on traits of character, in his account of *moral* approbation, plays a role in his accommodating the difference between the various effects a person might have that are properly seen as that person's doing, and for which the person is properly seen as responsible, and other effects that the person might have but that are not properly seen as being that person's doing.

17 For moral approval and disapproval alike, what is in play is an attitude directed at a person (the object), for his or her character (the subject), because of its impact (the subject's qualities).

his good services to you, but that approval, if it depends on a pleasure that comes not from sympathy but from a concern for yourself, will not be moral approval) and (2) the subject of moral approval is always ultimately a trait of character. To the extent that we restrict ourselves to sympathetic pleasures and we are focusing on a person's character traits, our approval (if we feel it) will count as moral approbation. Plenty can of course get in the way; we might be constantly focused on our own interests and the impact of someone's character on us, or we might, even when sympathetically engaged, be thinking not of the person's durable traits of mind and character but of his looks, or his wealth, or some other aspect of him that is not the subject of moral approval even if it is useful or agreeable to the person or others.

Hume's theory of the indirect passions, and so of moral approbation, is admittedly complex, to the point of striking many as implausibly baroque. So it is worth pausing to highlight an important virtue of Hume's view, a virtue that seems to call for just the sort of complexity Hume puts into play. Specifically, Hume is well placed to account for the idea that some of our attitudes (though certainly not all of them) are such that we can reasonably ask "what considerations underwrite the attitude?" or "what reasons do we have for them?" Certain attitudes are such that if you have them, there must be considerations that, from your point of view, make sense of, or serve as reasons for, your attitude. While the idea of free-floating pleasure makes sense, taking pride in nothing in particular and for no reason does not; nor, it seems, does feeling hate toward no one in particular, or toward someone but for no reason. Hume's theory of the indirect passions allows him to explain why certain feelings—including approbation, moral and otherwise—are such that we only have them when we see considerations as (so to speak) counting in their favor. If I approve of someone, Hume holds, it must be because I see her as related to something with features that I see in a favorable light. Similarly, if I disapprove of her, it must be because I see her as related to something with features that I see in an unfavorable light.

In the case of distinctively moral approbation, Hume holds that my approval must be of the person for her character, in light of what I see (without regard to my own interests) as its positive impact on her or relevant others (that is, those I see as being, in Hume's terms, in her "narrow circle"). When it comes to our approval of benevolent people, for instance, Hume sees us as approving of a benevolent person, for her benevolence, because of (what we see as) the benefits her benevolence brings to others (with whom we are sympathetically engaged). Obviously, this proposal is compatible with noting that different people may take different groups to be relevant, may differ in what they see as the impact of a person's character on that person and on others, and may differ in what engages their sympathy and so what they see in a favorable light.[18] Still, whenever we are morally approving of someone, Hume claims, it will be because we approve of that person, for her character, because of her character's effects on her and others, considered without regard to our personal interest.

Significantly, any account of reason-related attitudes that have intentional objects, and are felt only when the person takes there to be considerations in light of which they make sense, will end up with as many moving parts as Hume introduces, and for the same reasons that motivate Hume's introduction of them. So while Hume's account of the indirect passions may be baroque, its complexities are unavoidable if we are to do justice to the phenomena.

Perhaps it is worth noting that Hume's particular views (1) that we succeed in considering something without regard to our own interests, yet in ways that engage our interest, only thanks to sympathy and (2) that sympathy works by transforming the idea of someone's pleasures or pains into pleasures or pains, end up giving such feelings, and our ideas of them, an especially prominent role in his theory of moral approbation. But one could work with the general outline of his theory, while

---

[18] It may well be, for instance, that some people do not approve of benevolence because, for instance, they think its effects, contrary to popular opinion, are not beneficial.

holding (for instance) that we can be impersonally engaged independently of the workings of sympathy or that when sympathy works it is not always via having an idea of the pleasures or pains of others.[19]

As Hume is well aware, our distinctively moral approvals, despite being restricted to the effects of sympathy and focused exclusively on durable traits of mind and character, will vary dramatically according to whom we consider in thinking of the effects of the person's character and how vividly we consider their pleasures and pains, which will in turn be heavily influenced by resemblance, contiguity, and cause and effect. The upshot is that we will find people's *feelings* of moral approval shifting in ways that reflect these influences, even when they are genuinely relying on sympathy and putting to one side considerations that do not relate to people's characters. At the same time, as Hume notes, people's moral *judgments* do not exhibit the same variability. So it becomes an important part of Hume's overall theory to make sense of the difference between *feeling* moral approval and *judging* that something is morally approvable. But before we turn to that part of his theory, we should look at Smith's account of moral approval.

4.2. Smith

Smith's conception of approval is much simpler than Hume's, while giving an even more central place to sympathy. In developing his account of moral approval Smith turns his attention first to our approval of another person's *opinions*:

> To approve of another man's opinions is to adopt those opinions, and to adopt them is to approve of them. If the same arguments which convince you convince me likewise, I necessarily approve of your conviction; and if they do not, I necessarily disapprove of it:

---

[19] Smith's account of sympathy may well be one according to which we might sympathize with others without having an idea of their pleasures and pains, simply by successfully putting ourselves in their situation and finding ourselves feeling a certain way.

neither can I possibly conceive that I should do the one without the other. To approve or disapprove, therefore, of the opinions of others is acknowledged, by every body, to mean no more than to observe their agreement or disagreement with our own.

And then he extends the idea: "this is equally the case with regard to our approbation or disapprobation of the sentiments or passions of the others" (*TMS*, 17).

Pressing the same line, Smith argues that "[e]very faculty in one man is the measure by which he judges of the like faculty in another. I judge of your sight by my sight, of your ear by my ear, of your reason by my reason, of your resentment by my resentment, of your love by my love. I neither have, nor can have, any other way of judging about them" (*TMS*, 19). According to Smith, then, we approve of someone's sentiments when we recognize that we sympathize with that person's sentiments, that is, that we share the sentiments (perhaps, though not necessarily, as a result of putting ourselves in the person's place). What matters to approval is the recognition of fellow-feeling, not the process by which we come to share the same feeling: "To approve of the passions of another . . . as suitable to their objects, is the same thing as to observe that we entirely sympathize with them; and not to approve of them as such, is the same thing as to observe that we do not entirely sympathize with them" (*TMS*, 17). It is important to Smith's view that the approval does not consist in sharing passions but comes with noticing or observing or thinking that one does. As Smith points out,

> in the sentiment of approbation there are two things to be taken notice of; first, the sympathetic passion of the spectator; and, secondly, the emotion which arises from his observing the perfect coincidence between this sympathetic passion in himself, and the original passion in the person principally concerned. This last emotion, in which the sentiment of approbation properly consists, is always agreeable and delightful. The other may be agreeable or disagreeable, according

to the nature of the original passion, whose features it must always, in some measure, retain. (*TMS*, 46)[20]

As Smith recognizes, this view needs some adjustment to take account of the ways in which we might approve of someone's sentiments even when we do not happen, actually, to sympathize with them. To take just one example, "[w]e may often approve of a jest," he notes, "and think the laughter of the company quite just and proper, though we ourselves do not laugh, because, perhaps, we are in a grave humour, or happen to have our attention engaged with other objects" (*TMS*, 17).

Smith handles these cases by introducing the idea of a conditional sympathy, of the sympathy we would feel if we were to consider the "situation, fully and in all its parts," which we often do not do (*TMS*, 18). We approve of others' sentiments, Smith then holds, if we observe that we would, if we were fully considering their circumstances, be in sympathy with them.

On Smith's view, distinctively moral approval has as its focus the "sentiment or affection of the heart" from which actions proceed, when these sentiments and affections are "considered under two different aspects, or in two different relations; first, in relation to the cause which excites it, or the motive which gives occasion to it; and secondly, in relation to the end which it proposed, or the effect which it tends to produce" (*TMS*, 18). Reflection on the first—the cause of sentiments—shapes whether we approve of some action as *proper*. We do so, Smith thinks, as long as we (think that we) would, under the agent's circumstances, share the agent's "sentiment or affection of the heart." When we find that we do (or would) sympathize with the agent's sentiment or affection, we approve of the agent as acting properly. Alternatively,

---

20 This is in response to a worry pressed by Hume that Smith could not hold both that sympathy is always agreeable and yet that we can sympathize with unpleasant sentiments. Hume's concern was that sympathizing with unpleasant sentiments must be unpleasant. Smith's reasonable response is to distinguish the unpleasant sympathetic feelings from the pleasant feeling of observing the agreement in feeling.

though, if we find that we do not (or would not) sympathize with the agent's sentiment or affection, we disapprove of the agent for acting improperly.

Reflection on the second relation—on what the intended end is or its usual effects are—shapes whether we approve of person as acting *meritoriously*. We do so when we (think that we) would feel gratitude if we were in the circumstances of those who are or would be subject to the effects of the action. When we find that we do (or would) sympathize with their gratitude we approve of the agent as having acting meritoriously. Alternatively, though, if we find that we do (or would) sympathize with the resentment of those who are (or would be) affected, we disapprove of the agent as acting blamably.[21]

The pleasure we take in being in sympathy with others—the pleasure of approving of others—works also, Smith thinks, to shape our own sentiments (or at least our willingness to show them) so as to make them more likely to be sympathized with by others.

> Our first moral criticisms are exercised upon the characters and conduct of other people; and we are all very forward to observe how each of these affects us. But we soon learn, that other people are equally frank with regard to our own. We become anxious to know how far we deserve their censure or applause, and whether to them we must necessarily appear those agreeable or disagreeable creatures which they represent us. We begin, upon this account, to examine our own passions and conduct, and to consider how these must appear to them, by considering how they would appear to us if in their situation. (*TMS*, 112)

As a result, he notes, we tend to temper our expressions of sadness to bring them to a level with which others can sympathize and we work to

---

[21] As Smith emphasizes, whether we will sympathize with someone's gratitude or resentment is sensitive to whether we see the actions of those to whom they are grateful or resentful as proper (*TMS*, 71–73).

bring our attitudes into line with what others will find they can sympathize with. "It is indecent," he observes, "to express any strong degree of those passions which arise from a certain situation or disposition of the body; because the company, not being in the same disposition, cannot be expected to sympathize with them" (*TMS*, 27). More generally, he claims, "if we consider all the different passions of human nature, we shall find that they are regarded as decent, or indecent, just in proportion as mankind are more or less disposed to sympathize with them" (*TMS*, 27).[22]

Importantly, as Smith notes, man "desires, not only praise, but praiseworthiness; or to be that thing which, though it should be praised by nobody, is, however, the natural and proper object of praise. He dreads, not only blame, but blame-worthiness; or to be that thing which, though it should be blamed by nobody, is, however, the natural and proper object of blame" (*TMS*, 114). This poses the challenge of figuring out what it takes to be praiseworthy (or blameworthy). And this leads Smith to distinguish *judging* that someone has acted properly or meritoriously (or improperly or blamably) from *feelings* of approval (and disapproval) we might have toward them.

5. Moral Judgment

Hume and Smith both recognize that there is an important difference between something securing approval and being approvable. And they recognize the need for an account of moral thought and talk to accommodate the distinction and explain what it is for something to be approvable, and not merely approved. In broad outlines, as I have said,

---

[22] Smith uses this phenomenon to explain an important difference between the unsocial passions ("hatred and resentment and all their modifications" [*TMS*, 34]) and the social passions ("[g]enerosity, humanity, kindness, compassion, mutual friendship and esteem, all the social and benevolent affections"). The former, he argues, "must always be brought down to a pitch much lower than that to which undisciplined nature would raise them" in order to secure the sympathy of others, while the latter are such that we "have always . . . the strongest disposition to sympathize with the benevolent affections" (*TMS*, 39).

they adopt the same general view. They both work to identify conditions in which approval (which they have already explained) is veridical. Their shared idea is that for something to be approvable is for it to be such that it would garner approval under the appropriate conditions.

The model for this approach is familiar from accounts of what it is for something to be, say, blue, that appeal to it looking a certain way, under normal light, to a person with a normal visual system, under normal circumstances. These accounts start with the fact that we have certain reactions to the world (color perceptions, in this case) and then mark the difference between something merely seeming or looking blue and it actually being blue by appeal to how it would look under privileged circumstances. The idea, it is worth emphasizing, is not that the privileged ("normal") conditions are those in which we happen to be able to see a thing's true color, where we have some independent way of identifying its true color, and so a way of confirming the conduciveness of the circumstances to seeing it. Rather, the idea is that being blue just is being such as to look a certain way under the specified conditions. There is no independent standard; the standard is set by how things appear when the privileged conditions are met.[23]

Significantly, since the privileged conditions are not privileged because they are those under which we get things right, some other argument must be offered for thinking they are the conditions that set the standard. While Hume and Smith offer quite different arguments for the standard they defend, they are sensitive to many of the same features of moral judgment—especially its demand for impartiality, but also its independence from the vagaries that, both acknowledge, influence individual patterns of approval.

---

[23] Hume is explicit about the model for judgments of color and about extending it to his account of moral judgment. He makes clear as well that he thinks the general model extends to a range of other judgments that have their origin in our perceptions, including judgments concerning not merely "secondary" but also "primary" qualities. See, for instance, *Enquiry*, 227–28. And Smith emphasizes that, when it comes to moral judgments, the "precise and distinct measure can be found nowhere but in the sympathetic feelings of the impartial and well informed spectator" (*TMS*, 294).

5.1. Hume

Hume's approach to identifying the standard of moral judgment (which is set by what he calls the "General Point of View") involves starting with what he takes to be the pattern of our moral judgments, and our judgments (as correct or not) of other people's moral judgments. Then, in light of that pattern, he extrapolates a standard that makes sense of, and explains, why the judgments exhibit the pattern they do.

In the process, Hume marks the ways in which our judgments often break free from our approvals. For instance, our approvals, thanks in part to their dependence on the workings of sympathy, vary significantly, making them parochial and variable in ways that our moral judgments are not. He notes, for instance, that in thinking about a person's character and its effects, we are influenced by our relation to him (including resemblance and contiguity) as well as by the vividness with which those effects are presented. As a result, our approvals are influenced "by our acquaintance or connexion with the persons, or even by an eloquent recital of the case" (*Enquiry*, 230). In our moral judgments, however, though the differential effects of sympathy are *felt*, and our actual approvals are influenced accordingly, we *judge* people of the same character as morally the same. With this in mind, Hume points out that "[a] statesman or patriot, who serves our own country in our own time has always a more passionate regard paid to him, than one whose beneficial influence operated on distant ages or remote nations" because the latter "affects us with a less lively sympathy." But he notes that "[w]e may own the merit to be equally great, though our sentiments are not raised to an equal height, in both cases" (*Enquiry*, 227). In the same way, "[o]ur servant, if diligent and faithful, may excite stronger sentiments of love and kindness than Marcus Brutus, as represented in history; but we say not upon that account, that the former character is more laudable than the latter" (*Treatise*, 582).

From this Hume infers that we are relying on a standard for our judgments that, in some way, abstracts from, or controls for, the variable influences of sympathy caused by our connection with those we judge and by differences in how vivid the case is to us. He thinks this is accomplished by turning our attention from our own actual feelings of approbation to the approbation we would feel if we were to take up a privileged point of view—a point of view from which we are considering not a particular person and the actual effects of her character, but instead the usual effects of the kind of character she has. So while we judge her for her character, our judgments turn not on the actual effects of her particular character, nor on her relation to us, but on a more general view of the effects of the kind of character she has.

This aspect of our privileged point of view has another advantage, as an explanation of our judgments, in that it makes sense of why "[v]irtue in rags is still virtue; and the love, which it procures, attends a man into a dungeon or desart, where the virtue can no longer be exerted in action, and is lost to all the world" (*Treatise*, 584). So, for instance, we judge benevolence to be a virtue, even where it happens not to find expression in benefits to others, despite our sympathy being less engaged, and our feelings of approval less strong, than they would have been had there been actual benefits. Benevolence's standing as a virtue depends on how we are engaged not by reflection on the effects of a specific person's benevolence, as they turn out to be, but by reflection on the usual or expected effects of benevolence.

> [T]he tendencies of actions and characters, not their real accidental consequences, are alone regarded in our moral determinations or general judgments; though in our real feeling or sentiment, we cannot help paying greater regard to one whose station, joined to virtue, renders him really useful to society, than to one, who exerts the social virtues only in good intentions and benevolent affections. (*Enquiry*, 228)

Hume makes the same point in the *Treatise*: "Where a person is possess'd of a character, that in its natural tendency is beneficial to society, we esteem him virtuous, . . . even tho' particular accidents prevent its operation and incapacitate him from being serviceable to his friends and country." We praise equally, for instance, the character of people equally honest, despite knowing that the honesty of one actually benefits people while the honesty of the other does not. "'Tis true," Hume acknowledges, "when the cause is compleat, and a good disposition is attended with good fortune . . . , which renders it really beneficial to society, it gives a stronger pleasure to the spectator, and is attended with a more lively sympathy. We are more affected by it; and yet," he recognizes, "we do not say that it is more virtuous, or that we esteem it more" (*Treatise*, 585).

Moreover, Hume recognizes, our moral judgments suppose a common standard, one sharable (and often shared) with others we recognize as being of the same mind with us about virtue and vice, and such that it delivers the same verdict for us all. This introduces the idea that the relevant point of view must both be accessible to us all and be, in its deliverances, insensitive to our individual differences. As a result, he argues that the general point of view, properly understood, not only restricts the relevant reactions of approval and disapproval to those prompted by sympathy (which leaves to one side the influence of individual differences), and limits attention to the usual effects of the character type in question, but also introduces a common focus for that attention, fixing "our view to that narrow circle, in which any person moves, in order to form a judgment of his moral character" (*Treatise*, 602).[24] Who exactly counts varies according to which kind of character is under consideration. So, for example, the virtues of a parent are measured mostly by a character's effects on those in his or her family, while those of a statesmen are answerable to the effects on a much broader audience (albeit not always the effects on everyone).[25]

---

[24] In other places, thinking of the same restriction, Hume talks of those who have "a connexion" with the person judged (*Treatise*, 591 and 602) rather than of those in the "narrow circle."

[25] So, for instance, "When the interests of one country interfere with those of another, we estimate the merits of a statesman by the good or ill, which results to his own country from his measures and councils, without regard to the prejudice which he brings on its enemies and rivals" (*Enquiry*, 225).

Hume, as I have said, extrapolates the standard for our moral judgments (as set by the general point of view) from what he sees as the pattern of those judgments, and the pattern of our judgments of other peoples' moral judgments, arguing that the standard he identifies explains those patterns. He sees the resulting standard as being insensitive to the influences of self-interest, special relations, and actual sympathetic engagement. Yet he recognizes that our actual moral judgments (as well as our judgments of other people's moral judgments) can be, and often are, influenced by these factors. Still, on his account, and—if he is right, by our own lights—our moral judgments go wrong when this happens. This is because the standard for the *correctness* of our moral judgments, even if not our actual moral judgments, is insensitive to these influences, and rightly so.[26] That the standard is *rightly* insensitive to such influence is, I will argue at the end of this chapter, important to the plausibility of Hume's view. First, however, we should look at Smith's account of moral judgment.

5.2. Smith

Once the distinction between someone being approved and that person being approvable is recognized, Smith faces the challenge of explaining what marks the difference. With Hume, he sees the challenge as one of identifying the standard that governs our judgments of approvability. The standard in question is a standard we use in judging how things—people, actions, institutions—*ought* to be, not how they happen to be.

Smith's approach to identifying the standard of moral judgment (which is set by what he calls the "impartial spectator") involves starting with the observation that we desire "not only praise, but praiseworthiness; or to be that thing which, though it should be praised by

---

Keeping this in mind is important for seeing how and why Hume does not evaluate character traits by appeal to their contribution to overall utility, taking everyone into account.

26 For a more detailed discussion of Hume's account of moral judgment and the "General Point of View," see my "On Why Hume's 'General Point of View' Isn't Ideal—and Shouldn't Be," *Social Philosophy and Policy* 11. 1 (1994): 202–28.

nobody, is, however, the natural and proper object of praise" (*TMS*, 114). Then, keeping that desire in mind, he identifies a standard for what counts as praiseworthy (or approvable) by looking at what satisfies that desire. He argues that the desire finds satisfaction when, but only when, we would secure the approval of an impartial spectator who is fully informed about our actions, motives, and circumstances.

Smith points out that the desire to be praiseworthy is not satisfied when we secure the praise of those who are not appropriately informed impartial spectators: "It is by no means sufficient that, from ignorance or mistake, esteem and admiration should, in some way or other, be bestowed upon us.... The man who applauds us either for actions which we did not perform, or for motives which had no sort of influence upon our conduct, applauds not us, but another person. We can derive no sort of satisfaction from his praises" (*TMS*, 115–16). The approval of those who are not appropriately informed does not satisfy the desire for praiseworthiness.

Nor is it sufficient, Smith notes, for us to secure the admiration and approval of those influenced by self-interest or bias. So, for instance, Smith argues that in weighing someone else's interests against our own, "[w]e must view them, neither from our own place nor yet from his, neither with our own eyes nor yet with his, but from the place and with the eyes of a third person, who has no particular connexion with either, and who judges with impartiality between us" (TMS, 135). The approval of those who are not impartial also does not satisfy the desire for praiseworthiness.

What does satisfy the desire for praiseworthiness is knowing that one *would* secure the approval of an appropriately informed spectator, whether or not one actually enjoys such approval.[27] In using this standard people are appealing not to what garners approval but to "a much

---

27 "We are pleased to think that we have rendered ourselves the natural objects of approbation," Smith observes, "though no approbation should ever actually be bestowed upon us: and we are mortified to reflect that we have justly merited the blame of those we live with, though that sentiment should never actually be exerted against us" (*TMS*, 115–16).

higher tribunal, to the tribunal of their own consciences, to that of the supposed impartial and well-informed spectator, to that of the man within the breast, the great judge and arbiter of their conduct" (*TMS*, 130).

Once we have on board the standard set by the impartial spectator, we are in a position to consider our own patterns of approval to determine which ones meet that standard and which ones do not. And we are able to distinguish between what we happen to approve of and what is genuinely approvable, allowing our judgments to be governed by the latter, rather than the former.[28] Like Hume, Smith recognizes that it is important that the standard we rely on in drawing the distinction itself emerges as, in the appropriate sense, approvable.[29] More about this requirement shortly.

6. Ratifying the Standard of Moral Judgment

Hume and Smith share the idea that we should understand thinking of something as approvable in terms of the thing being such that it would secure approval—not approval from just anyone under any circumstances, but approval from someone appropriate under suitable circumstances. And they share a view, at least in general outline, about what someone has to be like, and what her circumstances need to be, in order for her approval to matter. She must be informed, for instance, and impartial, and engaged by the welfare of others. These are features of someone taking up the general point of view, or serving as the impartial spectator, that are crucial to her role in setting a standard for our moral judgments.

---

28 In turning our attention to the reactions of an impartial spectator, when we make judgment concerning what is approvable, "habit and experience have taught us to do this so easily and so readily, that we are scarce sensible that we do it; and it requires, on this case too, some degree of reflection, and even of philosophy, to convince us" (*TMS*, 135–36).

29 For a more detailed discussion of Smith's account of moral judgment and the impartial spectator, see my "Sentiments and Spectators: Adam Smith's Theory of Moral Judgment," in *The Philosophy of Adam Smith*, ed. Vivienne Brown and Samuel Fleischacker (Abingdon, U.K.: Routledge, 2010), 124–44.

Importantly, Hume and Smith both suggest a further, explicitly normative, condition on an appropriately specified standard for moral judgment. According to them both we neither can nor should rest content finding that we happen to rely on some standard in making our moral judgments; the standard must itself be morally good, appropriate, or justified. This means that the standard we rely on (whether set by the general point of view or by the impartial spectator) must itself meet the standard it sets. Were we to discover that the standard we rely on is (by our own lights) morally defective, we would, they think, have grounds for thinking the standard defective.[30]

So, for instance, at the end of the *Treatise*, Hume claims (without elaboration) that "not only virtue must be approv'd of, but also the sense of virtue: And not only that sense, but also the principles from whence it is derived" (*Treatise*, 619). Smith, in turn, criticizes Francis Hutcheson's account of moral judgment on the grounds that he treats as irrelevant—even absurd—the question of whether the standard on which we rely is, itself, morally evaluable as proper or appropriate.[31] Smith goes on to argue not only that we can and do make such evaluations, but that a mark of correct moral sentiments is that they "naturally appear in some degree laudable and morally good" (*TMS*, 323). Exactly what is required for a standard to meet this requirement is left unexplored by both Hume and Smith.

In Hume's case, it seems that he is sensitive to the worry that, when it comes to determining virtue, it is not enough to show that a character trait garners the approval of those taking the general point of

---

30 This marks an important difference between the standard of moral judgment and the standards for other judgments, say of color or size. In the case of the latter, the standards themselves, and the judgments we make using them, are not within the scope of those standards (such standards and judgments have no color or size) nor need the standards be morally good, appropriate, or justified in order to be the right standards for these nonmoral judgments.

31 Stressing the analogy between moral judgments and judgments of taste or size, Hutcheson's view is that a person cannot "apply *moral Attributes* to the very *Faculty* of perceiving *moral Qualities*; or call his *moral Sense morally Good* or *Evil*, any more than he calls the *Power of Tasting*, *sweet*, or *bitter*; or of *Seeing*, *strait* or *crooked*, *white* or *black*." Francis Hutcheson, *An Essay on the Nature and Conduct of the Passions and Affections, with Illustrations on the Moral Sense*, ed. Aaron Garrett (1742; Indianapolis: Liberty Fund, 2002), 149.

view, it must also merit the approval it garners. And, on Hume's account, it will count as meriting that approval if, but only if, the fact that the trait garners the approval it does (from the general point of view) itself garners approval from the general point of view. That it will garner such approval is not trivial. Given Hume's account of approbation, when we take up a particular general point of view, from which we feel approval of various traits, we might find that, as our attention is shifted to the pattern of our resulting approvals, we feel disapproval. In such a case, though the putative virtue is "approv'd of," *the sense of virtue*, and "the principles from whence it is derived," are not. If this were to happen, we would be in the position of thinking, of what meets the standard (by garnering approval from the general point of view), that it does not merit that approval—not because we have wheeled in some new standard, but because our own standard does not count the approval approv*able*. In such cases, the standard on offer will fail to meet the requirement Hume has introduced.

Clearly, in cases in which the sense of virtue, and the principles from which it derives, are approved of, from the general point of view, we might wonder whether *that* approval is merited. So a potential regress looms. Hume is explicit that making the first step is mandatory—to insure that what is approved by our standard merits, by that standard, the approval it receives. Yet he says nothing about successive steps. Hume can reasonably treat each successive step as optional, though he should hold that an acceptable standard must pass at each level, however far back one goes. So the requirement is not that we must take an infinite number of steps, but that for each one taken we do not find that the approval in question is not merited.

Smith, as I have indicated, imposed a very similar normative condition on the adequacy of the standard we rely on in making our moral judgments (whether it is set by the impartial spectator or not). It is unclear, however, how this condition should be seen as applying to his account of the impartial spectator. What did he think that standard needed to do in order to count as appropriately ratified?

One possibility might be that Smith thought a particular conception of the impartial spectator meets the normative condition as long as we find that the impartial spectator approves of her own (pattern of) approvals. This would fit nicely with what seems to be Hume's view. Yet Smith's account of approbation, which is significantly different from Hume's, makes this test trivially satisfied (in a way it is not trivially satisfied, on Hume's account). After all, for Smith, to approve of something, say some (pattern of) approval, is just to recognize that one would, under the same circumstances, feel the same approval. But of course an impartial spectator, reflecting on her own (pattern of) approval, will inevitably discover that she would feel exactly the same as she in fact does feel. If this is all it took for the standard to count as "laudable and morally good," one might well worry about the significance of the requirement. So it is worth noting that, even if Smith's account of the standard of moral judgment meets the test easily, if other accounts—say Hutcheson's or Hume's—end up failing the test, that would be important.

Alternatively, though, Smith might hold that an impartial spectator's approvals are successfully defended only when they would secure the approval of some *other* spectator, different in some relevant respect from ours. This would make the test nontrivial. However, it would raise significant worries about how we should understand the relation between the two spectators, and the standards that would then be in play, such that one is an appropriate standard for our moral judgments but another one is the appropriate standard not for such judgments but for the standard for such judgments. If the latter standard is the appropriate one for determining the standard for our moral judgments, why is it not itself an appropriate standard for our moral judgments? What qualifies the second spectator's approvals for one role but not the other?

The challenge here is analogous to the challenge facing indirect rule utilitarians who hold that overall utility is the right standard for judging among rules, but not among actions, which should be judged by appeal to the rules sanctioned by overall utility. In fact, one might think that Smith actually embraces the standard of overall utility as the appropriate standard for impartial spectators; after all, Smith often highlights the good consequences that come from regulating our moral judgments by appeal to the impartial spectator. On such an interpretation, when it comes to the question of whether the standard set by the impartial spectator can be defended as proper or appropriate, the answer is found by appeal to the consequences of using that standard. Yet there are two strong reasons for thinking that this interpretation gets Smith wrong. First, if Smith were to appeal to overall utility in defense of the impartial spectator, he would be relying on just the sort of independent standard of moral judgment that he rejects in giving his account of our reliance on the impartial spectator. Second, if Smith were relying on such a standard, he would need to count as valuable certain states of affairs, or actions, or feelings, independent of whether they would secure the approval of an impartial spectator. Yet Smith is clear that the value of, say, pleasure is crucially conditioned by whether it is proper or merited. On his view, not all pleasure is equally valuable; whether some pleasure is valuable, and how valuable it is (when it is valuable), depends on whether it would be approved of by the impartial spectator. Absent an appeal to the impartial spectator, there is, according to Smith, no criterion for distinguishing between what is and what is not a valuable consequence.[32] Needless to say, once the standard of value set by the impartial spectator is in place, there is no obstacle to Smith offering utilitarian arguments in favor of various practices and institutions, as he often does. But these appeals to utility all play out against the standard set by the impartial spectator, so they

---

32 Smith draws a sharp distinction between his view and one that gives priority to utility. Both views, he supposes, offer a measure of when various sentiments and affections are felt to the appropriate degree. The difference is that the one he rejects "makes utility, and not sympathy, or the correspondent affection of the spectator, the natural and original measure of this proper degree" (*TMS*, 306). And an appeal to our judgments of when sentiments and affections are proper or not, Smith holds, reveals that utility is not the natural and original measure, while "the correspondent affection of the [impartial] spectator" is.

will not provide an independent standard for judging the impartial spectator.[33]

Yet Smith does not need to appeal to some other, independent, standard (set either by another impartial spectator or considerations of overall utility) in order to raise and address the question of whether the impartial spectator sets a proper or appropriate standard in a way that is nontrivial. He can, and should, rely on the impartial spectator, but see the question not as whether the impartial spectator approves of her own (pattern of) approval, which she inevitably will, but whether the impartial spectator approves of our relying on the deliverances of the impartial spectator in making our moral judgments. Once the candidate object of approbation is not the impartial spectator's (pattern of) approval but our using that approval as the standard for our moral judgments, we have a nontrivial test that might be failed. Nothing in Smith's account of approbation or in his characterization of approbation or of the impartial spectator ensures, *ex ante*, that such a spectator will approve of us using the spectator's reactions as a standard for judgment.

At the same time, the results of such a test are important. If we were to discover that, by our own standard, our relying on that standard is improper or inappropriate, we would have reason to revise our standard. After all, we would be thinking that there is something improper in judging ourselves, and others, as proper and meritorious in the way we have been. If, however, we were to discover that, by our own standard, relying on that standard is proper or appropriate, we would be in a position to ask and answer, with some significance, the question that Hutcheson mistakenly thought was irrelevant.

If we do interpret Smith's normative condition this way, two things are worth noting. The first is that Hume could make sense of, and embrace, the condition understood in this way. Whether relying on

---

33 See, for instance, Smith's famous discussion of how a well-structured economy will promote the public interest even though those within in it are acting only with the intention of promoting their own interests. See Smith's *Wealth of Nations*, 1. 456.

the general point of view will satisfy this condition is not a foregone conclusion; but it may well satisfy it, and if it does, that looks to be significant. The second thing worth noting is that if it is our reliance on the standard that is up for evaluation, we will not be concerned with showing that what garners approval merits that approval. Instead, we will be concerned with showing that it is morally good (or appropriate, or justified) to use the fact that something garners approval (or disapproval) from a privileged point of view as the standard for our judgments. Perhaps both concerns are important to address.

However that works out, finding that the standard we are using is, by our own lights, defensible as morally good, or appropriate, or justified is not to find independent grounds for the standard. Yet it is to show that the standard does not suffer a serious defect—of being such that, even by our own lights, it is not an appropriate standard for our judgments.

7. Conclusion

My concern in this essay has been to sort out three distinct elements of the theories offered by David Hume and Adam Smith—their theories of sympathy, of approbation, and of moral judgment. Too often the differences between these three elements are simply confounded and too often, also, the differences between Hume's and Smith's theories of these elements are missed altogether. At the same time, many have read the sentimentalists (including Hume and Smith) as if they had no account of moral *judgment* at all, or as if whatever account they had was simply a nonstarter. Neither view does justice to the aims, subtlety, or plausibility of the theories Hume and Smith developed.

I have stressed in particular that Hume and Smith have accounts of the difference between *feeling* approval and *judging* that something is approvable, proper, or meritorious. This is crucial to the plausibility of their sentimentalist approach to moral theory. To lose the contrast between having a moral feeling and making a moral judgment is to lose something essential to understanding moral practice, even if (as the sentimentalists hold) there is a deep connection between feeling and judging. Fortunately, Hume and Smith do not lose the contrast. Which of their accounts is right, if either, of course matters greatly, and I have not here taken a position on the adequacy of either. Yet with them, and for the reasons highlighted in the last section, I think neither Hume's account nor Smith's will be adequate unless the standard of judgment it offers can itself be defended as morally approvable (in light of the standard itself). At the same time, though, I suspect they might each have the resources to show that their standards meet this normative requirement—or, at least, that suitable variations of their standards will.

Reflection
TRACING A LINE OF SYMPATHY FOR NATURE IN GOETHE'S *WAHLVERWANDTSCHAFTEN*
Elizabeth Millán

In a seminal essay from 1924–25 on Goethe's *Wahlverwandtschaften* (1809), Walter Benjamin uses Goethe's novel to present the task of the critic. In his essay, Benjamin observes that "[c]ritique seeks the truth content of a work of art; commentary, its material content."[1] Benjamin likens the work of the commentator to that of the chemist: if the work is like a burning funeral pyre, for the commentator wood and ash are objects of analysis. The work of the critic is like that of an alchemist: faced with the burning funeral pyre, for the critic the flame itself preserves an enigma, that of what is alive, and presenting that flame in its movement and in its heat is the task of the critic. As Benjamin tells us, "Thus, the critic inquires into the truth, whose living flame continues to burn over the heavy logs of what is past and the light ashes of what has been experienced."[2] We see at once that the task of the critic will involve an act of deep sympathy with and for the material; such care for the material keeps the flame of its meaning alive.[3]

---

1 Walter Benjamin, *Selected Writings*, vol. 1, *1913–1926* (Cambridge, MA: Harvard University Press, 1996), 297. The essay was written in 1919–22 and published in *Neue Deutsche Beiträge*, 1924–25, as *Goethes Wahlverwandtschaften*.
2 Benjamin, *Selected Writings*, 298.
3 The theme of hermeneutic sympathy is developed by Friedrich Schleiermacher during the late 1700s, and it is found in the writing of other early German romantics as well, especially in the concepts

For a certain contemporary of Goethe's, one Goethe admired for his scientific innovations and accomplishments, preserving life was also a central task. I refer to Alexander von Humboldt, who in his presentation of nature valued life as much as Benjamin's critic, writing: "The breath of life should not be eliminated from the depiction of nature. And yet the mere enumeration of a series of general results is productive of just such a wearying impression, that is, the accumulation of too many individual details of observation."[4] A merely empirical depiction of nature indicates a lack of appreciation for nature's meaning, the sort of approach that ignores the breath of nature's life. Humboldt approaches nature as a critic rather than merely as a commentator. These themes of criticism, commentary, life, nature, and understanding bring us, albeit along an unconventional path, to the insights about sympathy that are developed in Goethe's novel *Elective Affinities*.

It is no accident that Goethe's *Wahlverwandschaften* would be a place where an affinity between Humboldt and Benjamin would be found. Of course, the novel is not about the affinities between Humboldt and Benjamin, but rather orbits around its four main characters: Eduard, Charlotte, the Hauptmann, and Ottilie. Eduard and his wife, Charlotte, test their relationship by opening it to the presence of Eduard's friend, the Hauptmann (the captain), and Charlotte's young, pure charge, Ottilie. As the affinities or attractions that define much of the focus of the novel develop, we find ourselves in the midst of love triangles that turn tragic, as Eduard and Ottilie perish (along with Charlotte's infant son, who curiously resembles both Ottilie and the Hauptmann). Goethe's interest in the concept

---

of symphilosophy and sympoetry that Friedrich Schlegel develops. See *Schleiermacher: Hermeneutics and Criticism and Other Writings*, ed. Andrew Bowie (Cambridge: Cambridge University Press, 1998); and *Friedrich Schlegel: Philosophical Fragments*, trans. Peter Firchow (Minneapolis: University of Minnesota Press, 1991).

4 Alexander von Humboldt, *Kosmos*, ed. Hanno Beck (Stuttgart: Brockhaus, 1978), xxvi. I refer above, with some alteration, to the English translation, *Cosmos: A Sketch of the Physical Description of the Universe*, trans. E. C. Otté (Baltimore: Johns Hopkins University Press, 1997), 1.9.

of elective affinities stemmed from his studies of the natural sciences. It is a term he took from chemistry, a term that in his poetic hands took on some alchemist tones. Just as the natural world operates in part via the formation and dissolution of certain bonds between molecules, our social world is also affected by bonds of affection and antipathy between individuals. Of course, in contrast to the natural realm, in the realm of social relations the laws that govern our attachments are the function of our freedom. At first glance it might seems that in using a term describing chemical bonds born of natural necessity as a title for a novel featuring love's successes and failures, Goethe is confusing two distinct realms. However we do well to recall Goethe's eloquent reminder in "Natur und Kunst":

Wer Grosses will, muss sich zusammenraffen;
In der Beschraenkung zeigt sich erst der Meister,
Und das Gesetz nur kann uns Freiheit geben.[5]

In *Elective Affinities*, Goethe presents the affinity or sympathy born of our freedom, a freedom bound by law, as all freedom must be. Hence, Goethe allows us to see that elective affinities in the chemical sense and those attachments of the heart detailed in the novel have a common root.

Just as Benjamin's view of commentary and criticism links chemistry to alchemy, Goethe's novel links the natural sciences to poetry in order to uncover truths about nature as a whole. Martin Swales writes that in the *Wahlverwandtschaften*, "there is a level of thematic statement which has to do with nature, nature both within and outside the human sphere."[6] Let us go to part 2 of the novel, to a subsection of chapter 7, a passage from Ottilie's diary.

---

5 Johann Wolfgang von Goethe, *Aus dem Nachlaß* (Weimar: Böhlau, 1887–1919), rpt. in *Werke*, ed. Erich Trunz (Munich: DTV, 1998): "Whoever strives for something great, must pull himself together / Mastery shows itself first in self-limitation / Only the law can give us freedom" (my trans.; *Werke*, 1.245).
6 Martin Swales, "Goethe's Prose Fiction," in *The Cambridge Companion to Goethe*, ed. Lesley Sharpe (Cambridge: Cambridge University Press, 2002), 129–46, at 137.

This passage takes us directly to the theme of nature, both within and outside the human sphere, and also takes us to an aspect of hermeneutical sympathy that I would like to highlight:

> At times when a longing and curiosity about such strange things has come over me, I have envied the traveler who sees such marvels in living, everyday connection with other marvels. But he, too, becomes another person. No one wanders under palm trees unpunished; and attitudes are certain to change in a land where elephants and tigers are at home.
>
> Only the naturalist deserves admiration, who knows how to describe and present [*darstellen*] to us the strangest and most exotic things in their locality, always in their own special element, with all that surrounds them. How much I would enjoy just once hearing Humboldt speak![7]

This passage continues a theme of Ottilie's overall chapter 7 diary entry: the theme of our true relation (*wahres Verhältnis*) to nature, a relation uncovered, in part, via the study of particular humans, which Ottilie links to the study of humanity itself ("das eigentliche Studium der Menschheit ist der Mensch"). For Goethe, the true relation to nature could only be uncovered by a method that fused the natural and human sciences. As Daniel Steuer points out, "Goethe's views on the systematic investigation of nature were

---

[7] Johann Wolfgang von Goethe, *Elective Affinities*, trans. James Anthony Froude, in *Novels and Tales*, trans. R. Dillon Boylan and Froude (London: Henry G. Bohn, 1854), 170–72. I have altered the translation slightly. The German text is as follows: "Manchmal, wenn mich ein neugieriges Verlangen nach solchen abenteurlichen Dingen anwandelte, habe ich den Reisenden beneidet, der solche Wunder mit andern Wundern in lebendiger alltäglicher Verbindung sieht. Aber auch er wird ein anderer Mensch. Es wandelt niemand ungestraft unter Palmen, und die Gesinnungen ändern sich gewiß in einem Lande, wo Elefanten und Tiger zu Hause sind.

Nur der Naturforscher ist verehrungswert, der uns das Fremdeste, Seltsamste mit seiner Lokalität, mit aller Nachbarschaft, jedesmal in dem eigensten Elemente zu schildern und darzustellen weiß. Wie gern möchte ich nur einamal Humboldten erzählen hören." (Johann Wolfgang Goethe, *Die Wahlverwandtschaften* [Leipzig: Insel, 1972], 174).

informed by his belief that science once developed out of poetry, and that one day these two human faculties might well meet again to their mutual advantage."[8] Goethe's novel, in its use of a chemical term (elective affinities) to uncover the laws of human sympathies and antipathies, is a model of just what such an attempt to join poetry and science might look like. Further in Ottilie's diary entry, we read that the best guide for us in the quest toward an understanding of humanity is the teacher who can arouse in us a feeling for the world around us. The praise for Humboldt expressed by Ottilie is due in part to the fact that we find in him the sort of teacher who values life and displays the sort of hermeneutical sympathy for his subject matter that would infuse his students with the feelings (in particular sympathy) for a true understanding of the world. Following Ottilie's musings, the study of nature is a way to uncover its effects on human sensibilities, more particularly, the influence of nature on the emotions. Hence, a great naturalist would be a person able to teach us about human feelings: one of Humboldt's greatest accomplishments was the sympathy he awakened in European readers for the landscape of Latin America.

Humboldt is signaled out in Ottilie's diary entry for his ability to perform a hermeneutic act of great dexterity, demonstrating not only an understanding of the exotic but also an ability to present the unfamiliar to a reading public unacquainted with the palms and other marvels of foreign lands. Ottilie highlights a feature of Humboldt's work that the political leaders of the newly independent countries of Latin America also appreciated and recognized, namely that Humboldt was after a just presentation of America, a task carried out through a dedication to unveiling the meaning of the natural landscapes of Spanish America (as the region Humboldt explored from 1799 to 1804 was known until

---

8 Daniel Steuer, "In Defence of Experience: Goethe's Natural Investigations," in *The Cambridge Companion to Goethe*, ed. Lesley Sharpe (Cambridge: Cambridge University Press, 2002), 160–78, at 160.

independence), which was a dedication to the process of coming to an understanding of Spanish America. Without sympathy for the landscape, no such understanding could take place; "the strangest and most exotic things" would remain foreign, even threatening, and be presented as thus, hindering a view that would clear the way for the European public to appreciate America.[9]

Humboldt wandered (punished most severely by mosquitoes of the Amazon jungle) under the Spanish-American palms. Upon his return from the journey to the equinoctial regions of the earth (more blandly, Spanish America) in 1804, Humboldt was welcomed back to Europe as a figure uniquely situated to present the exotic and unfamiliar territories of America to Europeans, and Goethe was one of Humboldt's most ardent supporters. Humboldt did indeed "describe and present... the strangest and most exotic things in their locality, always in their own special element, with all that surrounds them." Ottilie lingers on this achievement, in part, because she recognizes (as did Goethe) that the tasks of science and of poetry were related by a band of sympathy: without a desire to truly understand the world around us, neither the natural scientist nor the poet would present anything more than dead remains, remains utterly incapable of arousing any feeling in others, let alone of clarifying anything about the world. Both Humboldt and Goethe realized the importance of presentation (*Darstellung*) for both the natural sciences and for poetry. In both Goethe and Humboldt's work, *Darstellung* is used as a way to create a *Zusammenhang* or context for understanding that which is presented (*dargestellt*). *Darstellung* is a way to allow the relations between objects of nature to emerge, so *Darstellung* is not merely an explanation of the object but rather provides a context that

---

[9] This matter of sympathy for nature and its implications for environmental ethics is addressed in great detail by Patrick R. Frierson, "Adam Smith and the Possibility of Sympathy with Nature," *Pacific Philosophical Quarterly* 87.4 (2006): 442–80.

allows the meaning of the presented object to emerge. Goethe's presentation of the characters of the *Wahlverwandtschaften* and the rich context he provides for their presentation as they suffer the slings and arrows of fortune's fate is what enables the deeper meaning of the human condition to emerge; a sympathetic portrait of the human condition emerges in beautiful detail.

CHAPTER EIGHT

Sympathy in Schopenhauer and Nietzsche

Bernard Reginster

Schopenhauer's "morality of compassion" and Nietzsche's critique of it arguably constitute an important stage in the history of the philosophical engagement with compassion.[1] Schopenhauer's claim that "compassion for all that suffers" is the "basis of morality" (*BM* §16) is a substantive challenge to the Kantian idea that this basis is found in respect for the dignity of humanity. He argues that acting out of reverence for the categorical imperative cannot account for the full range of actions and attitudes we consider morally worthy, including actions and attitudes toward nonhuman animals (*BM* §7, 89–91, §19, 169–75). Nietzsche's attack on Schopenhauer's doctrine of compassion may in turn be taken

---

[1] While the term "sympathy" is an acceptable translation of the German term *Mitleid* used by both Schopenhauer and Nietzsche, translators and scholars of both philosophers have tended to prefer the Latinate "compassion" instead. To avoid confusion, I will follow this convention as well in this essay, using "compassion" as a translation for *Mitleid*. Abbreviations of Schopenhauer's and Nietzsche's works are listed at the beginning of the bibliography.

as a critique of the value of the morality it underwrites: the indiscriminate condemnation of suffering in all its forms it advocates poses a serious threat to the possibility of important forms of human "greatness." All this has created the impression that the main issue of contention in Nietzsche's dispute with Schopenhauer is the *value* of compassion. This impression is misleading. Some appearances to the contrary, Nietzsche does not deny the value of compassion any more than Schopenhauer does. His misgivings concern primarily Schopenhauer's conception of the *nature* of compassion. Specifically, he argues that Schopenhauer misconceives both the proper object of compassion and the kind of attitude it is. In this study, I shall examine both lines of objection, though I will spend more time on the latter, which is more elusive and less well understood.

1. Compassion and Suffering

Schopenhauer argues that the proper object of compassion (*Mitleid*) is "all that suffers," or suffering *as such*. The valuation of compassion is therefore an expression of the view that suffering as such is evil, and ought to be avoided or alleviated. Nietzsche concludes that the cult of compassion is therefore also and essentially a cult of comfortableness:

> if you experience suffering and displeasure as evil, hateful, worthy of annihilation, and as a defect of existence, then it is clear that besides your religion of compassion you also harbor another religion in your heart that is perhaps the mother of the religion of compassion: the *religion of comfortableness*. How little you know of human *happiness*, you comfortable and benevolent people, for happiness and unhappiness are sisters and even twins that either grow up together or, as in your case, *remain small* together. (*GS* 338; cf. *D* 174; *BGE* 202)

Nietzsche objects to the value of compassion only insofar as its proper object is understood as suffering as such. And his objection is that when it is so understood compassion may be harmful to the individual at whom it is directed.[2] Strictly speaking, the issue is not that on this conception compassion is not sufficiently altruistic—it may well be motivated by a concern for the good of another for its own sake—but that it fundamentally misunderstands the character of this good. Here is how he describes the issue:

> our dear compassionate friends...wish to *help* and have no thought of the personal necessity of distress, although terrors, deprivations, impoverishments, midnights, adventures, risks and blunders are as necessary for me and for you as are their opposites. It never occurs to them that, to put it mystically, the path to one's heaven always leads through the voluptuousness of one's own hell. (*GS* 338)

Certain forms of suffering in certain circumstances may be necessary for the good of another. Admittedly, even the end of alleviating suffering could justify letting another undergo certain forms of suffering in certain circumstances. The pains of growing up are genuine pains, for instance, but parents motivated by Schopenhauerian compassion would still recognize that it is necessary for their children to undergo these pains now in order to avoid these or greater sufferings later in life. The parents' compassion would therefore not induce them to alleviate the pain of their children; indeed, it would motivate them not to intervene and let the children deal with it. Nietzsche's objection goes deeper than this. His point is not merely that certain forms of suffering in certain circumstances might be necessary to achieve the good life as he takes Schopenhauer to understand it, namely, as "comfort" or "contentment,"

---

[2] Nietzsche also objects that compassion may be harmful to the compassion subject himself, apparently by distracting or diverting him from his own pursuit of greatness (e.g., *GS* 325, 338). However, this objection does not seem to touch on the character of compassion as much as on its importance relative to other pursuits. Thus, even if we conceive compassion in what Nietzsche would consider the right way, it may still be that, in his view, we ought to subordinate its exercise to the pursuit of great achievements. Since this essay aims to focus exclusively on the issue of the character of compassion, I will leave out further consideration of this objection.

or at least the absence of suffering. He argues that suffering is an *essential ingredient* of the good life, once it is properly understood.

As Nietzsche believes we should understand it, a good life is a life that includes great creative achievements. In his view, an achievement counts as "great" only if it involves the confrontation and overcoming of resistance or difficulty. And the experience of such resistance is what suffering consists of. It follows that a measure of suffering is a constitutive ingredient of any great achievement.[3] The compassion that condemns and seeks to eliminate all suffering indiscriminately is thus bound to threaten the possibility of greatness: "sometimes compassionate hands can interfere in a downright destructive manner in a great destiny" (*EH* I 4).

As I noted earlier, Nietzsche does not simply deny all value to compassion; he simply proposes an alternative conception of its proper object, aligned with his conception of the human good. He explicitly contrasts this new conception with that advocated by Schopenhauer and others:

> Whether it is hedonism or pessimism, utilitarianism or eudaimonism—all these ways of thinking that measure the value of things in accordance with *pleasure* and *pain*... are ways of thinking that stay in the foreground and naivetés on which anyone conscious of *creative* powers and an artistic conscience will look down upon not without derision, not without compassion. Compassion with *you*—that, of course, is not compassion in your sense.... *Our* compassion is a higher and more farsighted compassion: we see how *man* makes himself smaller, how *you* make him smaller—and there are moments when we behold *your* compassion with indescribable anxiety, when

---

[3] This is not to say that any difficult achievement is great or that greatness requires any manner of suffering. I have explored these and related issues in greater detail in *The Affirmation of Life: Nietzsche on Overcoming Nihilism* (Cambridge, MA: Harvard University Press, 2006) and "The Will to Power and the Ethics of Creativity," in *Nietzsche and Morality*, ed. B. Leiter and N. Sinhababu (Oxford: Oxford University Press, 2007), 32–56.

we resist this compassion—when we find your seriousness more dangerous than any frivolity. You want, if possible—and there is no more insane "if possible"—*to abolish suffering*. And we? It really seems that *we* would rather have it higher and worse than ever. Well-being as you understand it—that is no goal, that seems to us an *end*, a state that soon makes man ridiculous and contemptible—that makes his destruction *desirable*. The discipline of suffering, of *great* suffering—do you not know that only *this* discipline has created all enhancements of man so far? (*BGE* 225)

The proper object of compassion is not the suffering of another *as such*, and the properly compassionate attitude is not simply motivated by the desire "to abolish suffering." The correct conception of the good of another, which is supposed to govern compassion, is not the elimination of suffering as such, but the "enhancement of man" brought on by "creative powers and an artistic conscience," which require "the discipline of suffering." Far from seeking to abolish suffering, Nietzsche's own brand of compassion "would rather have it higher and worse than ever." This remains genuine compassion, however, insofar as it is still very much driven by a concern to benefit the other: "But if you have a suffering friend, be not a resting place for his suffering, but a hard bed as it were, a field cot: thus you will profit him best" (*Z* II 3).

In explicit contrast with Schopenhauer's view, Nietzschean compassion is therefore not necessarily aroused by the sufferings of others, nor does it necessarily imply a condemnation of them: "*My kind of 'compassion'.*—This is a feeling for which I find no name adequate: I sense it when I see precious capabilities squandered.... Or when I see anyone halted, as a result of some stupid accident, at something less than he might have become" (*WP* 367). Compassion is a response not primarily to suffering, but to whatever might interfere with, or undermine, the pursuit of great creative achievement. Indeed, compassion could even be a proper response to people who do not suffer in any way, but lead very comfortable lives, when such lives remain mired in mediocrity or squander "precious capabilities." Paradoxically, then, Nietzschean compassion could be aroused by the *lack* of suffering since true "happiness," the happiness found in achievement, necessarily involves suffering, or "unhappiness" in the ordinary sense: "happiness and unhappiness are sisters and even twins that either grow up together or... *remain small together*" (*GS* 338).

I should emphasize that none of this implies that Nietzsche's own brand of compassion could not be aroused by the sufferings of others. It only implies that it will no longer be a response to suffering *as such*, but to the suffering that causes "precious capabilities" to be "squandered," or "halts" someone at "something less than he might have become." Not all kinds of suffering are constitutive of greatness, after all, and some forms of it may be antithetical to it. Under such conditions, Nietzsche would presumably regard compassion as a proper response to suffering.

2. The Character of Altruism

In Nietzsche's view, Schopenhauer's conception of compassion goes wrong not simply by directing it at the wrong object. It also goes wrong in its characterization of the attitude the compassionate agent is expected to take toward this object. Specifically, Schopenhauer supposes that the defining attitude of the compassionate agent is one of selflessness, understood as a relative devaluation of his own interests by the compassionate agent. The precise nature of Nietzsche's objection to this aspect of Schopenhauer's view is quite elusive. He does not seem to deny that genuine compassion should be, in some sense, altruistic, or that it should involve a concern with the good of another for its own sake. His chief misgiving appears to focus on Schopenhauer's assumption that the altruistic character of compassion requires the selflessness of the agent.

Schopenhauer argues explicitly that "if my action is to be done simply and solely *for the sake of another*" (*BM* §16, 143), I must devalue my own interests, at least relatively to those of others. Nietzsche dismisses this view as "thoughtlessness": "Out of compassion: at that moment, we are thinking only of the other person—thus says thoughtlessness.... Out of compassion: at that moment we are not thinking of ourselves—thus says the same thoughtlessness" (*D* 133). Although he initially appears to reject the possibility of altruism on the ground that the selfless motivation it requires is impossible for human beings (see *HH* I 1, 57, 103, 133; *D* 133), he also seems inclined to a different and subtler objection, concerning now the nature of altruism. Altruism does not require selflessness, and indeed might even be incompatible with it (*D* 148; *GM* Preface, 5; *WP* 296, 362, 388). This is the line of thought I propose to examine here: Nietzsche objects that the selflessness Schopenhauer takes to be essential to altruism is actually incompatible with it.

As Schopenhauer defines it, the fundamental "problem" of the analysis of compassion is to account for its altruistic character:

> But now if my action is to be done simply and solely *for the sake of another*, then his *weal and woe* must be *directly my motive*, just as *my* weal and woe are so in the case of all other actions. This narrows the expression of our problem, which can be stated as follows: How is it possible for *another's* weal and woe to move my will immediately, that is to say, in exactly the same way in which it is usually moved by my own weal and woe?... Obviously only through the other man's becoming *the ultimate object* of my will in the same way as I myself otherwise am.... But this requires that I am in some way *identified with him*, in other words, that this entire *difference* between me and everyone else, which is the very basis of my egoism, is eliminated, to a certain extent at least. (*BM* §16, 143–44)

This passage is remarkable in the particular manner in which it formulates, and proposes to solve, the problem of altruism. As Schopenhauer conceives of it, this problem is to determine how I could be "moved" by the weal and woe of another as "directly" as I am by my own. This is remarkable because it rules out, from the outset, two natural ways of understanding altruism: according to one, the altruist would be motivated by his recognition of the intrinsic value of the happiness of others; according to the other, the altruist would be motivated by a (noninstrumental) desire to make others happy. Schopenhauer rejects both of these conceptions of compassion.

An action is altruistic if it is done "simply and solely *for the sake of another.*" This implies that the compassionate agent must somehow find the happiness of others to be good independently of its contribution to the satisfaction of his own desires. But Schopenhauer rejects any notion of goodness beyond what contributes to the satisfaction of one's desires: "we call everything good that is just as we want it to be" (*WWR* I §65, 360). In other words, he rejects the notion of "intrinsic value" (see *PP* II §146, 287). This implies that there can be no motivated desires, or desires based on the recognition of the intrinsic value of their objects. This rules out the notion that the compassionate agent could be motivated by the recognition of the intrinsic value of the happiness of others. And if all desires are unmotivated, their objects can have value for the agent only insofar as they are desired or, more precisely, insofar as their possession eliminates the pain associated with the desire for them (*WWR* I §57, 312–14; §58, 319). It follows that even if an agent has an unmotivated noninstrumental desire to make others happy, their happiness will matter to him only insofar as it gratifies his desire for it and not for its own sake—it will be, so to speak, only a scratch to his itch.

If my compassion is motivated by one of my desires, including the noninstrumental desire to make others happy, it cannot be altruistic, and therefore genuine compassion, for I remain moved only by my own weal and woe. My compassion will be altruistic, therefore, only if it is not motivated by any of *my* desires ("*my* weal and woe"), but is motivated "directly" by the desires of the other ("*another's* weal and woe"). And this, Schopenhauer claims, "requires that I am in some way *identified with him*, in other words, that this entire *difference* between me and everyone else, which is the very basis of my egoism, is eliminated, to a certain extent at least."

Following Schopenhauer's own suggestion, we might begin our analysis of the concept of identification with an examination of the concept of egoism. He defines it as the condition in which an individual "makes himself the center of the world, and refers everything to himself" (*BM* §14, 132). This definition is ambiguous. On the one hand, the egoist would simply be the individual whose practical perspective on the world is dominated by the "unqualified desire to preserve his existence, to keep it absolutely free from pain and suffering, which includes all want and privation" (*BM* §14, 131). Egoism, in this case, describes a psychological condition of self-absorption: the unqualified desire for existence and well-being is so powerful that it blinds the individual to any other consideration, and fosters a certain perspective on the world, where everything in it is interpreted in terms of its impact on his existence and well-being. On the other hand, the egoist would also be someone who believes his own existence and well-being to be more important than anyone else's: "he finds himself to be the holder and possessor of all reality, and nothing can be more important to him than his own self" (*BM* §14, 132). What relation, if any, do these two claims about egoism bear to one another?

It might be tempting to describe the egoist as someone who judges his interests to be more important than those of others. Such a conception of egoism would involve a number of substantial assumptions. In the first place, the egoist would be assumed to grasp fully the reality of other individuals with their own interests and to judge his own interests to be more important. Moreover, he would presumably have to judge his own interests to be more important solely *because they are his own*, and not because of their particular content: for there would be nothing distinctively egoistic in placing my interest in the advancement of knowledge, for example, above your interest in collecting obscure sports memorabilia because I judge knowledge—the particular content of my interest—to be the more valuable end. I am an egoist insofar as I regard my interests to be more valuable than yours simply in virtue of their being *my own*.

Schopenhauer agrees that the egoist overvalues his own interests, but he rejects the notion that he does so on the basis of a comparison between his interests and those of others, in which the fact that his interests are his is the decisive consideration. In his way of thinking, rather, the egoist "regards himself alone as *real*, at any rate from the practical point of view, and all others to a certain extent as phantoms" (*BM* §14, 132). In other words, it is *because* "he finds himself to be the holder and possessor of all reality" that "nothing can be more important to him than his own self." The overvaluation of his own interests by the egoist is thus explained in terms of the perspective he takes on himself and his world: he cares only about his own interests because he fails to recognize or appreciate fully the reality of others with interests of their own.

Schopenhauer takes this peculiar blindness to be rooted in a fundamental feature of human psychology: "This is due ultimately to the fact that everyone is given to himself *directly*, but the rest are given to him only *indirectly* through their representation in his head; and the directness asserts its right. Thus in consequence of the subjectivity essential to every consciousness... everything is always closely associated with self-consciousness" (*BM* §14, 132). Schopenhauer acknowledges here the fact that I bear a special "direct" conscious relation to those mental states, such as a desire or an interest, that are mine. He draws a fundamental distinction between the consciousness of "things" in the "external world" and "self-consciousness," or consciousness of something as me or mine. This distinction arises paradigmatically in relation to the experience of my own body: "this body is given in two entirely different ways. It is given in intelligent perception as representation, as an object among objects, liable to the laws of these objects. But it is also given in quite a different way, namely as what is known immediately to everyone" (*WWR* I §18, 100). I can be conscious of my body as a portion of space, an "object among objects," but this consciousness is not yet self-consciousness, or a consciousness of this body as *my* body: "it has become clear to us that something in the consciousness of everyone distinguishes the representation of *his own body* from all others that are in other respects quite like it. That is that the body occurs in consciousness in quite another way, *toto genere* different" (*WWR* I §18, 100; first emphasis mine).

Schopenhauer thus follows a venerable Cartesian tradition in supposing that I have a privileged epistemic access to my own self. However, he does not appear to conceive of this epistemic privilege primarily in terms of immunity to error. It consists rather of the fact that I have a special "immediate" or "direct" knowledge of myself, that is to say, a knowledge that is not based on observation or inference, and cannot be "deduced as indirect knowledge from some other more direct knowledge" (*WWR* I §18, 102). Insofar as I know my body merely as "an object among objects," my access to it is no more immediate than the access others have to it, or than the access I have to their bodies. But I also have an immediate epistemic access to my own body, which gives me a particularly intimate acquaintance with it:

> It is just this double knowledge of our own body which gives us information about that body itself, about its action and movement following on motives, as well as about its suffering through outside impressions, in a word, about what it is, not as representation, but as something over and above this, and hence what it is *in itself*. *We do not have such immediate information about the nature, action, and suffering of any other real objects.* (*WWR* I §18, 103; last emphasis mine; cf. II xxii, 281)[4]

The special "direct" access I have to my own self, particularly to my own interests and desires, is manifested in two respects relevant to the

---

4 Schopenhauer unfortunately assumes that the kind of immediate, non-inferential, and not "purely" representational experience I have of my own body must also be an experience of it as it is "in itself" since it does not answer to the strictures of the principle of sufficient reason. This appears to confuse the *manner* of knowing ("immediately") with its *content* (the "thing-in-itself"). The value of his insight, however, can be separated from this particular way of formulating it.

explanation of egoism. In the first place, it indicates an epistemic proximity that gives those interests and desires a vividness and urgency that is denied to my merely "indirect" representation of the interests and desires of others. While his own suffering "lies near to him [*liegt ihm... nahe*]," the suffering of others is "strange" or "foreign [*fremd*]" to him (*WWR* I §68, 379). It is this vividness and urgency that explains my overvaluation of my desires and interests by granting them their special "right" in my eyes. In other words, in Schopenhauer's view, the egoist overvalues his own interests because he fails to recognize or otherwise fully appreciate the "reality" of others with interests of their own.

In the second place, the epistemic proximity that gives my interests their vividness and urgency also accounts for the special role they play in my consciousness generally. As Schopenhauer puts it, "in consequence of the subjectivity essential to every consciousness... everything is always closely associated with self-consciousness" (*BM* §14, 132). In speaking of the "subjectivity essential to every consciousness," Schopenhauer refers to the fact that my own interests shape the consciousness I take of the surrounding world: everything in that world is represented in relation to my "self-consciousness," that is to say, in terms of its impact on the pursuit of my interests.

This suggests that the distinctive blindness of the egoist is not simply that he fails to recognize the "reality" of others with interests of their own. In fact, Schopenhauer calls this stance "theoretical egoism," and dismisses it as requiring "not so much a refutation as a cure" (*WWR* I §18, 104). It is only "in a practical respect" that the egoist "regards and treats only his own person as a real person, and all others as mere phantoms" (*WWR*, I §18, 104). It is not altogether clear what this distinction between theoretical and practical egoism amounts to.[5] The most

---

5 The distinction is important in Kant, where it assumes a particular significance: the "practical point of view" is the point of view of agency and deliberation, from which I must regard myself as free (see his *Groundwork for a Metaphysics of Morals*, in *Practical Reason*, ed. Mary Gregor [Cambridge: Cambridge University Press, 1996], 448); by contrast, the "theoretical point of view" is the point of view from which I consider myself an object in the world, subject to the laws regulating it. It is doubtful that Schopenhauer would use this distinction in the same way since in his view, the "practical point of

promising suggestion is that, although the egoist recognizes the existence of others with interests of their own, his view of them remains fundamentally framed by his interests: others and their interests appear only as potential obstacles or instruments for the satisfaction of his interests, that is to say, as mere objective complications, which his deliberations about how to achieve his ends have to take into account. Thus, the egoist may well be aware that those others whose interests conflict with his own will suffer from their frustration, but this fact is granted a purely practical—that is to say, from this perspective, instrumental—significance. In the last analysis, Schopenhauer notes, the egoist "ultimately regards only his own person as truly real, looking upon others virtually only as phantoms, attributing to them only a relative existence insofar as they may be a means or an obstacle to this ends" (*BM* §22, 213).

Schopenhauer appears drawn to this conception of egoism—on which the overvaluation of his interests by the egoist does not rest on an evaluative comparison with the interests of others, in which the decisive consideration is that his interests are *his*—because he assumes that the bare fact that my interests are mine, and those of others are theirs, could not make any meaningful ethical difference. This assumption appears in turn to rest on the notion that the special significance my interests have for me reduces to their epistemic proximity to me, which accounts for the framing role they play in my consciousness of others and their interests. It thus seems plausible to suppose that the egoist's overvaluation of his interests is the consequence of a cognitive illusion created by their epistemic proximity.

It should be no surprise, then, that Schopenhauer proposes to define compassion as a condition in which I manage to have as direct an acquaintance with the interests of others as I have with my own, that is to say, a condition in which I come to have a different appreciation of the sufferings of others. They no longer are merely objects of indirect

---

view" is one from which I regard myself as the only person, and it is hard to see how such a point of view could be constitutive of agency.

acquaintance, which are apprehended as instrumental complications in the pursuit of my own interests, but they rather move me as directly as my own interests do. The distinctive mark of compassion, for Schopenhauer, is that "another's suffering in itself and as such *directly* becomes my motive": compassion thus consists of a "wholly *direct* and even instinctive participation in another's sufferings" (*BM* §18, 163; my emphases). Here is how he characterizes the perspective of the compassionate person:

> No suffering is any longer strange or foreign to him. All the miseries of others, which he sees and is so seldom able to alleviate, all the miseries of which he has indirect knowledge, and even those he recognizes as merely possible, affect his mind just as do his own.... Wherever he looks, he sees suffering humanity and the suffering animal world, and a world that passes away. Now all this lies as near to him [liegt ihm jetzt so nahe] as only his own person lies to the egoist. (*WWR* I §68, 379)

This view of compassion elicits the following question:

> But how is it possible for a suffering which is not *mine* and does not touch *me* to become just as directly a motive as only my own ordinarily does, and to move me to action? As I have said, only by the fact that although it is given to me merely as something external, merely by means of external perception or knowledge, I nevertheless *feel it with him, feel it as my own,* and yet not *within me,* but *in another person....* But this presupposes that to a certain extent I have identified myself with the other man, and in consequence the barrier between ego and non-ego is for the moment abolished; only then do the other man's affairs, his need, distress, and suffering, directly become my own. I no longer look at him as if he were something given to me by empirical intuitive perception, as something strange and foreign, as a matter of indifference, as something

entirely different from me. On the contrary, I share the suffering *in him*, in spite of the fact that his skin does not enclose my nerves. Only in this way can *his* woe, *his* distress, become a motive *for me;* otherwise it can be absolutely only my own. (*BM* §18, 165–66)

Schopenhauer's proposal is that identification leads me to experience the sufferings of others just as I experience my own, that is, as sufferings calling "immediately" for condemnation and, whenever possible, for alleviation. Without such identification, I can still recognize that others are suffering, but these sufferings do not affect me in the same way. The chief difficulty of this proposal lies in understanding what this "identification" amounts to. The most common view is that Schopenhauer invokes the ideality of the "principle of individuation" (the transcendental forms of space and time) to make room for the possibility of an insight into the essential identity of all individuals. The required sort of identification with others would consist of precisely this insight (*BM* §22, 209–10; see *WWR* I §66, 372). According to this common interpretation, Schopenhauer's reasoning would go as follow: I cannot be moved by anything other than my own weal and woe; when I am selfish, I am duped by the illusion of individuation, which leaves me indifferent to the weal and woe of others; on some occasions, I manage an insight into the identity of all beings, and come to recognize that the weal and woe of others is also my own; my egoism is then replaced with genuine compassion.

There are well-known difficulties with this reasoning. For example, it rests on what Nietzsche calls "the unprovable doctrine of the *One Will*" (*GS* 99), a false inference from the ideality of space and time to the unity of the world as it is in itself.[6] But the most damaging objection denies that compassion so construed can be genuinely altruistic. This objection comes in two forms.

---

6 See Georg Simmel, *Schopenhauer and Nietzsche*, trans. H. Loiskandl, D. Weinstein, and M. Weinstein (Cambridge, MA: University of Massachusetts Press, 1986), ch. 3.

Nietzsche presents the first form of this objection in his early works. He observes that if compassion were to rest on a numerical identification with the sufferer, then the pain felt by the compassionate agent at the sight of the pain of another would have to be identical with it. But, as Nietzsche stresses repeatedly, this is obviously not in keeping with the phenomenology of compassion: "That compassion... is the *same kind of thing* as the suffering at the sight of which it arises, or that it possesses an especially subtle, penetrating understanding of suffering, are propositions contradicted by *experience*" (*D* 133). For instance, "what a difference there nonetheless remains between a toothache and the ache (compassion) that the sight of a toothache evokes" (*HH* I 104). And if we were to concede to Schopenhauer the notion that our compassionate acts can only be motivated by the pain caused in us by the pain of another, it would follow that our compassion can be really nothing more than covert egoism:

> It is misleading to call the suffering [*Leid*] we may experience at such a sight, and which can be of varying kinds, compassion [*Mit-Leid*], for it is under all circumstances a suffering which he who is suffering in our presence is *free* of: it is our own, as the suffering he feels is his own. But it is *only this suffering of our own* which we get rid of when we perform deeds of compassion. (*D* 133; see *HH* I 103, 133)

According to the second version of this objection, if compassion rests on the recognition by the compassionate person of his (numerical) identity with the sufferer, then it can amount to nothing more than enlightened egoism. As one recent commentator puts it, "after all, the altruist *does* act for the sake of his own interests, the only difference between him and the egoist being that he acts for the sake of the interests of his *metaphysical* rather than his empirical self, so, we might put it, the empirical altruist turns out to be a metaphysical egoist."[7]

---

7 Julian Young, *Schopenhauer* (London: Routledge, 2005), 183.

Both of these versions of the objection might seem too quick, however, for they ignore an important passage in which Schopenhauer criticizes the conception of compassion proposed by Ubaldo Cassina.[8] According to Cassina, compassion rests on a peculiar "deception of the imagination" whereby "we put ourselves in the position of the sufferer, and have the idea that we are suffering *his* pains in our person" (*BM* §16, 147). Schopenhauer rejects this view on the ground that compassion requires that "at every moment we remain clearly conscious that *he* is the sufferer, not *we*; and it is precisely in *his* person, not in ours, that we feel the suffering, to our grief and sorrow. We suffer *with* him and hence *in* him; we feel his pain as *his* and do not imagine that it is ours" (*BM* §16, 147).

The rejection of Cassina's view bears on both versions of the objection we just considered. In rejecting this view, Schopenhauer at least implicitly acknowledges that the pain the sight of another's pain evokes in me when I feel compassion is not identical with it.[9] And he at least implicitly recognizes that if I were to take the pain of another to be my own, my response to it would become inevitably egoistic. The same problem arises in a variety of cases in which the very distinction between my own interests and those of others becomes blurred. For example, an overanxious mother can instill in her child a strong aversion to danger, which may not have been there to begin with. In this case, the interest of the mother acquires for the child the same vividness and urgency as his own, simply because, through a process known as internalization, it actually *becomes* his own. But when the interest of the mother, once it is so internalized, motivates the child to avoid some perceived danger, the resulting action can hardly be thought to be motivated by his altruistic concern for *her* well-being. For his action to be altruistic, he would have to recognize that the interest from which he

---

[8] Ubaldo Cassina (1736–1824), a professor or moral philosophy at Parma, published the *Analytical Essay on Compassion* (*Saggio analitico su la compassione* [Parma, 1772]).

[9] See David Cartwright, "Schopenhauer's Compassion and Nietzsche's Pity," *Schopenhauer-Jahrbuch* 69 (1988): 557–67, at 562.

acts is hers, and not his own. (That is not sufficient, of course, as he must also attend to her interests for their own sake, not to secure some personal benefit.)

Schopenhauer's rejection of Cassina's view seems to imply that compassion cannot be thought to rest on a numerical identification with others. And in fact, several of his other formulations suggest that compassion actually rests on a qualitative type of identification: "compassion...would consist in *one* individual's again recognizing in *another* his own self, his true inner nature" (*BM* §22, 209); or: "virtue must spring from the intuitive knowledge that recognizes in another's individuality the same nature as in one's own" (*WWR* I §66, 368). Although I am numerically different from others, I share the same nature with them. At first glance, qualitative identification looks to provide a promising account of compassion. For to be moved by the sufferings of another, I must first see him as a being whose nature is identical to my own, that is to say, a being with interests of his own, and a susceptibility to suffering when they are frustrated.

But such a qualitative identification is certainly not sufficient for compassion. For one thing, I remarked earlier that on any plausible account of egoism, even the egoist is capable of recognizing that others are susceptible to suffering. And for another, cruelty, which consists in taking pleasure in the sufferings of others, would simply not be possible without such recognition. Moreover, even when such qualitative identification elicits a sense of solidarity with those beings who are, like me, susceptible to suffering, it is still not evident that the resulting concern to alleviate their sufferings will necessarily be genuinely altruistic.[10] As Nietzsche once subtly observes, I could, out of what plausibly looks like solidarity with them, be motivated to alleviate the suffering of those beings with whom I share a condition not because I am concerned for their well-being but because I wish to alleviate my own anxiety

---

10 David Cartwright, "Compassion and Solidarity with Sufferers: The Metaphysics of *Mitleid*," *European Journal of Philosophy* 16.2 (2008): 292–310, proposes to think of Schopenhauerian compassion in terms of solidarity.

about my condition by convincing myself that it is not as fragile and vulnerable as their plight might make it appear to be (*D* 133).

The insufficiency of qualitative identification to account for compassion may well explain why Schopenhauer continues to insist that it also requires numerical identification, the insight that "we are all one and the same entity," and that to the compassionate individual, "the others are not a non-ego for him, but an 'I once more'" (*BM* §22, 210–1; see *WWR* I §66, 372). Since the cruel individual is able to take pleasure in the sufferings of others only if he sees these as similar to his own, but located in some numerically different individual, then numerical identification, which would make him see the sufferings of others as his own, would undercut cruelty and leave compassion as the only possible response (see *BM* §22, 204–5).

Schopenhauer's conception of numerical identification appears to oscillate between two views. The first, suggested by his metaphysical monism (the world in itself is will, and the will is one), is a strict identification, whereby I *am* the other and the other is me. The second, suggested by some of his actual examples of compassion (such as the case of Arnold von Winkelried, which I discuss later in this chapter), is that I see myself as part or member of a single entity; I recognize that others are also members of the same entity, but I do not have to see them as identical with me. In this case, I am able to see what happens to the entity, or to other members of it, as happening to me. The problem with this conception of identification in both its forms is that, as we saw earlier, by Schopenhauer's own lights, it has unwelcome consequences: it deprives compassion of its essential altruistic character. For I care about what is happening to another only insofar as I represent it as happening to me.

We might find one way out of this difficulty by reconsidering the objection of egoism, and the manner in which Schopenhauer's critique of Cassina bears on it. The objection simply assumes that what I have called here numerical identification turns compassion into a form of "metaphysical egoism" that is, for all practical purposes, similar to the ordinary "empirical egoism" Schopenhauer denounces. But it is possible to read in the critique of Cassina a challenge to this very assumption.

One possible way of construing Schopenhauer's challenge is that, in his view, Cassina would take the "deception" of the compassionate individual to consist of an expansion of the boundaries of his individual empirical ego so as to encompass those others who are the objects of his compassion. By remaining mired in the illusion of individuation, he would therefore also remain an egoist of the ordinary "empirical" kind. By contrast, in the view Schopenhauer advocates, compassion rests on a *dissolution* of the boundaries of individuation: it is not that I mistakenly take others to be a part of me, it is rather than there is, in some sense, no me and them any longer. For Cassina, compassion involves an expansion of my sense of self—it is far more encompassing than the narrow view of the ordinary egoist suggests—while for Schopenhauer compassion requires dissolution of my (individuated) sense of self. And his insistence that when we feel compassion for another we must "remain clearly conscious that *he* is the sufferer, not *we*," is only meant to apply to our ordinary empirical view of things, a view we maintain but also recognize to be illusory.[11] As a consequence, there would be something fundamentally wrong in the suggestion, on which the objection rests, that compassion is a kind of "metaphysical egoism," which is nothing more than "empirical egoism" under a different guise.

In the terms of Schopenhauer's metaphysics, the distinction between expanding the boundaries of one's individual ego and dissolving them is conceptually permissible. But what a dissolution of the boundaries of individuation precisely amounts to as a matter of actual concrete experience is much less clear. Schopenhauer's view is that it essentially consists of an insight: "He perceives that the distinction between himself and others, which to the wicked man is so great a gulf, belongs only

---

[11] I can rightly suspect that there is something wrong with my perception if I fail to see the stick in the water as bent, even though I know this perceptual impression to be an illusion. Likewise, I can rightly suspect that something has gone wrong if I confuse (empirically) my suffering with the suffering of others, even though I also know the distinction between me and them to be an illusion.

to a fleeting, deceptive phenomenon" (*WWR* I §66, 372). Although Schopenhauer officially bases this insight on his own version of transcendental idealism—the "deceptive phenomenon" is the transcendental forms of space and time—we might also suppose that it results from a certain appreciation of the roots of egoism. I overvalue my own interests because I stand in a special epistemic proximity to them and because they frame my representation of others and their interests, in a way that is bound to limit my appreciation of them. Since I am naturally absorbed in the interests with which I am "directly" acquainted, and thus represent others and their interests only in terms of their impact on the realization of those interests, I am naturally unable to *see* the well-being of others as an object of independent concern.

The recognition of these epistemic facts at the root of my egoism would contribute to disabling it, presumably, by inducing me to deny those interests that are my own any special importance. And it does so, presumably, by exposing the truth that the personal significance of those interests—of the fact that they are *mine*—amounts to nothing more than that I happen to stand in a special epistemic proximity to them, which in turn accounts for the framing role they play in my consciousness of the rest of the world, including others and their interests. If all there is to those interests' being mine is that I am "directly" acquainted with them, then I can see why they would have a special vividness for me, and why I would be in a particularly good position to feel their motivational pressure, but I can also see that it does not give them a higher standing than interests with which I am not so directly acquainted.

Schopenhauer's preferred example of compassion—the man who dies for his country out of an identification with it (*BM* §22, 212–13)—does not really shed any light on the idea of a dissolution of the boundaries of individuation. For it might certainly be taken to suggest that identification is in fact the expansion of one's sense of self, so as to include in it an identity as citizen of a country. Arguably, however, the point of this analogy would rather be to evoke a condition where the concern for suffering remains as strong as it is for the egoist but where the spatio-temporal *location* of this suffering, or whether the agent stands in special epistemic proximity to it, has become insignificant.

3. *Selflessness and Compassion*

If Nietzsche's critique of the Schopenhauerian conception of altruistic selflessness often looks scattered and tentative, it may well be because he has understandable difficulties in circumscribing it. His main challenge, as I suggested, is to the notion that altruism requires selflessness, but the manner in which Schopenhauer conceives of this selflessness remains elusive. Nietzsche's earliest version of this challenge is based on psychological egoism, the view that human agents are incapable of selfless motivation. His argument goes roughly as follows: he would grant that some actions are altruistically good, deny that actions can ever be selfless, and conclude that altruistic goodness cannot depend on selflessness. As he puts it, "our counter-reckoning is that we shall restore to men their goodwill towards the actions decried as egoistic and restore to these actions their *value*" (*D* 148). His arguments for psychological egoism look inadequate,[12] but they gain greater appeal if we locate them in the context of his critique of Schopenhauer. Given that Schopenhauer rejects the notion of intrinsic goodness (and the associated notion of motivated desire), his difficulties in supplying a compelling account of compassionate identification invite the suggestion that compassion should be construed as a covert form of "self-enjoyment" (*HH* I 104; see 133).

Nevertheless, Nietzsche soon adopts a different strategy, which consists in granting the possibility of selflessness, examining the various guises it might assume, and asking whether selflessness is, under any of these possible guises, actually consistent with, let alone necessary for, altruism:

---

[12] I review some of these difficulties in "Nietzsche on Selflessness and the Value of Altruism," *History of Philosophy Quarterly* 17.2 (2000): 177–200, at 179–84.

There is no other way: the feelings of devotion, self-sacrifice for one's neighbor, the whole morality of self-denial must be questioned mercilessly and taken to court.... There is too much charm and sugar in these feelings of 'for others', '*not* for myself', for us not to need to become doubly suspicious at this point and to ask: 'are these not perhaps—*seductions?*' (*BGE* 33)

In one way of understanding it, selflessness is the attitude of the individual who has a determinate sense of self, in the form of specific interests and desires, which he deliberately ignores or denies. This is selflessness as self-denial, the devaluation of one's own self, of one's interests and desires. I observed earlier that I can regard my interests as worth less than those of others either because of their content or because they are mine. There is nothing particularly selfless about favoring the ends of others when I judge their content more valuable than that of my own ends. Sacrificing my interests for the sake of others just because they are mine, by contrast, comes closer to one plausible way of understanding altruistic selflessness. But it also highlights the strangeness of this attitude, which Nietzsche describes as "the apparently crazy idea that a man should esteem the actions he performs for another more highly than those he performs for himself" (*WP* 269).

The strangeness of this idea inclines Nietzsche to suspect that hidden ulterior motives must animate those whose valuation of the well-being of others is directly linked to a devaluation of their own. Here are two representative examples. Nietzsche sometimes takes this type of self-devaluation to be symptomatic of a narcissistic pathology, involving an excessive preoccupation with one's self-esteem. Vitiated as it is by this pathology, the motivation for benevolence is itself narcissistic—the need to restore the disrupted self-esteem:

> Let us for the time being agree that benevolence and beneficence are constituents of the good man; only let us add: 'presupposing that he is first benevolently and beneficently inclined *towards himself!*' For

without this—if he flees from himself, hates himself, does harm to himself—he is certainly not a good man. For in this case all he is doing is rescuing himself from himself *in others*: let those others look to it that they suffer no ill effects from him, however well disposed he may want to appear! (*D* 516)

I say to you: your love of the neighbour is your bad love of yourselves. You flee to your neighbour from yourself and would like to make a virtue out of that: but I see through your 'selflessness'.... You cannot endure yourself and do not love yourselves enough: now you want to seduce your neighbour to love and then gild yourselves with his error. (*Z* I 16)

On other occasions, Nietzsche argues that the compassionate service of others should be seen not as a consequence of self-denial but as a deliberate cause of it. In this view, "self-sacrifice" or "self-denial" are opportunities for the gratification of the agent's "will to power," though in circumstances in which this gratification is significantly constrained by his "weakness" (*GM* II 16, III 14). In the terms of the *Genealogy*, the will to power is "a desire to overcome, a desire to throw down, a desire to become master, a thirst for enemies and resistances and triumphs" (*GM* I 13)—that is to say, a desire for the overcoming of resistance. Unable to overcome resistance outside themselves, the "weak" turn their will to power inward, by creating in themselves, through the deliberate frustration of their desires ("cruelty turned *against oneself*"), the very resistance they proceed to overcome (*GM* II 16; see III 10, *HH* I 141). This would show that the "seduction" of "self-sacrifice for one's neighbor" has nothing to do with an altruistic concern for his well-being:

> This hint will at least make less enigmatic the enigma of how contradictory concepts such as *selflessness, self-denial, self-sacrifice* can suggest an ideal, a kind of beauty; and one thing we know henceforth— I have no doubt of it—and that is the nature of the *delight* that the selfless man, the self-denier, the self-sacrificer feels from the first:

this delight is tied to cruelty. So much for the present about the origin of the moral value of the 'unegoistic', about the soil from which this value grew: only the bad conscience, only the will to self-maltreatment provided the conditions for the *value* of the unegoistic. (*GM* II 18)

These cases, of course, merely suggest that the agent who appears to act out of compassion may have ulterior, non-altruistic motives, such as eliciting a good opinion in others, with which he can bolster his self-esteem, or demonstrating the power he has over himself. But they point to some deeper misgivings about the role of selflessness—"the unegoistic"—in compassion. We get an initial insight into these misgivings by returning to Schopenhauer's most common and most compelling example of compassionate identification.

This is the case of the individual who sacrifices himself for the sake of his country out of an identification with it (*BM* §22, 212–13): "when Arnold von Winkelried exclaimed, 'Comrades, true and loyal to our oath, care for my wife and child in remembrance thereof', and then clasped in his arms as many hostile spears as he could grasp, some may imagine that he had a selfish intention, but I cannot" (*BM* §15, 139). If this identification were construed as an expansion of his sense of self so as to include in it, in addition to his identity as husband and father, an identity as citizen of a fatherland, Nietzsche observes, it would undermine the altruistic character of his sacrifice. His sacrifice would not be "self-sacrifice" but only the sacrifice of one portion of his self for the sake of another:

A solider wishes he could fall on the battlefield for his victorious fatherland; for his supreme desire is victorious in his fatherland's victory.... But are these all unegoistic states? Are these deeds of morality *miracles* because they are, in Schopenhauer's words, 'impossible, yet real'? Is it not clear that in all these instances man loves *something of himself*, an idea, a desire, an offspring, more than *something else of himself*, that he thus *divides* his nature and sacrifices one part of it to the other? (*HH* I 57)

Nietzsche also considers Schopenhauer's view that in compassion the individual does not expend his sense of self so much as he *dissolves* it. As one possible example of such dissolution, he suggests that Arnold von Winkelried could also be seen as an individual who has no sense of self outside his identification with another, or with a group of others: he thinks of himself only as a "function" or extension of others, or of a group of others (*GS* 116). Even so conceived, however, Nietzsche argues that such a "selfless" individual would remain incapable of genuine altruism. Here is a relevant passage:

> *No altruism!*—In many people I find an overwhelmingly forceful and pleasurable desire to be a function: they have a very refined sense for all those places where precisely *they* could 'function' and push in those directions. Examples include those women who transform themselves into some function of a man that happens to be underdeveloped in him, and thus become his purse or his politics or his sociability. Such beings preserve themselves best when they find a fitting place in another organism; if they fail to do this, they become grumpy, irritated, and devour themselves. (*GS* 119)

As Nietzsche defines it in the preceding sections (*GS* 116–17), a selfless individual is one who lacks a "sense of self" (*GS* 117), insofar as he does not think of himself as a full-blown individual, but sees himself only as a "function" of another individual, or of a group of individuals, with whom he has identified. Nietzsche insists that the attitudes and actions of such a "selfless" individual cannot be regarded as altruistic. He sometimes favors, in this connection, the image of the parasite: "In many cases of feminine love, perhaps including the most famous ones above all, love is merely a more refined form of parasitism, a form of nestling down in another soul, sometimes even in the flesh of another—alas, always decidedly at the expense of 'the host'!" (*CW* 3)

Leaving aside the misogynistic overtones of both passages, we should ask in precisely what way this selfless individual fails to be altruistic. For thinking of oneself as a "function" of another certainly seems to imply that one will be motivated to do everything in what one believes to be the other's interest. It seems as though this selfless individual would be the quintessential altruist. Indeed, inasmuch as he lacks a sense of self, this individual cannot have selfish or self-interested motives for the assistance he brings others, in the way the ordinary egoist does. Since he has no sense of self other than that of being a "function" of some other or group of others, he cannot think of the only interests he recognizes as *his*—they are only the interests of the other, or the group of others, with whom he is identified.[13] We might gain greater understanding of this perplexing view by considering further characterizations of that species of selflessness: the selfless ideal is an "ideal slave," a psychological type Nietzsche describes in the following terms: "*The ideal slave* (the 'good man').—He who cannot posit *himself* as a goal, nor posit any goals for himself whatever, bestows honor upon *selflessness*—instinctively" (*WP* 358). Such an individual, he adds elsewhere, "can be only a means, he has to be *used,* he needs someone who will use him" (*A* 54).

Why would such a condition make the individual in it incapable of genuine altruism? Though Nietzsche offers no clear, fully articulated view on this matter, some clues he tosses our way inspire the following conjecture. To begin, we must note that, for him, altruism is a matter of both motivation and competence. The altruistic agent must act out

---

[13] Nietzsche declares that the individual who turns himself into a "function" of another, or of a group, manages, in this way, to "preserve himself" (*GS* 119). This is odd given that the individual in question precisely lacks the sense of a self to preserve in the first place. The statement is odd only if we think of self-preservation in the customary way, which assumes an individual with a determinate sense of self whose attitudes and actions aim at preserving it. But in the sense in which Nietzsche uses it in this context, self-preservation might be a matter of maintaining *any* sense of self at all: the selfless individual manages to have a sense of self only through his association or identification with the other or group of which he makes himself a function. This also suggests that, even though gaining and preserving a sense of self is the aim of identification, it is not necessarily its *motivation*.

of a concern for the well-being of others, but he must also possess certain competences, including in particular a certain kind of knowledge or experience, without which he will not be able to appreciate what that well-being requires, and so will be unable, despite his best intentions, to contribute to it adequately.

Since the particular kind of selfless individual Nietzsche is inviting us to consider here cannot really act out of self-interest as the ordinary egoist does (for, to repeat, he has no sense of self other than that of being a "function" of some other or group of others), his defect must be found in the lack of some basic competence essential to altruism. Consider an agent who is unable to "posit goals" for herself, or herself as a goal. Following Nietzsche, let us imagine, as an instance of such a selfless character, the blandly devoted wife who selflessly works for the sake of her husband's happiness.[14] For whatever reason (early on, Nietzsche often mentions the relentless conditioning of the "morality of customs" as a cause of such self loss [see D 9, 107; GS 116]), she has no sense of self outside her association with her husband, and so cannot posit ends of her own, which means that she is unable to attach any *personal* significance to the ends she does pursue. Having no ends of personal significance, she is bereft of a certain sort of capacity: she has no appreciation of the personal significance their ends have to those others she wants to help.

But, Nietzsche objects, the ability to appreciate the personal significance the interests of others have for them is a necessary condition of genuine altruism. And a selfless agent who has no interests of personal significance to her, and co-opts the interests of others as a way of achieving a sense of self, is unable to acknowledge and appreciate the fact that the interests of others are actually *theirs*, which implies that she is also unable to appreciate the personal significance these interests have for them. She is single-mindedly devoted to the fulfillment of their interests,

---

14 This is an example proposed by Jean Hampton, "Selflessness and the Loss of Self," in *Altruism*, ed. E. F. Paul, F. Miller, and J. Paul (Cambridge: Cambridge University Press, 1993), 135–65.

but in a way that displays no appreciation of the personal significance these interests have for them.[15]

Think, for example, of the overbearing wife who identifies too closely with her husband's achievements and in this way might very well successfully help him to become, say, a first-rate violinist. If she fails to appreciate, in the process, the basic fact that becoming a virtuoso was *her husband's* interest, we will rightly suspect that her efforts in fulfilling this interest possess no altruistic value. Indeed, the husband himself might grow uncomfortable with this sort of help, even if it proves most useful, and not feel properly cared for, as he senses that *he*, or his happiness insofar as it is *his*, is not the proper focus of his wife's concern.[16] This interpretation of Nietzsche's objection sheds some light on otherwise elusive statements like the following:

> It is richness in personality, abundance in oneself, overflowing and bestowing, instinctive good health and affirmation of oneself, that produce great sacrifice and great love...and if one is not firm and brave within oneself, one has nothing to bestow and cannot stretch out one's hand to protect and support. (*WP* 388; cf. *EH* III, 5: "that gruesome nonsense that love is supposed to be something 'unegoistic'.—One has to sit firmly upon *oneself*,...otherwise one is simply *incapable* of loving.")

How does the discussion of this peculiar form of selflessness bear on the critique of Schopenhauer? If compassionate identification is to

---

15 Consider this observation by Hampton in "Selflessness" about such a character: "he and others like him not only have a poor sense of self-worth and a poor grip on what they owe to themselves..., but also a dearth of plans, projects, and goals that are uniquely their own. Thus, they decide to satisfy the ends of others because they have so few ends of their own to pursue. This explanation accounts for why those of us who have received help from such obsessive care-givers frequently resent and feel violated by the help: it is as if our own ends of action have been seized and taken away from us by these 'helpers' when they insist on pursuing them for us" (149).

16 In fact, the kind of identification I have been considering also makes the kind of qualitative identification Schopenhauer regards as an essential condition of compassion impossible, at least in the following respect: to appreciate the frustrations of others, one must also appreciate the personal significance the frustrated interests have for them, something that is presumably impossible to do for someone who has no interests of personal significance to begin with.

consist of a dissolution of the boundaries of individuation, rather than an expansion of them, then the selflessness of the Schopenhauerian altruist may well bear a close resemblance to the selflessness under consideration in Nietzsche's discussion. If the man who sacrifices himself for his countrymen is not simply acting out of an expanded understanding of his own interests, then he would have to be an individual who does not think of himself as a full-blown individual, but sees himself only as a "function" of his countrymen, with whom he has identified. And what he does for them could not be, for the reasons Nietzsche lays out, genuinely altruistic.

Whether or not this construal of selflessness adequately captures Schopenhauer's elusive conception of compassionate selflessness, it does point to a potential deep problem with it. For at least the following seems clear about this conception. Through identification, the compassionate individual ceases to see himself and the other as separate individuals. It is not that he takes the two of them to form a single individual, as Cassina had supposed, it is rather that he now regards the boundaries of individuation as insignificant illusions. This means not that the other is part of me, or that I am part of the other, but that there really is no me and him anymore. All that remains, and all that matters, in this perspective, is suffering. In deploring and seeking to relieve this suffering, as the compassionate individual does, it matters not at all that it is located in this or that region of time and space: his sole concern is with *deindividuated* suffering. All that matters, in Schopenhauerian compassion, is that suffering be deplored and, whenever possible, removed; but it does not matter *whose* suffering it is. Such compassion would thus constitute an instance of what Nietzsche calls "unselfing [*Entselbstung*]" (both of the compassionate agent and of those others who are the object of his compassion). At the heart of the Nietzschean objection I am now considering lies the question of whether deploring and seeking to relieve the sufferings of others with no thought of the individuals whose sufferings they are still captures something that plausibly remains altruistic compassion.

Nietzsche's repeated emphasis on the capacity to posit ends "for himself" or "himself" as an end, that is to say, on the personal significance to the agent of the ends he pursues, though itself quite elusive, points to a possible diagnosis for the problem he has with Schopenhauer's view. It would overlook the personal significance to the agent of the interests out of which he ordinarily acts. Schopenhauer appears to suppose that the special significance assumed by my own interests is nothing over and above the fact that I stand in close epistemic proximity to them. If, by contrast, we take the special significance my own interests have for me to be more than a psychological effect of their epistemic proximity (which would itself be at most a necessary consequence of the fact that those interests are mine, and not what their being mine consists of), then it could not be so easily discounted either in myself or in those others who are the objects of my compassion.

Schopenhauer's own critique of Cassina's conception of compassion rests on the intuition that it is a requirement of altruism that the interests of others be regarded as *theirs*. But Schopenhauer himself seems to have overlooked one appealing possible interpretation of this intuition, namely, that the genuine altruist is not one who simply seeks to fulfill the interests of others, but one who helps *others* to fulfill their interests. The altruist's focus is not on the interests themselves, but on the well-being of others, and on their interests only insofar as their fulfillment contributes to it. The genuine altruist, in other words, is required to appreciate the personal significance the interests of others have for them, and this presumably involves more than appreciating the mere fact that they are more intimately acquainted with their own interests than they are with the interests of others. In contrast, by Schopenhauer's own lights, the compassionate agent should arguably *not* show any appreciation for a fact that, in fostering the illusion on which egoism and malice rest, is the ultimate cause of immorality. In the final analysis, the deep problem Nietzsche comes to see, however dimly, in Schopenhauer's analysis of compassion is that it operates with too impoverished a conception of the personal significance each agent's interests have for him. This would explain why Schopenhauer regards this personal significance as ultimately nothing more than a discountable illusion, and why the "compassion" that results from the discounting of this illusion fails to be, in Nietzsche's view, genuinely altruistic.[17]

---

[17] This chapter is a revised and expanded version of an essay previously published under the title "Compassion and Selflessness" in *Nietzsche, Naturalism, and Normativity*, ed. C. Janaway and S. Robertston (Oxford: Oxford University Press, 2012), 160–82. I thank Oxford University Press for permission to use these materials here.

CHAPTER NINE

From *Einfühlung* to Empathy

SYMPATHY IN EARLY PHENOMENOLOGY
AND PSYCHOLOGY

Remy Debes

What is the difference between "sympathy" and "empathy"? Serious students of either concept must eventually ask this question, but it proves frustrating to answer.[1] Ever since the American psychologist Edward Titchener (1867–1927) introduced the term "empathy" into English in 1909 as a translation of the German concept *Einfühlung* (feeling into), "empathy" has either been used synonymously with "sympathy," or, even if distinguished from sympathy by one author, nevertheless defined in ways that other authors happily reverse, ignore, contradict, reject, dilute, delimit, and in general,

---

[1] Etymology isn't very helpful for clarifying the modern meaning of "empathy," which strictly comes from the Greek *en* + *pathos*, and thus either means that the person is *in* a state of pathos (experience), or has a pathos *in* him or her (and, by extension, the emotion one feels in response to that experience). Neither really suits the purposes to which the term is usually put, including Titchener's.

redefine.[2,3] In short, like "sympathy," the concept of "empathy" has a complicated, even convoluted history, never mind its comparative youth.

To be fair, as we will see, a case can be made for a principled distinction by the earliest terminological innovators, like Titchener or his likely source of inspiration, the German aesthetician-cum-psychologist, Theodore Lipps (1851–1914), who wrote extensively on *Einfühlung*. Nevertheless, as also will be made clear, these early accounts of empathy and *Einfühlung* failed to establish any stable paradigm of usage for turn of the century theorists. Nor have the intervening years helped much. At present, anyway, 'empathy' and 'sympathy' are eclectic concepts, which only the most dogmatic or ignorant pretend to separate objectively and without stipulation.[4]

So here is how I will proceed. After a brief historical overview, I shall narrow my focus to late nineteenth- and early twentieth-century phenomenology and psychology, where the terminological and conceptual innovations of Lipps and Titchener had an immediate effect, and where interest in the related phenomena of *Einfühlung*, empathy, and sympathy spread with startling speed.[5] My discussion will intentionally

---

2 Edward Titchener, *Lectures on the Experimental Psychology of Thought-Processes* (New York: MacMillan, 1909), 21. The *Oxford English Dictionary* currently falsely attributes the coining of "empathy" to Vernon Lee. See n. 21 below. Curiously, a reference to Titchener's translation (albeit with a typographical error), appears two years earlier in Oscar Ewald's (1908) annual *Philosophical Review* roundup of German philosophy ("German Philosophy in 1907." *Philosophical Review* 17.4: 400–426). I have not been able to confirm Ewald's source, though presumably it was a draft of Titchener's *Lectures*.

3 Etymology fails us here. "Empathy" translates from the Greek as "in passion" or "in feeling," and was sometimes used to connote a strong passionate response. This obviously doesn't track the meaning of "empathy," however eclectic a meaning "empathy" may have.

4 Every so often a valiant effort is made to establish a consensus distinction. See, for example, Lauren G. Wispé, "The Distinction between Sympathy and Empathy: To Call Forth a Concept, a Word Is Needed," *Journal of Personality and Social Psychology* 50.2 (1986): 314–21; or Daniel Batson, "These Things Called Empathy: Eight Related but Distinct Phenomena," in *The Social Neuroscience of Empathy*, ed. Jean Decety and William Ickes (Cambridge, MA: MIT Press, 2011), 3–13. But honest scholars, like Wispé and Batson, are well aware that their efforts ride on a healthy dose of stipulation.

5 My choice is partly guided by what I take to be already well-covered aspects of this history. For those looking to round out their study, I recommend conjoining my essay with (1) George Pigman, "Freud and the History of Empathy," *International Journal of Psychoanalysis* 76.2 (1995): 237–56; (2) Hans Kögler and Karsten Stueber, introduction to *Empathy and Agency: The Problem of Understanding in the Social Sciences* (Boulder: Westview Press, 1999); (3) Gustav Jahoda, "Theodor Lipps and the Shift

end with a focus on early twentieth-century American social psychology. For therein is one particular thread of the relevant conceptual history that simultaneously helps clarify the relationship of sympathy to empathy, early psychology to early phenomenology, and all this historical study to something loaded with present meaning. To foreshadow, consider the following: Part and parcel of the fundamental maxims of the modern egalitarian society is usually classed some kind of *recognition* for the distinctive value, status, or "dignity" belonging to individual persons. This recognition is often construed in rational terms, for example as a certain kind of deliberative attention we owe to other persons, especially in our decisions about how to act with respect to them. Recently, however, many scholars have asked what such recognition might amount to, or require at a psychologically descriptive, precognitive, or phenomenological level. There is no consensus reply to this question. However, at first blush it seems the answer must involve reference to some ability to experience other persons as just that—as "other." That is, we must be able to "see" other individuals not merely as individuals, but as individuals apart from oneself—even if also "like" oneself in some sense. How interesting, then, that something like this idea is woven into, on the one hand, turn-of-the-century phenomenological conceptions of *Einfühlung* and empathy, and, on the other hand, early American social psychological conceptions of sympathy. So let us tug at this thread all the way through. Thankfully, it will become increasingly easy to follow, and in turn increasingly unnecessary to make it a subject of second-order analysis, as I've just done.

1. At the Dawn of Psychology: A Little Bit of History

Psychology is conceptually ancient. But it was not until 1879, when Wilhelm Wundt established the first experimental psychology lab at

---

from Sympathy to Empathy," *Journal of the History of the Behavioral Sciences* 41 (2005): 151–63; and (4) Dan Zahavi, "Empathy, Embodiment, and Interpersonal Understanding: From Lipps to Schultz," *Inquiry* 53.3 (2010): 285–306. Finally, see chapter 8 in this volume.

the University of Leipzig, that it became a bona fide academic discipline (some say 1883 when the lab was officially recognized as an academic department).[6] The lab proved monumentally important, partly in virtue of Wundt's own voluminous contributions, but largely in virtue of the sheer number of doctoral students who matriculated there, many of whom went on to lead prominent careers or form labs of their own in and out of Continental Europe.[7] Edward Titchener was one such student, and the lab he ran at Cornell, dedicated to promoting his elementalist psychological theory of "structuralism," was one of the largest in America at the time.[8] Titchener is also notable for his role in disseminating Wundt's introspective experimental methods to the English-speaking world, which methodology grounded Titchener's own theory. Thus Titchener argued that psychology properly understood is the study of consciousness, or the stream of human mental experiences, from the point of view of the experiencing agent.[9] Moreover, this stream of experiences can be resolved into certain delimited kinds of basic elements, and this resolution, and the study of the elements themselves, is and must be through introspective analysis. "[W]ithin the sphere of psychology," Titchener wrote in his *Outline of Psychology*, "introspection is the final and only court of appeal."[10]

---

6 Also hugely important to the "founding" of modern psychology was William James's *Principles of Psychology*, published in 1890 (New York: Dover, 1950). Notably, James briefly visited Wundt's lab prior to the publication of the *Principles*.

7 For a record of Wundt's students, see Miles Tinker, "Wundt's Doctorate Students and Their Theses 1875–1920," *American Journal of Psychology* 44.4 (1932): 630–37.

8 Titchener received his Ph.D from Wundt in 1892. He is sometimes said to have founded the Cornell lab. In fact, he took over a lab founded by Frank Angell, a fellow student from Leipzig.

9 According to Titchener (*Lectures*, 16), "mind" is the "sum-total of mental processes." "Consciousness," when used properly, is synonymous with "mind" in this sense. (Titchener rejects using "consciousness" to indicate "something more than mind," e.g. the Lockean "perception of what passes in a man's own mind," on the grounds that to talk of "the mind's awareness of itself" has misleading homuncular implications.) However, for ease of argument Titchener further stipulates that "consciousness" refers to "present" mental experiences, i.e., "the sum-total of mental processes occurring *now*" (18–19). Also important, Titchener claimed that psychological explanations cannot be wholly descriptive. Mental experiences must ultimately get parallel physiological ones (see e.g. 36–41). For his more nuanced taxonomy of psychology, see Edward Titchener, "The Postulates of a Structural Psychology," *Philosophical Review* 7.5 (1898): 449–65.

10 Edward Titchener, *An Outline of Psychology* (New York: MacMillan, 1896), 341. Titchener added with futile optimism, "On this point all psychologists would be agreed."

Titchener was not, however, a perfect disciple of Wundt. As is better appreciated now, he skewed Wundt's theory to his own ends insofar as he concealed or downplayed anti-elementalist and anti-sociological components of Wundt's psychology as well as Wundt's own strict limitations on introspection[11] (Wundt rejected that introspection was the exclusive and ultimate court of appeal for psychology).[12] Still, Wundt did defend introspection; and this shared methodology is important.

In the first place, methodology helps explain Titchener's easy appropriation of *Einfühlung* from, we presume, Theodor Lipps. Titchener actually never clearly explained whose theory of *Einfühlung* he had in view or exactly why he chose the term "empathy," but Lipps was the preeminent German proponent of *Einfühlung*, and Titchener would have known this. Moreover, Titchener and Lipps shared a fundamental methodology. Thus, although Lipps was not a student of Wundt, Lipps also relied on introspective principles in developing his theory of *Einfühlung* to explain aesthetic pleasure.[13] In fact, Lipps claimed that aesthetics was a part of psychology precisely because he believed aesthetics, and by definition also the experience of *Einfühlung*, could be studied

---

[11] Two excellent essays by Kurt Danziger articulate these points: (on introspection) "The History of Introspection Reconsidered," *Journal of the History of the Behavioral Sciences* 16 (1980): 241–62; and (on Titchener's misleading portrayal of Wundt's antielementalist social psychology) "The Positivist Repudiation of Wundt," *Journal of the History of the Behavioral Sciences* 15 (1979): 205–30.

[12] Wundt defined "folk or ethnic" psychology in the introduction to his very first book, *Contributions toward a Theory of Sense Perception*, published in 1862 (*Beiträge zur Theorie der Sinneswahrnehmung* [Leipzig: Winter]). He clarified the concept in his more famous *Principles of Physiological Psychology* (*Grundzüge der physiologischen Psychologie* [Leipzig: Engelmann, 1874]). Moreover, he devoted the end of his career to his ten-volume *Volkerpsychologie* (Cultural or ethnic psychology) (Leipzig: Engelmann, 1900–1909). It is thus absurd that Titchener claimed social psychology was not at the heart of Wundt's interests, a distortion that was perpetuated by Titchener's student Edward Boring in his *A History of Psychology*, first published in 1929 and reprinted in a new edition with great success in 1950 (New York: Appeton-Century-Crofts, 1950). Indeed, as a few contemporary historians have pointed out, it is less Titchener's distortion and more the fame of Boring's book, which was for decades the standard history of the subject, that directly contributed to almost a century of misunderstanding of Wundt, at least in Anglo-Saxon circles.

[13] At least one prominent historian of psychology, David Hothersall, has mistakenly said otherwise; see his *History of Psychology* (Philadelphia: Temple University Press, 1984), 87. Perhaps Hothersall was misled by the fact that Wundt did supervise the dissertation of a different Lipps—Gottlob Friedrich Lipps—in 1888.

experimentally,[14] and, in particular, through "internal" experiments involving "the free presentation to oneself of all kinds of experiences, the internal variation, the addition of parts, and also abstraction," all of which is made possible by introspection.[15] Unsurprisingly, then, Titchener articulated "empathy" as a kind of introspective mental experience—a kinesthetic one to be exact—that we have upon observing certain kinds of objects or action, especially affective human expressions: "Not only do I see gravity and modesty and pride and courtesy and stateliness, *but I feel or act them in the mind's muscles*. This is, I suppose, a simple case of empathy, if we may coin that term as a rendering of *Einfühlung*; there is nothing curious or idiosyncratic about it; but it is a fact that must be mentioned."[16] Of course, many others were curious about this phenomenon. And Titchener's blasé tone foreshadows his eventual obscurity on the subject. The passage also suggests Titchener had an impoverished understanding of the German literature on *Einfühlung*. At a minimum, given that Lipps articulated several forms of *Einfühlung*, Titchener's narrow concept of "empathy" indicates he didn't well understand Lipps's theory even if he was familiar with it. Moreover, Titchener sometimes used "sympathy" synonymously alongside

---

14 "Aesthetics," Lipps wrote, "is either psychological aesthetics or it is the statement about the requirement of individual taste, accidental mood, or fashion. It is psychological aesthetics or it is a sum of declarations of an individual who possess a sufficiently loud voice to show his private enthusiasms [or fancies] or his dependence on fashion to its best advantage" ("Psychologie und Aesthetik," *Archiv für die gesamte Psychologie* 9 [1907]: 91–116, at 111–12). I originally learned of this quote from a translation in John Fizer, *Psychologism and Psychoaesthetics: A Historical and Critical View of Their Relations* [Amsterdam: John Benjamins, 1981], 224 n. 15. However, after a careful copyeditor to this chapter noted that Fizer's own citation is to a nonexistent p. 117, I conferred with my colleague Hoke Robinson over the original. He discovered the true location of the quote and supplied me with the translation I've used, and for this help I am deeply grateful.

15 Theodor Lipps, *Leitfaden der Pscyhologie*, 3rd ed. (Leipzig: Engelmann, 1909 [1903]), 58; trans. in Danziger, "History of Introspection," 253.

16 Titchener, *Lectures*, 21; first emphasis added. Curiously, there is evidence that Titchener had already started using "empathy" in this context at least a year prior to its use in the *Lectures* (which were delivered in March 1909 and published in November the same year). Thus, in his 1908 review of "German Philosophy in 1907," Oscar Ewald notes that Titchener had suggested, perhaps privately to him, using "empathy" as a translation of *Einfühlung* in his comments on recent work on the subject, instead of Ewald's preferred "sympathy" (407). I have not been able to chase up this curiosity further, but doubt it would prove conceptually illuminating.

"empathy" in his *Lectures*, further confusing his usage. Granted, as already mentioned, Titchener didn't explain his source for the concept of *Einfühlung*.[17] So it is possible Titchener assumed *Einfühlung* to have a generalized meaning, as opposed to being especially owed to Lipps.[18] But this doesn't help restore Titchener's reputation, given that at this point *Einfühlung* did not, in fact, have a generalized meaning in German circles, if ever it did.[19] I'll return to substantiate this point in the next section. But first, a last point on introspection is worth noting.

Both Titchener's and Lipps's work was eventually eclipsed, but to different degrees. In Titchener's case the fade was swift, nearly total, and lasting. And his reliance on introspection is largely to blame. The fin de siècle boom of positivism (which, ironically, Titchener himself espoused), the associated rise of behaviorism, and certain discoveries related to imageless thought, the unconscious, and animal psychology, all told relatively immediately against an assertion of the principled authority of one's own inner awareness of his or her mental states for establishing reliable, duplicable psychological experimental data.[20] Titchener's work thus floundered as soon as he could no longer personally defend it. Even bracketing this general eclipse, however, Titchener had almost no substantive impact on the development of empathy theory in particular. This is borne out by the relative dearth of attention paid to him on the psychology of empathy, substantively or

---

17 This is not always well observed in conceptual histories of empathy. See e.g. the entry on "Sympathy and Empathy" by Lauren Wispé in the *International Encyclopedia of the Social Sciences* (Detroit: MacMillan, 1968, 441–47); republished online, Encyclopedia.com, 2014. Wispé doesn't explicitly attribute Lipps as Titchener's source, but she implies it.

18 Titchener certainly knew of Lipps's work, occasionally citing him, including in the *Lectures*. But (1) he does not cite Lipps as a source of his idea of "empathy"; (2) a review of Titchener's various indexes of names and subjects, both in the *Lectures* and his other works, does not suggest a great interest in Lipps; and (3) by the time Titchener used the term there was already a vigorous body of German literature on *Einfühlung*, including some discussion by Wundt. See also Jahoda, "Theodor Lipps and the Shift."

19 Compare Jørgen Hunsdahl, "Concerning Einfühlung (Empathy); A Concept Analysis of Its Origin and Early Development," *Journal of the History of the Behavioral Sciences* 3 (1967): 180–91; Pigman, "Freud and the History of Empathy"; Jahoda, "Theodor Lipps and the Shift"; and Juliet Koss, "On the Limits of Empathy," *Art Bulletin* 88 (2006): 139–57.

20 For an excellent discussion of this point, see Danziger, "Positivist Repudiation of Wundt."

nominally, either by his contemporaries or those who came after.[21] Titchener introduced the word, and little more. Correspondingly, we too shall pay little more attention to him.

Lipps's case, however, is more complicated.[22] Speaking generally, the story resembles Titchener's. Lipps was arguably the principal player in the broad flurry of late nineteenth-century German research on *Einfühlung*, which flurry ended rather suddenly around the turn of the century, and once again largely as a result of the diminished interest in introspective methodology in a burgeoning climate of experimental psychology. Thus recall Lipps's own invitation to draw aesthetics into the fold of experimental psychology through introspective study. The implication was the ability to generalize claims about aesthetic value from the reports of individual "internal" reports—that is, to make objective claims about aesthetic value based on the armchair reflection of the theorist. But actual laboratory study on the basis of such reports, which was definitional to experimental psychology, contradicted this expectation. Experiments indicated both varying reports by the same observer in response to the same objects and wide differences between individual observers within groups, which results seemed to confound the aspiration to explain objective aesthetic value—at least from a psychological perspective. This as much as anything probably explains why most contemporary general histories of psychology take little or no notice of Lipps, despite the great praise he received in his own day by the reputed fathers of this new discipline.[23]

---

21 The terminology of "empathy" did catch on quickly in Anglo-American aesthetics. However, Titchener's influence here was at best nominal. For example, although it is certain that the famous aesthetician Vernon Lee (a.k.a. Violet Piaget) adopted the term "empathy" from Titchener in her own translations of *Einfühlung*, her own diary entries make it clear that substantively it was Lipps, Wundt, and other German theorists of *Einfühlung*, who influenced Lee. Titchener had a similarly nominal influence on dramatic theory; see George Gunkle, "Empathy: Implications for Theatre Research," *Educational Theatre Journal* 15.1 (1963): 15–23.

22 The following remarks owe much to Koss's excellent "Limits of Empathy," on the history of "empathy" in modern aesthetics.

23 Wundt, James, and Freud all highly praised Lipps. Yet several prominent general histories of psychology barely notice him, like Boring, *A History*; Hothersall, *History of Psychology*; and George Mandler, *A History of Modern Experimental Psychology: From James and Wundt to Cognitive*

On the other hand, some particularities of Lipps's life and work complicate his historical legacy, and demand a broader evaluation of his influence. Most important, Lipps posited multiple forms of *Einfühlung*, including an interpersonal form that he elaborated into an answer to the general epistemological problem of other minds (the problem of how we know that there are other "minded" creatures besides ourselves, and what this knowledge consists in).[24] Such richer, more subtle, and in a word more philosophical elements of Lipps's work on *Einfühlung* had more lasting influence than Titchener's trite treatment of "empathy." This longevity is most notable in psychoanalysis and phenomenology. The former influence, which can't be expanded here, is due to Lipps's underappreciated direct influence on Freud (an oversight that goes hand in hand with a general neglect of the import of empathy in Freudian theory).[25] Lipps's influence on early phenomenology was even greater and bears special relevance for our study. Lipps himself trained several early phenomenologists, including Adolf Reinach. For a time Lipps even participated in the "Munich Circle," one of the first phenomenological societies, which also included another prominent early phenomenologist, Max Scheler. Scheler later departed to Göttingen, where he met his informal student Edith Stein, and both went on to write

---

Science (Cambridge, MA: MIT Press, 2006). Hothersall also incorrectly places him in Wundt's lab (see n. 13).

24 To be fair, some aspects of Titchener's descriptions of empathy suggest he may have had something of Lipps's interpersonal form in view. But even if he did, he ran it together with Lipps's more straightforwardly kinesthetically based aesthetic form of *Einfühlung*.

25 Anglo-American students of Freud might easily miss this, given that the Standard Edition of Freud translates *Einfühlung* as "empathy" only about half the time, and never does so in a clinical context, despite Freud's emphasis on *Einfühlung* as a necessary condition for correctly judging when to begin treatment. See esp. Pigman, "Freud and the History of Empathy," 246. Thus, according to Freud, clinicians should begin "making communications to the patient" only when a proper "rapport" is established, which in turn is only established by taking up the standpoint of "*Einfühlung*" (Sigmund Freud, "On Beginning the Treatment [Further Recommendations on the Technique of Psycho-Analysis I]," in *The Standard Edition of the Complete Psychological Works of Sigmund Freud*, vol. 12, trans. and ed. James Strachey [London: Hogarth Press, 1958 (1913)], 121–44, at 139–40). Now by this point Freud clearly was using *Einfühlung* in a particular way, namely, as a process by which one puts oneself, unconsciously or consciously, into the place or viewpoint of another. Strachey, however, in the *Standard Edition*, translates this standpoint as one of "sympathetic understanding," a translation that is bound to mislead both casual and trained readers.

major treatises on sympathy and empathy, in which Lipps's concept of *Einfühlung* was closely critiqued. Central to these critiques was Lipps's application of *Einfühlung* to the classic epistemological problem of other minds. This is doubly remarkable. In the first place, although I've framed my own inquiry into the relation between "sympathy" and "empathy" around a decidedly *practical* theme—namely, as a part of a broader puzzle in moral and political philosophy about the nature of interpersonal recognition—it is worth noting that practical philosophy wasn't the principal source for the contemporary revival of interest in empathy. This credit goes to theoretical philosophy. Thus, it is primarily within the context of the problem of other minds that empathy (and by extension sympathy) first reemerged in the contemporary Anglo-American scene, namely as a central point in the relatively recent debate between so called Theory Theories and Simulation Theories of "mind reading." In this debate empathy has figured prominently in attempts to explicate and vindicate so-called folk psychology, or our ability to interpret and predict the behavior of others as *minded* creatures. Second (and ironically given the history I've just related), it is remarkable that for nearly two decades of this contemporary mind reading debate the main players almost totally neglected the long tradition of phenomenological investigation into the problem of other minds.[26] Thankfully, this neglect is now being remedied, and in turn, Stein and Scheler (among others in the phenomenological tradition) are getting better recognition. Perhaps Lipps will too.

2. Muddy Waters

"[I]s is hard to imagine," George Pigman remarked in his recent excellent analysis of empathy in Freudian theory, "the prominence of *Einfühlung*

---

26 But see Dan Zahavi's recent "Empathy," which is an excellent overview of the phenomenological discussion of empathy. And around the same time Vittorio Gallese (one of the discovers of so-called mirror neurons; see n. 68) started to cite Lipps as a forerunner of Simulation Theory. But before that, as the debate between Simulation Theory and Theory Theory went on from the mid '80s through the '90s, no one was seriously looking at phenomenological theory.

in aesthetics and psychology at the end of the nineteenth and beginning of the twentieth century."[27] He is right, too, as is evident from even a cursory review of the period, albeit, as I said, this blast of research fanned out relatively suddenly.[28] Pigman's remark, however, is not meant as mere description. It is a warning against too-simple-to-be-true accounts of the origin and meaning of *Einfühlung* and "empathy" (indeed, Pigman corrects a few such accounts himself).[29] For, the usual corollary to such energetic scholarship is the diffusion of meaning; and turn-of-the-century scholarship on *Einfühlung* and empathy was no exception. Indeed, both concepts became blurred almost upon introduction.

Einfühlung first came to the fore in German aesthetics after Robert Vischer introduced the term in 1873, following the then hugely influential Hermann Lotze (Lotze used the verb form *einfühlen*, as had, even earlier, the German romantic Johann Herder).[30] Lotze and Vischer instantly bred a lively industry of scholarship on *Einfühlung*, which flurry of work provoked an equally quick expansion in meaning.[31] Vischer himself was party to this expansion, having introduced *Einfühlung* alongside a set of closely related concepts including *Anfühlung* (attentive feeling), *Nachfühlung* (responsive feeling), and *Zufühlung* (immediate feeling)—and all in explicit addition to *Mitfühlung* or "sympathy."[32] When Lipps joined this milieu a few years later he further

---

27 Pigman, "Freud and the History of Empathy," 237.

28 Pigman himself notes a 1911 article that listed 161 different scholarly articles and books ("Freud and the History of Empathy," 237). The article is by the phenomenologist Moritz Geiger, who also wrote in psychology and aesthetics, which is telling. For Pigman might well have added phenomenology alongside aesthetics and psychology, given how often the three fields initially intertwined, in part due to shared interest in *Einfühlung*.

29 It also reminds us to pay careful attention to these moments, if for no other reason than to avoid mistakes about their origin. Pigman documents a few such mistakes in his own footnotes (see e.g. "Freud and the History of Empathy," 237).

30 This was in Vischer's doctoral thesis. See Robert Vischer, "On the Optical Sense of Form: A Contribution to Aesthetics," in *Empathy, Form, and Space: Problems in German Aesthetics, 1873–1893*, ed. Harry Francis Mallgrave and Eleftherios Ikonomou (Santa Monica, CA: Getty Center, 1994), 89–123.

31 See Koss, "Limits of Empathy."

32 For more on this historical moment, see Zahavi, "Empathy." Zahavi points out that Scheler would later try to play off Vischer's same "distinctions" (among others), but arguably not consistently and thus at the cost of obfuscating his already delicate sense of *Einfühlung*.

complicated matters by offering at least four types of *Einfühlung*, all of which, it seems, could be "positive" or "negative."[33] Moreover, Lipps failed to draw a neat distinction with sympathy (which Lipps did not, by contrast with Vischer, always render as *Mitfühlung*). Indeed, Lipps often used the two terms synonymously[34]—a conflation, by the way, Titchener replicated when he introduced "empathy." In any event, the proliferation of meaning was so quick that as early as 1898 the pioneering German psychologist and philosopher William Stern (who invented the "intelligence quotient" or IQ), felt compelled to object to the "paradoxical" and "slogan"-like character of the term *Einfühlung*.

It was into this swamp that Titchener dropped "empathy." As already noted, Titchener's own musings on empathy/*Einfühlung* didn't influence many in a substantive way. However, his translation did. Thus by 1932 Gardner Murphy (later elected president of the American Psychological Association) was able to say, speaking mostly with reference to English-language scholarship, that "*Einfühlung* (empathy)" had come into "general psychological use." And yet, as one might expect, the addition of "empathy" only added complication. Three years after Murphy's pronouncement, the prominent psychoanalyst Theodor Reik complained about the ever-expanding taxonomy of meanings for "empathy," a complaint that was retrospectively confirmed in 1957 by famed Gestalt researcher Abraham Luchins, who, in reviewing the intermediate years, declared that "empathy" had become so thin, "[c]onsideration of the status of the construct of empathy first requires *stipulation* of its meaning." Luchins first noted three primary uses that the "new" term "empathy" was alternatively used to pick out: (1) a kind of interpersonal "understanding," (2) an "awareness" of emotional qualities of objects and events, or (3) the process by which this "understanding" or "awareness" comes about. He then quickly added a jumble of further explicit theoretical candidates, covering everything from Lipps's own

---

33 See Hunsdahl, "Concerning Einfühlung."
34 See also Jahoda, "Theodor Lipps and the Shift."

notion of inner motor imitation to early sociological models of sympathy from William McDougall and George Mead, to Gestalt psychological concepts of "direct perception of emotions," to the doctrine of *Verstehen* offered by Wilhelm Dilthey and Eduard Spranger, to Freud's psychoanalytic distinction between a kind of "genuine" empathy and a process of "identification" (albeit Luchins also noted that "some psychologists use identification as synonymous with empathy"). And presumably this list is only illustrative. Without unreasonably bending his explicitly social psychological perspective, we might well add John Stuart Mill, Herbert Spencer, and Charles Cooley from the Anglo-Saxon tradition, and Théodule Ribot, Max Scheler, and Edith Stein from the European one.[35]

To reiterate, however, the point of the foregoing historical review is *not* that nothing of conceptual value can be discerned in such muddy waters. The point is that whatever is extracted, namely, the nature of empathy/*Einfühlung*, can't be generalized to the time period. It must speak for itself and in light of independent considerations and interests we have now, from our current vantage point looking back.

On that note, jump to the relative present and the social psychologist Lauren Wispé's distinction between sympathy and empathy: "Empathy, unlike sympathy, denotes an active referent. In empathy one attends to the feelings of another; in sympathy one attends to the suffering of another, but the feelings are one's own. In empathy I try to feel your pain. In sympathy I know you are in pain, and I sympathize with you, but I feel my sympathy and my pain, not your anguish and your pain."[36] Now compare Wispé's definition to another prominent recent suggestion from the philosopher Stephen Darwall. "Sympathetic concern or sympathy," Darwall writes, is

> a feeling or emotion that (a) responds to some apparent threat or obstacle to an individual's good or well-being, (b) has that individual

---

[35] For more on the British scene at roughly the same period, see chapter 10 in this volume.
[36] Wispé, "Sympathy and Empathy."

himself as object, and (c) involves concern for him, and thus for his well-being, for his sake. Seeing the child on the verge of falling, one is concerned for his safety, not just for its (his safety's) sake, but for his sake. One is concerned for him. Sympathy for the child is a way of caring for (and about) him.... Sympathy differs in this respect from several distinct psychological phenomena usually collected under the term 'empathy' which need not involve such concern.[37]

Whatever their differences, there are some striking convergences between Wispé and Darwall. First, with respect to sympathy, both clearly if only generally associate sympathy with negatively valenced emotions. Sympathy, when we feel it as spectators, is primarily directed at the suffering or pain of another person (some actor). Empathy, by contrast, doesn't clearly have this generic constraint, according to Wispé and Darwall (thus making "empathy" prima facie closer to what Hume and Adam Smith said of "sympathy," namely that it was a "fellow-feeling with any passion whatever").[38] Second, and still regarding sympathy, for both Wispé and Darwall, the suffering of the other (what we might call the object emotion) is not the only affect or emotion felt by the spectator. Instead, sympathy involves some *further* feeling of care or concern—some proactive motivational affect—directed at the object emotion or the person expressing it. In other words, to put it crudely, "sympathy = empathy + care." Darwall is admittedly more explicit about this, but in her later writing Wispé would essentially and more clearly press the same point.[39]

But my real interest isn't this agreement about sympathy. Instead, I introduce these contemporary viewpoints for what they suggest about one possible conception of empathy. Both Wispé and Darwall identify as a distinguishing feature of "empathy" some kind of direct attention

---
37 Stephen Darwall, "Empathy, Sympathy, Care," *Philosophical Studies* 89.2–3 (1998): 261–82, at 261.
38 That is how Smith famously defined sympathy, anyway, at the outset of *The Theory of Moral Sentiments*.
39 Wispé, "Distinction between sympathy and empathy."

to or regard for the other (or at least her experiences) *as* other; that is, unburdened by any motivational care *for* or interest *in* the other or her experiences. Empathy, in this sense, is thus potentially primary with respect to sympathy. Empathy is the awareness of, or attention to, or participation in, the emotions and experiences of others prior to, or at least in distinction from, any attitude we take *toward* those emotions or the actors who express them, whether that attitude be the peculiar caring of sympathy or anything else. Thus Darwall later elaborates: "[In empathy] it is the *other's* standpoint that is salient, in this case, the child's as he faces the prospect of falling down the well. Empathy consists in feeling what one imagines he feels, or perhaps should feel (fear, say), or in some imagined copy of these feelings, whether one comes thereby to be concerned for the child or not."[40] Thus Darwall, like Wispé, highlights a peculiar focus on the other as a distinguishing feature of empathy. In doing so, both authors turn out to follow a thread that, as we will see, runs continuously through the twisted path from *Einfühlung* to empathy, and even pulls together the *Einfühlung*-empathy narrative with turn-of-the-century theorizing about sympathy. Admittedly, it is a rather thin thread, with substantive differences dividing all the accounts in question. On the other hand, there are no thick threads here. Moreover, it would be a mistake to confuse thinness with import. As I said at the outset, for anyone invested in liberal or egalitarian ideals, there is a morally urgent need to explicate the nature of interpersonal recognition, especially the sense in which individuals are recognized *as* individuals. And now it seems that at least part of this explanation lies in the empathy-sympathy knot.

Before moving on, however, I must place a marker. Anyone remotely familiar with the literature on sympathy and empathy will recognize at once that Darwall, in virtue of rendering empathy as a process of imaginative perspective taking, aligns himself with a "simulationist" theory of the phenomena in question—that is, with that camp which claims

---

40 Darwall, "Empathy, Sympathy, Care," 261, emphasis added.

that our knowledge, understanding, recognition, and so on, of the mental states of other minded beings depends on using "the resources of [our] own minds to simulate" the mental states of that other being.[41] This is hardly a new or minority view. Adam Smith appears to distinguish his theory of sympathy from Hume's precisely on simulationist grounds, and ever since many have seen fit to situate their theories using a similar distinction, whether they label it "sympathy," "empathy," or anything else. A relevant exception, however, is the field of phenomenology. Many in this tradition will not wish to explain empathy in this way, for reasons that will become clearer later.

3. AESTHETIC *EINFÜHLUNG*: A CLOSER LOOK AT LIPPS

As already noted, Lipps postulated more than one kind of *Einfühlung*, and it isn't especially clear how they all relate. I will limit myself in this section to the primary form that he used to explain aesthetic experience. This "aesthetic" *Einfühlung* combines two innate psychological "instincts" or "impulses": projection and motor mimicry or imitation. The result is a mechanistic process of "inner imitation" (though Lipps later regretted that description), whereby we project our own kinesthetic feelings aroused by some object we are attending to, that is, through the instinctive imitation, back *into* that object—whether that object be Baryshnikov leaping across the stage or Rodin's *Le penseur* frozen in contemplation or even the flying buttresses of a basilica.[42]

Exactly how Lipps arrived at his initial views is not clear. Given that he translated Hume's *Treatise of Human Nature* into German, one wonders if something of Hume's mechanistic theory of sympathy impressed Lipps. But if Hume's influence on Lipps is unexplored scholarly

---
41 Martin Davies and Tony Stone, eds., *Mental Simulation* (Oxford: Blackwell, 1995), 3.
42 Lipps gives a concise explanation of his view in, "Empathy, Inner Imitation, and Sense Feelings (*Einfühlung, innere Nachahmung, und Organempfindungen*)," *Archiv für die gesamte Psychologie* 1 (1903), trans. Max Schertel and Melvin Rader, in *A Modern Book of Esthetics*, 5th ed., ed. Rader (Holt, Rinehart, and Winston: New York, 1979), 371–78. For more on Lipps's second thoughts about the description "inner imitation," see Jahoda, "Theodor Lipps and the Shift."

terrain, a point of consensus is that Lipps closely followed the German art historian, Robert Vischer.[43] Vischer also distinguished *Einfühlung* as an imitative process conjoined to some kind of instinctual projection. In his words, a spectator unconsciously displaces "its own bodily form—and thereby also the soul—into the form of the object."[44] Moreover, and crucially, Vischer and Lipps both assert that the end result of the imitative-projective process (which is not yet aesthetic experience) is a psychological identification with the object (which identification is at least partly aesthetic experience; namely, as we will see in a moment, what Lipps calls the "grounds" of aesthetic experience). Lipps, in particular, emphasized this identification. He also insisted that this identification is constituted by an essentially subjective experience. Thus, he contrasted it to, on the one hand, what we perceive to be in the object, like color; and, on the other hand, what we perceive to be in our bodies, like hunger. As Lipps puts it, "the doing or the activity, the endeavor, the striving, the succeeding, that I feel [in *Einfühlung*]. These belong to the ego; more than that, they are the ego or constitute it: I feel *myself* active."[45]

For example, suppose you observe someone stretching out her arm. According to Lipps you are innately disposed to imitate this movement. Now, you may do so deliberately, by actually stretching out your own arm. In this case you have two representations: on the one hand

---

43 Evidence suggests that Lipps began by "reworking" a set of notes and index to a translation of *Treatise* book 1, made by an Else Koettgen. This seems to have grown into a translation of the entire Treatise. Thus a translation of books 2 and 3, published in 1906 by Lipps, *Hume's Traktat über die menschliche Natur (Treatise on [sic!] human nature)* (Hamburg: Leopold Voss, 1906), is described as "based on a translation by Mrs. J. Bona Meyer" (who was, incidentally, the professor at Bonn under whom Lipps wrote his habilitation). This edition was reviewed by Paul Wuest in "Zu Theodor Lipps' Neuausgabe seiner deutschen Bearbeitung von Hume's Treatise of Human Nature," *Kant-Studien* 14 (1909): 249–73. In 1973 the whole translation was edited (by Reinhard Brandt, a well-known Kant scholar at Marburg) and republished by Philosophische Bibliothek (Hamburg) under the title *David Hume, Ein Traktat über die menschliche Natur (A Treatise on [sic!] human nature)*. ,which presumably means this translation, at least *mostly* by Lipps, is still the standard in German. (For tracking down this information, I am deeply indebted to my colleague Hoke Robinson.)

44 Robert Vischer, *Ueber das optische Formgefühl: Ein Beitrag zur Aesthetik* (Leipzig: Credner, 1873), translated by Jahoda in "Theodor Lipps and the Shift," 7.

45 Lipps, "Empathy, Inner Imitation, and Sense Feelings," 373.

you have some impression or "mental image" of what the person is doing (through observation) combined with some knowledge (based on your experience) of the other person's experience of her arm stretching (some sense of her "freedom" and "pride" of action, Lipps says); and on the other hand you also experience your own movement and feel your own "activity," "freedom," "pride."[46] But this complex—this "opposition" of representations—is not *Einfühlung*. In *Einfühlung*, "this opposition is absolutely done away with. The two are simply one.... And it is just because of this that I feel myself performing this movement in the other's movement."[47] Thus, in a case of observing a person stretching out her arm, to imitate *inwardly* is to experience a sense of activity or "striving" as part and parcel of the experience of observation. That is, as Gustav Jahoda helpfully interprets Lipps, you experience "a feeling of effort without actually moving."[48] But again, you don't experience this imitation consciously, as if it were "inward." You project this kinesthetic feeling back onto the object you are observing (in this case the person stretching her arm). Lipps writes with a flourish:

> In a word, I am now with my feeling of activity entirely and wholly *in* the moving figure. Even spatially, if we can speak of the spatial extent of the ego, I am in its [the figure's] place. I am transported into it. I am, so far as my consciousness is concerned, entirely and wholly identical with it. Thus feeling myself active in the observed human figure, I feel also in it free, facile, proud. This is esthetic imitation and it is at the same time esthetic empathy [*Einfühlung*].[49]

Notice the qualitative elaboration in the penultimate sentence, already foreshadowed in the description of outward imitation. What begins as a claim about the inner imitation of the observed movement per se,

---

46 Lipps, "Empathy, Inner Imitation, and Sense Feelings," 375.
47 Lipps, "Empathy, Inner Imitation, and Sense Feelings," 375.
48 Jahoda, "Theodor Lipps and the Shift," 155.
49 Lipps, "Empathy, Inner Imitation, and Sense Feelings," 375, emphasis added.

becomes a much thicker emotive description, one that is laden with positive value connotations: free, facile (i.e., easy and successful), proud. From this one senses how Lipps will arrive at a neat explanation of aesthetic pleasure—which explanation could in turn be conjoined straightforwardly to a theory about judgments of beauty. For such feelings—the freedom, ease, achievement, pride—are not only prima facie pleasing but also identical with the projected experience. Thus the object is perceived *as* pleasing.

Two elaborations of the general idea are worth mentioning. First, *Einfühlung* theories stand as a counterpoint to romantic conceptions of sympathy, like those expressed by Herder, wherein it was suggested that aesthetic experience involved something closer to a real (i.e., metaphysical as opposed to psychological) union with external objects, both animate and inanimate. Or at least, Lipps clearly intended *Einfühlung* this way.[50] Thus Lipps argued explicitly that whatever we feel through the inner imitation of *Einfühlung* was but the grounds of aesthetic experience. The aesthetic object (the object of the aesthetic experience) is, by contrast, an *expression* of these psychological grounds, that is, of *Einfühlung*. Indeed, Lipps asserted that the connection between *Einfühlung* and *Ausdruck*, or "expression," is definitional. As Lipps puts it, in *Einfühlung* we "press out" our feelings onto external objects. The aesthetic object thus ends up "an ex-pression, an out- pressing, a squeezing out, as of grapes to make wine." Hence, "[i]n aesthetic experience, a sensuous object distinct from me 'expresses' [*ausdruckt*] something interior or soul-like."[51] Ultimately, then, and contra romantic views, the object of aesthetic experience remains the aesthetic object itself, which

---

50 There is disagreement about whether Vischer was opposed to such panpsychist aesthetics. In "Theodor Lipps and the Shift," Jahoda suggests Vischer had his own romantic "flights." But David Depew argues the other way persuasively ("Empathy, Psychology, and Aesthetics: Reflections on a Repair Concept," *Poroi* 4.1 [2005]: 99–107). Either way, Jahoda unfortunately glosses over the same question for Lipps.

51 Theodore Lipps, *Aesthetik: Die ästhetische Betrachtung und die bidende Kunst* (Hamburg: Voss, 1906), trans. Depew in "Empathy, Psychology, and Aesthetics," 1. I follow Depew here in stressing the connection between *Einfühlung* and *Ausdruck* for Lipps.

we contemplate from a suitable "distance."[52] There is no metaphysical implication to *Einfühlung*.

Second, although Lipps initially ran together his description of *Einfühlung* with his account of aesthetic pleasure, he later distinguished "natural" *Einfühlung* as the basic process of imitation and projection prior to any felt pleasure.[53] Correspondingly, Lipps also later clarified that not all *Einfühlung* was pleasing. So what exactly are the conditions under which *Einfühlung* is pleasing? It would be misleading to suggest Lipps provides a clear answer to this crucial question. Roughly, he seems to suggest that what one can inwardly imitate in some sense "successfully" or "easily" gives pleasure; otherwise discomfort. The question thus becomes what constitutes or conditions "easy" or "successful" imitation? But to this question, Lipps seems to offer different answers. Sometimes Lipps seems to imply a physiologically reductive possibility. This presumably stems from Vischer, who argued, for example, that spectators feel physical discomfort while looking at a single vertical line on a blank page. "A horizontal line is pleasing because the eyes are positioned horizontally," he declared, whereas a "vertical line, by contrast, can be disturbing when perceived in isolation for... it contradicts the binocular structure of the perceiving eyes and forces them to function in a more complicated way."[54] This characterization would get picked on later, but in any event was overshadowed by two other explanations Lipps discusses at greater length.

On the one hand, Lipps postulates a third psychic drive behind *Einfühlung*, in addition to projection and imitation. "In the instinctive urge of *self-activity*," he writes, "lies its ultimate base."[55] However, Lipps

---

52 Lipps, "Empathy, Inner Imitation, and Sense Feelings." See also Depew, "Empathy, Psychology, and Aesthetics."
53 Eric Schliesser argues that a similar conflation can be found in Smith's account, in "The Piacular, or on Seeing Oneself as a Moral Cause in Adam Smith," in *Contemporary Perspectives on Early Modern Philosophy: Nature and Norms in Thought*, vol. 29, ed. M. Lenz and A. Waldow (Dordrecht, Netherlands: Springer, 2013), 159–77.
54 Vischer, "On the Optical Sense of Form," 97.
55 Lipps, "Empathy, Inner Imitation, and Sense Feelings," 376.

immediately adds that it is equally psychologically fundamental that this desire for self-activity can be satisfied by contemplating the object that stimulated the imitative process of *Einfühlung* in the first place; for example, by attending to another person's arm reaching, I can both "arouse" and satisfy an fundamental desire to *be* active. In saying so, Lipps seems to imply that some objects strike the mind with a clear idea of *productive* activity. That is, Lipps seems to be appealing to a normative notion of "activity," which itself turned on the idea of success. Or at least, reading Lipps this way yields a ready answer to the question, what conditions "easy" or "successful" imitation? For a given object, if the inward imitation itself suggests (is of) "successful" activity (understood broadly as activity that is itself easy, unencumbered, unobstructed, etc.), then these just are the objects we easily imitate, or imitate successfully. In turn, we will take pleasure in such objects and find them beautiful. By contrast, objects that can only be imitated through some kind of "frustrated" activity (understood broadly as activity that is impeded, awkward, unwilling, etc.) will be the ones we struggle to imitate, and in turn find painful and ugly. And this does indeed fit some of what Lipps says. Lipps thus offered examples like gazing on Doric columns: "The self-raising of the column is its 'proper activity.' Thereby the term activity is meant in its full sense: exertion, effort, use of force; a use of force that achieves something." Again, Jahoda helpfully interprets Lipps: "What we immediately and unreflectively perceive as its achievement, he alleged, is the carrying of its own weight and that of the wall it supports. In other words, we involuntarily arrive at a mechanical interpretation, and this, in turn, constitutes an analogy based on our personal experience of acting on our environment."[56] Lipps thus summarizes: "I *sympathize* [sympatisire] with the manner the Doric column behaves or testifies to an inner liveliness, because I recognize therein a natural mode of behavior of my own that gives me happiness. Thus, all pleasure produced by spatial forms, and we, can add, any kind

---

56 Jahoda, "Theodor Lipps and the Shift," 157–58.

of aesthetic pleasure, is a feeling of sympathy [Sympathiegefühl] that makes us happy."[57] The terminology of "sympathy" is striking here, and reminds us that Lipps was prone to using sympathy and *Einfühlung* synonymously. But it also hints at the second sense that Lipps seems to have offered to explain why some inner imitation is "easy" or "successful" and thus pleasurable.

Lipps explicitly distinguished a "positive" form of *Einfühlung* from a "negative" one on the basis of whether what has been "sensuously ascertained" in *Einfühlung* is in "agreement with my innermost nature" or a "negation" of it. This is admittedly cryptic. Worse, it arguably cuts against Lipps's aspiration to establish an objective account of aesthetic experience, insofar as it would prima facie seem to invite a relative standard for the "agreement" in question—unless Lipps was essentializing human nature, which doesn't seem to have been his intent. This worry aside, Lipps did sometimes explain "positive" *Einfühlung* less mysteriously as an "experience of harmony" with the object, and even allowed that this experience could for this reason be called "sympathetic *Einfühlung*" (with negative *Einfühlung* being an experience of discord).[58] Importantly, the harmony in question was psychic, in the sense of an "ego experience." It is a harmony between a "foreign" life and ego and my own life and ego—literally my own drives, needs, and sense of self. Lipps went so far as to identify cases of "full" positive *Einfühlung*, wherein the experience is the existence of a single "I."[59] His principal example was a case of having one's attention "spontaneously" and "wholly concentrated" on the movements of an acrobat. This is a more accessible, intuitive description. Certainly, most of us can think of experiences that we loosely call "empathy" and would describe (albeit reflectively) as

---

57 Theodor Lipps, *Raumästhetik und geometrisch-optische Täuschungen* (Leipzig: J. A. Barth, 1897); trans. Jahoda, "Theodor Lipps and the Shift," 158.
58 Lipps, *Aesthetik*, 21; trans. Jahoda, "Theodor Lipps and the Shift," 158–59.
59 Here I follow Hunsdahl, "Concerning *Einfühlung*," and his translated excerpts of Lipps, *Asthetik. Systematische Philosophie* (Liebzig: B.G. Teubner, 1908), 351–90, esp. 365.

marked by both total absorption and lacking a clear self-other distinction with the object in question. Thus while I suspect gazing upon Doric columns doesn't resonate with such an experience, the idea of being "lost" in the characters of a book or movie theater performance does. This armchair intuitive appeal, however, would not prove sufficient to give Lipps's view much staying power.

4. Interpersonal *Einfühlung*: The Phenomenological Twist

There are plenty of reasons to worry about Lipps's view. His descriptive appeal to the degree of contemplative absorption in the object as a means to help flesh out his account of the conditions for successful imitation sits uncomfortably with other normative elements he offered like his claim that it is an activity "in agreement with one's innermost nature." There is also the difficulty of trying to reconcile the aesthetic form of *Einfühlung* examined in the last section with the various other forms of *Einfühlung* Lipps posited—a difficulty most scholars describe pessimistically. Also recall that insofar as Lipps took himself to be articulating the principles of an objective aesthetics that is properly part of psychology, and thus amenable to empirical validation, his view failed miserably when put to laboratory tests by his contemporaries.

In addition to this heap of problems, Lipps's views were dealt a further blow by the rise of abstractionism in art and aesthetic theory in the early twentieth century. The whole story is complicated.[60] But insofar as *Einfühlung* is concerned, the essential chapter turns again on *why* imitation-to-projection produces pleasure. In particular, abstractionism was diametrically opposed to the idea that what is aesthetically pleasing is always easily imitated inwardly, as well as the tightly conjoined claim that easily imitated objects are those that we psychically

---

[60] I direct readers to Koss's excellent "Limits of Empathy," on which my summary here is closely based.

harmonize, or comfortably identify with, in projection. On the contrary, abstractionism was premised on the idea that there can be pleasure in estrangement or alienation from the objects we attend to, such that we don't easily imitate the object, let alone identify with it in a final act of "objectified self-enjoyment," as Lipps sometimes describes the result of aesthetic *Einfühlung*. Indeed, in its most sophisticated form abstractionism posited that some objects of contemplation please us because of their ability to make us feel estranged from ourselves. Thus Wilhelm Worringer, in his 1908 *Abstraction and Empathy* (not published in English until 1953) argued explicitly against the *Einfühlung* camp that it could not account for the aesthetic beauty of abstract art because it totally overlooked a "directly opposed" impulse, namely an "urge to abstraction."[61] Worringer further claimed that both the impulse towards *Einfühlung* (objectified self-enjoyment) and this countervailing impulse to abstraction arise out of a common, more fundamental human need, the "need for self-alienation."[62] Thus, he duly noted that Lipps himself had described *Einfühlung* as an identity with something external, and thus (in Lipps's words) a kind of "liberation" from the "real I" (Worringer quotes Lipps's 1906 *Aesthetik*). In any event, Worringer concludes that it is precisely the countervailing urge to abstraction that abstract art seeks to take advantage of.

As abstractionism strengthened and spread, *Einfühlung* theories weakened and contracted. By 1917, and almost half a century after Vischer presumed to explain why a simple vertical line is aesthetically displeasing, the Russian artist Olga Rozanova made a more symbolic argument for Worringer's same point: a small painting that consists only of a green vertical stripe on a white background. She declared, "We propose to liberate painting from its subservience to the ready-made forms of reality, and to make it first and foremost a creative,

---

61 Wilhelm Worringer, *Abstraction and Empathy* (Chicago: Ivan R. Dee, 1997), 14. (NB: the original German title is *Abstraktion und Einfühlung*.)
62 Worringer, *Abstraction and Empathy*, 23–25.

not a reproductive, art."[63] She might have said an "imitative" art, and really tugged the noose tight on the *Einfühlung* camp—whoever, that is, was still in it.

And yet Lipps's work continued to influence. As noted already, Lipps had an important effect on Freud, and through Freud on the development of psychoanalytic theory. Lipps's more explicitly psychological work seems to have impressed his peers, as evidenced in particular by a glowing review of his 1885 *Psychological Studies* by William James.[64] A later review of the same work (newly translated) also credits Lipps for influencing early Gestalt theory.[65] Even Lipps's aesthetic theory seems to have found a second life in Anglo-American dramatic theory, albeit only to suffer, under the guise of "empathy," a speedy dissent into ambiguity.[66] But even beyond these influences, Lipps's work became a central focus for two young phenomenologists, Max Scheler and especially Edith Stein. However, these phenomenologists had particular agendas. They were interested in what could be called interpersonal *Einfühlung*, which spun off Lipps's explicit address of what is now known as the problem of "other minds."

At the time, it was widely accepted within philosophy that our knowledge of other creatures as "minded" is based on an inference from analogy, namely to our experience as minded. According to Lipps, however, no such inference is justifiable as the foundation of such knowledge. For, on the one hand, such an inference would require a generic or general notion of self, but, on the other hand, prior to the experience of any other "self" we could have no such generic notion. There must be, at least initially, some experience of other minds that precedes such an analogy, by serving as the basis of a generalization or abstraction to a concept of "self." Thus enters *Einfühlung*, which, according to Lipps,

---

63 Olga Rozanova, "Extracts from Articles" (1918), in *Russian Art of the Avant-Garde: Theory and Criticism*, trans. and ed. John E. Bowlt (New York: Thames and Hudson, 1988), 148.
64 William James, "Lipps's Psychological Studies," *Science* 6.140 (1885): 308–10.
65 H. Meltzer, "Lipps' Pre-Gestalt studies," *Journal of Educational Psychology* 18.2 (1927): 131–33.
66 See Gunkle, "Empathy." Gunkle has a facile understanding of Lipps's notion of *Einfühlung*, but this doesn't undo the article.

makes possible an immediate experience of other minds—or better, other egos or personalities.

Two points of Lipps's view must be highlighted. First is the sense of "otherness" at issue. What *Einfühlung* makes possible is precisely an experience of a *foreign* ego—something strange and not me. Thus Lipps writes that a man's "sensuous manifestations," that is, his bodily and especially affective expressions, "are not the 'man,' they are not the *strange personality* with his psychological equipment, his ideas, his feelings, his will, etc. All the same, the man is linked to these manifestations.... This connection is created through *Einfühlung*."[67] This point is notable, however, not simply because Lipps himself stresses it, but because it would later become a point of contention for early phenomenologists, as will become clear in a moment. Second, it is crucial to appreciate that Lipps intends a further challenge to analogical arguments. According to Lipps, even after we acquire a generic notion of "self" we still don't typically rely on an inference by analogy to understand (in some sense) that the creature facing us is minded. Instead, in typical experience we display a capacity for immediate understanding. That is, we can immediately "grasp" the mental states of some creatures, part and parcel of our observation of them and prior to any reflection, which reflection would of course be needed for any inference. Indeed, it is precisely this immediacy of comprehension that he thought *Einfühlung* could explain. In *Einfühlung* we grasp such expressions, "immediately and simultaneously with the perception, and that does not mean that we see it or apprehend it by means of the senses. We cannot do that, since anger, friendliness, or sadness cannot be perceived through the senses. We can only experience this kind of thing in ourselves."[68] We might charitably reformulate this comment to get the following argument for *Einfühlung*:

---

67 Lipps, *Asthetik, Systematische Philosophie*, 361, emphasis added; trans. in Hunsdahl, "Concerning *Einfühlung*," 184. Hunsdahl, however, doesn't pay much attention to the import of this part of Lipps's theory.
68 Theodor Lipps, "Das Wissen from fremden Ich," in *Psychologische Untersuchungen*, ed. Lipps (Leipzig: Engelmann, 1907), 1.713; trans. in Jahoda, "Theodor Lipps and the Shift," 156.

1. Certain sensory objects are immediately graspable.
2. That is, in some cases, perception and comprehension of an object occur at once.
3. Affective appearances (e.g. anger) or affective changes (i.e., real-time changes in affective expression, e.g. from calm to angry) are one such object.
4. But of course, we don't see anger or hear anger. That is, we don't see or hear the mental state. We see and hear its expression.
5. Thus, if we do immediately comprehend what we see or hear, then simultaneous with the perception of the affective expression we must *experience* the affect itself internally. That is, we must imitate it inwardly, even if unconsciously.

The simplicity of this argument is attractive. Not only that, but in light of recent neuroscientific research, Lipps comes off looking prescient. I am alluding to the 1996 discovery of so-called mirror neurons in monkeys and the subsequent wave of research documenting a corresponding mirroring "system" in humans.[69] In short, this research strongly suggests that humans are endowed with a variety of cortical pathways that display congruent patterns of stimulation when certain actions, sensations, or emotions are performed or felt and when those actions, sensations, or emotions are merely observed. For example, when you observe someone tapping her finger or gagging in disgust; the stimulated regions of your brain and the signal patterns of those regions are strikingly similar to the regions and patterns that would be stimulated were it really you tapping or you feeling disgust. And so now the connection to Lipps: such "mirroring" has been argued to explain precisely the sort of immediate comprehension of *what* other beings are

---

[69] The discovery of "mirror neurons" was announced in a pair of articles by the Italian researchers Giacomo Rizzolatti, Luciano Fadiga, Vittorio Gallese, and Leonardo Fogassi. See Remy Debes, "Which Empathy? Limitations in the Mirrored 'Understanding' of Emotion," *Synthese* 175.2 (2010): 219–39.

experiencing, which Lipps was crediting to *Einfühlung*. Of course, to actually praise Lipps on this account would be anachronistic. Moreover, if the objections we are about to consider from his phenomenological detractors prove fitting, then the mirroring evidence will suddenly seem ill adapted to Lipps's view (or, I suppose, we learn a potential shortcoming of mirroring theories).

To be clear, neither Scheler nor Stein is entirely critical of Lipps. Scheler, for example, clearly thinks Lipps is closer to getting things right when it comes to the interpersonal phenomena associated with "sympathy" (Scheler did not follow Lipps's terminology of *Einfühlung*) than many more famous historical proponents like Hume or Smith.[70] Indeed, Scheler levels a number of what he takes to be "knock down" objections to Hume and Smith. And though none of them clearly are so devastating (in fact some clearly depend on wrongheaded readings of Hume and Smith), the point is that Scheler doesn't take a similarly dismissive tone toward Lipps. On the contrary, he not only lauds Lipps for rejecting analogical solutions to the problem of other minds, he also credits Lipps for perceiving the distinct modern import of solving this very problem, namely that "only by the solution of this question can *sociology* be established on a philosophical basis."[71]

But let us concentrate on Stein, whose reply to Lipps is more focused and for that reason more instructive. Boiled down, Stein's complaint is that Lipps has the basic phenomenology wrong when it comes to "empathy" (and for ease, I'll refer to her discussion of the relevant interpersonal phenomena in terms of 'empathy,' for that is how she is typically translated). Thus, Stein insists the correct starting point is to acknowledge that, from the perspective of an experiencing agent, there is no "problem" of other minds. Technically this is because experiences of empathy (specifically, of other minds) survive the Husserlian method

---

70 Scheler's own terminology aims for a far more exacting division of the phenomena, but is arguably too clever by half; see Zahavi, "Empathy," for criticism on this point.

71 Max Scheler, *The Problem of Sympathy*, trans. P. Heath (Hamden, CT: Archon Books, 1970), 213. This is obviously a nontrivial claim, but one I can't follow up here.

of "phenomenological reduction," in virtue of the fact that empathic experiences are "given" in one's pure (subjective) consciousness. To gloss crudely the complicated and disputed details of phenomenological reduction, the crucial point of Stein's claim is just this: empathic experiences are parts of experience that can't be doubted. "The phenomenon of foreign psychic life," Stein writes, "is indubitably there."[72]

So far there is no challenge to Lipps. But Stein elaborates her view in ways that clearly and explicitly cut against his view. First, Stein gives a more nuanced reformulation of Lipps's description of empathy as an encounter with a "strange personality" in order to bring home the point that the "otherness" of the other is part and parcel of the empathic experience itself. Thus, what is "given" in experience is not simply a physical body, Stein claims, but:

1. A sensitive, living body belonging to an "I" that senses, thinks, feels, and wills.
2. An "I" which is itself the center of orientation of a phenomenal world.
3. An "I" that "faces this world" and "communicates with me."[73]

The upshot, in her words, is that although the act of empathy—the experiencing of others' experiences—is given "primordially" (immediately) in one's experience, the *content* of that experience is *not* experienced primordially. Instead, the content is experienced *as* belonging to another—that is, as belonging to a foreign ego or nonprimordial "I."[74] Or as Scheler would describe the same basic "fact" but without the "primordial" terminology: what is given to us in our experience of others is "an individual self distinct from our own"—an individual "steeped" in its own psychic experience. Part and parcel of this, Scheler elaborates, is that we experience others as having, like ourselves, "a sphere of

---

72 Edith Stein, *On the Problem of Empathy*, trans. Waltraut Stein (Washington, DC: ICS Publications, 1989), 5.
73 Stein, *On the Problem of Empathy*, 5.
74 Stein, *On the Problem of Empathy*, 8.

absolute personal privacy, which can never be given to us." And yet, Scheler hastens to add, as if to remind us of Stein's starting point, "that 'experiences' occur there [in that being we observe] is given for us *in* expressive phenomena—again, not by inference, but directly, as a sort of primary 'perception.' It is *in* the blush that we perceive shame, *in* the laughter joy."[75] Indeed, it is precisely this juxtaposition that marks empathic experience: in empathy we directly experience others as experiencing, minded subjects, but nevertheless as (to some degree) unknowable, private, distinct, foreign, or in a word, individual.

Of course, this still doesn't substantially contradict Lipps's own description of interpersonal *Einfühlung* as the encounter with a "strange personality." As it happens, however, this is precisely what Stein hopes we will say. For this sets up her next move, which is decidedly critical. Thus Stein is keen to remind us that undergirding Lipps's view is a projective mechanism. So how, she asks, could any such account, which turns on the projection of the "I"—one's own ego—ever fully explain the way we experience the "otherness" of others, as she has fleshed out that experience? Indeed, didn't Lipps insist that *Einfühlung* involves a "dissolution" of the self-other distinction in virtue of a real identification or unity with the object? If so, then how could *Einfühlung* possibly explain the interpersonal phenomena in question?

To be clear, Stein does allow for experiences of "self-forgetfulness," wherein absorbed contemplation of some object leads to a "dissolution" of the self.[76] Stein also allows for cases of imitation, namely a kind of "contagion" or "transference" of feeling, wherein we "live in" and thus in a sense "unite" or "identify" with some feeling we witness (passively or actively) in another person. But none of these are cases of empathy, strictly speaking. Empathy, as far as Stein is concerned, is limited to precisely the kind of interpersonal experience with a foreign ego Lipps himself picked out. Thus Stein argues, for example, that in contagion whatever we feel is,

---

75 Scheler, *Problem of Sympathy*, 10.
76 Stein, *On the Problem of Empathy*, 17.

by the time we experience it, wholly one's own and primordial. That is why it is classified as a kind of transference in the first place. We don't experience anything foreign. On the contrary, in contagion we remain "in ourselves."[77] In short, in empathy there can be no psychic merging with the other—not in normal adult cases anyway.[78] Such a merging would bluntly contradict the whole point at issue, namely, of a fundamental and immediate experience of others *as other*, a point Lipps himself first suggested. Stein's objection is thus devastating to Lipps's account of interpersonal *Einfühlung*.

Of course, Stein's account has its own problems. In particular, its brevity and focus is often purchased at the expense of clarity, and many points needing more detail are left vague. However, it would distract too much to linger in a review of these worries. Instead, I close this section by turning to a last objection Stein raises about competing theories of empathy—though this time about the view offered by Adam Smith (albeit what Smith described as "sympathy"). Thus shall I pick up a marker dropped near the outset of this essay, namely, on the phenomenological challenge to simulationist accounts of empathy.

Drawing once again on the key theme of "otherness," Stein makes the following remark (almost as an afterthought): "[I]f, as in memory, we put ourselves in the place of the foreign 'I' and suppress it while we surround ourselves with its situation, we have one of these situations of 'appropriate' experience. If we then again concede to the foreign 'I' its place and ascribe this experience to him, we gain a knowledge of his experience."[79] Essentially, this is Stein's description of a simulationist model of "sympathy" like that espoused by Adam Smith, or, for that matter, the "empathy" of Stephen Darwall. More exactly, it is a translation of the sort of perspective-taking explanation of empathy (sympathy) into her phenomenological terminology. But to what effect?

---

77 Stein, *On the Problem of Empathy*, 23.
78 Scheler is keen to point out, as a criticism of both Lipps and Stein, that in certain idiopathic and heteropathic cases we may well experience certain kinds of full-blown identifications. But for the same reason in such cases we are essentially dealing with a different phenomenon. See Scheler, *Problem of Sympathy*, 18.
79 Stein, *On the Problems of Empathy*, 14.

Obviously, Stein does not reject such a model as *a* route to knowledge of other minds. Nevertheless, her comment is potentially devastating. For, what Stein does reject, implicitly here and explicitly just after, is that simulation can yield an experience of the other *as other*—that is, that it can yield the sort of experience of the "foreignness" of the other that we've been tracking. On the contrary, simulation, Stein charges, "suppresses" the foreign psyche or consciousness in favor of our own. By its own admission, simulation uses our own psyche and consciousness as a "surrogate" for getting at the experience of a foreign consciousness, which experience, it is crucial to recall, Stein treats as an indubitable fact. We *do* experience others as foreign. In our experiences, others do appear as so many strange personalities. That much Lipps had exactly right. Or so Stein argues.

Now, Stein herself didn't develop this into an explicitly ethical challenge. But Scheler did, even going so far as to imply that simulation models are deeply egoist, for essentially the very reason Stein identifies.[80] Scheler's worry is perhaps easier to appreciate if we translate the point now on the table back into the initial terms I used to frame my inquiry, as follows: for Scheler (and by extension for Stein), simulationist models of empathy (or sympathy) can never ground any sense of respect for others that is grounded on, or meant to embody, a recognition of the *individuality* of other persons. Because simulation cannot yield any understanding of others as distinctly *other*, any account of respect or recognition a simulationist theory of empathy (or sympathy) is argued to deliver will fall short of what is needed to satisfy the demands of human dignity.

Determining whether this objection holds up is beyond the scope of this chapter.[81] But as the objection has yet even to receive serious attention,

---

80 I'm interpreting here. But the combination of Scheler, *Problem of Sympathy*, 8–12 and 31–36, speaks in this direction.

81 Moreover, the objection itself must be situated against a paradox Scheler himself notes (*Problem of Sympathy*, 31–36), namely that to fully recognize the individuality of others requires a forgetfulness of one's own individuality (and thus dignity), given that it is precisely one's own individuality—one's own distinctness of ego and self—that psychically anchors us from really *identifying* with others, as opposed to merely empathizing with them.

especially in the Anglo-American analytic scene, airing it is already progress.

5. The Rise of American Social Psychology

As the phenomenological discussion about empathy was developing in Continental Europe, a parallel discussion in terms of sympathy was developing in North American social psychology. It is easy to overlook this coincidence, and not just because of the obvious terminological mismatch or ostensive difference in discipline. There was also virtually no mutual referencing between these two discussions (that is, explicitly on the subject of sympathy). Moreover, sympathy wasn't exactly in the limelight of early American psychology. It was an important piece in the contending systematic theories of social psychology, but social psychology itself was as yet not well defined, and largely overshadowed in America by the more quickly rooted empirical wing of the field.

Yet there was definitely a parallel. First, early American social psychology and early Continental phenomenology shared certain explanatory goals, if only thinly. Phenomenology understood itself to be fundamental to all sciences. And with respect to inquiries into *Einfühlung*, empathy, and sympathy, phenomenology took itself to be fundamental to sociology in particular, as we saw. But, of course, to aim at founding sociology is only a few degrees from aiming at founding social psychology, if indeed there is any difference at all. Second, and more important, it turns out that early American social psychology conceptualized "sympathy" in a way that aligned it with the distinctive notion of "empathy" we found in Scheler and Stein. Or so I will suggest in this final section.

The conceptual convergence is most clear in George Mead (1863–1931). But it was Charles Cooley (1864–1929) who set the stage. In the first place, Cooley stressed sympathy's centrality to social psychology, while at the same time rejecting the closest contending theory of sympathy as far as Anglo-American sociological debate was concerned, namely the notion of Herbert Spencer's fully mechanized and utilitarian understanding of sympathy. At the same time, Cooley rejected any identification of sympathy with, as he put it, "pity or other 'tender emotion.'"[82] Now, that Cooley needed such conceptual ground clearing is somewhat ironic, given that Adam Smith had essentially cleared the same ground nearly two centuries earlier. In any event, the upshot was to open the way for a much richer and more general concept of sympathy. Cooley took this opportunity to link "sympathy" to a kind of interpersonal "understanding." Thus Cooley concluded, sympathy does not operate only over "crude emotion," but rather, "[t]he content of [sympathy]... is chiefly thought and sentiment."[83] And thus social psychology more or less made an inroad into the space of interpersonal empathy.

Now enter Mead. Mead approaches the subject of sympathy with caution, acknowledging explicitly the ambiguity of the concept.[84] Mead also straightaway acknowledges his own tendency to talk of sympathy in terms of an "immediate attitude of care" (perhaps reflecting the onset of some rigidity to the connotation Darwall would later identify strictly with "sympathy"). Despite this tendency, however, Mead ultimately follows Cooley's invitation to allow a broader concept, one closer to what I've conceptualized as interpersonal empathy.

This generalized notion became increasingly important to Mead's greater theory. Thus consider the following crucial claim, near the end of a discussion entitled "The Nature of Sympathy": "To take a distinctively human, that is, self-conscious, social attitude toward another individual, or to become aware of him *as such*, is to identify yourself sympathetically with him, by taking his attitude toward, and his role in, the given social situation, and by thus responding to that situation implicitly as

---

82 Charles Cooley, *Human Nature and the Social Order* (New York: Scribner's, 1922), 137.
83 Cooley, *Human Nature and the Social Order*, 137–38.
84 George H. Mead, "The Nature of Sympathy," in *Mind, Self, and Society from the Standpoint of a Social Behaviorist*, ed. Charles Morris (Chicago: University of Chicago Press, 1934), section 38, 298–303, but see esp. 299.

he does or is about to do explicitly."[85] In this passage we find no definitional commitment to sympathy as a kind of caring attitude. But that is really the lesser reason for quoting it. For what we must also not fail to notice in this passage is the idea that sympathy with another person is constituted by an awareness of the other "as such." That is a peculiar turn of phrase. By it, Mead seems to suggest that what is at issue is an awareness of the distinctiveness or individuality of the other. It is, in other words, a gesture at the idea that sympathy focuses us on others *as other*, familiar to us now from early phenomenology.

Granted, cutting against this potential convergence is a simulationist tone in the same passage. Indeed, at first blush it might seem as if Mead endorses a strong perspective-taking sense of simulation. However, this would be to mistake Mead's view. At least, there are good reasons to think he was not advocating an essentially perspective-taking theory. Mature sympathy may well operate at times through perspective taking. But it is not originally a perspective-taking phenomenon. To see why, consider, for a start, the way Mead concludes the same passage in question: "Human society endows the human individual with a mind; and the very social nature of that mind requires him to put himself to some degree in the experiential places of, or to take the attitudes of, the other individuals belonging to that society."[86] This hints at a quite different way of reading Mead's concept of sympathy. Socialization—literally the development of a social mind—doesn't just allow for sympathy, it "requires" it. As he says elsewhere, "Social consciousness is the *presupposition* of imitation"[87]—that is, it is the presupposition of sympathy (Mead often uses the term "imitation" synonymously with "sympathy"). The point is akin to one made by Lipps. In order to become aware of others as minded, social creatures, we must likewise have a social

---

85 Mead, "Nature of Sympathy," 300; emphasis added.
86 Mead, "Nature of Sympathy," 300.
87 George H. Mead, "Social Psychology as Counterpart to Physiological Psychology," *Psychological Bulletin* 6 (1909): 401–408, at 406.

mind. But to have a social mind one must *already* be able to sympathize. But that implies sympathy must originally operate in some simpler, less robust form than full-blown perspective taking, which starts with a general concept of mind.

Mead's explanation of this claim is roughly the following: sympathy is most essentially the "arousing" or "calling out" (as he sometimes puts it) of a congruent attitude *in* an observer *with* an actor. Drawing directly on Wundt, Mead argues that this works through the medium of "gestures," which, in its most sophisticated form, is vocal language. Mead thus writes, "The gesture [in one form] calls out a gesture in the other form which will arouse or call out the same emotional attitude and the same idea [as in the original gesturer]."[88] And if this gesture "has parallel with it a certain psychical state which is the idea of what the person is going to do," and "if this gesture calls out a like gesture in the other individual and calls out a similar idea," then it "becomes a significant gesture. It stands for the idea in the minds of both of them."[89] Mead then adds, now against Wundt:

> [I]f, as Wundt does, you presuppose the existence of mind at the start, as explaining or making possible the social process of experience, then the origin of minds and the interaction among minds become mysteries. But if, on the other hand, you regard the social process of experience as prior (in a rudimentary form) to the existence of mind and explain the origin of minds in terms of the interaction among individuals within that process, then not only the origin of minds, but also the interaction among minds (which is thus seen to be internal to their very nature and presupposed by their existence or development at all) cease to seem mysterious or miraculous.[90]

---

88 George H Mead, "Wundt and the Concept of the Gesture," in *Mind, Self, and Society,* section 7, 42–51, at 48. See also Mead, "The Mechanism of Social Consciousness," *Journal of Philosophy, Psychology, and Scientific Methods* 9 (1912): 401–6.

89 Mead, "Wundt," 48.

90 Mead, "Wundt," 50. Eric Schliesser made the intriguing suggestion to me that Mead's argument here has strong affinities to the arguments of part 3 of Adam Smith's *Theory of Moral Sentiments*.

In the light of these claims, Mead's conception of "sympathy" no longer looks essentially simulationist. On the contrary, we need sympathy in order to acquire a concept of mind, which concept would be needed for any sense of perspective taking. In fact, Mead is suggesting that sympathy is required for *us* to have a mind in the first place. At the root sympathy is, as he says, "the origin of minds" precisely because minds arise *out of* social interaction. Or to put the point even more clearly, minds arise out of *sympathetic* social interaction.

Much more work would be needed to clarify how Mead's theory works and to determine whether Mead's view is, in the end, closer to the phenomenological conception of empathy we found in Stein and Scheler or in fact some very sophisticated simulation theory. That said, if it does turn out to be simulationist, Mead's theory might well harbor resources for defending simulation theory against the sharpest part of the phenomenological challenge. Either way, what *is* clear is that Mead agreed with Stein and Scheler that what (at least partly) distinguishes sympathy is the peculiar way it allows us to experience others *as* others— as individuals and distinctly "other." Correspondingly, we've got one more lead on what is arguably the most important contribution the tradition of sympathy currently has to offer contemporary moral and political philosophy. Of course, once again it is a lead that would be otherwise hidden from us if we dogmatically adopt any proposal to establish an objective, nonstipulated distinction between "empathy" and "sympathy"—a distinction it now seems never really existed anyway.[91]

---

91 I'm grateful to Eric Schliesser for comments on the penultimate draft of this chapter, but even more for his support and encouragement since our first meeting years ago, when I was a new professor. Such kindness can never fully be repaid. I also benefited from discussion with Hoke Robinson, John Kirby, Shaun Ghallagher, and all the participants at the Richmond workshop where early drafts for this volume were presented. Finally, I am indebted to the graduate students in my "Empathy" seminar during the spring of 2012, where I worked out the foundations of the analysis in this chapter.

CHAPTER TEN

Sympathy Caught between Darwin and Eugenics

David M. Levy and Sandra J. Peart

> Mr. Darwin's anecdotes of animal societies are marvelous. There exists solid evidence which abundantly proves the capacity of animals to constitute admirably organized societies. They have co-operation for a common end. They have subordinate ranks. They have monarchs to rule, soldiers to defend, artisans to work, cattle to milk, and they hold slaves in bondage. They have some good characteristics of human societies, and they have some bad ones. But they are stationary, while an increasing purpose runs through human history, and our thoughts "are widened with the process of the suns." We have emancipated our slaves. No Wilberforce or Clarkson has appeared among the ants.
>
> WILLIAM BINNS, "*Science, Theology, and the Evolution of Man*"

1. INTRODUCTION

Sympathy became a central topic of discussion in the post-Darwinian evolutionary literature when Alfred Russel Wallace asked in 1864 whether the survival principles of "natural selection" applied to humans.[1] In a paper first presented at the Anthropological Society and then widely reprinted, Wallace asserted that natural selection stopped at the edge

---

[1] We benefited from discussions at the conference on sympathy sponsored by the Adam Smith Program of the Jepson School of Leadership Studies in June 2012. Jane Perry helped by carefully correcting the manuscript. We thank the editor for encouraging us to take on the project and for his detailed suggestions. All the remaining errors are our responsibility.

of civilization because humans are connected by sympathetic bonds and accordingly they would not let the disabled perish. Moreover, with the division of labor that codefines civilization, people find occupations that suit a wide variety of capacities and thereby support themselves and their children. The discussion that informed Wallace's argument emphasized the importance of sympathy for creating a sphere of rights for individuals.

To make the case in *Descent of Man* (1871) that humans evolved from nonhuman animals, Charles Darwin stressed a twofold continuity between animals and humans. First, he asserted that the social instinct in animals develops into sympathy and a moral sense among humans. Second, he takes sexual selection in animals and humans to be largely the same principle. The most systematic challenge to Darwin was offered by St. George Mivart in a series of publications. In his *Quarterly Review* essay, Mivart argued that sexual selection can occur with or without consent. Sexual selection without consent, Mivart noted, can be thought of as another form of natural selection, one that challenges Darwin's continuity thesis. Another challenge—that while the social insects are so much like us as to even have slaves, there has been no Wilberforce ant equivalent as emancipator of either the aphids or the black ants—also argues against the continuity thesis. Human societies, unlike social insects, can reform themselves and the reforms at issue, the requirement for consent in marriage and the requirement for consent in the division of labor, depend on a reciprocity principle that respects the individual. This principle is at work in Adam Smith's version of sympathy; it is presupposed in Wallace's discussion but not that of Darwin. We shall argue that taking the continuity thesis as a normative guide removes the constraint of justice from social reform.

Darwin's "Moral Sense" chapter in *Descent* pays tribute to Smith's pioneering exploration of the sympathetic principle but he does not know Smith's work very well, believing as he does that Smith's system cannot explain why our affection for family would be stronger than affection for strangers.[2] Perhaps more importantly, Darwin uses a sympathetic principle to explain how *praise* motivates. For the utilitarians who were most influenced by Smith, James Mill and John Stuart Mill, Smith's great contribution was showing how *praiseworthiness* motivates. Motivation by praise, a commonplace in folk wisdom, can explain how small connected groups function, and it can be plausibly extended to affective motivation outside language as Darwin suggested. The utilitarian project was to escape from small groups, to explain what can motivate for the greatest happiness. For this, one needs to work with praiseworthiness or to disregard undeserved praise for acts that benefit a smaller group at the expense of the larger.

There is an aspect of Smith's work on sympathy that perhaps escaped even the Mills. While Smith did not disagree that the greatest happiness ought to guide reform, he offered a subtle objection to putting much trust in reform proposals. His argument was simple and spare: time is so scarce that people fail fully to understand how a proposed reform bears on the well-being of others. For Smith a time-economizing social reform might be effected by advancing a model in which society's ends are collapsed to a simple goal. But Smith offers a caution to the reader. With the ends being made tractable, model builders, Smith's men "of system," then detail how means are to be used to implement these ends. These reformers may become so fascinated by the system as

---

[2] The 1870 volume of Darwin's correspondence (*The Correspondence of Charles Darwin: 1870*, ed. Frederick Burkhardt, James A. Secord, Sheila Ann Dean, Samantha Evans, Shelley Innes, Alison M. Pearn, and Paul White [Cambridge: Cambridge University Press, 2010], 18.396) contains the manuscript report: "On the verso of this letter is a note by CD mentioning the explanation for the basis of sympathy given in Smith [Adam Smith, *The Theory of Moral Sentiments*, 1759] and Bain [Alexander Bain, *Mental and Moral Science: A Compendium of Psychology and Ethics*, 1868]. CD notes that neither work can account for the fact that sympathy is stronger when excited by a loved one rather than a stranger." This is an odd reading since Smith is famous for the sympathetic gradient that follows from his definition of affection as habitual sympathy and the necessary truth that we are mortals so our time is finite (Sandra J. Peart and David M. Levy, *The "Vanity of the Philosopher": From Equality to Hierarchy in Post-Classical Economics* [Ann Arbor: University of Michigan Press, 2005]; Levy and Peart, "Adam Smith and the State: Language and Reform," in *Oxford Handbook on Adam Smith*, ed. Christopher Berry, Maria Paganelli and Craig Smith [Oxford: Oxford University Press, 2013], 372–93). Unfortunately, there is no listing of *Theory of Moral Sentiments* in the record of his marginalia (Mario A. Di Gregorio and N. W. Gill, *Darwin's Marginalia* [New York: Garland, 1990]).

to use it as a guide to perfection even at the expense of overall happiness. Sympathy for the ends of individuals, about whom we know so little, might be sacrificed for the temptation to pursue the vision of social perfection that seems so clear.[3] We shall employ this aspect of Smith's teaching to consider how Darwin's continuity thesis removes the constraint of justice from political reform proposals.

We view Darwin's models of artificial (or human) and natural selection as contending methods of possible political reform. To simplify a bit: when transferred to a model for public policy to emulate, "artificial" selection is undertaken to attain the happiness of the humans who *choose*; "natural" selection is undertaken as part of a twofold struggle for existence and for mates. Reread from this perspective, in *On the Origin of Species* (1859) the contention is between natural and artificial selection of nonhumans; in *Descent* the contention is between human selection of their own descendants and the principles of "natural" selection. While the issue of human sympathy is obliquely raised in *Origin*, as Darwin explains why he thinks artificial selection is inferior to natural selection for racial improvement, sympathy moves to front and center in *Descent*. Darwin here worries that sympathy will interfere with natural selection as people pursue their own happiness. Because both human happiness and racial improvement are taken as worthwhile goals, Darwin now posits an explicit trade-off between sympathy and racial improvement. By "racial" of course we refer to the human race, not any subset.

As Wallace would later explain, the "science" of eugenics arose as an artificial replacement for the "failure" of natural selection. His 1864 essay initiated the public discussion of the importance of deadening sympathy for the surviving "unfit" in order to attain the goals of racial perfection supposedly effected by "natural" selection. The remainder of his life was filled with responses to eugenic proposals. The challenges immediately offered to Darwin's continuity thesis explain why

---

3 Levy and Peart, "Adam Smith and the State."

social Darwinism's most important reform proposals can be described as variations on a eugenic theme. Later writers were far less careful than Darwin. It is all too easy to find published defenses of the desired eugenic properties of war and famine. Among many post-Darwinian highly educated persons, the sympathy for the "lesser" had ended; all that remained was to remake humanity in the image of the model's idealization.

We discuss two public controversies. The first began with George Darwin's 1874 proposal to go beyond Francis Galton's proposal to subsidize children of an elite and W. R. Greg's handwringing to begin a systematic policy of negative eugenics by prohibiting marriage of an antielite. Here we shall see that the debate quickly moved from biological theories to policy advocacy. The second occurred because of a letter from Charles Darwin to Charles Bradlaugh that puts the trade-off between happiness and natural selection in sharp relief. Bradlaugh and Annie Besant stood trial in 1877 for distributing an "obscene" manual on contraception. In response to their entreaty that he might testify on their behalf, Darwin declined and called attention to what he had written about the trade-off between the goals of individuals in avoiding misery for their children and the goal of racial perfection by means of natural selection.

2. The Mills on Sympathy and Motivation by Praiseworthiness

James and John Stuart Mill read *Theory of Moral Sentiments [TMS]* as part of their research in psychology. James Mill read *TMS* when he was a student of Dugald Stewart, Smith's first biographer.[4] Although controversy has arisen over whether Stewart downplayed Smith's

---

4 Alexander Bain, *James Mill: A Biography* (London, Longmans, Green, 1882), 18–19, gives a list of the books James Mill took out from the Theological Library. It has both volumes of *TMS*. Bain documents Mill's affection for Stewart.

radicalism,[5] Stewart's reading of *TMS* is precise. In *TMS* Smith was careful to define "affection" as habitual sympathy, and Stewart called attention to the importance of this step in Smith's argument.[6]

James Mill's 1820 "Government" is perhaps the classic text on the problem of small groups exploiting large groups.[7] His 1829 *Analysis of the Phenomena of the Human Mind* applied sympathetic considerations to explain group organization. The comments added in 1869 by John Stuart Mill in his edition are particularly helpful.[8] We begin with James Mill's account of our affections for others. He starts with "[a]ctions give birth to a set of Associations" and goes on to examine "acts contemplated as causes of such alterations in the States as render them to a greater or less degree causes of our pleasures or pains" (2: 270). J. S. Mill amplifies the argument in a way that suggests James Mill had understated the impact of sympathetic motivation by neglecting the interactions of agents: "the fact that a feeling is shared by all or many of those with whom we are in frequent intercourse, strengthens, by an obvious consequence, all the associations, both of resemblance and of contiguity, which give that feeling its force. This is the well-known influence of sympathy, so strikingly evinced by the vehement feelings of a crowd" (2: 274–75). James Mill considers why members of small groups confuse the interest of their part of society with that of the whole;

---

[5] See Emma Rothschild, *Economic Sentiments: Adam Smith, Condorcet and the Enlightenment* (Cambridge, MA: Harvard University Press, 2002), 52–71.

[6] Dugald Stewart, *The Philosophy of the Active and Moral Powers of Man*, in *The Works of Dugald Stewart in Seven Volumes* (1828; Cambridge: Hilliard and Brown, 1829), vol. 5, comments: "'What we call affection' says Mr. Smith, 'is nothing but an habitual sympathy.' I will not go quite so far as to adopt this proposition in all its latitude, but I perfectly agree with this profound and amiable moralist in thinking, that the experience of this sympathy is the chief foundation of friendship, and one of the principal sources of the pleasures which it yields" (59–60). This link between sympathy and affection is central to modern interpretative debates over the relationship between Smith's argument in *TMS* and that in *Wealth of Nations* (Levy and Peart, "Adam Smith and the State," 376).

[7] James Mill, "Government," in *Essays* (1820; London: Innes, 1824–25), 3–32. Mill argues: "Whenever the powers of Government are placed in any hands other than those of the community, whether: those of one man, of a few, or of several, those principles of human nature which imply that Government is at all necessary, imply that those persons will make use of them to defeat the very end for which Government exists" (8).

[8] Citations to quotations from both Mills in this section are to *Analysis of the Phenomena of the Human Mind*, ed. John Stuart Mill, 2 vols. (1829; London: Longmans, Green, Reader and Dyer, 1869).

their part contains all those to whom they are sympathetically connected: "Where the inhabitants of a country are divided into classes, a Ruling Class, and a Subject Class, the members of the Ruling Class have hardly any sympathies, except with one another; in other words, have agreeable associations with the pleasures, and removal of the pains, of hardly any persons, but those who belong to the same class" (2: 275). Education is offered as a means by which people come to identify with a larger group to "control the narrow associations, growing out of a particular position" so they are "always identified with that of the community at large" (2: 276). Can we hope for the "Love of Mankind"?[9] (2: 278). This is the challenge for education, to widen sympathy (2: 278).

For utilitarian purposes, we require praiseworthy action, not praised action. Mill makes the point across two paragraphs that we run together. The goal of education is motivation by praiseworthiness:

> that remarkable phenomenon of our nature, eloquently described, but not explained, by Adam Smith, that, in minds happily trained, the love of Praiseworthiness, the dread of Blameworthiness, is a stronger feeling, than the love of actual Praise, the Dread of actual Blame.... It has reference, not to what is, or to what shall be, but to what ought to be, the sentiments of mankind. (2: 298–99)

J. S. Mill takes great care in an editorial comment to make sure the point is made and that James Mill's words are not misread. And here at the center of the motivational theory of utilitarianism we find the impartial spectator:

> the desire of undeserved praise is greatly counteracted by the thought that people would not bestow the praise if they knew all. That what has now been stated was really the author's meaning, is proved by his

---

9 The word "philanthropy" was used to criticize utilitarians in the debates over reform (Peart and Levy, *Vanity of the Philosopher*).

going on to say, that praiseworthiness and blameworthiness, as motives to action, have reference "not to what is, or to what shall be, but to what ought to be, the sentiments of mankind." (2: 298–99)

Praise depends on the group in which an individual happens to fall. There is no reason to believe that motivation by praise is deserved, that it will serve ends with any connection beyond that of the immediate group. For utilitarian motivation, one needs to have the concerns of the largest group serve as motivation.[10] What links Smith and the two Mills is their focus on praiseworthiness as motivation.[11]

3. The Biological Background to Darwin

In nineteenth-century evolutionary biology, sympathy was the key to passing from self-interest to group interest in matters of justice and beneficence.[12] Erasmus Darwin's 1803 *Temple of Nature* appealed to the principle of sympathy:

> How Love and Sympathy the bosom warm,
> Allure with pleasure, and with pain alarm,
> With soft affections weave the social plan,
> And charm the listening Savage into Man.
>
> (canto 1: 219–23)

---

10 See Arthur N. Prior, review of C. S. Lewis, *Abolition of Man*, *Landfall* 1 (1947): 63–67, at 66: "There is no reason ... why such disinterestedness should not be made the *defining characteristic* of ethical sentiments, as it has in fact been made by the more circumspect subjectivists from Adam Smith onwards."

11 Smith, *TMS* VII.vi.24: "And as we cannot always be satisfied merely with being admired, unless we can at the same time persuade ourselves that we are in some degree really worthy of admiration; so we cannot always be satisfied merely with being believed, unless we are at the same time conscious that we are really worthy of belief. As the desire of praise and that of praise-worthiness, though very much a-kin, are yet distinct and separate desires; so the desire of being believed and that of being worthy of belief, though very much a-kin too, are equally distinct and separate desires."

12 The literature is extensive as one can discover by searching for "sympathy" in JSTOR's collection of anthropology journals. We restrict ourselves to those Darwin would have known. Jumping from Smith directly to Darwin, e.g., John Laurent and Geoff Cockfield, "Adam Smith, Charles Darwin and the Moral Sense," in *New Perspectives on Adam Smith's* Theory of Moral Sentiments, ed. Geoff Cockfield, Ann Firth, and John Laurent (Cheltenham, UK: Edward Elgar, 2007), 141–62, misses Spencer's revival of *Theory of Moral Sentiments* to explain justice.

In a note to canto 3: 466 Darwin adds: "From our aptitude to imitation arises which is generally understood by the word sympathy, so well explained by Dr. Smith of Glasgow" (122–23). Darwin's earlier *Botanic Garden* (1791) contained a reproduction of his friend Josiah Wedgewood's 1787 medallion created for the antislavery movement, the celebrated visualization of the question "Am I not a man and a brother?" (fig. 10.1). As the antislavery movement marks the beginning of modern democratic politics, it is appropriate that its most enduring image is one that asks for an act of sympathetic imagination that Smith described.

The fullest evolutionary discussion of sympathy begins with the work of Herbert Spencer. Relying explicitly on Smith, Spencer argues in his 1851 *Social Statics* that sympathy is the foundation for our perception that others possess *rights*, and hence it forms the basis for moral action:

FIGURE 10.1. "Am I not a man and a brother?"

Seeing, however, that this instinct of personal rights is a purely selfish instinct, leading each man to assert and defend his own liberty of action, there remains the question—Whence comes our perception of the rights of others?

The way to a solution of this difficulty has been opened by Adam Smith in his "Theory of Moral Sentiments." It is the aim of that work to show that the proper regulation of our conduct to one another, is secured by means of a faculty whose function it is to excite in each being the emotions displayed in surrounding ones... the faculty, in short, which we commonly call Sympathy. (96)

After a two-page discussion extending Smith's account, Spencer explains that justice and beneficence are both rooted in sympathy (98). Although Spencer and J. S. Mill disagreed on the content of utilitarianism as an intellectual enterprise,[13] Mill fully agreed with Spencer on the importance of sympathy. To explain justice in *Utilitarianism*, Mill appealed to an extended sense of sympathy: "Human beings, on this point, only differ from other animals in two particulars. First, in being capable of sympathising, not solely with their offspring, or, like some of the more noble animals, with some superior animal who is kind to them, but with all human, and even with all sentient, beings."[14] Wallace made the case in 1864 in "The Origin of Human Races" that if sympathy was extended to the weak among us, the principle of natural selection would not apply to humans. Moreover, the division of labor supported by a system of legal rights allowed a huge variation of what is sufficient for survival. The "uniform standard" that natural selection was taken to enforce among nonhumans simply fails to exist in humans with a division of labor supported by rights.

---

13 Peart and Levy, *Vanity of the Philosopher*, 214–15.
14 John Stuart Mill, *Utilitarianism*, in *Essays on Ethics, Religion and Society*, ed. John M. Robson, vol. 10 of *Collected Works of John Stuart Mill* (1861; Toronto: University of Toronto Press, 1969), 203–59, at 248.

If a herbivorous animal is a little sick and has not fed well for a day or two, and the herd is then pursued by a beast of prey, our poor invalid inevitably falls a victim. So in a carnivorous animal the least deficiency of vigour prevents its capturing food, and it soon dies of starvation. There is, as a general rule, no mutual assistance between adults, which enables them to tide over a period of sickness. Neither is there any division of labour; each must fulfill all the conditions of its existence, and, therefore, "natural selection" keeps all up to a pretty uniform standard.

But in man, as we now behold him, this is different. He is social and sympathetic. In the rudest tribes the sick are assisted at least with food; less robust health and vigour than the average does not entail death.... Some division of labour takes place.... The action of natural selection is therefore checked.[15]

Wallace's closing footnote acknowledges his debt to *Social Statics*.[16] His letter to Darwin in 1864 about the importance of *Social Statics* makes clear how Wallace read the political economic literature of the time.[17]

Wallace's argument that natural selection is checked by human sympathy marks the beginning of the eugenics movement. W. R. Greg responded that since sympathy blocked the "salutary" effects of natural selection, sympathy should therefore be suppressed:

---

15 Alfred R. Wallace, "The Origin of Human Races and the Antiquity of Man Deduced from the Theory of 'Natural Selection,'" *Journal of the Anthropological Society of London* 2 (1864): clviii–clxxxvii, at clxii.

16 Wallace, "Origin of Human Races," clxx: "The general idea and argument in this paper I believe to be new. It was, however, the perusal of Mr. Herbert Spencer's works, especially Social Statics, that suggested it to me." The acknowledgment was removed in later versions, e.g., Alfred Russel Wallace, "The Development of Human Races under the Law of Natural Selection," in *Contributions to the Theory of Natural Selection*, 2nd ed. (1864; London: Macmillan, 1871), 303–31.

17 Wallace's letter of 2 January 1864 to Darwin encourages Darwin to look into *Social Statics*. Wallace views Spencer as a political economist of the first order: "I am utterly astonished that so few people seem to read Spencer, & the utter ignorance there seems to be among politicians & political economists of the grand views & logical stability of his works. He appears to me as far ahead of John Stuart Mill as J.S.M. is of the rest of the world, and I may add as Darwin is of Agassiz" Charles Darwin, *The Correspondence of Charles Darwin: 1864*, ed. Frederick Burkhardt, Duncan M. Porter, Sheila Ann Dean, Paul S. White, and Sarah Wilmot (Cambridge: Cambridge University Press, 2001), 5. Michael Shermer, *In Darwin's Shadow: The Life and Science of Alfred Russel Wallace* (New York: Oxford University Press, 2002), 239, cites the letter to Darwin and the acknowledgment to Spencer.

> My thesis is this: that the indisputable effect of the state of social progress and culture we have reached, of our high civilization in its present stage and actual form, is to counteract and suspend the operation of that righteous and salutary law of "natural selection" in virtue of which the best specimens of the race—the strongest, the finest, the worthiest—are those which survive... and propagate an ever improving and perfecting type of humanity.[18]

Much of the eugenics rhetoric was an attempt to show that the "unfit" were a breed apart and therefore undeserving of sympathy. Greg described the Irish, who in his and many of his contemporaries' hands for all intents and purposes were thought subhuman relative to their human counterpart, the Scots: "careless, squalid, unaspiring Irishman, fed on potatoes, living in a pig-stye, doting on a superstition, multiply like rabbits or ephemera."[19] Late in his life Wallace remembered Galton's proposals for positive eugenics.[20] He was much more critical of Galton's disciples who proposed negative eugenics, policies to reduce births among the "unfit."

If natural selection serves a norm specifying an ideal trajectory of human "progress"—"fitness" in Spencer's terminology (not the modern sense)—then the failure of natural selection tells us that there is something "wrong" with human beings as we find them. It is in this context that we find Darwin opposing an augmentation of the "preventive check" that would make "natural" selection less effective. We quote Wallace's report of a conversation with Darwin:

> In one of my latest conversations with Darwin he expressed himself very gloomily on the future of humanity on the ground that in our modern civilization natural selection had no play, and the fittest did

---

18 W. R. Greg, *Enigmas of Life* (Boston: James R. Osgood), 119.
19 [W. R. Greg], "On the Failure of 'Natural Selection' in the Case of Man," *Fraser's Magazine for Town and Country* 78: 353–62, at 360.
20 Alfred Russel Wallace, *Social Environment and Moral Progress* (London: Cassell, 1913), 127.

not survive. Those who succeed in the race for wealth are by no means the best or the most intelligent, and it is notorious that our population is more largely renewed in each generation from the lower than from the middle and upper classes.[21]

The passage continues with Wallace discussing the emerging debate about how one might replace "natural selection" with human policies to remove the unfit:

> As a recent American writer [Hiram M. Stanley] well puts it, "We behold the melancholy spectacle of the renewal of the great mass of society from the lowest classes, the highest classes to a great extent either not marrying or not having children. The floating population is always the scum, and yet the stream of life is largely renewed from this source. Such a state of affairs, sufficiently dangerous in any society, is simply suicidal in the democratic civilization of our day."

4. Natural versus Human Selection

In *Origin of Species* Darwin details his belief that natural selection is superior to human selection (83). As the argument will be presupposed in *Descent of Man*, we quote at length. In artificial selection, humans interfere with what Darwin will later call sexual selection. Then, in a step that speaks to human sympathy, they refuse to kill ("rigidly destroy") lesser creatures for whom they are responsible. The question of what they will do with lesser humans is not asked.

> He does not allow the most vigorous males to struggle for the females. He does not rigidly destroy all inferior animals, but protects during each varying season, as far as lies in his power, all his productions.

---

[21] Alfred Russel Wallace, "Human Selection," in *Studies Scientific and Social* (1890; London: Macmillan, 1900), 1.509–26, at 509.

He often begins his selection by some half-monstrous form; or at least by some modification prominent enough to catch his eye, or to be plainly useful to him. Under nature, the slightest difference of structure or constitution may well turn the nicely-balanced scale in the struggle for life, and so be preserved. (83–84)

Appealing to the difference in time between natural and artificial selection, Darwin draws the normative conclusion: "Can we wonder, then, that nature's productions should be far 'truer' in character than man's productions; that they should be infinitely better adapted to the most complex conditions of life...?" (84).

We turn now to the *Descent of Man*. The reader is here warned as early as the second chapter that one distinguishing characteristic of mankind has been our uncontrolled breeding: "In another and much more important respect, man differs widely from any strictly domesticated animal; for his breeding has never been long controlled, either by methodological or unconscious selection."[22] The question, uncontrolled by whom or by what, will be important because Darwin proposed a new standard of morality, that of racial perfection; the "general good" was to replace the greatest happiness principle of utilitarianism. The critical step in his argument is the continuity thesis of the social instincts:

> The term, general good, may be defined as the means by which the greatest possible number of individuals can be reared in full vigour and health, with all their faculties perfect, under the conditions to which they are exposed. As the social instincts both of man and the lower animals have no doubt been developed by the same steps, it would be advisable, if found practicable, to use the same definition in both cases, and to like as the test of morality, the general good or

---

22 Charles Darwin, *The Descent of Man; or, Selection in Relation to Sex* (London: John Murray, 1871), 1.112.

welfare of the community, rather than the general happiness; but this definition would perhaps require some limitation on account of political ethics. (1: 98)

The question then is what connects marriage for our happiness with the goal of racial perfection? In the second edition, Darwin provides a classical gloss on how self-interested calculations interfere with projects of biological improvement: "The Grecian poet, Theognis, who lived 550 B.C., clearly saw how important selection, if carefully applied, would be for the improvement of mankind. He saw, likewise, that wealth often checks the proper [*sic*] action of sexual selection."[23] Sympathy is vital in Darwin's account of the development of the human race. In chapter 4 of part 1 in the first edition he uses the sympathetic principle to move between individual and group interests. He questions whether sympathy has survival value in the next chapter, which opens with a discussion of Wallace's 1864 essay:

> It is extremely doubtful whether the offspring of the more sympathetic and benevolent parents, or of those who were the most faithful to their comrades, would be reared in greater numbers than the children of selfish and treacherous parents belonging to the same tribe. He who was ready to sacrifice his life, as many a savage has been, rather than betray his comrades, would often leave no offspring to inherit his noble nature. The bravest men, who were always willing to come to the front in war, and who freely risked their lives for others, would on an average perish in larger numbers than other men. Therefore it hardly seems probable, that the number of men gifted with such virtues, or that the standard of their excellence, could be increased through natural selection, that is, by the survival of the fittest. (1: 163)

---

23 Charles Darwin, *The Descent of Man; or, Selection in Relation to Sex*, ed. James Moore and Adrian Desmond (1874; London: Penguin Books, 2004), 47.

It is important to recognize that biological perfection is the new norm. Darwin does his best to make this clear when he asks whether we ought to check sympathy in the section entitled "Natural Selection as Affecting Civilised Nations" (1: 167–80). Here he asks the Platonic question anew: if we are interested in biological perfection, why do we breed cattle but not men (*Republic* 459). Darwin's context is the question of vaccinations. For a utilitarian for whom all are sympathetically connected, the life of a person is better than her or his death and the answer is trivial. But what about an answer from the standpoint of biological purity?

> There is reason to believe that vaccination has preserved thousands, who from a weak constitution would formerly have succumbed to small-pox. Thus the weak members of civilised societies propagate their kind. No one who has attended to the breeding of domestic animals will doubt that this must be highly injurious to the race of man. It is surprising how soon a want of care, or care wrongly directed, leads to the degeneration of a domestic race; but excepting in the case of man himself, hardly any one is so ignorant as to allow his worst animals to breed. (1: 168)

Darwin blames this misdirection of effort on sympathy but he accepts a good deal of biological imperfection at the cost of our being moral agents. The hope of racial improvement rests on sexual selection, in which the better men have more children than the worse men:

> The aid which we feel impelled to give to the helpless is mainly an incidental result of the instinct of sympathy, which was originally acquired as part of the social instincts, but subsequently rendered, in the manner previously indicated, more tender and more widely diffused. Nor could we check our sympathy, even at the urging of hard reason, without deterioration in the noblest part of our nature.... We must therefore bear the undoubtedly bad effects of the weak

surviving and propagating their kind; but there appears to be at least one check in steady action, namely the weaker and inferior members of society do not marry so freely as the sound; and this check might be indefinitely increased by the weak in body or mind refraining from marriage, though this is more to be hoped for than expected. (1: 169)

As the chapter continues, Darwin cites the arguments of Greg and Galton against the Malthusian recommendation to increase human happiness by delaying marriage:

A most important obstacle in civilised countries to an increase in the number of men of a superior class has been strongly insisted on by Mr. Greg and Mr. Galton, namely, the fact that the very poor and reckless, who are often degraded by vice, almost invariably marry early, whilst the careful and frugal, who are generally otherwise virtuous, marry late in life. (1: 173–74)

Darwin returns to these themes when the book concludes. The Platonism returns, complete with scorn at the ability of self-government without expert guidance:

Man scans with scrupulous care the character and pedigree of his horses, cattle, and dogs before he matches them; but when he comes to his own marriage he rarely, or never, takes any such care.... When the principles of breeding and inheritance are better understood, we shall not hear ignorant members of our legislature rejecting with scorn a plan for ascertaining whether or not consanguineous marriages are injurious to man. (2: 402–03)

Second, we find the claim of a trade-off between our sympathy and biological betterment:

The advancement of the welfare of mankind is a most intricate problem: all ought to refrain from marriage who cannot avoid abject poverty for their children; for poverty is not only a great evil, but tends to its own increase by leading to recklessness in marriage. On the other hand, as Mr. Galton has remarked, if the prudent avoid marriage, whilst the reckless marry, the inferior members tend to supplant the better members of society. Man, like every other animal, has no doubt advanced to his present high condition through a struggle for existence consequent on his rapid multiplication; and if he is to advance still higher, it is to be feared that he must remain subject to a severe struggle. Otherwise he would sink into indolence, and the more gifted men would not be more successful in the battle of life than the less gifted. Hence our natural rate of increase, though leading to many and obvious evils, must not be greatly diminished by any means. (2: 403)

After Darwin sent this passage to Charles Bradlaugh, six years later, it would be featured in an important trial over the legality of distributing contraception information.

5. The Continuity Hypothesis

Darwin's account of the movement from animal to human depends on the motivation by praise and approbation. These, he argues, depend on sympathy.[24] The continuity hypothesis is more than an empirical claim

---

24 Darwin, "Descent of Man," 1871 ed., 1:42. Darwin writes: "Animals manifestly feel emulation. They love approbation or praise; and a dog carrying a basket for his master exhibits in a high degree self-complacency or pride. [1:42] ... Instinctive sympathy would, also, cause him to value highly the approbation of his fellow-men; for, as Mr. Bain has clearly shewn, the love of praise and the strong feeling of glory, and the still stronger horror of scorn and infamy, 'are due to the workings of sympathy.' Consequently man would be greatly influenced by the wishes, approbation, and blame of his fellow-men, as expressed by their gestures and language. [1:86] ... We may therefore conclude that primeval man, at a very remote period, would have been influenced by the praise and blame of his fellows. It is obvious, that the members of the same tribe would approve of conduct which appeared to them to be for the general good, and would reprobate that which appeared evil. To do good unto others—to do unto others as ye would they should do unto you,—is the foundation-stone of morality. It is, therefore, hardly possible to exaggerate the importance during rude times of the love of praise and the dread of blame [1:165]."

that animals' social instincts have evolved into a sense of "right" and "wrong." If it is understood as a norm that underwrites Darwin's conception of racial perfection, it implies that people do not have to worry about justice to individuals. They may sympathize with their inferiors but they do not owe them justice because justice is not well defined in the goal of racial perfection. This is very different from the utilitarianism defended by J. S. Mill and his teachers. The discussions among the members of the antislavery coalition made it clear that the greatest happiness principle was the same as the golden rule of Christianity.[25] Reciprocity norms presuppose individuals with claims against others. A norm of racial perfection where individuals have no such claims dispenses with justice.

Ant slavery. Darwin's discussion of the enslaving nature of ants was a central topic of Samuel Wilberforce's, the son of the famous abolitionist, in his review of the *Origin* for the *Quarterly Review* in 1860.[26] There are over thirty instances of "slave" in the review. Here's a specimen:

> Or take the following admirable specimen of the union of which we have spoken, of the employment of the observations of others with what he has observed himself, in that which is almost the most marvellous of facts—the slave-making instinct of certain ants. We say nothing at present of the place assigned to these facts in Mr. Darwin's argument, but are merely referring to the collection, observation, and statement of the facts themselves:—Slave-making Instinct.—This remarkable instinct was first discovered in the Formica (Polyerges) rufescens by Pierre Huber, a better observer even than his celebrated father. This ant is absolutely dependent on its slaves; without their aid the species would certainly become extinct in a single year. The males and fertile females do no work. The workers or sterile females, though most energetic and courageous in capturing slaves, do no

---

25　Peart and Levy, *Vanity of the Philosopher*, 163–79.
26　[Samuel Wilberforce], "On the Origin of Species," *Quarterly Review* 30 (1860): 225–64, at 227–28.

other work. They are incapable of making their own nests or of feeding their own larvae.

Wilberforce calls attention to what Darwin reports about the color difference in the master and the slaves: "The slaves are black, and not above half the size of their red masters, so that the contrast in their appearance is very great" (228). The problem for the continuity thesis advanced in *Descent*, if it is interpretative as a fact of how biological evolution has worked, is trivial: if sympathy and the moral sense in humans are continuations of the social instincts, where is the ant equivalent of his father, William Wilberforce? This we find advanced in the contemporary discussion of *Descent of Man*: gregarious does not give justice. More generally, if moral sense is a continuation of the social instincts, where is the sense of justice in the social instincts described by Darwin?[27]

Sexual selection. Two of the early reviews of *Descent* by Darwin's fellow naturalists Wallace and Mivart pointed out a serious problem with the continuity hypothesis in Darwin's account of sexual selection. Wallace in "Physical Science and Philosophy" questioned the imputation of mate choice from the fact of bodily functions:

> Many parts of the body have been modified to enable the male to seize and hold the female; and this is adduced as an argument that the female exerts a choice, and has the power of rejecting any particular male. But this hardly seems to follow, for it may well be maintained that when the more active male seizes a female, she cannot escape, and that she has no means of rejecting him and practically never does.[28]

---

[27] See, e.g., Charles Elam, "Automatism and Evolution," *Contemporary Review* 29 (1876): 117–46, at 141: "it needs no discussion to show that the religious sentiment has no representative whatever, nor such abstract ideas as truth and justice; and Mr. Darwin's abortive attempt to trace back the 'moral sense' to some development of gregarious or social instinct is so completely beside the mark, that it really presents no point for criticism. Professor Huxley, with great sagacity, says nothing about it." See also the passage from William Binns, "Science, Theology, and the Evolution of Man," *Modern Review* 2 (1880): 245–78, at 268, quoted in the epigraph to this chapter.

[28] Alfred Russel Wallace, "Physical Science and Philosophy," *The Academy and Literature* 2 (1871): 177–83, at 179.

Mivart's criticism is much more systematic and sustained.[29] Like Wallace in "Physical Science" (177), he emphasizes the centrality of sexual selection to Darwin's argument.[30] In "Descent of Man," he sharpens the distinction that Wallace made:

> Under the head of "sexual selection" Mr. Darwin includes two very distinct processes. One of these consists in the action of superior strength of activity, by which one male succeeds in obtaining the possession of mates and in keeping away rivals. This is, undoubtedly, a *vera causa;* but may be more conveniently reckoned as one kind of "natural selection" than as a branch of "sexual selection." The second process consists in alleged preference or choice, exercised freely by the female in favour of particular males on account of some attractiveness.... It is this second kind of "sexual selection"... that is important for the establishment of Mr. Darwin's views, but its valid action has to be proved. (53)

Mivart specialized in primates. His skepticism of the Darwinian supposition of an evolutionary pathway that passed through the gorilla on the way to the fully human became a twentieth-century commonplace.[31] The characterization of the Darwinian position in his primate book as "highest of the apes—close ally of the Negro"[32] catches perfectly the

---

29 Perhaps the most detailed account of the technical issues is provided by Peter J. Vorzimmer, *Charles Darwin: The Years of Controversy* (Philadelphia: Temple University Press, 1970), 225–31. He does not discuss the George Darwin episode.
30 [St. George Mivart], "The Descent of Man, and Selection in Relation to Sex," *Quarterly Review* 131: 47–89, at 53.
31 Mivart's position is now widely accepted as an instance of parallel evolutionary pathways. See William L. Straus Jr., "The Riddle of Man's Ancestry," *Quarterly Review of Biology* 24 (1949): 200–23, at 204; W. C. Osman Hill, "Man's Relation to the Apes," *Man* 50 (1950): 161–62, at 161; and Malcolm Jay Kottler, "Alfred Russel Wallace, the Origin of Man, and Spiritualism," *Isis* 65 (1974): 144–92, at 160–61. Jacob W. Gruber, *A Conscience in Conflict: The Life of St. George Jackson Mivart* (New York: Columbia University Press, 1960), 126–27, gives a helpful summary of the argument in *Apes and Men*. There is no natural order one can make out in the primates.
32 St. George Mivart, *Apes and Man, an Exposition of Structural Resemblances and Differences Bearing upon Questions of Affinity and Origin* (London: Robert Hardwicke), 5.

attitude identifying both Africans and Irish with the gorilla as evolutionary way stations to that peak of humanity in North Britain.[33] His question about "sexual selection" is particularly pointed in the case of apes. In "Descent of Man," he notes the male teeth as instruments of domination (57). The technical, biological point in Mivart's response would take over a century to appreciate. Thomas Huxley took Mivart to be close to accepting the "inmost heart" of Darwinianism, the "ape ancestry of...the body of man."[34] The persistence of the Darwinian trajectory from ape to human is revealed in the great surprise that greeted the publication of the physiology of *Ardipithecus ramidus* in the 2 October 2009 issue of *Science*. *Ardi's* attenuated sexual dimorphism is far more human than ape; the teeth are a particularly important part of the evidence.[35]

Mivart singles out one argument by which Darwin presses the sexual selection principle in birds. We quote at length from "Descent of Man" as it shows the central supposition in Darwin's approach:

Let it be granted that the female does not select; yet the display of the male may be useful in supplying the necessary degree of stimulation to her nervous system, and to that of the male. Pleasurable sensation, perhaps very keen in intensity, may thence result to both. There would be no difficulty in suggesting yet other purposes if we were to ascend into higher speculative regions. Mr. Darwin has given us in one place a very remarkable passage; he says:—

'With respect to female birds feeling a preference for particular males, we must bear in mind that we can judge of choice being exerted,

---

33 Peart and Levy, *Vanity of the Philosopher*; David M. Levy and Sandra J. Peart, "Charles Kingsley and the Theological Interpretation of Natural Selection," *Journal of Bioeconomics* 8 (2006): 197–218.

34 Thomas Huxley, "Mr. Darwin's Critics," *Contemporary Review* 18 (1871): 443–76. Huxley writes that "high watermark of intelligence among those most respectable of Britons, the readers of the *Quarterly Review*, has now reached such a level, that the next tide may lift them easily and pleasantly on to the once-dreaded shore of evolution. Nor, having got there, do they seem likely to stop, until they have reached the inmost heart of that great region, and accepted the ape ancestry of, at any rate, the body of man" (458–59).

35 C. Owen Lovejoy, "Reexamining Human Origins in Light of *Ardipithecus ramidus*," *Science* 326 (2009): 74.

only by placing ourselves in imagination in the same position. If an inhabitant of another planet were to behold a number of young rustics at a fair, courting and quarrelling over a pretty girl, like birds at one of their places of assemblage, he would be able to infer that she had the power of choice only by observing the eagerness of the wooers to please her, and to display their finery', (vol. ii.: 122).

Now here it must be observed that, as is often the case, Mr. Darwin assumes the very point in dispute, unless he means by "power of choice" mere freedom of physical power. If he means an internal, mental faculty of choice, then the observer could attribute such power to the girl only if he had reason to attribute to the rustics an intellectual and moral nature similar in kind to that which he possessed himself. Such a similarity of nature Mr. Darwin, of course, does attribute to rational beings and to brutes. (62)

Darwin's observer from another planet cannot tell the difference between human consent and biophysical attraction. Therein lies the problem with the continuity thesis; in humans, consent does not follow automatically from attraction. In a world of monogamy one can be attracted to many, but consent only to one.

6. George Darwin's Negative Eugenics

The Darwinian involvement in the eugenic reform movement begins soon after the publication of *Descent* with George Darwin's 1873 "Beneficial Restrictions to Liberty of Marriage."[36] Both Mivart's sharp reaction and the public and private responses from both Darwins suggest that the support of negative eugenics policies flows from their understanding of biological theory laid out in the passage from *Descent* quoted

---

[36] George Darwin, "On Beneficial Restrictions to Liberty of Marriage," *Contemporary Review* 22 (1873): 412–26. See Gruber, *Conscience in Conflict*, 98–110; and Gregory P. Elder, *Chronic Vigour: Darwin, Anglicans, Catholics and the Development of a Doctrine of Providential Evolution* (Lanham, MD: University Press of America), 100–104.

above, in which the great hope of continued racial improvement depended on "the weak in body or mind refraining from marriage."[37] George Darwin starts his argument with Francis Galton's that from a policy point of view, people are similar to cattle (414). This is the strong version of the continuity thesis. George Darwin makes an important distinction that separates his proposal from Galton's. In contrast to Galton's positive eugenic proposals, George Darwin's offers an early proposal for what is called "negative" eugenics. His prediction that this will be the future course of eugenic policy was correct:

> The second and less efficient method is by the prevention of breeding from the inferior members of the race,—a result brought about by one form of "Unconscious Selection" among savages, when they kill off their inferior dogs and other domestic animals to support themselves in times of famine. This is the method which forms my groundwork in the present article, and I for my part feel little doubt that it will be the one which will be adopted, at least at the beginning. I am desirous of pointing out some of the ways in which our liberty of marriage may be affected by the adoption of this method, and not so much to indicate definite schemes of legislation, as to bring to a focus some of the considerations to be taken in initiating such schemes. (415–16)

The motivating fear expressed in the article is the inheritance of insanity. But that is just the beginning of his plans for the future of mankind. He appeals to his father's book:

---

[37] Evidence for this position is that Darwin often used surrogates for debating purposes. George Darwin had previously written the response to Wallace for his father (Vorzimmer, *Charles Darwin*, 208). Darwin's "third party" debating strategy is now the subject of a specialist study (John Angus Campbell, "The Invisible Rhetorician: Charles Darwin's 'Third Party' Strategy," *Rhetorica: A Journal of the History of Rhetoric* 7 [1989]: 55–85). The family support of eugenic policy, most famously by Leonard Darwin, who served almost two decades as the chair of the British Eugenics Society, was articulated as late as in the centennial of the *Origin of Species* at the University of Chicago by Sir Charles Galton Darwin, "Can Man Control His Numbers?" in *The Evolution of Man*, ed. Sol Tax, vol. 2 of *Evolution after Darwin: The University of Chicago Centennial* (Chicago: University of Chicago Press, 1960), 463–73, at 471.

we need a substitute to replace the weakened influence of Natural Selection.... There can be no doubt that the health of large numbers in our present highly civilized condition is alarmingly feeble, and that the advance of medical science will, by the preservation of the weak, only aggravate the evil for future generations. The extent to which, in the present age, the weak are placed almost on a par with the strong in the struggle for life has been pointed out in the "Descent of Man." (419)

In addition to describing Galton's "positive" eugenics as inefficient, he finds Greg's worry about the importance of consent simply liberal defeatism (421).

Mivart's response to this proposal was not long in coming. He wrote for a Christian audience, who would have heard the words from the *Book of Common Prayer* that proclaimed the marriage sacrament as a remedy for the sin of fornication. The abolition of marriage thus condemns some to a life of sin. Mivart also makes the point in *Apes and Man*, independent of Christian ethics, that marriage as a civil institution enforces consent in a world with an imperfectly attenuated sexual dimorphism:

> Another triumph of the same Christian period has been the establishment of at least a pure theory of the sexual relations and the protection of the weaker sex against the selfishness of male concupiscence. Now, however, marriage is the constant subject of attack, and unrestrained licentiousness theoretically justified. Mr. George Darwin proposes that divorce should be made consequent on insanity, and coolly remarks that, should the patient recover, he would suffer in no other respect than does anyone that is forced by ill-health to retire from any career he has begun[!]; although, of course, the necessary isolation of the parent from the children would he a peculiarly bitter blow. Elsewhere he speaks in an approving strain of the most oppressive laws, and of the encouragement of vice in order

to check population. There is no hideous sexual criminality of Pagan days that might not be defended on the principles advocated by the school to which this writer belongs. This repulsive phenomenon affords a fresh demonstration of what France of the Regency and Pagan Rome long ago demonstrated; namely, how easily the most profound moral corruption can co-exist with the most varied appliances of a complex civilisation. (80)

The Darwins responded immediately. George Darwin published an outraged note denying that he was intentionally advocating immorality; Charles Darwin ceased all further communication with Mivart.[38] The modern commentary has neglected Mivart's position.

7. Natural versus Human Selection in the Court of Law

Mivart's question of sexual morality was important in the nineteenth-century debates over contraception. When T. R. Malthus recommended delay of marriage until a couple could support their children, the immediate objection from many Christians was that this would encourage prostitution.[39] Francis Place's contraceptive proposal was defended by the argument that encouraging early marriage would reduce the demand for prostitutes.[40] Unregulated contraception is in many ways the epitome of human selection and in the nineteenth century was part of the liberal amelioration program. A couple could marry early in life in accordance with community norms without then demanding

---

38 G. Darwin, "Beneficial Restrictions"; on C. Darwin's reaction, see Gruber, *Conscience in Conflict*, 103–4; and Elder, *Chronic Vigour*, 101–2.

39 David M. Levy, "Some Normative Aspects of the Malthusian Controversy," *History of Political Economy* 10 (1978): 271–85, and "Christianity or Malthusianism: The Invisibility of a Successful Radicalism," *Historical Reflections/Réflexions Historiques* 25 (1999): 61–93.

40 Francis Place, *Illustrations and Proofs of the Principle of Population*. ed. Norman E. Himes (1822; London: Allen & Unwin, 1930), 177. Place argues, "Much even of that sort of promiscuous intercourse carried on by means of open prostitution, now so excessively and extensively pernicious, would cease."

support from others in the community to support their family. The critical question for public policy in the nineteenth century was whether discussion of contraceptive methods was obscene or not.

The 1877 trial of Charles Bradlaugh and Annie Besant for the "crime" of republishing a forty-year-old text on birth control—Charles Knowlton's *Fruits of Philosophy*—helps to make clear the difference between the utilitarian greatest happiness and Darwin's general good. The substantial question debated at the trial concerned the *means* by which Bradlaugh and Besant were disseminating contraceptive information. The question for the jury was this. Stipulating that contraceptive information, when presented in medical books at thirty shillings or sold to the wealthy patients of physicians at two shillings, sixpence, was entirely legal, did publishing this information in a sixpence pamphlet constitute an obscenity?[41] The high price and dissemination using physicians as intermediaries served as control mechanisms. Debate focused on whether birth-control material constituted something that people could read and understand on their own or whether it should be dispensed to those deemed by a physician capable of understanding?

The jury decided the sixpence pamphlet was obscene. When Bradlaugh's and Besant's conviction was reversed on appeal, the publication of birth-control material in Britain went unhindered. Mailed from a British address, contraceptive information could go to any other country, regardless of its laws on the matter, without legal risk to the sender. Consequently, the Bradlaugh-Besant trial has received much attention as a critical moment in the international birth-control movement.[42]

Before the trial, Bradlaugh wrote to ask whether Darwin might support the defendants at the trial. Darwin responded that he hoped not to testify because his health was suspect. He emphasized that the principle of "natural selection" ought *not* to fail when it comes to human

---

41 *Queen v Bradlaugh & Besant* [1877] 1878: 139, 147.
42 See Sripati Chandrasekhar, *"A Dirty, Filthy Book"* (Berkeley: University of California Press, 1981).

beings and he insisted that, were he called to testify at the trial, he would *oppose* Bradlaugh and Besant rather than support them.

Six years earlier, Darwin had sketched his opposition to contraception in his *Descent of Man*. Thus, when he sent Bradlaugh the passage from the first edition of *Descent of Man* that we noted above (2: 403), in which he quoted Galton's concern about the fate of the race when only the "prudent" consciously limit their numbers, Darwin reasserted his position that a goal of racial perfection attained by means of "natural selection" ought to replace the goal of human happiness attained by means of individuals' conscious choices.

The question of whether Darwin viewed "natural selection" as progressing toward some goal has focused on his published work.[43] The letter to Bradlaugh expresses Darwin's considered opinion on this issue in a serious legal context and helps clarify that Darwin was much troubled by the idea of leaving selection among humans to the unimpeded judgment of individuals.

Darwin's involvement in the trial has been reported for a century with some puzzling variation concerning what his position actually was.[44] The puzzle may have resulted from the fact that there are two parts of the communication: the then unpublished letter and an extract from *Descent of Man*. In the latter, Darwin expressed his published opposition to birth control. In the letter, he explained the meaning of the extract. In addition, as we will see, Darwin went beyond his published work in the letter to express concern about how the

---

43 See Dov Ospovat, *The Development of Darwin's Theory: Natural History, Natural Theology, and Natural Selection, 1838–1859* (Cambridge: Cambridge University Press, 1981); Ernst Mayr, *One Long Argument: Charles Darwin and the Genesis of Modern Evolutionary Thought* (Cambridge, MA: Harvard University Press, 1991); Robert J. Richards, *The Meaning of Evolution: The Morphological Construction and Ideological Reconstruction of Darwin's Theory* (Chicago: University of Chicago Press, 1992); Michael Ruse, *Afterwards: Two Decades Later*, in *The Darwin Revolution: Science Red in Tooth and Claw*, 2nd ed. (Chicago: University of Chicago Press, 1999); and Stephen Jay Gould, *The Structure of Evolutionary Theory* (Cambridge, MA: Harvard University Press, 2002).

44 See Hypatia Bradlaugh Bonner, *Charles Bradlaugh; A Record of His Life and Work* (London: T. F. Unwin, 1895), 1.24; Gloria Mc Connaughey, "Darwin and Social Darwinism," *Osiris* 9 (1950): 397–412, at 408; and Adrian J. Desmond and John Moore, *Darwin* (New York: Warner Books, 1991), 627–28.

diffusion of birth control information might affect chastity and the institution of marriage.

At the trial itself, Besant discussed the letter from Darwin at length. She defended *her* position against that of Darwin by appeal to John Stuart Mill's *Political Economy*. The public discussion of the letter speaks to the relationship between political economy and biology of the nineteenth century.[45] As we read the historical record, the Malthusian political economists favored allowing individuals consciously to limit their family size. The question of the *means* of limitation—late marriage or contraception—was much debated.[46]

Mill and Bradlaugh before the trial. That Mill admired Bradlaugh was well known in their time. Mill's ten pound contribution to Bradlaugh's 1868 parliamentary campaign was an important factor in his own election defeat.[47] This episode serves as the penultimate paragraph in Mill's 1873 *Autobiography* when he explains the election result.[48]

---

45 See S. S. Schweber, "The Origin of the Origin Revisited," *Journal of the History of Biology* 10 (1977): 229–316, and "Darwin and the Political Economists: Divergence of Character," *Journal of the History of Biology* 13 (1980): 195–289; Donald Winch, "Darwin Fallen among Political Economists," *Proceedings of the American Philosophical Society* 145 (2001): 415–37; Peart and Levy, *Vanity of the Philosopher*; Shermer, *In Darwin's Shadow*; and Levy and Peart, "Charles Kingsley."

46 James P. Huzel, *The Popularization of Malthus in Early Nineteenth-Century England: Martineau, Cobbett and the Pauper Press* (Aldershot, UK: Ashgate, 2006).

47 See Bonner, *Charles Bradlaugh*, 1: 274–75; Bruce L. Kinzer, Ann P. Robson, and John M. Robson, *A Moralist in and out of Parliament: John Stuart Mill at Westminster, 1865–1868* (Toronto: University of Toronto Press, 1992). Mill and Bradlaugh are even linked in the political cartoons of the time. One such is discussed and reproduced by Kinzer, Robson, and Robson, *Moralist*, 289–90. Another one is found in the publication *Judy* of September 30, 1868, in which horrific violence is being done to Bradlaugh. Mill is, contrary to his usual image in *Judy*, gendered masculine (Peart 2009). Mill's role in the trial did not pass unnoticed. We have published a black-and-white reproduction of the most remarkable color image from the *Cope's Tobacco Plant's* 1878 advertising "card," *In Pursuit of Diva Nicotina*. In this we find the likeness of Mill in close proximity to the very book at issue at the Bradlaugh and Besant trial, *Fruits of Philosophy*. Mill is being trampled by a crowd of pleasure seekers (Peart and Levy, *Vanity of the Philosopher*, 158, 227). There is no mystery to the connection between *Cope's Tobacco Plant* and the Bradlaugh and Besant trial. The poet James Thomson, who wrote his most acclaimed verse under the initials B. V. for Bradlaugh's *National Reformer*, was an important contributor to John Fraser's *Cope's Tobacco Plant* in that period (W. D. Schaefer, introduction to *The Speedy Extinction of Evil and Misery: Selected Prose of James Thomson (B. V.)*. ed. Schaefer [Berkeley: University of California Press, 1967], 4). Thomson seems to have lost his position at *National Reformer* because of the growing influence of Annie Besant (Henry S. Salt, *The Life of James Thomson ("B.V.")* [Port Washington, NY: Kennikat Press, 1889], 125).

48 John Stuart Mill, *Autobiography and Literary Essays*, ed. John M. Robson and Jack Stillinger, vol. 1 of *Collected Works of John Stuart Mill* (Toronto: University of Toronto Press), 289.

If the jury had forgotten this, Bradlaugh certainly reminded them.[49] This history frames Besant's testimony that their position reflected Mill's understanding of political economy, at the time widely accepted at universities.[50] Although Mill had passed away four years earlier, there could be no doubt that the defendants were able exponents of his political economy.

7.1. The Letter from Darwin to Bradlaugh

We present the letter from Darwin to Bradlaugh, as transcribed by the Darwin Correspondence Project at Cambridge University.[51]

> June 6 1877
> Sir
> I am much obliged for your courteous notice. I have been for many years much out of health & have been forced to give up all Society or public meetings, & it would be great suffering to me to be a witness in a court.—It is indeed not improbable that I might be unable to attend.
>
> Therefore I hope that if in your power you will excuse my attendance. I may add that I am not a medical man. I have not seen the book in question, but from notices in the newspapers, I suppose that it refers to means to prevent conception. If so I sh^d be forced to express

---

49 Bradlaugh testified, "I have been a journalist for the last nineteen years, and in my first prospectus I put forward the Malthusian view as part of the editorial intention of that journal, and lest the jury should think that we now take up this struggle in any mere desire for novelty or notoriety, I may mention that the late Mr. John Stuart Mill left me, written by himself, in his autobiography, a few lines stating that I commended myself to him because I took upon myself the advocacy of these Malthusian views when they were even more unpopular than to-day." *Queen v Bradlaugh & Besant* [1877] 1878, 156.

50 *Queen v Bradlaugh & Besant*, 111.

51 Charles Darwin Correspondence Project, Cambridge University transcription of calendar number 10988, draft of a letter from Charles Darwin to Charles Bradlaugh, 6 June 1877, supplied to David M. Levy and Sandra J. Peart, 6 October 2004. The transcription is at a prepublication stage and thus the Project cannot be held responsible for any errors of transcription remaining. A photographic reproduction of the letter is provided in Sandra J. Peart and David M. Levy, "Darwin's Unpublished Letter at the Bradlaugh-Besant Trial: A Question of Divided Expert Judgment," *European Journal of Political Economy* 24 (2008): 243–53.

in court a very decided opinion in opposition to you & Mrs Besant; though from all that I have heard I do not doubt that both of you are acting solely in accordance to what you believe best for mankind.— I have long held an opposite opinion, as you will see in the enclosed extract, & this I sh^d think it my duty to state in court.

When the words "any means" were written I was thinking of artificial means of preventing conception. But besides the evil here alluded to I believe that any such practices would in time spread to unmarried women & w^d destroy chastity on which the family bond depends; & the weakening of this bond would be the greatest of all possible evils to mankind; & this conclusion I sh^d likewise think it my duty to state in Court; so that my judgment, would be in the strongest opposition to yours;

On Friday the 8th I leave home for a month & my address for the 8th to.... will be at my sisters house & from the 13th at my sons house,

PS. If it is not asking too great a favour, I sh^d be greatly obliged if you w^d inform me what you decide; as apprehension of the coming exertion would prevent the rest which I receive doing me much good. Apologising for the length of this letter.
Sir your obed.
C. R D.

7.2. *The Public Record*

The public record of the trial in *Queen v. Bradlaugh & Besant* highlights the differences between Darwin and Mill on the public dissemination of contraceptive information. In her testimony at the trial, Annie Besant focused on the question of what is "natural" about natural selection. She constructed her case to show that access to contraceptive information and the prevention of misery it entailed was as "natural" as natural selection accompanied by premature death. She placed Malthus and Mill on the side of preventive checks that arise from foresight, and Darwin on the side of unthinking natural selection, which, she maintained, was not a salutary result, whether "natural" or artificial.

What is "natural" about natural selection? Besant considered this question in some detail. On the first day, she located the neo-Malthusian approach inside the larger body of Malthusian thinking. She argued that since it was uncontroversial that any species, whether human or otherwise, can grow exponentially, some "check" to population was needed. Besant identified Malthus's "positive" check—misery and starvation—with the "natural" check. This is consistent with both Darwin's and Wallace's views on the matter.[52] The positive check was "natural," she argued, only to the extent that it is a general check operating on all species:

> Those checks are divided into what are called "positive" checks, and what are called "preventive" checks. Positive checks for a moment I will call "natural" checks, following out the line of thought which the learned Solicitor-General kindly draws for my guidance, but they are "natural" only in the sense of being general throughout Nature; that is to say, it is the death-producing check which is the positive check, the check that produces death. You find it in the vegetable kingdom; you find it in the animal kingdom; the trees produce a number of seeds more than can ever grow into plants, animals produce far more young than ever can grow into maturity. If any of you have taken an interest in natural history, you will have seen there (and even without that you must know it from the common everyday matters of life), that the death producing check is the one check that acts throughout nature on all the young brought into the world, not one tithe survives to grow up into maturity; but that check is only a natural check in the sense that nature is opposed to art, to science, or to men's reason. (72–73)

---

52 Levy and Peart, "Charles Kingsley."

Besant continued to develop a profound argument. In humans, "positive checks" are "natural" only when "nature" is understood as nature *unmodified by man's reason*. She then developed the counterargument at some length, suggesting that reason and foresight offer the additional opportunity of "preventive checks" for humans.

Besant opposed the "natural" check to population and argued for the Malthusian "preventive" or "artificial" check. All the while, she insisted that her case was constructed from Malthus:

> I have pleaded that our intent is good, and that the purpose at which we aim is good, because it conduces to human and to social happiness. I have shown you from Malthus—and he has never yet been disproved—what the law of population is. I have shown that some checks must prevail, either positive or preventive. (73)

On the second day of the trial, Besant returned to the idea of Malthus's "positive" check. She identified the "positive check"—the "difficulty of subsistence and of getting food"—with Darwin:

> in his great work on the "Origin of Species," p. 61, he remarks that "of the many individuals of any species which are periodically born, but a small number can survive," and on p. 63, he says: "A struggle for existence inevitably follows, from the high rate at which all organic beings tend to increase. Every living being which, during its natural lifetime, produces eggs or seeds, must suffer destruction during some period of its life, and during some season or occasional year; otherwise, on the principle of geometrical increase, its numbers would quickly become so inordinately great that no country could support the product. Hence, as more individuals are produced than can possibly survive, there must, in every case, be a struggle for existence, either one individual with another of the same species, or with individuals of distinct species, or with the physical conditions of life. It is the doctrine of Malthus applied with manifold force to the whole

animal and vegetable kingdoms, for in this case there can be no artificial increase of food, no prudential restraint from marriage." (75–76)

In Besant's view, the only argument against the preventive check was that of natural selection:

One argument only of those which are used against the checks which we propose to introduce is deserving of smallest consideration. Mr. Darwin in his "Origin of Species" puts that argument in the strongest light. Mr. Darwin thinks rightly, with reference to the lower animals, that the application of "natural" checks upon the natural rate of increase is really for the welfare and progress of the various classes of brutes; and Mr. Darwin thinks this "natural" check good for the human species, and in this he is supported to a certain extent by Mr. Herbert Spencer. I will venture to lay before you what I consider to be his strongest statement of that argument, and therefore of any possible objection.

This, too, she opposed, having first placed Darwin on the side of natural selection and in opposition to birth control. At this point in the trial, Besant quoted at length from Darwin's letter to Bradlaugh:

Mr. Darwin, writing to us a few days since, pointed our attention to the following extract from his "Descent of Man," p. 618:—"The enhancement [sic] of the welfare of mankind is a most intricate problem; all ought to refrain from marriage who cannot avoid abject poverty for their children, for poverty is not only a great evil, but tends to its own increase by leading to recklessness in marriage. On the other hand, as Mr. Galton has remarked, if the prudent avoid marriage, whilst the reckless marry, the inferior members tend to supplant the better members of society. Man, like every other animal, has no doubt advanced to his present high condition through a struggle for existence, consequent on his rapid multiplication, and if he is to advance still higher it is to be feared that he must remain subject to a severe struggle; otherwise he would sink into indolence, and the more gifted men would not be more successful in the battle of life than the less gifted. Hence our natural rate of increase, though leading to many and obvious evils, must not be greatly diminished by any means." That is Mr. Darwin's position, and, putting aside for a moment the awful amount of human misery which it accepts as the necessary condition of progress, let us see if the position be defensible. (96)

Darwin's name attracted the attention of the court. In an exchange between Besant and the lord chief justice, the chief justice agreed with Besant that Darwin had failed fully to appreciate the case for "scientific" means to check population.

> Mrs. Besant:....it seems to me that in his argument Mr. Darwin has altogether overlooked this aspect of the question, which is fatal to the ground that he has taken up—the ground that the natural checks should be sufficient in the human as in the animal kingdoms to overcome the tendency to over-population. We have not, therefore, to deal with natural so much as with scientific checks.
>
> The Lord Chief Justice: I think that is a point very well worth the serious consideration of Mr. Darwin. Whether there may result, as a consequence of the struggle for existence among mankind, the survival of a smaller number of the strongest, or a larger number of the weaker, and whether, should it be found that the weaker survive, the race is not by that means in process of deterioration. The process might result in a few of a higher race, but the effect on the masses would be an increase of suffering and of misery.
>
> Mrs. Besant: That, my lord, is just the point that I have been endeavouring to make. (97–98)

Besant's goal was to "enable people to marry early, and, at the same time, to avoid those evils which come by over-population" (110). She found an ally in the political economists of the time, notably John Stuart Mill, whose *Principles* she quoted next (111–12).

The report in the Times. The *Times* reported extensively on the case of "The Queen v Bradlaugh and Another," hiding Besant's name apparently in order to protect her reputation. Not surprisingly, given the sketch of the trial and the letter from Darwin reproduced above, the coverage emphasized that the trial centered on a conflict between Mill and Darwin. Unlike Darwin, the *Times* reported, Mill advocated "the substitution of prudential and scientific checks for these natural or positive checks" to population growth as a means of reducing poverty.[53]

8. The Long Shadow of Eugenic Philosophy

Eugenic reforms in their idealized form were advanced without concern for obtaining the consent of the persons to be harmed. Taking the continuity thesis as norm and natural selection as the method of racial progress, then such a constraint would be an unnecessary impediment. This view is evident in F. Y. Edgeworth's blend of Darwin and utilitarianism in which it would be better for society if low-capacity individuals were not allowed to have children.[54] This is a remarkable demonstration of the power of systems of thought, since Edgeworth's model is populated by sympathetic agents who might well care when those with whom they are sympathetically connected were harmed by an empowered modeler.

---

53 "The Queen v Bradlaugh and Another," *London Times*, 20 June 1877: 11.
54 F. Y. Edgeworth, *Mathematical Psychics* (London: Kegan Paul, 1881), 70–77; Peart and Levy, *Vanity of the Philosopher*, 226–30.

CHAPTER ELEVEN

Fair and Impartial Spectators in Experimental Economic Behavior

USING SYMPATHY TO DRIVE ACTION

Vernon L. Smith and Bart J. Wilson

> If he would act so as that the impartial spectator may enter into the principles of his conduct...he must...humble the arrogance of his self-love, and bring it down to something which other men can go along with.
> —ADAM SMITH, *Theory of Moral Sentiments*, II.ii.2.1

1. INTRODUCTION

Our primary purpose in this essay is to draw on the literature of classical liberal economy to show how it informs and is informed by results from experimental economics.[1] Adam Smith's first great book, *The Theory of Moral Sentiments* (hereafter *TMS*), serves as our chief source of insights for understanding and interpreting modern laboratory research in terms of the conventions that govern human conduct in personal exchange.[2] At the same time, we wish to demonstrate how today's economic experiments elucidate a reading of Adam Smith.

---

1 This chapter is a modified version of the article of the same title originally published in the *Review of Behavioral Economics* and reprinted here with permission.
2 Page numbers cited from *The Theory of Moral Sentiments* (1759) are to the edition of D. D. Raphael and A. L. Macfie (Indianapolis: Liberty Fund, 1984).

We report results from a variety of two-person laboratory experiments motivated originally by game-theoretic predictions. In these economic environments we see property rights, in the sense of rights and wrongs of taking certain actions. In personal exchange environments, these property rights are involved as mediators of choice; that is, they emerge as conventions, or a form of mutual consent, that are recognized implicitly, or not, within the group by the interacting individuals, and that determine whether cooperative outcomes are realized or not. In impersonal market exchange, these socially grown rights have become codified in externally imposed and enforced rules, defining an institution that governs exchange and outcomes.[3] This insight into the social origins of property rights is captured in Hayek's quotation from Julius Paulus, a third-century AD Roman jurist: "What is right is not derived from the rule, but the rule arises from our knowledge of what is right."[4]

2. Principles of Action in *TMS*

The arguments that follow make use of our interpretation of Adam Smith's theory of the mental and emotional states that serve to mediate the individual actions that produce those states; accordingly, we provide a very brief overview of these principles of action.

Humans desire and seek praise and praiseworthiness; also to avoid blame and blameworthiness.[5] Praise and praiseworthiness are connected, but the latter is not derived from the former and the two are somewhat

---

[3] See Vernon L. Smith, "Adam Smith: From Propriety and *Sentiments* to Property and *Wealth*," *Forum for Social Economics*, 16 July 2013, http://www.tandfonline.com/doi/abs/10.1080/07360932.2013.798241#.UiizvtIqh8E, for further discussion of *TMS* as providing a theory of the transformation of the rules of propriety in small groups into property rights for the civil order based on third-party enforcement and setting the stage for Smith's *An Enquiry into the Nature and Causes of the Wealth of Nations*. In this critical sense, *Wealth of Nations* presupposes *TMS*, and the two works define a coherent Smithian "humanomics."

[4] Friedrich A. Hayek, *Law, Legislation and Liberty*, vol. 1: *Rules and Order* (Chicago: University of Chicago Press, 1973), 162.

[5] *TMS*, III.2.1, 114. All citations such as this in the text are to *TMS*, with the final number representing page number in the Raphael and Mcfie edition.

independent (III.2.2–3, 114). Thus praise yields little pleasure if, in ignorance or error, we judge it—via the impartial spectator—to be undeserved (III.2.4, 114–15). Similarly, we find satisfaction in our praiseworthy conduct, even if no such praise is likely to be bestowed on us (III.2.5, 115–16). In these passages it is important for modern economic readers to avoid thinking of words like "satisfaction" and "pleasure" as being equivalent to or yielding "utility," which for Smith meant merely and only "useful" (IV.1.6, 180). For Smith what was satisfying or pleasing was the conformance of our conduct with social propriety in choosing an action.

Concerning action for the self, Smith followed the Stoics in arguing that "self-love" is recommended to all by the requirements of self-preservation, but its arrogant forms must at all times be humbled in order to pursue actions that conform to the judgments of one's impartial spectator (II.ii.2.1, 82–83; VII.ii.1.15, 272).[6]

3. The Impartial Spectator

Our actions are subject to a discipline of self-command by principles that operate through the metaphor of the "fair and impartial spectator," or simply the impartial spectator:

---

[6] Formally, we might think of a beneficent action taken by individual i as depending on its propriety, given the circumstances:

$$a_i(\text{Propriety}|C) = \alpha_i(C)(PR) + \beta_i(C)(PR)\cdot(PW) + \gamma_i(C)(PW) + \delta_i(C),$$

where PR and PW are (0, 1) indicator variables that an action deserves social praise (1), or not (0), and is praiseworthy (1), or not (0); and $\alpha_i, \beta_i, \gamma_i,$ and δ_i are nonnegative functions. In the second term, PW adds leverage to PR, while the third term expresses the TMS sentiment that PW may yield stand-alone value even where it can never receive praise. C defines the circumstances—the game structure, including i's choice of alternatives and their payoffs. Each action is based on conduct that is more or less satisfying or pleasing conditional on circumstances, and the action chosen is the one most satisfactory according to these socially mediated criteria. The term $\delta_i(C)$, independent of the social indicators, allows "self-love" to be part of the evaluation of action. This function is defined only on own payoffs. One implication is that where i's information is limited regarding the choice or payoffs of other individuals, then i cannot infer the intent of other individuals and thereby reward beneficence, although she may still value her decision as praiseworthy; hence $\alpha_i = \beta_i = 0$, and $\delta_i(C)$ looms larger than otherwise in determining the choice. A formal treatment similar to the above would apply where blame and blameworthiness were elements to be applied to the evaluation of some actions. Even where payoffs are large, self-love may be constrained by considerations of blame and blameworthiness.

We endeavour to examine our own conduct as we imagine any other fair and impartial spectator would examine it. If, upon placing ourselves in his situation, we thoroughly enter into all the passions and motives which influenced it, we approve of it, by sympathy with the approbation of this supposed equitable judge. If otherwise, we enter into his disapprobation, and condemn it. (III.1.2, 110)

The words "fair," "impartial" and "equitable" were chosen, we believe, quite deliberately by Smith to represent judgment by a neutral referee as to whether an action was fair or foul under the applicable rules of interaction given the circumstances. Within Smith's metaphor of the impartial spectator is the sports metaphor of judgment under the rules of the game.[7] Smith repeatedly makes reference to actions that "other people" or "mankind," or the "impartial spectator," "can go along with" (or not). The Impartial Spectator constitutes an internalization of what is approved or not approved by others. We are encouraged to take actions that others can go along with, and deterred from actions that they cannot and find objectionable: others "always mark when they enter into, and when they disapprove of (our) sentiments" (III.1.3, 110). This characterization of human sociality serves to mediate human action, however imperfectly.[8] As a social-psychological restraint it emerges first in our families, extended families, and friendship enclaves, but ultimately appears in the laws codified by civil society (VI.ii.introduction,1, 218–27; II.ii.2.2–3, 83–85).

---

7 For a discussion of "fair" as playing within the rules of social practice, see Bart J. Wilson, "Contra Private Fairness," *American Journal of Economics and Sociology* 71 (2012): 407–35, particularly note 7, which discusses the eighteenth-century meaning of the word. Adam Smith's usage of "fairness" stands in sharp contrast to the interpretation and discussion in Nava Ashraf, Colin Camerer, and George Lowenstein, "Adam Smith, Behavioral Economist," *Journal of Economic Perspectives* 19.3 (2005): 131–45, at 136–37.

8 The impartial spectator is not, however, equivalent to our conscience because "[t]he word conscience does not immediately denote any moral faculty by which we approve or disapprove. Conscience supposes, indeed, the existence of some such faculty, and properly signifies our consciousness of having acted agreeably or contrary to its directions" (*TMS*, VII.iii.3.15, 326). Ashraf, Camerer, and Lowenstein miss this distinction in their reading of *TMS* when they argue that "[i]n social situations, the impartial spectator plays the role of a conscience" (132).

The impartial spectator enters in two ways: our judgments of the actions of others and judgments of, and actions by, ourselves. Propositions concerning our judgments of the actions of others include the following:

- Properly motivated beneficent actions alone require reward. Why? Because it is these actions alone that inspire our gratitude (II.ii.1.1, 78).
- Improperly motivated hurtful actions alone deserve punishment. Why? Because these actions alone provoke resentment (II.ii.1.2, 78).
- The want of beneficence cannot provoke resentment.[9] Why? Because beneficence is always free (voluntarily given) and "cannot be exhorted by force" (II.ii.1.3, 78–79).

In *TMS* the emotion of resentment has a central role in expressing disapproval and emerges in human social interactions, providing common experience and a consensual foundation for rights to take action in social groupings. Thus, resentment safeguards justice by provoking the punishment of an injustice already done to another, while protecting against injustice by deterring others who fear punishment if they commit a like offense (II.ii.1.4–5, 79–80). Retaliation is a law of nature that requires the violator of the laws of justice to feel the evil done to another; he who simply observes and does not violate the laws of justice merits no reward, but only respect for his innocence (II.ii.1.9–10, 82).

Judgments of, and actions by, ourselves are governed by the principles of approval (or disapproval) of our own conduct:

- These reflect the judgments we apply to others as we endeavor to exchange, mirror-like, our perspective with that of others,

---

[9] Thus, as we interpret it, if I pass up an opportunity to trustingly benefit you this would or need not be cause for your resentment. But if I should accept the opportunity, and you take advantage of my trust, then I have just cause for resentment of your action. Vernon L. Smith and Bart J. Wilson, "*Sentiments,* Conduct, and Trust in the Laboratory," Economic Science Institute Working Paper, Chapman University, 2013; and Jan Osborn, Bart J. Wilson, and Bradley R. Sherwood, "Conduct in Narrativized Trust Games," *Southern Economic Journal,* forthcoming, test these conjectures.

and "[t]o see oursels as ithers see us"[10] in which we imagine our conduct examined by any other fair and impartial spectator.
- We possess no other looking glass with which to examine our own conduct.
- In this, each becomes as two persons—the first is the impartial spectator, the judge; the second is the agent, himself the person judged (III.1.2–6, 109–13).[11]

4. Traditional Game Theory and Experimental Economics

Initially, many of the experimental game results were interpreted through the loss of game theory; subsequently, experiments were designed to better understand why the initial results so often deviated from game-theoretic predictions. Hence, we begin with a simple reduced form representation of a game as in Joel Sobel's article "Interdependent Preferences and Reciprocity" of 2005.[12] We then modify that framework with a formalization that we believe corresponds more accurately to the way Adam Smith constructed a process view of human sociality in *TMS*.

Suppose that individual $i = 1,...,n$ selects an action, x_i, in a stage game to maximize $Z_i(x)$, where $x = (x_1,... x_i,... x_n)$ are strategy choices by n players:

$$Z_i(x) = (1-d)u_i(x) + dV_i[H(x)], \qquad (1)$$

where $1 > d > 0$ is the discount rate, $H(x)$ is the history of play, u_i is i's self-loving "utility" outcome from the choice x_i in the stage game, and V_i is the value to i of continuation of play. (In the discussion below our examples are for $n = 2$ persons.)

---

10 From Robert Burns, "Ode to a Louse." Burns, we should note, was born the year *TMS* was published.

11 "We suppose ourselves the spectators of our own behaviour, and endeavour to imagine what effect it would, in this light, produce upon us. This is the only looking-glass by which we can, in some measure, with the eyes of other people, scrutinize the propriety of our own conduct. If in this view it pleases us, we are tolerably satisfied" (III.1.5, 112).

12 Joel Sobel, "Interdependent Preferences and Reciprocity," *Journal of Economic Literature* 93 (2005): 392–436.

$Z_i(x)$ is interpreted as the criterion of judgment for decision making by i in a single sequential repetition of the same stage game with the same well-identified other individual. $Z_i(x)$ is described as i's discounted current plus future utility in a pairing created by the experimenter. Hence, $H(x)$ includes all history, as well as the shadow of i's anticipated future history of play with the other. As described by Sobel: "Repeated-game theory incorporates strategic context, not by changing preferences but by changing the way people play. In order to obtain equilibria distinct from repetitions of equilibria of the underlying static game, the history of play must influence future play. History does not influence preferences, but it does influence expectations about behavior" (412). To achieve this, actions may take the form of punishments and rewards, contingent on actions by the other, that shape the self-loving behavior of the other so as to enable i to maximize her long-term self-loving interest over the horizon of the repeated game.

In this development, V_i is an endogenous function of the history of play. If V_i is positive and d is sufficiently large (near enough to 1), then in maximizing $Z_i(x)$, i must take care not to spoil her self-loving future interaction with this particular other person by her choice in the present—a care that in traditional repeated game theory exhausts the content of actions that are social; that is, her sociality is defined and confined relative to her historical and anticipated future interactions with the particular person with whom she has been paired.

In game theory repetition is essential for long-term strategic success in achieving cooperative results, but laboratory experiments have long recorded significant levels of cooperation in single plays of a stage game in which the anonymous players forgo larger payoff for themselves in favor (or expectations) of a cooperative outcome. Therefore, as noted by Sobel, "[b]ecause laboratory experiments carefully control for repeated-game effects, these results need a different explanation" (411). That is, in a single play of the stage game a rational i is *assumed* to set $V_i = 0$ when matched with an unknown other person who therefore is presumed to be a "stranger" whom person i cannot identify and thereby build on any relevant personal history. Hence, both *i* and the other are predicted to choose self-loving dominant outcomes, whatever the circumstances defined by the game.

The "different explanation" commonly offered for experimentally observed cooperative outcomes is the postulate of other-regarding or "social preferences" that rationalize the observed behavior by each player attributing his own utility (or envious disutility) to money assigned to the other, as well as money assigned to one's self in a single play of the stage game.

In this explanation any generosity, positive or negative, has been accounted for by simply augmenting post hoc the decision maker's utility function in an appropriate way. But we cannot infer utility from decision choice. The "if" in the scientific proposition "if preferences are social then choices will be other regarding" is replaced by "if and only if." It is the latter proposition that has been widely adopted by theorists and experimenters since the predictive failures of game theory started to accumulate.

Adam Smith carefully and thoughtfully modeled human interactions of this kind, not as governed by one's own versus other utilitarian considerations, but by *conduct*—rules conditioned by propriety.[13] In following these principles the individual is pleased by the actions driven by her self-judgment, but "pleased" does not map into a utilitarian reward. Even if one can identify a formal case-by-case technical equivalence between outcome utilities and actions motivated by conduct rules, following such mechanical curve fitting involves an omitted essential step, and risks failing to articulate a process that disciplines our understanding of how and why context matters in games and life.[14] Adam Smith, who

---

13 Two articles, Bart J. Wilson, "Language Games of Reciprocity," *Journal of Economic Behavior and Organization* 68 (2008): 365–77, and "Social Preferences Aren't Preferences," *Journal of Economic Behavior and Organization* 73 (2010): 77–82, use the insights of Ludwig Wittgenstein to make the related point that rules of conduct cannot be represented by utilitarian preferences, but are rather embedded in language games, the lifelong social intercourse that each of us has with the rest of humankind. The impartial spectator is Adam Smith's version of that intercourse with oneself.

14 Evidence of the failure of utilitarianism is prominent in the ubiquitous observation that varying payoffs for a given context matters much less than varying the contextual circumstances given payoffs. See Colin Camerer, *Behavioral Game Theory* (Princeton, NJ: Princeton University Press, 2003), 60–61,

believed *TMS* was his most important work, provides a meaningful systematic approach to experimental testing as an alternative to extending utilitarianism.

In (1), if H is "history," a decision must be informed by one's entire cultural and social experience, and the exploration of this social experience may expose thinking to non-preference-based forms of other-regarding behavior. In this development, actions are only intelligible in reference to moral judgments of one's own and others' actions in past and anticipated future interactions. What is important about the actions is the conduct (including intentions) they signal, and not merely the outcomes the actions yield.

Such a pathway is provided by Smith's program in *TMS*. That pathway not only includes a continuation value, which we will now call $W_i[H(x)]$ where the stage game is to be repeated, but also sympathetically modifies the self-loving first term, $u_i(x)$, in equation (1). Moreover, W_i is now based on expected future conduct, both one's own and the other's, and not only on outcomes.

In *TMS*, individuals are motivated to seek praise and praiseworthiness, and to avoid blame and blameworthiness, in all social interactions. And in judging her own conduct, a person i will always imagine that conduct as being examined by a fair and impartial spectator. Her actions will vary with circumstances, based on experience, but require that her conduct serve personal long-term (reputation) ends across a wide variety of human social encounters. When she knows little of a particular other she may be cautious, and more preserving of immediate

---

for a report of the minor effects on ultimatum game outcomes of varying the stakes by factors of 10 and much higher; and Armin Falk, Ernst Fehr, and Urs Fischbacher, "On the Nature of Fair Behavior," *Economic Inquiry*, 41.1 (2007): 20–26, for an examination of the importance of intentions. In Elizabeth Hoffman, Kevin McCabe, Keith Shachat, and Vernon L. Smith, "Preferences, Property Rights, and Anonymity in Bargaining Experiments," *Games and Economic Behavior* 7.3 (1994): 346–80, ultimatum game choices vary significantly with circumstances, whereas in Elizabeth Hoffman, Kevin McCabe, and Vernon L. Smith, "On Expectations and the Monetary Stakes in Ultimatum Games," *International Journal of Game Theory* 25.3 (1996): 289–301, a tenfold increase in payoff levels yields an insignificant effect on choices. Yet these games have been ritualistically modeled by attempts to refit explanatory utility functions to the shifting circumstances recorded by experiments.

Stoic care for herself, but, even so, she knows it is another human, recruited from a group whose characteristics may not be that dissimilar from her own, and she relies on self-command principles that have served her well on average in the past. Her action x_i will generate a current value that we will designate $U_i[x|H_i(\text{o})]$, where $H_i(\text{o})$ is her current entry-level personal historical state (after reading the instructions of the experiment). U_i values i's conduct in taking immediate action x_j; part of that valuation is the resulting payoffs. But the value attained is derived from the judgment of the impartial spectator as to the propriety of her action, albeit including that the payoffs *are deserved and justified by the circumstances*.

That our description of $U_i[x|H_i(\text{o})]$ captures baseline elements in Smith's criterion for weighing the present against the future by a prudent person, under the self-commanding judgment of the impartial spectator, seems plainly evident in the following quotation from *TMS*:

> [I]n his steadily sacrificing the ease and enjoyment of the present moment for the probable expectation of the still greater ease and enjoyment of a more distant but more lasting period of time, the prudent man is always both supported and rewarded by the entire approbation of the impartial spectator, and of the representative of the impartial spectator, the man within the breast. The impartial spectator does not feel himself worn out by the present labour of those whose conduct he surveys; nor does he feel himself solicited by the importunate calls of their present appetites. To him their present, and what is likely to be their future situation, are very nearly the same: he sees them nearly at the same distance, and is affected by them very nearly in the same manner. He knows, however, that to the persons principally concerned, they are very far from being the same, and that they naturally affect *them* in a very different manner. He cannot therefore but approve, and even applaud, that proper exertion of self-command, which enables them to act as if their present

and their future situation affected them nearly in the same manner in which they affect him. (VI.i.11, 215)

Instead of equation (1) we now have a sympathy-derived criterion of action

$$S_i(x) = (1-d)U_i\left[x|H_i(0)\right] + d \cdot W_i\left[H(x)\right] \qquad (2)$$

If $W_i = 0$, as in an advertised one-shot game, max $S_i(x)$ does not reduce to max $Z_i(x)$; that would occur only for an *i* raised in isolation from all contact with other humans, or who is otherwise barren of all socialization: "To a man who from his birth was a stranger to society, the objects of his passions, the external bodies which either pleased or hurt him, would occupy his whole attention" (III.1.3, 110).

With $W_i > 0$, equation (2) allows action to accommodate the knowledge that the interaction will be repeated, and thereby enables the relationship with the other to be influenced by possible futures that the two are able to create beyond the self-command principles that would apply to a single encounter that already contains baseline considerations of futurity as in the above quote from *TMS*. Under repetition, judgments by the impartial spectator of each person in his shared interaction will be updated based on how each reads the intentions conveyed sequentially by the other.

5. Ultimatum Games

In this game people are recruited to the lab in groups, say of twelve, and are randomized into pairs, and at random one person is selected to be the proposer, the other the responder. The task of each pair is to determine the allocation of a fixed sum of money, *M*, say ten dollars or one hundred dollars (consisting of ten one-dollar bills or ten ten-dollar bills) between them, under the following rules: The proposer chooses an amount *y* for herself, with the understanding that $M - y$ is allocated to the responder. Play then passes to the responder, who either accepts the allocation, in which case the indicated payments will be made to each, or he rejects the allocation, in which case each receives zero from the interaction.[15] The subgame perfect equilibrium of the game is for the proposer to offer one dollar (the minimum unit of account), and for the responder to accept. The latter should accept any amount that is better than zero, and, in awareness of this, the proposer offers that amount. The data tend to show very high rejection rates of one dollar, and rejections of amounts up to three dollars are not uncommon. But proposers appear to anticipate this behavior and very few offer low amounts. In experiments described as a "divide $\$M$" game the average offer is commonly about 45 percent of M, but offers change substantially with variations in the context and instructions.[16]

The first thought, for those schooled in *TMS*, might be that this behavior suggests that the impartial spectator of each player is at work evaluating the propriety of their actions. But this is a strange game to consider as a test of the propositions from *TMS* summarized above. Smith informs us emphatically that "[b]eneficence is always free, it cannot be extorted by force, the mere want of it exposes to no punishment; because the mere want of beneficence tends to do no real positive evil" (II.ii.1.3, 78). Rethinking the ultimatum game in this light, we can say:

- As in most lab experiments, people are recruited to the lab not knowing the experiment that is to occupy them.
- They arrive and are not offered a choice between alternative experimental games.

---

15 The ultimatum game originated with Werner Güth, Rolf Schmittberger, and Bernd Schwarze, "An Experimental Analysis of Ultimatum Bargaining," *Journal of Economic Behavior and Organization* 3.4 (1982): 367–88, and has spawned a vast literature. See, for example, Robert Forsythe, Joel L. Horowitz, N. E. Savin, and Martin Sefton, "Fairness in Simple Bargaining Experiments," *Games and Economic Behavior* 6.3 (1994): 347–69; Hoffman et al., "Preferences, Property Rights"; Hoffman, McCabe, and Smith, "On Expectations"; and for a partial survey, Camerer, *Behavioral Game Theory*, 48–59.
16 See Vernon L. Smith, *Rationality in Economics: Constructivist and Ecological Forms* (New York: Cambridge University Press, 2008); Camerer, *Behavioral Game Theory*.

- These procedures are carefully designed to control for self-selection bias, but as we see, other conditions may be inadvertently controlled for.
- These procedures, however, are hardly sacred: the first rule of any experimentalist should be that the experiment and its design be relevant to its purpose. One should backward induct from the purpose, and the question, to the design of the experiment.
- Playing the ultimatum game does not constitute a voluntary action. Have we gathered much data on pairs of "reluctant duelists," without this being part of our intention?
- Borrowing Adam Smith's words, should we not think of the ultimatum game as an "extortion game." The proposer under the terms of her participation must decide on y, with $M - y$ awarded to the responder. Is her choice motivated by beneficence? Is the responder rewarding beneficence by his acceptance of $M - y$? Is he punishing "want of beneficence" by rejecting it?
- The circumstances of the game—to which the impartial spectator must always be sensitive in the light of experience—are such that our answers to these questions are surely, "No," or at least "Mmm." From the perspective of *TMS* this is a mixed motive game.

These considerations cannot be dismissed with the convenient ex post argument that "in many situations one must play a game, even against one's wishes."[17] Rather the question is whether it is useful to think about the ultimatum game from a broader perspective, such as that in *TMS*, for there are experiments showing clearly that it matters

---

17 The quotation is from Daniel Ellsberg, "Theory of the Reluctant Duelist," *American Economic Review*, 46.5 (1956): 909–23, who notes that minimax strategies were not satisfactory solutions to zero-sum games, because if that were the solution to playing the game, and a person had the option to refuse play, then "[h]e would never play" (922).

how one arrives at the circumstance of deciding on a take-it-or-leave-it offer. Timothy Salmon and Bart J. Wilson's article of 2008 on second-chance offers is a case in point.[18] In their experiment motivated by observations on eBay, they embed an ultimatum game in a context of multiple buyers competing for purchases from a single seller. The seller has two units of the same good for sale, the first of which is auctioned off to the highest bidder in a typical English (ascending price) auction. For the second unit, the seller then makes a take-it-or-leave-it offer to the bidder with the highest losing bid (the second highest bidder). If the buyer accepts, he receives a profit equal to the difference between his randomly drawn value and the seller's offer. If he rejects, neither the seller nor the buyer earn anything on that unit.

Salmon and Wilson find that in a treatment with only two competing bidders, only 12 of 273 offers (4.4 percent) are rejected. Moreover, 93 of those offers are greater than the buyer's final (but losing) bid, and only 6 of those are rejected. In other words, the seller is attempting to extract even more surplus out of the buyer and the buyers still do not reject the offers. With four bidders, 111 profitable offers are made to the bidders and only 4 (3.6 percent) are rejected. But here's the kicker. The median accepted surplus is a mere sixty-one cents and thirty-nine cents in the two- and four-bidder treatments, respectively. In contrast, Elizabeth Hoffman and colleagues in "Preferences, Property Rights" find that 10.4 percent of all offers are rejected, usually for amounts of two dollars and three dollars, even when the ultimatum game is framed as a one-shot buyer-seller negotiation over a price.[19]

Why are the Salmon and Wilson results so strikingly different relative to the standard ultimatum game? Because, in our interpretation of

---

18 Timothy C. Salmon and Bart J. Wilson, "Second Chance Offers Versus Sequential Auctions: Theory and Behavior," *Economic Theory* 34 (2008): 47–67.

19 Hoffman, McCabe, and Smith, "On Expectations," report rejections of thirty dollars offered from stakes of one hundred dollars; John List and Todd L. Cherry, "Learning to Accept in Ultimatum Games: Evidence from an Experimental Design that Generates Low Offers," *Experimental Economics* 3.1 (2000): 11–29, report rejections of offers of one hundred dollars where the stakes are four hundred dollars.

TMS, the ultimatum game over the second unit is not a game of extortion mixed with beneficence from receiving a windfall. The second unit is a game of prudence with an immediate history, and the context that invokes the virtue of prudence is distinct from those that call for the virtues of beneficence or justice (*TMS*, part 6). There is no open-ended question as to whether the seller is being beneficent enough with his offer to the buyer because he's not beneficently splitting a windfall with the buyer. He's prudently attempting to sell the second unit of a commodity to a buyer who couldn't pay as much as some other buyer for the first unit. Unlike the traditional ultimatum game, we observe that there's simply no beneficence to assess in a seller's take-it-or-leave-it offer.

Likewise, there is also no room for resentment of the seller's offer, for "[r]esentment seems to have been given us by nature for defence, and for defence only" (II.ii.i.4, 79). In a reluctant game of extortion, a proposer may go too far in extracting money from the windfall and thus an offer of two dollars may "prompt us to beat off the mischief which is attempted to be done to us, and to retaliate that which is already done" (II.ii.i.4, 79). But in the Salmon and Wilson markets, where is the mischief on the part of the seller? The buyer has just demonstrated he is unwilling to name and pay a price as high as someone else and in the process he has revealed approximately how much he is willing to spend. So when faced with take-it-or-leave-it, the buyer takes it nearly every time. Notice, in comparing observations from the two different experimental designs, that the process is governed by "fairness" in the sense of the rules of conduct given the circumstances, not whether the outcomes are fair.

Paul Pecorino and Mark Van Boening in a 2010 article embed the ultimatum game in the context of a litigation dispute.[20] A plaintiff and a defendant are bargaining over how to split the cost savings of not

---

20 Paul Pecorino and Mark Van Boening, "Fairness in an Embedded Ultimatum Game," *Journal of Law and Economics* 53 (2010): 263–87.

going to trial, 75¢ to the plaintiff and 75¢ to the defendant. To avoid this cost, the defendant makes a pretrial settlement offer to the plaintiff. If the plaintiff accepts the settlement offer, neither incurs the trial costs. The plaintiff receives the offer as payment and the defendant incurs the cost of his wrongdoing (which is subtracted as a lump sum given to him by the experimenter). If the plaintiff rejects the offer, then the plaintiff receives a judgment from which the trial costs are subtracted, and the defendant incurs the trial cost and the cost of judgment. In the baseline comparison treatment, a proposer and a responder play a traditional ultimatum game with $M = \$1.50$. Both versions are repeated for ten rounds.

In the embedded game, the median offer by the defendant is 8 percent of $1.50, or 12¢. In Pecorino and Van Boening's replication of the traditional ultimatum game, the median proposer offer is 50 percent of $1.50, or 75¢. For similar offers of 0–25¢, 23 percent of the offers are rejected in the litigation game and 100 percent in the traditional game. Thus, defendants offer less and plaintiffs accept more often than their counterparts in the traditional ultimatum game. How does the *TMS* framework help us understand this? In the litigation game, the motives are no longer mixed. The proposing defendant is attempting to avoid a loss with an offer to the plaintiff that corresponds to the plaintiff avoiding the cost of a trial. While the experimenter has thrown them into a dispute, albeit an unavoidable one (which might explain the high rejection rates of 21–25 percent), mutually avoiding a cost is not a matter of beneficence on the part of the defendant.[21] In the litigation game, prudence in the form of accepting an offer equal to her opportunity cost is a virtue for the plaintiff, and not a matter of how beneficent the defendant is in his offer. Regardless of what happens, the defendant is minimizing the depletions from his upfront windfall.

---

21 Nancy Buchan, Rachel Croson, Eric Johnson, and George Wu, "Gain and Loss Ultimatums," in *Advances in Behavioral and Experimental Economics*, ed. John Morgan (San Diego: Elsevier, (2005), 1–24, observe similar differences between ultimatum games over gains versus losses, though not to such a stark extent.

6. Trust Games: Single Play

Consider the following two-person game commonly studied by experimental economists in a variety of forms and summarized in figure 11.1. Person 1 chooses to either (a) end the interaction sending each person on his or her way with an additional ten dollars or (b) forgo his sure ten dollars and turn the decision making over to Person 2. If Person 1 chooses (b), then Person 2 decides between (a′) the experimenter paying her twenty-five dollars and Person 1 fifteen dollars or (b′) the experimenter paying her forty dollars and sending Person 1 on his way with nothing by way of the outcome from the interaction in this game.[22]

If Person 1 is fully aware of the choice that Person 2 faces, and vice versa, how do we understand what two anonymous people do when faced with this situation? Adam Smith notes that unless the situation calls for a rule of justice "our conduct should rather be directed by a certain idea of propriety, by a certain taste for a particular tenor of conduct, than by any regard to a precise maxim or rule" (III.6.10, 175). If that sounds fairly "loose, vague, and indeterminate" (III.6.11, 175), then that is because "there are no rules by knowledge of which we can infallibly be taught to act upon all occasions with prudence, with just magnanimity, or proper beneficence" (III.vi.11, 176). Consequently, Smith

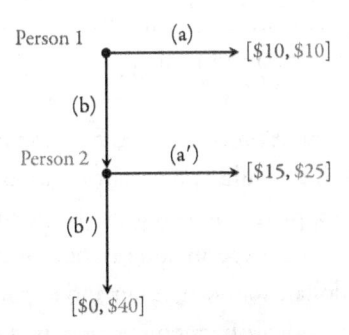

FIGURE 11.1. A Two-Person Trust Game in Extensive Form

---

[22] Experimentalists commonly pay subjects a fixed show-up payment when they arrive, which is for each person to keep whatever the outcomes of the subsequent experiment.

implicitly recognizes here that the rule a particular individual might follow can be expected to vary with the circumstances that constitute particular "occasions."

This rules out as being pertinent for all occasions the modern economist's rather precise and accurate concept of subgame perfect equilibrium, which predicts that Person 1 would immediately end the game and receive ten dollars because, if given the opportunity to make the decision, Person 2 would choose forty dollars over twenty-five dollars for herself, thereby leaving Person 1 with nothing. Fortunately, "[n]ature ... [has not] abandoned us entirely to the delusions of self-love. Our continual observations upon the conduct of others, insensibly lead us to form to ourselves certain general rules concerning what is fit and proper either to be done or to be avoided" (III.4.7, 159).

What general rules of fit and proper behavior are applicable to this game and to the experiences of this community of participants? And what would the rules predict? Let's first consider, as subgame perfection does, Person 2. If given the opportunity to make a decision, Person 2 would "endeavor to examine [her] own conduct as [she] imagines any other fair and impartial spectator would examine it. If, upon placing [herself] in his situation, [she] thoroughly enter[s] into all the passions and motives which influenced it, [she] approve[s] of it, by sympathy with the approbation of this supposed equitable judge. If, otherwise, [she] enter[s] into his disapprobation, and condemn[s] it" (III.1.2, 110).

In this game the question is whether, by sympathy with the impartial spectator, Person 2 would approve or disapprove of choosing (a′) and approve or disapprove choosing of (b′). Choosing (a′) yields a higher payment from the experimenter to both individuals as Person 1 forwent a sure ten dollars for both. A fair and impartial spectator could thus approve of (a′); both are better off because of the actions of Person 1 and Person 2. Choosing (b′), however, sends Person 1 home with nothing after forgoing a sure ten dollars. In light of (a′), Person 2 is better off, regardless of what she does, because Person 1 passed the play to her.

Thus however anonymous the participants may be in this interaction, an impartial spectator could reasonably disapprove of (b′). Now consider Person 1. From experience with friends and classmates, he expects that "[n]ature, which formed men for that mutual kindness, so necessary for their happiness, renders every man the peculiar object of kindness, to the person to whom he himself has been kind" (VI.ii.1.19, 225; hereafter, principle of reciprocal beneficence). In other words, experience has taught him that if he kindly passes the play for a mutual gain for the both of them, a Person 2 may kindly reciprocate him, the person to whom he himself has just been kind.

But must the impartial spectator disapprove of (b′)? Not necessarily, if our conduct is indeed directed by a certain idea of propriety and not a precise rule. Recall that Person 1 has the choice of (a) or (b), and if Person 1 chooses (b), Person 2 has the choice of (a′) or (b′). An impartial spectator could reason that the experimenter's rules are the rules, and everyone, including Person 1, knows the rules and has agreed to participate in this experiment. Thus, if Person 1 willingly chooses (b) an impartial spectator could also approve of (b′), for if the experimenter did not wish to observe whether Person 2 might actually choose (b′) the experimenter would not have given her the option.

TMS thus informs the experimental economist that the rules of interaction in the trust game merely "present us with a general idea of the perfection we ought to aim at, [rather] than afford us any certain and infallible directions for acquiring it" (III.6.11, 175–76), and this general idea of perfection is founded on our autobiographical experiences "of what, in particular instances, our moral faculties, our natural sense of merit and propriety, approve, or disapprove of" (III.4.8, 159). Different people, either with different experiences or different interpretations as to how their experience applies to the game in question, may converge on different responses, especially in a one-shot game.

In the laboratory the replicable facts from three different studies are that of ninety-eight first movers, fifty-two choose (a) and forty-six choose (b), and that of the forty-six second movers who have the opportunity to make a decision, thirty-one (67 percent) choose (a′) and fifteen (33 percent) choose (b′).[23] So while *TMS* modestly makes no specific prediction about what people will do in the trust game,[24] experimental economics can inform Smith's theory of the general principles with which impartial spectators approve and disapprove of (a), (b), (a′), and (b′). By randomly assigning participants to conditions with systematic variations in the procedures, we can trace out the contextual principles that excite and mediate whether more impartial spectators approve or disapprove of (a), (b), (a′), and (b′).

Typically in a laboratory experiment, subjects make decisions anonymously with respect to each other, but the experimenter knows by name what each subject did so as to pay them (privately) what they earn. This is the protocol for the data reported above. In a second condition, James Cox and Cary Deck in "On the Nature of Recipropal Motives" implement an elaborate procedure to ensure that the subjects also make their decisions anonymously with respect to the experimenter. The experimenter cannot match decisions to specific individuals. Interestingly, this change in procedures asymmetrically affects the decisions of Persons 1 and 2. First movers pass the play by choosing (b) at the same rate in both conditions. However, ten of fourteen (71 percent) second movers choose (b′) with double anonymity but only eight of twenty-five (32 percent) choose (b′) with single anonymity. It seems that increasing the private character of the interaction is one aspect of the context that excites more impartial spectators to approve of (b′). An unresolved question is why Persons 1 do not anticipate that

---

[23] Kevin McCabe and Vernon L. Smith, "A Comparison of Naïve and Sophisticated Subject Behavior with Game Theoretic Predictions," *Proceedings of the National Academy of Arts and Sciences* 97.7 (2000): 3777–81; James C. Cox and Cary A. Deck, "On the Nature of Reciprocal Motives," *Economic Inquiry*, 43 (2005): 623–35; and Anthony S. Gillies and Mary L. Rigdon, "Epistemic Conditions and Social Preferences in Trust Games," Working paper, University of Michigan, 2008.

[24] The critic who asserts that a Smithian analysis of this game is unhelpful because it does not make a specific prediction has the burden of providing and demonstrating a set of rules for this interaction that are, in the words of Adam Smith, "precise, accurate, and indispensable" (III.6.11, 175). When the experimental games on which we are reporting first began to be studied in the 1980s, the predictions of game theory performed very poorly.

Persons 2 are more disposed to choosing (b′) over (a′) with double anonymity.[25] Hence, empirical support for Smith's principle of beneficent reciprocity is strong under single, but not double, anonymity; it seems important whether people other than your matched counterpart can know your behavior.

Anthony Gillies and Mary Rigdon in "Epistemic Conditions and Social Preferences in Trust Games" consider how knowledge of the payoffs affects the play of Persons 1 and 2. In what they call a "Private Game," each person only knows his or her own payoffs associated with (a), (b), (a′), and (b′). As shown in figure 11.2, Person 1 only knows that he receives ten dollars from choosing (a) and that if he passes the play, Person 2 is choosing between fifteen dollars and zero for him. The catch is that Person 1 does not know what Person 2's payoffs are from choosing (a′) and (b′) and Person 1 knows that Person 2 does not know what his payoffs are from choosing (a′) and (b′). Likewise, Person 2 does not know what Person 1's payoff is from choosing (a), only that her payoff is ten dollars from Person 1 choosing (a).

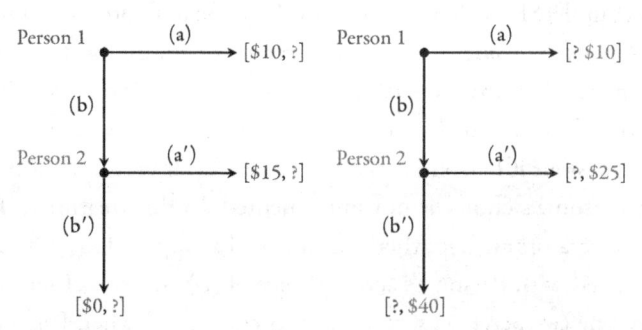

Panel (a). Person 1's View of the Game   Panel (b). Person 2's View of the Game

FIGURE 11.2. Private Knowledge of Payoffs in the Trust Game

---

25 Person 2's conduct in choosing (a′), under double anonymity, may be merely praiseworthy and thus weakened in conduct value compared with single anonymity; similarly, Person 2's choice of (b′) may be less discouraged by being merely blameworthy compared with single anonymity. Any such second-order effects may be more difficult for Persons 1 to anticipate.

Without knowledge of how his decision affects Person 2, Person 1 is unable to conclude from experience that Person 2 will reciprocate a trusting action of (b) with a trustworthy one of (a′), and that is what Gillies and Rigdon observe. Fifteen of forty-five (33 percent) first movers play down in the "private game" as opposed to twenty-one of fifty (42 percent) first movers in the full common knowledge game.

More dramatic is the response of Person 2's impartial spectators. Only three of fifteen (20 percent) second movers play (a′) in the "private game" in contrast to fourteen of twenty-one (67 percent) who do so in the full common knowledge game. More impartial spectators approve of (b′), taking the higher payoff of forty dollars, when they are unaware of what Person 1 forwent in choosing (b) and unaware of what Person 1 will receive (zero). Since neither player knows the payoff of the other, the sentiments of praise and praiseworthiness, and the principle of reciprocal beneficence, cannot enter into judging the propriety of each other's actions; hence their self-love cannot be "humbled" by the impartial spectator and is necessarily more important under such game circumstances.

In the complete knowledge version of the game in figure 11.1, Gillies and Rigdon also consider in a separate treatment condition how Persons 2 behave when they are asked to make their decision assuming that Person 1 has chosen (b). Persons 2, however, are only paid based on those decisions if Person 1 actually chooses (b). If Person 1 chooses (a), then Person 2's choice is not implemented. In this treatment the impartial spectators are hypothetically invoked as opposed to being explicitly excited with Person 1's actual choice of (b). Whereas fourteen of twenty-one (67 percent) second movers choose (a′) when Person 1 has actually chosen (b), only twenty of forty-three (47 percent) Persons 2 choose (a′) when asked to assume Person 1 has chosen (b).[26] The distinction made in these experiments corresponds to games played in

---

26 Marco Casari and Timothy N. Cason, "The Strategy Method Lowers Measured Trustworthy Behavior," *Economics Letters* 103.3 (2009): 157–59 observe similar behavior in a trust game with different parameters.

extensive versus normal (or strategic, i.e., contingent play) form. Traditional game theory treated the two as equivalent, but many experimental studies have reported data rejecting this postulated equivalence.[27] The two game forms are cognitively much different in that in the extensive form Person 1 conveys to Person 2 her intentions before the latter is required to choose. TMS is particularly relevant in this interpretation because intentions are central to the capacity of the impartial spectator to form an appropriate judgment of the other person's action, and therefore in judging an appropriate response.

7. Trust Games: Repeat Play

Figure 11.3 presents another simple trust game that has been used to study single as well as repeat play versions of the same basic stage game. In single play, if Person 1 chooses to end the game, each receives twenty dollars; if Person 1 passes to Person 2, the latter chooses between (a′) twenty-five dollars for each or (b′) fifteen dollars for Person 1 and thirty dollars for Person 2. As in the first trust game above (figure 11.1), the subgame perfect equilibrium is for Person I to end the game and each leave with twenty dollars apiece, but in the laboratory we observe 63 percent passing to Person 2. And twice as many people in the Person 2 position (65 percent) choose (a′) over (b′). As before, both persons are choosing cooperatively in a manner consistent with the principle of reciprocal beneficence in *TMS*. Kevin McCabe, Mary Rigdon, and Vernon Smith in a 2003 article use this game to answer the following question: how will these results be affected if in a second treatment condition, Person 1 cannot voluntarily choose between ending the game and passing to Person 2, with passing being required of Person 1?[28]

---

27 For a discussion and several references, see Smith, *Rationality*, 264–67,); and for earlier experiment results see Kevin McCabe, Stephen Rassenti, and Vernon L. Smith, "Game Theory and Reciprocity in Some Extensive Form Experimental Games," *Proceedings of the National Academy of Arts and Sciences* 93 (1996): 13421–28.
28 Kevin McCabe, Mary L. Rigdon, and Vernon L. Smith, "Positive Reciprocity and Intentions in Trust Games," *Journal of Economic Behavior and Organization* 52.2 (2003): 267–75.

Person 2 faces the same alternatives as before, but sees that Person 1 gives up nothing. Consequently, under these conditions, the impartial spectator in Person 2 is prevented from forming the same intentional "kindness" judgment of the conduct of person 1 as in the first treatment. Consistent with this reasoning, under the second treatment conditions the results from the first experiment are reversed: now only 33 percent of the Persons 2 choose (a′) over (b′).[29]

Rigdon, McCabe, and Smith in a 2007 article have also studied behavior in repeat play of the stage game as shown in figure 11.3.[30] Their experiments examine decision behavior under two different conditions that vary only the protocols for matching subject pairs after each round of play. In both protocols, the subjects are not informed as to the number of repetitions; without warning, play is stopped after twenty rounds. In the first protocol the subjects are simply repaired at random. In the second a scoring algorithm uses their previous decisions to enable all Persons 1 and Persons 2 to be separately rank ordered from most cooperative to least. The highest in each rank are then matched with each other for the next round; the second highest are matched with each other for the next round, and so on down the list. A cooperative choice by Person 1 means that she passed to Person 2; a cooperative choice by Person 2 occurs whenever option (a′) is selected. It is very important to keep in mind that the subjects in these experiments *were not informed of the matching procedure.* In both treatments all the participants were told simply that they would be repaired with a person in the room each period. In all sessions there were sixteen people in the room with eight Persons 1 (and eight Persons 2) to be repaired either at random or by application of the scoring algorithm.

If indeed "kindness begets kindness" as in Adam Smith's principle of reciprocal beneficence, then the scoring rule allows those interacting

---

29 But remarkably many Persons 2 still choose to be generous to Persons 1, perhaps leaving ample room for the *TMS* sentiment of acting in a praiseworthy manner even without the implied praise when kindness is returned by kindness.
30 Mary L. Rigdon, Kevin A. McCabe, and Vernon L. Smith, "Sustaining Cooperation in Trust Games." *Economic Journal* 117.522 (2007): 991–1007.

over the twenty repetitions to "discover" by experience that they are in an environment characterized by "kindness." Over time each person's impartial spectator would be updated and reflect any experiential tendencies toward kind behavior. Rigdon, McCabe, and Smith had no assured expectation as to how effective the scoring rule would be. This is why they used a comparison control that implemented random repairing. An open question was how effective the two protocols would be in separating the two different pools of subjects with respect to their frequency of cooperative choice.[31]

The data show that the primary research hypothesis was strongly supported, as the two treatment groups bifurcated significantly across repeat trials in exhibiting cooperative responses: in trials 1–5, the ratio

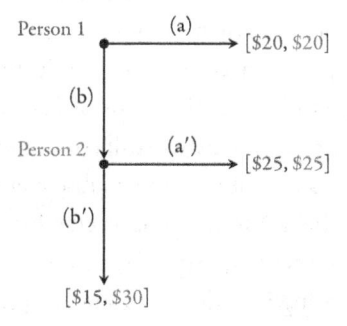

```
           Person 1    (a)
                  •────────▶ [$20, $20]
                  │
              (b) │
                  ▼
           Person 2    (a′)
                  •────────▶ [$25, $25]
                  │
             (b′) │
                  ▼
              [$15, $30]
```

FIGURE 11.3. Another Two-Person Trust Game in Extensive Form

---

31 The research reported in Rigdon, McCabe, and Smith, "Sustaining Cooperation" was done at the University of Arizona at the turn of the millennium, appearing as a working paper in 2002, and was delayed in publication. Why? Principally, the procedure—subjects not being informed of the rank order rule for rematching pairs—was the source of many explanations and discussions with seminar participants and in the editor-refereeing process. Many had difficulty grasping why we did not make the comparison with subjects given full knowledge of the cooperative matching procedure. There is a body of constructivist economic theory—irrelevant and distractive from the perspective of this study—that argues that a small in-group of cooperators can invade a population of defectors, and being able to identify each other, outperform their out-group peers. Yes, and if our subjects knew the circumstances of their matching and we observed more cooperation than in the randomly repaired group, what would we learn? Only, we feared, that when it is made plain to people that in repeat interaction cooperation is individually optimal, then people are likely to choose optimally. In that case we would learn yet again that in games that essentially reduce rationally to games against nature, people tend to go to the top of the profit hill. If this exercise is to be meaningful, the question must be what will people do if they find themselves—without knowledge of why—in a climate of relative cooperation, compared to a climate of relative defection? Will cooperation and profitability build experientially and "insensibly" in the former à la *TMS* or will it deteriorate in attempted mutual exploitation à la game-theoretic self-loving behavior?

of percentage cooperative choice by Persons 1 in the treatment to the percentage cooperation in the random control was 1.05; for Persons 2, the ratio was 1.10; that is, there was essentially very little treatment difference in the first five trials. But cooperation steadily improved, so that in the last five trials, 16–20, these ratios respectively were 1.94 and 1.63, corresponding to increases respectively of 1.94/1.05 = 185 percent for Persons 1 and 1.63/1.10 = 150 percent for Persons 2. According to *TMS* the latter percentages are less than the former because regardless of treatment, Persons 2, experiencing the largest of Persons 1, tend to honor the principle that "[a]ctions of a beneficent tendency, which proceed from proper motives, seem alone to require reward; because such alone are the approved objects of gratitude, or excite the sympathetic gratitude of the spectator" (II.ii.1.1, 78).

Rigdon, McCabe, and Smith in "Sustaining Cooperation" also report the finding of a very pronounced regularity in the behavior of people in both treatments: the individual decisions of Persons 1 to trust or not and for Persons 2 to respond trustworthily or not *on the first trial* were strongly and significantly related to their subsequent tendency to show trust or trustworthy behavior in repeat interactions. Thus, in equation (2) we can say that in these experiments, each person after reading the instructions and entering into the first round of play makes a decision conditional upon her or his history, $H_i(0)$, and her or his anticipated future interactive behavior, $H(x)$. What we learn across all the subjects is that their sympathetic state is marked indelibly by their first decision, and is predictive of their subsequent behavior in the remaining nineteen trials. In the language of game theory, they are "typed" by their decision on the first trial, and their type significantly accounts for their subsequent decisions, although these vary significantly with their subsequent experience and the experimental treatment condition.[32]

---

32 Thomas A., Rietz et al., "Transparency, Efficiency and the Distribution of Economic Welfare in Pass-Through Investment Trust Games," *Journal of Economic Behavior and Organization* 94 (2013): 257–67, have extended this finding to three-person trust games in which an independent single-play game, as distinct from first-trial behavior in repeat play, significantly types people's subsequent cooperation across all repeat play decisions in the same game.

8. Concluding Remarks

Adam Smith's *Theory of Moral Sentiments* is much more than a source of ornamental quotations for modern research in economics. *TMS* is a primary source of insights for understanding what modern, logico-deductive economics cannot account for—our human passions and motives, the edifice on which our morality is built. Adam Smith is a theorist in the original sense of the Greek word *theoria*, meaning "to view or behold." He importantly begins, not ends, with acute observations on everyday human intercourse qua axiom, which he then organizes as elements in a rule-governed system of morality. Rules of conduct, not outcomes, are the focus of his analysis. Adam Smith uses the word *society* 157 times in the *TMS*, roughly once every other page. Why? Because his overarching concern with understanding human rules of conduct is how, in an ever-fluxional world, society orders itself via morality, which is "indeed the result of human action but not the execution of any human design."[33]

---

[33] Adam Ferguson, *An Essay on the History of Civil Society* (Middlesex, UK: Echo Library, 1767/2007), at 102.

Bibliography

ABBREVIATIONS

Alesse = Francesca Alesse, ed. 1997. *Panezio di Rodi: Testimonianze*. Naples: Bibliopolis.
Edelstein and Kidd = Ludwig Edelstein and Ian G. Kidd, eds. 1989. *Posidonius*. Vol. 1: *The Fragments*. 2nd ed. Cambridge: Cambridge University Press.
FDS = Karlheinz Hülser, ed. 1987–88. *Fragmente der Dialektik der Stoiker*. 4 vols. Stuttgart: Frommann-Holzbog.
Giannantoni = Gabriele Giannantoni. 1990. *Socratis et socraticorum reliquiae*. Naples: Bibliopolis.
Helmreich = G. Helmreich. 1884–93. *Claudii Galeni Pergameni scripta minora*. 3 vols. Leipzig: Teubner; 1907–9. *Galeni De usu partium libri XVII*. 2 vols. Leipzig: Teubner.
Kühn = C. Kühn. 1964–65. *Claudii Galeni opera omnia*. 20 vols. repr. Hildesheim: Olms.
Littré = E. Littré. 1839–61. *Œuvres complètes d'Hippocrate*. 10 vols. Paris: Baillière.
LS = Anthony A. Long and David N. Sedley. 1987. *The Hellenistic Philosophers*. 2 vols. Cambridge: Cambridge University Press.

Nickel = D. Nickel. 2001. *Galeni De foetuum formatione, CMG* V 3,3. Berlin: Akademie.
Pfaff = E. Wenkebach and F. Pfaff. 1934. *Galeni In Hippocratis Epidemiarum libri I et II, CMG* V 10,1. Leipzig: Teubner.
SVF = Hans von Arnim, ed. 1903–5. *Stoicorum veterum fragmenta*. Vols. 1–3. Leipzig: Teubner.

WORKS BY NIETZSCHE

German edition of Nietzsche's works: *Friedrich Nietzsche: Sämtliche Werke, Kritische Studienausgabe*. 1967–77. Ed. Giorgio Colli and Mazzino Montinari. 15 vols. Berlin: De Gruyter.
A = *The Anti-Christ*. 1968. Trans. R. J. Hollingdale. Harmondsworth, UK: Penguin.
BGE = *Beyond Good and Evil*. 1966. Trans. W. Kaufmann. New York: Random House.
CW = *The Case of Wagner*. 1967. Trans. W. Kaufmann. New York: Random House.
D = *Daybreak*. 1982. Trans. R. J. Hollingdale. Cambridge: Cambridge University Press.
EH = *Ecce Homo*. 1969. Trans. W. Kaufmann. New York: Random House.
GM = *On the Genealogy of Morals*. 1969. Trans. W. Kaufmann. New York: Random House. See also: *On the Genealogy of Morality*. Trans. M. Clark and A. J. Swensen. Indianapolis: Hackett, 1998.
GS = *The Gay Science*. 1974. Trans. W. Kaufmann. New York: Random House.
HH I, II = *Human, All Too Human*. 1986. Trans. R. J. Hollingdale. Cambridge: Cambridge University Press.
Selected Letters of Friedrich Nietzsche. 1996. Ed. and trans. C. Middleton. Indianapolis: Hackett.
WP = *The Will to Power*. 1968. Trans. W. Kaufmann and R. J. Hollingdale. New York: Random House.
Z = *Thus Spoke Zarathustra*. 1978. Trans. W. Kaufmann. Harmondsworth, UK: Penguin.

WORKS BY SCHOPENHAUER

German edition of Schopenhauer's works: *Arthur Schopenhauer Sämtliche Werke*. 1949. Wiesbaden: Eberhard Brockhaus.
BM = *On the Basis of Morality*. 1995. Trans. E. F. J. Payne. Providence, RI: Berghahn.
FR = *On The Fourfold Root of the Principle of Sufficient Reason*. 1974. Trans. E. F. J. Payne. La Salle, IL: Open Court.

PP I, II = *Parerga and Paralipomena*. 1974. Trans. E. F. J. Payne. New York: Oxford University Press.
WWR I, II = *The World as Will and Representation*. 1969. Vols. 1 and 2. Trans. E. F. J. Payne. New York: Dover.

ARCHIVAL SOURCE

Charles Darwin Correspondence Project. Cambridge University transcription of calendar number: 10988, draft of a letter from Charles Darwin to Charles Bradlaugh, 6 June 1877, supplied to David M. Levy and Sandra J. Peart, 6 October 2004.

GENERAL BIBLIOGRAPHY

Primary Sources

Agrippa von Nettesheim, Heinrich Cornelius. 1531. *De occulta philosophia: Liber primus*. Paris: Wechilus.
Agrippa von Nettesheim, Heinrich Cornelius. 1533. *De occulta philosophia libri tres*. Cologne: Johannes Soter.
Agrippa von Nettesheim, Heinrich Cornelius. 1992. *De occulta philosophia libri tres*. Ed. V. Perrone Compagni. Leiden: Brill.
Aquinas, Thomas. 1981. *Summa Theologica*. 5 vols. Trans. Fathers of the English Dominican Province. New York: Christian Classics.
Aquinas, Thomas. 1975. *Summa Contra Gentiles*. Trans. and ed. James F. Anderson Notre Dame, IN: University of Notre Dame Press.
Arnim, Hans von, ed. 1903–5. *Stoicorum veterum fragmenta*. Vols. 1–3. Leipzig: Teubner.
Bacon, Francis. 1626. *Sylua Syluarum; or, A Naturall Historie in Ten Centuries... Published after the authors death, by William Rawley Doctor of Diuinitie, late his Lordships chaplaine*. London: John Haviland and Augustine Mathewes for William Lee.
Bacon, Francis. 1869–72. *Works*. Ed. James Spedding, Robert Leslie Ellis, and Douglas Denon Heath. 15 vols. New York: Hurd and Houghton.
Bain, Alexander. 1882. *James Mill: A Biography*. London: Longmans, Green.
Bandello, Matteo. 1567. *Certaine Tragicall Discourses Written out of Frenche and Latin...* Trans. Geoffrey Fenton. London: Thomas Marshe.
Bandello, Matteo. 1898. *Certain Tragical Discourses of Bandello*. Tudor Translations. Ed. Robert Langton Douglas. 2 vols. London: Nutt.

Benjamin, Walter. *Selected Writings*. Vol. 1, *1913–1926*. Cambridge, MA: Harvard University Press, 1996.

Bentley, Richard. 1692–93. "The Folly and Unreasonableness of Atheism," Demonstrated from the Advantage and Pleasure of a Religious Life, the Faculties of Human Souls, the Structure of Animate Bodies, & the Origin and Frame of the World: in Eight Sermons Preached at the Lecture Founded by the Honourable Robert Boyle, Esquire. London: H. Mortlock.

Berkeley, Bishop George. 2008. "Three Dialogues." In *Philosophical Writings*, ed. Desmond Clarke. Cambridge: Cambridge University Press, 151–242.

Binns, William. 1880. "Science, Theology, and the Evolution of Man." *Modern Review* 2: 245–78.

Bonner, Hypatia Bradlaugh. 1895. *Charles Bradlaugh; A Record of His Life and Work*, London: T. F. Unwin.

Burke, Edmund. 2008. *A Philosophical Enquiry into the Origin of Our Ideas of the Sublime and Beautiful*. Ed. Adam Phillips. Oxford: Oxford University Press.

Butler, Joseph. 2006 [1867]. *Fifteen Sermons*. In *The Works of Joseph Butler*. London: William Tegg; reprint, Adamant Media.

Cabanis, Pierre Jean George. 1981. *On the Relations between the Physical and Moral Aspects of Man*. Trans. Margaret Saidi. Baltimore: Johns Hopkins University Press.

Cardano, Girolamo. 1556. *De rerum varietate libri XVII*. Lyon: Apud Stephanum Michaelum.

Cassina, Ubaldo. 1772. Saggio analitico su la compassione. Parma.

Cavendish, Richard. 1571. *The Image of Nature and Grace Conteynyng the Whole Course, and Condition of Mans Estate*. London: John Daye.

Chauvin, Stephanus. 1713. *Lexicon Philosophicum*. 2nd ed., Leeuwarden, repr. Düsseldorf.

Cicero. 1923. *De Senectute, De Amicitia, De Divinatione*. With English trans. William Armistead Falconer. Loeb Classical Library. Cambridge, MA: Harvard University Press.

Condillac, Etienne Bonnot de. 2001. *Essay on the Origin of Human Knowledge*. Ed. Hans Aarsleff. Cambridge: Cambridge University Press.

Conway, Anne. 1992. *The Conway Letters: The Correspondence of Anne Viscountess Conway, Henry Moore, and Their Friends (1642–1684)*. Ed. Marjorie Hope Nicholson and Sarah Hutton. New York: Oxford University Press.

Conway, Anne. 1996. *The Principles of the Most Ancient and Modern Philosophy*. Trans. Alison Coudert and Taylor Corse. Cambridge: Cambridge University Press.

Cudworth, Ralph, 1996. *Ralph Cudworth: A Treatise concerning Eternal and Immutable Morality with a Treatise of Freewill*. Ed. Sarah Hutton. Cambridge: Cambridge University Press.

Cullen, William. 1795. *Clinical Lectures, Delivered in the Years 1765 and 1766* London.

Darwin, Charles. 1964 [1859]. *On the Origin of Species by Natural Selection; or, The Preservation of Favoured Races in the Struggle for Life*. Ed. Ernst Mayr. Cambridge, MA: Harvard University Press.

Darwin, Charles. 1871. *The Descent of Man; or, Selection in Relation to Sex.* 2 vols. London: John Murray.

Darwin, Charles. 2004 [1874]. *The Descent of Man; or, Selection in Relation to Sex.* 2nd ed. Ed. James Moore and Adrian Desmond. London: Penguin.

Darwin, Charles. 2001. *The Correspondence of Charles Darwin: 1864*. Ed. Frederick Burkhardt, Duncan M. Porter, Sheila Ann Dean, Paul S. White, and Sarah Wilmot. Vol. 18. Cambridge: Cambridge University Press. 21 vols.

Darwin, Charles. 2010. *The Correspondence of Charles Darwin: 1870*. Ed. Frederick Burkhardt, James A. Secord, Sheila Ann Dean, Samantha Evans, Shelley Innes, Alison M. Pearn, and Paul White. 21 vols. to date. Cambridge: Cambridge University Press.

Darwin, Erasmus. 1791. *The Botanic Garden: A Poem in Two Parts. Part I Containing the Economy of Vegetation. Part II The Loves of the Plants, with Philosophical Notes.* London: Johnson.

Darwin, Erasmus. 1803. *The Temple of Nature; or, The Origin of Society: A Poem, with Philosophical Notes*, London: Johnson.

Darwin, George. 1873. "On Beneficial Restrictions to Liberty of Marriage." *Contemporary Review* 22: 412–26.

Darwin, George. 1874. "Note upon the Article 'Primitive Man—Taylor and Lubbock.'" *Quarterly Review* 137: 587–88.

De Boot, Anselmus. 1609. *Gemmarum et lapidum historia: qua non solum ortus, natura, vis et precium, sed etiam modus quo ex iis, olea, salia, tincturae, essentiae, arcana et magisteria arte chymica confici possint, ostenditur*. Hanover.

De Grouchy, Sophie. 2008. *Letters on Sympathy: A Critical Edition*. Ed. Karin Brown Philadelphia: American Philosophical Society, 2008.

De Grouchy, Sophie. 2010. *Les Lettres sur la sympathie (1798) de Sophie de Grouchy: Philosophie morale et réforme sociale*. Ed. Marc André Bernier and Deidre Dawson. Oxford: Voltaire Foundation.

Della Porta, Giambattista. 1658. *Natural Magick*. London: Thomas Young and Samuel Speed.

Descartes, René. 1974–86. *Oeuvres*. 11 vols. Ed. Charles Adam and Paul Tannery. Paris: Vrin/CNRS.

Descartes, René. 1985. *The Philosophical Writings of Descartes*. 3 vols. Ed. and trans. John Cottingham, Robert Stoothoff, and Dugald Murdoch. Cambridge: Cambridge University Press.

Diderot, Denis. 1968 [1757]. *Entretiens sur le Fils naturel*. In *Oeuvres esthétiques*, ed. P. Vernière. Paris: Garnier.

Diderot, Denis, and Jean d'Alembert, eds. 1747–65. Encyclopédie ou dictionnaire raisonné des sciences, des arts et des métiers. Paris.

Diels, Hermann. 1917. *Philodemus. Über die Götter. Drittes Buch. 2. Erläuterung des Textes*. Berlin: Akademie der Wissenschaften.

Digby, Sir Kenelm. 1644. *Two Treatises: In the One of Which, the Nature of Bodies, in the Other, the Nature of Mans Soule, is Looked Into, in the Way of Discovery, of the Immortality of Reasonable Soules*. Paris: Gilles Blaizot.

Digby, Sir Kenelm. 1658a. *Discours fait en une célèbre assemblée, touchant la guérison des playes par la poudre de sympathie*. Paris: Augustin Courbé and Pierre Moet.

Digby, Sir Kenelm. 1658b. *A Late Discourse... Touching the Cure of Wounds by the Powder of Sympathy: With Instructions How to Make the Said Powder*. Trans. R. White. London: Lownes and Davies.

Doughty, John. 1752. *Christian Sympathy*. London.

Edelstein, Ludwig, and Ian G. Kidd, eds. 1989. *Posidonius*. Vol. 1: *The Fragments*. 2nd ed. Cambridge: Cambridge University Press.

Edgeworth, F. Y. 1881. *Mathematical Psychics*. London: Kegan Paul.

Egger, Émile, 1850. *Essai sur l'histoire de la critique chez les Grecs*. Paris: Durand.

Elam, Charles. 1876. "Automatism and Evolution." *Contemporary Review* 29: 117–46.

Erasmus, Desiderius. *Opera omnia*. 1969. Vol. 1.3. Amsterdam: North-Holland.

Erasmus, Desiderius. 1997. *Colloquies*. Trans. Craig R. Thompson. *Collected Works of Erasmus*. 2 vols. Toronto: University of Toronto Press. Vol. 2.

Euclid. 1956. *The Thirteen Books of the Elements*. New York: Dover.

Ewald, Oscar. 1908. "German Philosophy in 1907." *Philosophical Review* 17(4): 400–426.

Ferguson, Adam. 2005 [1792]. "Of Man's Progressive Nature." In *Selections from the Scottish Philosophy of Common Sense*, ed. George A. Johnston. Chicago: Open Court, 196–217.

Ferguson, Adam 2007 [1767]. *An Essay on the History of Civil Society*. Middlesex, UK: Echo Library.

Ficino, Marsilio. 1532. "Commentarium." In *Convivium, Platonis Opera*. Basel, 1532, 401.

Ficino, Marsilio. 1989. *Three Books on Life*. Trans. and ed. Carol V. Kaske. Binghamton, NY: Center for Medieval and Early Renaissance Studies.

Ficino, Marsilio. 2001–6. *Platonic Theology*. 6 vols. Trans. Michael J. B. Allen, ed. James Hankins and William Bowen. Cambridge MA: Harvard University Press.

Fordyce, David. 2003 [1748]. *The Elements of Moral Philosophy*. Ed. Thomas Kennedy. Indianapolis: Liberty Fund.

Fracastoro, Girolamo. 1546. *De sympathia et antipathia rerum liber unus. De contagione et contagiosis morbis et curatione libri iii.* Venice: Heredes Lucaeantonii Juntae Florentini.

Fracastoro, Girolamo. 2008. *De sympathia et antipathia rerum.* Ed. Concetta Pennuto. Studi e testi del Rinascimento europeo 31. Rome: Edizioni di storia e letteratura, 2008.

Freud, Sigmund. 1958 [1913]. "On Beginning the Treatment (Further Recommendations on the Technique of Psycho-Analysis I)." In *The Standard Edition of the Complete Psychological Works of Sigmund Freud,* vol 12, trans. and ed. James Strachey. London: Hogarth Press, 121–44.

Galen. 1984. *On the Doctrines of Hippocrates and Plato.* Ed. and trans. with commentary by Phillip De Lacy. 2nd ed. Berlin: Akademie Verlag.

Gangloff, Jacob Heinrich. 1669. *Disputatio physica de sympathiai.* Jena: Samuel Adophus Müller.

"George Jones of London, Student in the Art of Physick and Chyrurgery...." C. 1675. Wellcome Institute broadside collection, London.

Goclenius, Rudolph. 1608. *De Vita proroganda, hoc est animi corporisque vigore conservando salubriterque producendo tractatus.* Mainz: J. Albinus.

Goclenius, Rudolph. 1980 [1613]. *Lexicon Philosophicum.* Frankfurt; repr. Hildesheim: Georg Olms.

Goethe, Johann Wolfgang von. 1854. *Elective Affinities.* Trans. James Anthony Froude. In *Novels and Tales,* trans. R. Dillon Boylan and Froude. London: Henry G. Bohn, 1–246.

Goethe, Johann Wolfgang von. *Aus dem Nachlaß.* Weimar: Böhlau, 1887–1919.

Goethe, Johann Wolfgang von. 1972. *Die Wahlverwandtschaften.* Leipzig: Insel.

Goethe, Johann Wolfgang von. 1998. *Werke.* Ed. Erich Trunz. Munich: DTV.

[Greg, W. R.]. 1868. "On the Failure of 'Natural Selection' in the Case of Man." *Fraser's Magazine for Town and Country* 78: 353–62.

[Greg, W. R.]. 1869. "Realities of Irish Life." *Quarterly Review* 126: 61–80.

Greg, W. R. 1875. *Enigmas of Life.* Boston: James R. Osgood.

Hall, John. 1679. "Counsel 11: Hurt in the Eye." In *Select observations on English bodies of eminent persons in desperate diseases first written in Latin by Mr. John Hall...; after Englished by James Cook...; to which is now added, an hundred like counsels and advices, for several honourable persons, by the same author; in the close is added, Directions for drinking of the bath-water, and Ars cosmetica, or beautifying art, by H. Stubbs....* London: Benjamin Shirley.

Hartley, David. 1749. *Observations on Man.* London.

Hegel, G. W. F. 1995. *Lectures on the History of Philosophy.* 3 vols. Trans. E. Haldane. Lincoln: University of Nebraska Press.

Helvétius, Claude Adrien. 1989 [1773]. *De l'homme*. Paris: Fayard.
Hobbes, Thomas. 1996. *Leviathan*. Ed. Richard Tuck. Cambridge: Cambridge University Press.
Hobbes, Thomas. 2004. *The English Works of Thomas Hobbes of Malmesbury*. Ed. W. Molesworth. Yarmouth: Elibron Classics.
Huloet, Richard. 1572. *Huloets Dictionarie Newelye Corrected, Amended, Set in Order and Enlarged... by which you may finde the Latin or Frenche, of anye English woorde you will*. Ed. John Higgins. London: Thomas Marsh.
Humboldt, Alexander von. 1978. *Kosmos*. Ed. Hanno Beck. Stuttgart: Brockhaus.
Humboldt, Alexander von. 1997. *Cosmos: A Sketch of the Physical Description of the Universe*. Vol. 1. Trans. E. C. Otté, Baltimore: Johns Hopkins University Press.
Hume, David. 1975 [1751]. *Enquiries concerning Human Understanding and the Principles of Morals*. Ed. L. A. Selby-Bigge and P. H. Nidditch. Oxford: Oxford University Press.
Hume, David. 1978 [1738–39]. *A Treatise of Human Nature*. Ed. L. A. Selby-Bigge and P. H. Nidditch. Oxford: Oxford University Press.
Hume, David. 2000 [1738–39]. *A Treatise of Human Nature*. Ed. David Fate Norton and Mary J. Norton. New York: Oxford University Press.
Hume, David. 2007. *Enquiry Concerning the Principles of Morals*. Ed. Tom Beauchamp. Oxford: Oxford University Press.
Hutcheson, Francis. 2002 [1742]. *An Essay on the Nature and Conduct of the Passions and Affections, with Illustrations on the Moral Sense*. Ed. Aaron Garrett. Indianapolis: Liberty Fund.
Hutcheson, Francis. 2007. *Short Introduction to Moral Philosophy*. Ed. Luigi Turco. Indianapolis: Liberty Fund.
Huxley, Thomas H. 1871. "Mr. Darwin's Critics." *Contemporary Review* 18: 443–76.
James, William. 1885. "Lipps's Psychological Studies." *Science* 6.140: 308–10.
James, William. 1950 [1890]. *Principles of Psychology*. New York: Dover.
Johnson, Samuel. 1755. *A Dictionary of the English Language*. CD-rom. Oakland, CA: Octavo. (2005).
Kames, Henry Home, Lord. 2005a. *Elements of Criticism*. Ed. Peter Jones. Indianapolis: Liberty Fund.
Kames, Henry Home, Lord. 2005b. *Essays on the Principles of Morality and Natural Religion*. Ed. Mary Catherine Moran Indianapolis: Liberty Fund.
Kant, Immanuel. 1996a. *Groundwork of the Metaphysics of Morals*. In *Practical Reason*, ed. Mary Gregor. Cambridge: Cambridge University Press, 37–108.
Kant, Immanuel. 1996b. *The Metaphysics of Morals*. In *Practical Reason*, ed. Mary Gregor. Cambridge: Cambridge University Press, 353–604.

Kant, Immanuel. 2007. *Observations on the Feeling of the Beautiful and Sublime.* In *Anthropology History, and Education*, ed. Günter Zöller and Robert Louden. Cambridge: Cambridge University Press, 18–62.

La Chaussée, Pierre-Claude Nivelle de. 1970 [1777]. *Oeuvres.* 5 vols. Paris; Geneva: Slatkine Reprints.

Leibniz, G. W. 1875–90. *Die philosophischen Schriften von Gottfried Wilhelm Leibniz.* Ed. C. I. Gerhardt. 7 vols. Leipzig: Weidman.

Leibniz, G. W. 1923–. *Sämtliche Schriften und Briefe.* Darmstadt: Berlin Academy.

Leibniz, G. W. 1970. *Philosophical Papers and Letters.* Trans. Leroy E. Loemker. 2nd ed. Dordrecht: Reidel.

Leibniz, G. W. 1978 [1879]. *Die philosophischen Schriften von Gottfried Wilhelm Leibniz.* Ed. C. I. Gerhardt. 7 vols. Leipzig: Lorentz; repr. Hildesheim: Georg Olms.

Leibniz, G. W. 1985. *Theodicy.* Trans. E. M. Huggard. LaSalle, IL: Open Court.

Leibniz, G. W. 1989. *Philosophical Essays.* Ed. and trans. Roger Ariew and Daniel Garber. Indianapolis: Hackett.

Leibniz, G. W. 1992. *De Summa Rerum: Metaphysical Papers, 1675–76.* Ed. and trans. G. H. R. Parkinson. New Haven, CT: Yale University Press.

Leibniz, Gottfried Wilhelm. 1996 [1981]. *New Essays on Human Understanding.* Ed. and trans. Peter Remnant and Johatan Bennett. Cambridge: Cambridge University Press.

Lemnius, Levinus. 1576. *The Touchstone of Complexions Generallye Appliable, Expedient and Profitable for all Such, as be Desirous & Carefull of their Bodylye Health.* Trans. and ed. Thomas Newton. London: Thomas Marsh.

Lemnius, Levinus. 1587. *An Herbal for the Bible. Containing a Plaine and Familiar Exposition of such similitudes, parables, and metaphors, both in the olde Testament and the newe....* Trans. Thomas Newton. London: Edmund Bollifant.

Libavius, Andreas. 1593. *Tractatus duo physici; prior de impostoria vulnerum per unguentum armarium sanatione paracelsicis usitata commendataque; posterior de cruentatione cadaverum in justa caede factorum praesente, qui occidisse creditur.* Frankfurt: Joannes Saur.

Lipps, Theodor. 1897. *Raumästhetik und geometrisch-optische Täuschungen.* Leipzig: Barth.

Lipps, Theodor. 1906a. "Die aesthetische Betrachtung und die bildende Kunst." In *Aesthetik: Psychologie des Schönen und der Kunst, Zwither Teil.* Hamburg: Leopold Voss, vol. 2.

Lipps, Theodor. 1906b. Hume's Traktat über die menschliche Natur (A Treatise on [sic!] human nature). Hamburg: Leopold Voss.

Lipps, Theodor. 1907a. "Das Wissen vonfremden Ich." In *Psychologische Untersuchungen*, ed. Lipps. Vol. 1. Leipzig: Engelmann, 794–822.

Lipps, Theodor. 1907b. "Psychologie und Aesthetik." *Archiv für die gesamte Psychologie* 9: 91–116.
Lipps, Theodor. 1908. *Asthetik, Systematische Philosophie.* Liebzig: B. G. Teubner.
Lipps, Theodor. 1909 [1903]. *Leitfaden der Pscyhologie.* 3rd ed. Leipzig: Engelmann.
Lipps, Theodor. 1973 [1906]. *David Hume, Ein Traktat über die menschliche Natur (A Treatise on [sic!] human nature).* Ed. Reinhard Brandt. Hamburg: Philosophische Bibliothek.
Lipps, Theodor. 1979 [1903]. "Empathy, Inner Imitation, and Sense Feelings (Einfühlung, innere Nachahmung, und Organempfindungen)." Originally published in *Archiv für die gesamte Psychologie* 1. Trans. Max Schertel and Melvin Rader in *A Modern Book of Esthetics*, 5th ed., ed. Rader. New York: Holt, Rinehart, and Winston, 371–78.
Lipsius, Justus, 1604. *Manuductionis ad Physiologiae Stoicorum libri tres, L. Annaeo Senecae, aliisque scriptoribus illustrandis.* Antwerp: Moretus.
Mandeville, Bernard. 1988. "An Essay on Charity, and Charity-Schools." In *Fable of the Bees*, ed. F. B. Kaye. Indianapolis: Liberty Fund, 1988, 1.253–322.
Mayhew, Robert, trans. 2011. *Aristotle: Problems: Books 1–19.* Cambridge, MA: Loeb.
Mead, George H. 1909. "Social Psychology as Counterpart to Physiological Psychology." *Psychological Bulletin* 6: 401–8.
Mead, George H. 1912. "The Mechanism of Social Consciousness." *Journal of Philosophy, Psychology, and Scientific Methods* 9: 401–6.
Mead, George H. 1934a. "The Nature of Sympathy." In *Mind, Self, and Society: From the Standpoint of a Social Behaviorist*, ed. Charles Morris. Chicago: University of Chicago Press, section 38, 298–303.
Mead, George H. 1934b. "Wundt and the Concept of the Gesture." In *Mind Self and Society from the Standpoint of a Social Behaviorist*, ed. Charles Morris. Chicago: University of Chicago Press, section 7, 42–51.
Mercier, Louis-Sébastien. 1767. *La Sympathie, histoire morale.* Amsterdam.
Mill, James. 1824–25 [1820]. "Government." In *Essays.* London: Innes, 3–32.
Mill, James. 1869 [1829]. *Analysis of the Phenomena of the Human Mind.* Ed. John Stuart Mill. 2 vols. London: Longmans, Green, Reader and Dyer.
Mill, John Stuart. 1869. "Editorial Notes." In *Analysis of the Phenomena of the Human Mind*, by James Mill, ed. John Stuart Mill. London: Longmans, Green, Reader and Dyer.
Mill, John Stuart. 1965 [1873]. *Autobiography and Literary Essays.* Ed. John M. Robson and Jack Stillinger. Vol. 1 of *Collected Works of John Stuart Mill.* Toronto: University of Toronto Press.

Mill, John Stuart. 1969 [1861]. *Utilitarianism*. In *Essays on Ethics, Religion and Society*, ed. John M. Robson. Vol. 10 of *Collected Works of John Stuart Mill*. Toronto: University of Toronto Press, 203–59.

[Mivart, St. George]. 1871. "The Descent of Man, and Selection in Relation to Sex." *Quarterly Review* 131: 47–89.

Mivart, St. George. 1873. *Apes and Man, an Exposition of Structural Resemblances and Differences Bearing upon Questions of Affinity and Origin*. London: Robert Hardwicke.

[Mivart, St. George]. 1874. "Researches into the Early History of Mankind and the Development of Civilisation." *Quarterly Review* 137: 40–78.

More, Henry. 1654. *Immortality of the Soul, so farre forth as it is demonstrable from the Knowledge of Nature and the Light of Reason*. London: Flesher.

More, Henry. 1690. *An Account of Virtue*. London.

More, Henry. 1987. *Immortality of the Soul*. Ed. A. Jacob. Dordrecht: Martinus Nijhoff.

Mozart, Leopold. 2008. *The Art of the Violin*. Ed. Matthias Michael Beckmann, trans. Elisabeth Kaplan. [Salzburg]: Kunstverlag Polzer.

Patrizi, Francesco. 1593. *Magia philosophica hoc est Francesci Patricii summi philosophici Zoroaster. & ejus 320. oracula chaldaica. Asclepii dialogus. & Philosophia magna. Hermetis Trismegisti Pomoander... & alia miscellanea. Jam nunc primum ex bibliotheca Ranzoviana è tenebris eruta & latine reddita*. Hamburg: Jakob Wolff.

Paynell, Thomas. 1572. *The Treasurie of Amadis of Fraunce Conteyning Eloquente Orations, pythie epistles, learned letters, and feruent complayntes, seruing for sundrie purposes*. London: Henry Bynneman for Thomas Hacket.

Pepys, Samuel. 1659/60. *Diary*. 16 January. http://www.pepysdiary.com/diary/1660/01/15/. Accessed 10 September 2013.

Peucer, Caspar. 1553. *Commentarius de praecipuis divinationum generibus, in quo a prophetiis divina autoritate traditis, et physicis praedictionibus, separantur diabolicae fraudes et superstitiosae observationes, et explicantur fontes accausae physicarum praedictionum, diabolicae et superstitiosae confutatae damnantur, ea serie, quam tabula indicis vice praefixa ostendit*. Wittenberg: J. Crato.

Philo. 1952. *The Works of Philo*. Trans. C. D. Yonge. Peabody, MA: Hendrickson.

Pico della Mirandola, Giovanni. 1969 [1557]. *Opera omnia*. <*1557–1573.*>. Basel: Petrina; Hildesheim: G. Olms, 2 vols.

Pico della Mirandola, Giovanni. 1942. *De hominis dignitate; Heptaplus; De ente et uno; e scritti vari*. Ed. Eugenio Garin. Edizione nazionale dei classici del pensiero italiano 1. Florence: Vallecchi.

Pico della Mirandola, Giovanni. 1948. "Oration on the Dignity of Man." Trans. Elizabeth Livermore Forbes. In *The Renaissance Philosophy of Man*, ed. Ernst

Cassirer, Paul Oskar Kristeller, and John Herman Randall. Chicago: University of Chicago Press, 223–56.

Place, Francis. 1930 [1822]. *Illustrations and Proofs of the Principle of Population*. ed. Norman E. Himes, London: Allen & Unwin.

Plato. 1532. *Omnia divini Platonis opera translatione Marsilii Ficini....* Basel: Froben and Episcopius.

Plato. 1996. *Complete Works*. Ed. John M. Cooper. Indianapolis: Hackett.

Pliny. 1525. *Historia Mundi*. Ed. Desiderius Erasmus. Basel: Froben.

Plotinus. 1966–88. *Enneads*. With English trans. Arthur Hilary Armstrong. Loeb Classical Library. 7 vols. Cambridge, MA: Harvard University Press.

Plotinus. 1984. "On the Problems of Soul." *Ennead* IV.4.41. Trans. A. H. Armstrong. Loeb Classical Library. Cambridge, MA: Harvard University Press.

Plutarch. 1579. *The Lives of the Noble Grecians and Romanes Compared Together by That Graue Learned Philosopher and Historiographer, Plutarke of Chaeronea; translated out of Greeke into French by Iames Amyot...; and out of French into Englishe, by Thomas North*. London: Thomas Vautroullier and John Wight.

Porta, Giambattista della. 1658. *Natural Magick*. London: Thomas Young and Samuel Speed.

Pratt, Samuel Jackson. 1781. *Sympathy: A Poem*. 5th ed. London.

Proclus. 1964. *The Elements of Theology*. Ed. and trans. E. R. Dodd. Oxford: Oxford University Press.

The Queen v. Charles Bradlaugh and Annie Besant. 1878 [1877]. London: Freethought. [2 Q.B.D, 569; reversed 3 Q.B.D., 607.]

Rattray, Silvester, 1658. *Aditus Novus ad Occultas Sympathiae et Antipathiae Causas Inveniendas: Per Principia Philosophiae Naturalis, ex Fermentorum Artificiosa Anatomia hausta Patefactus*. Glasgow: Andreas Anderson.

Rousseau, Jean-Jacques. 1959–95. *Oeuvres completes*. Ed. Bernard Gagnebin and Marcel Raymond. 5 vols. Paris: Gallimard.

Rousseau, Jean-Jacques. 1997. *Discourse on the Origins of Inequality*. In *Discourses and Other Early Political Writings*, ed. Victor Gourevitch. Cambridge: Cambridge University Press, 129–222.

Rousseau, Jean-Jacques. 2009. *Emile*. Trans. Allan Bloom. In *The Collected Writings of Rousseau*, ed. Christopher Kelly and Roger D. Masters. Hanover, NH: University Press of New England, vol. 13.

Ryff, Walther Hermann. 1548. *In Caii Plinii Secundi Naturalis historiae argutissimi scriptoris I. & II. cap. libri XXX. commentaries....* Würzburg: Mylius.

Salt, Henry S. 1889. *The Life of James Thomson ("B.V.")*. Port Washington, NY: Kennikat Press.

Schegelius, Albertus. 1584. *De venenis et morbis venenosis tractatus locupletissimi variaque doctrina referti non solum medicis, verum etiam philosophis magnopere utiles Ex voce... Hieronymi Mercurialis... excepti, atque in Libros duos digesti.* Venice: Paolo Meietti.

Schlegel, Friedrich. *Friedrich Schlegel: Philosophical Fragments.* Trans. Peter Firchow. Minneapolis: University of Minnesota Press, 1991.

Schleiermacher, Friedrich. *Schleiermacher: Hermeneutics and Criticism and Other Writings.* Ed. Andrew Bowie. Cambridge: Cambridge University Press, 1998.

Shaftesbury, Anthony Ashley Cooper, Third Earl. 2001. "An Inquiry Concerning Virtue and Merit." In *Characteristicks*, ed. Douglas J. Den Uyl. Indianapolis: Liberty Fund, 2.1–101.

Shakespeare, William. 2002. *King Lear.* The Arden Shakespeare. Ed. R. A. Folkes. London: Thomson.

Smith, Adam. 1982 [1795]. "The History of Astronomy" In *Essays on Philosophical Subjects.* Indianapolis: Liberty Fund, .

Smith, Adam. 1976; 1984 [1759]. *The Theory of Moral Sentiments.* Ed. D. D. Raphael and A. L. Macfie. Oxford: Clarendon Press; Indianapolis: Liberty Fund.

Smith, Adam. 1981 [1776]. *An Inquiry into the Nature and Causes of the Wealth of Nations.* 2 vols. Indianapolis: Liberty Fund.

Spencer, Herbert. 1851. *Social Statics; or, The Conditions Essential to Human Happiness Specified, and the First of them Developed.* London: John Chapman.

Spinoza, Baruch. 1925. *Opera.* Ed. C. Gebhardt. 4 vols. Heidelberg: Winter.

Spinoza, Baruch. 1984. *The Collected Works of Spinoza.* Vol. 1. Ed. and trans. Edwin Curley. Princeton, NJ: Princeton University Press.

Spinoza, Baruch. 1992 *Ethics.* Trans. Samuel Shirley. Indianapolis: Hackett.

Spinoza, Baruch. 1995. *The Letters.* Trans. Samuel Shirley, ed. Steven Barbone, Jonathan Adler, and Lee Rice. Indianapolis: Hackett.

Stein, Edith. 1989. *On the Problem of Empathy.* Washington, DC: ICS Publications.

Stewart, Dugald. 1829 [1828]. *The Philosophy of the Active and Moral Powers of Man.* In *The Works of Dugald Stewart in Seven Volumes*, Cambridge: Hilliard and Brown, vol. 5.

Thatcher, Peter. 1794. *Christian Sympathy.* Boston.

Thevet, André. 1568. *The New Found Worlde, or Antarctike Wherin is Contained Wonderful and Strange Things.....* London: Henrie Bynneman for Thomas Hacket.

Thomasius, Jakob. 1676. *Exercitatio de Stoica Mundi Exustione.* Leipzig: Lanckisius.

Titchener, Edward. 1896. *An Outline of Psychology.* New York: MacMillan.

Titchener, Edward. 1898. "The Postulates of a Structural Psychology." *Philosophical Review* 7(5): 449–65.

Titchener, Edward. 1909a. *Lectures on the Experimental Psychology of Thought-Process.* New York: MacMillan.

Titchener, Edward. 1909b. *A Text-Book of Psychology*. New York: MacMillan.
Turnbull, George. 2005 [1740]. *The Principles of Moral and Christian Philosophy*. Ed. Alexander Broadie. Indianapolis: Liberty Fund.
Van Helmont, Jan Baptiste. 1632. *De magnetica vulnerum curatione*. In *Opera omnia*. Frankfurt: Johann Justus Erythropilus, §151, 701–33.
Van Helmont, Jan Baptiste. 1632. *Opera omnia*. Frankfurt: Johann Justus Erythropilus.
Vesalius, Andreas. 1568. *Chirurgia magna in septem libros digesta*. Venice: Officina Valgrisiana.
Vischer, Robert. 1873. *Ueber das optische Formgefühl: Ein Beitrag zur Aesthetik*. Leipzig: Credner.
Vischer, Robert. 1994. "On the Optical Sense of Form: A Contribution to Aesthetics." In *Empathy, Form, and Space: Problems in German Aesthetics, 1873–1893*, ed. Harry Francis Mallgrave and Eleftherios Ikonomou. Santa Monica, CA: Getty Center, 89–123.
Wallace, Alfred R. 1864. "The Origin of Human Races and the Antiquity of Man Deduced from the Theory of 'Natural Selection.'" *Journal of the Anthropological Society of London* 2: clviii–clxxxvii.
Wallace, Alfred Russel. 1871a [1864] . "The Development of Human Races under the Law of Natural Selection." In *Contributions to the Theory of Natural Selection*, 2nd ed. London: Macmillan, 303–31.
Wallace, Alfred Russel. 1871b. "Physical Science and Philosophy." *Academy and Literature* 2: 177–83.
Wallace, Alfred Russel. 1900 [1890]. "Human Selection." In *Studies Scientific and Social*. 2 vols. London: Macmillan. 1.509–26.
Wallace, Alfred Russel. 1913. *Social Environment and Moral Progress*. London: Cassell.
Wardle, David. 2006. *Cicero: On Divination Book 1*. Oxford: Oxford University Press, 2006.
[Wilberforce, Samuel]. 1860. "On the Origin of Species." *Quarterly Review* 30: 225–64.
Wollstonecraft, Mary. 2009. *A Vindication of the Rights of Woman*. 3rd ed. Ed. Deidre Shauna Lynch. New York: Norton.
Worringer, Wilhelm. 1997 [1908]. *Abstraction and Empathy*. Chicago: Ivan R. Dee.
Wundt, Wilhelm. 1862. *Beiträge zur Theorie der Sinneswahrnehmung*. Leipzig: Winter.
Wundt, Wilhelm. 1874. *Grundzüge der physiologischen Psychologie*. Leipzig: Engelmann.
Wundt, Wilhelm. 1900–1909. *Volkerpsychologie*. 10 vols. Leipzig: Engelmann.
Wüst, Paul. 1909. "Zu Theodor Lipps' Neuausgabe seiner deutschen Bearbeitung von Hume's Treatise of Human Nature." *Kant-Studien* 14: 249–73.

Secondary Sources

Alesse, Francesca, ed. 1997. *Panezio di Rodi: Testimonianze*. Naples: Bibliopolis.

Allen, Michael J. B., Valery Rees, and Martin Davies, 2002. *Marsilio Ficino: His Theology, His Philosophy, His Legacy*. Leiden: Brill.

Allison, Henry. 1987. *Benedict de Spinoza: An Introduction*. New Haven, CT: Yale University Press.

Altschuler, Sari. 2012. "From Blood Vessels to Global Networks of Exchange: The Physiology of Benjamin Rush's Early Republic." *Journal of the Early Republic* 32: 207–31.

Amaral, Pedro. 1988. "Harmony in Descartes and the Medical Philosophers." *Philosophy Research Archives* 13: 499–556.

Armstrong, Arthur Hilay. 1955. "Was Plotinus a Magician?" *Phronesis* 1: 73–79.

Armstrong, Lilian. 1983. "The Illustrations of Pliny's *Historia naturalis* in Venetian Manuscripts and Early Printed Books." In *Manuscripts in the Fifty Years after the Invention of Printing: Some Papers Read at a Colloquium at the Warburg Institute on 12–13 March 1982*, ed. J. B. Trapp. London: Warburg Institute, University of London, 97–106.

Ashraf, Nava, Colin Camerer, and George Lowenstein. 2005. "Adam Smith, Behavioral Economist." *Journal of Economic Perspectives* 19(3): 131–45.

Bailey, Michael David. Bailey, Michael David. 2013. *Fearful Spirits, Reasoned Follies: the Boundaries of Superstition in Late Medieval Europe*. Ithaca, NY: Cornell University Press.

Batson, Daniel. 2011. "These Things Called Empathy: Eight Related but Distinct Phenomena." In *The Social Neuroscience of Empathy*, ed. Jean Decety and William Ickes. Cambridge, MA: MIT Press, 3–13.

Bennett, Jonathan. 1984. *A Study of Spinoza's Ethics*. Indianapolis: Hackett.

Bernier, Marc André. 2007. "Eloquence du corps et sympathie: Les 'Tableaux de sensations' de Sophie de Condorcet." In *Les Discours de la sympathie: Enquête sur une notion de l'âge classique à la modernité*, ed. Thierry Belleguic, Eric Van der Scheuren, and Sabrina Vervacke. Quebec: Les Presses de l'Université Laval.

Bernier, Marc André. 2010. "Les Métamorphoses de la sympathie au siècle des Lumières." In *Les lettres sur la sympathie (1798) de Sophie de Grouchy: Philosophie morale et reforme sociale*, by Sophie de Grouchy, ed. Bernier and Deidre Dawson. Oxford: Voltaire Foundation, 1–17.

Beutel, Albrecht. 2003. "Life." In *The Cambridge Companion to Martin Luther*, ed. Donald K. McKim. Cambridge: Cambridge University Press, 3–19.

Blumenthal, Henry J. 1971. "World-Soul and Individual Soul in Plotinus." In *Le Néoplatonisme: Colloques internationaux du Centre de la recherche scientifique*, edited by Pierre-Maxime Schuhl and Pierre Hadot. Paris: CNRS, 55–63.

Bonar, James. 1894. *A Catalogue of the Library of Adam Smith*. London: Macmillan & Co.
Boring, Edward. 1929. *History of Psychology*. London: Genesis.
Botting, Eileen Hunt. 2006. *Family Feuds: Wollstonecraft, Burke and Rousseau on the Transformation of the Family*. Albany: SUNY Press.
Bowen, Alan C., and Robert B. Todd, trans. 2004. *Cleomedes' Lectures on Astronomy*. Berkeley: University of California Press.
Bowie, Andrew, ed. 1998. *Schleiermacher. Hermeneutics and Criticism and Other Writings*, Cambridge: Cambridge University Press.
Bréhier, Emile. 1927. *Plotin: Ennéades IV*. Paris: Les belles lettres.
Broecke, Steven Vanden. 2003. *The Limits of Influence: Pico, Louvain, and the Crisis of Renaissance Astrology*. Leiden: Brill.
Brouwer, René. 2008. "On the Ancient Background of Grotius's Notion of Natural Law." *Grotiana* 29: 1–24.
Brouwer, René. 2011. "Polybius on Stoic Tyche." *Greek, Roman, and Byzantine Studies* 51: 111–32.
Brouwer, René. 2014. *The Stoic Sage*. Cambridge: Cambridge University Pres.
Brown, Eric. 2000. "Socrates the Cosmopolitan." *Stanford Agora: An Online Journal of Legal Perspectives* 1: 74–87. Accessed 15 July 2013. http://agora.stanford.edu/agora/issue1/index.html.
Brulotte, Gaëtan. 2007. "La Sympathie et la littérature érotique dans la France du XVIIIe siècle." In *Les discours de la sympathieEnquête sur une notion de l'âge classique à la modernité*, ed. Thierry Belleguic, Eric Van der Scheuren, and Sabrina Vervacke. Quebec: Les Presses de l'Université Laval, 199–218.
Buchan, Nancy, Rachel Croson, Eric Johnson, and George Wu. 2005. "Gain and Loss Ultimatums." In *Advances in Behavioral and Experimental Economics*, ed. John Morgan. San Diego: Elsevier. 1–24.
Bullock, Marcus, and Michael W. Jennings, eds. 1996. *Walter Benjamin. Selected Writings*. Volume 1: *1913–1926*. Cambridge, MA: Harvard University Press.
Caird, John. 1888. *Spinoza*. London: William Blackwood and Sons.
Camerer, Colin F. 2003. *Behavioral Game Theory*. Princeton, NJ: Princeton University Press.
Campbell, John Angus. 1989. "The Invisible Rhetorician: Charles Darwin's 'Third Party' Strategy." *Rhetorica: A Journal of the History of Rhetoric* 7: 55–85.
Carriero, John. 1991. "Spinoza's Views on Necessity in Historical Perspective." *Philosophical Topics* 19(1): 47–96.
Carriero, John. 2005. "Spinoza on Final Causality." in (eds.), *Oxford Studies in Early Modern Philosophy*, ed. Daniel Garber and Steven Nadler. Oxford: Oxford University Press, 105–47.

Cartwright, David. 1988. "Schopenhauer's Compassion and Nietzsche's Pity." *Schopenhauer-Jahrbuch* 69: 557–67.
Cartwright, David. 2008. "Compassion and Solidarity with Sufferers: The Metaphysics of *Mitleid*." *European Journal of Philosophy* 16(2): 292–310.
Casari, Marco, and Timothy N. Cason. 2009. "The Strategy Method Lowers Measured Trustworthy Behavior." *Economics Letters* 103(3): 157–59.
Chandrasekhar, Sripati. 1981. *"A Dirty, Filthy Book."* Berkeley: University of California Press.
Cherniss, Harold. 1933. "Galen and Posidonius' Theory of Vision." *American Journal of Philology* 54: 154–61.
Cherpack, Clifton. 1958. *The Call of Blood in French Classical Tragedy*. Baltimore: Johns Hopkins University Press.
Chismar, Douglas. 1988. "Empathy and Sympathy: The Important Difference." *Journal of Value Inquiry* 22: 257–66.
Clucas, Stephen."John Dee's Annotations to Ficino's Translations of Plato." 2011. In *Laus Platonici Philosophi: Marsilio Ficino and His Influence*, by Clucas, Peter J. Forshaw, and Valery Rees. Brill's Studies in Intellectual History. Leiden: Brill, 227–47.
Cohen, Hendrik Floris. 1984. *Quantifying Music: The Science of Music at the First Stage of the Scientific Revolution, 1580–1650*. Dordrecht: Reidel.
Cook, R., G. Bird, C. Catmur, C. Press, and C. Heyes. 2014. "Mirror Neurons: From Origin to Function." *Behavioral and Brain Sciences* 37(2): 177–92.
Cooley, Charles. 1922. *Human Nature and the Social Order*. New York: Scribner's.
Copenhaver, Brian P. 1991. "A Tale of Two Fishes: Magical Objects in Natural History from Antiquity through the Scientific Revolution." *Journal of the History of Ideas* 52(3): 373–98.
Copenhaver, Brian P. 1998. "The Occultist Tradition and Its Critics." In *Cambridge History of Seventeenth-Century Philosophy*. Vol 1., ed. Daniel Garber and Michael Ayers. Cambridge: Cambridge University Press, 455–512.
Copenhaver, Brian P., and Charles B. Schmitt, eds. 1992. *Renaissance Philosophy*. Oxford: Oxford University Press.
Corrigan, Kevin. 1996. "Essence and Existence in the Enneads." In *The Cambridge Companion to Plotinus*, ed. Lloyd P. Gerson, Cambridge: Cambridge University Press, 105–29.
Cox, James C., and Cary A. Deck. 2005. "On the Nature of Reciprocal Motives." *Economic Inquiry* 43: 623–35.
Craven, William G. 1981. *Giovanni Pico della Mirandola, Symbol of His Age: Modern Interpretations of a Renaissance Philosopher*. Travaux d'humanisme et Renaissance. Geneva: Droz.

Curley, Edwin. 1969. *Spinoza's Metaphysics: An Essay in Interpretation*. Cambridge, MA: Harvard University Press.

Curley, Edwin. 1988. *Behind the Geometrical Method: A Reading of Spinoza's* Ethics. Princeton, NJ: Princeton University Press.

D'Amico, John F. 1988. *Theory and Practice in Renaissance Textual Criticism: Beatus Rhenanus between Conjecture and History*. Berkeley: University of California Press.

Dandey, Patrick. 2007. "Entre *medicinalia* et *moralia*: La Double Ascendance de la 'Sympathie.'" In *Les Discours de la sympathie: Enquête sur une notion de l'âge classique à la modernité*, ed. Thierry Belleguic, Eric Van der Scheuren, and Sabrina Vervacke. Quebec: Les Presses de l'Université Laval, 3–23.

Danziger, Kurt. 1979. "The Positivist Repudiation of Wundt." *Journal of the History of the Behavioral Sciences* 15: 205–30.

Danziger, Kurt. 1980. "The History of Introspection Reconsidered." *Journal of the History of the Behavioral Sciences* 16: 241–62.

Darwall, Stephen. 1998. "Empathy, Sympathy, Care." *Philosophical Studies* 89(2–3): 261–82.

Darwin, Charles Garlton. 1960. "Can Man Control His Numbers?" In *The Evolution of Man*, ed. Sol Tax. Vol. 2 of *Evolution after Darwin: The University of Chicago Centennial*. Chicago: University of Chicago Press, 463–73.

Davies, Martin, and Tony Stone, eds. 1995. *Mental Simulation*. Oxford: Blackwell.

Debes, Remy. 2010. "Which Empathy? Limitations in the Mirrored 'Understanding' of Emotion." *Synthese* 175(2): 219–39.

Debru, Armelle. 2008. "Physiology." In *The Cambridge Companion to Galen*, ed. R. J. Hankinson, Cambridge: Cambridge University Press, 263–83.

Debus, Allen G. 1977. *The Chemical Philosophy: Paracelsian Science and Medicine in the Sixteenth and Seventeenth Centuries*. 2 vols. New York: Science History Publications.

Debus, Allen G. 1987. "The Chemical Philosophers: Chemical Medicine from Paracelsus to Van Helmont." In *Chemistry, Alchemy and the New Philosophy, 1550–1700: Studies in the History of Science and Medicine*. III. London: Variorum.

Debus, Allen G. 1987. "Robert Fludd and the Use of Gilbert's *De Magnete* in the Weapon-Salve Controversy." In *Chemistry, Alchemy and the New Philosophy, 1550–1700*. Studies in the History of Science and Medicine. XII. London: Variorum.

De Lacy, Philip. 2005. *On the Doctrines of Hippocrates and Plato: Books I–V*. Berlin: Akademie.

Deleuze, Gilles. 1990. *Expressionism in Philosophy: Spinoza*. Trans. Martin Joughin. London: Zone.

Della Rocca, Michael. 1993. "Spinoza's Argument for the Identity Theory." *Philosophical Review* 102(2): 183–213.

Della Rocca, Michael. 1996. *Representation and the Mind-Body Problem*. Oxford: Oxford University Press.
Della Rocca, Michael. 2003. "Rationalist Manifesto: Spinoza and the Principle of Sufficient Reason." *Philosophical Topics* 31(1–2): 75–94.
Della Rocca, Michael. 2008. *Spinoza*. London: Routledge.
Depew, David. 2005. "Empathy, Psychology, and Aesthetics: Reflections on a Repair Concept." *Poroi* 4(1): 99–107.
Desmond, Adrian J., and John Moore. 1991. *Darwin*. New York: Warner.
DiGregorio, Mario A., and N. W. Gill. 1990. *Darwin's Marginalia*. New York: Garland.
Di Liscia, Daniel A. 2011. "Johannes Kepler." In *The Stanford Encyclopedia of Philosophy*, Summer 2011 ed., ed. Edward N. Zalta. http://plato.stanford.edu/archives/sum2011/entries/kepler/.
Donagan, Alan. 1988. *Spinoza*. Chicago: University of Chicago Press; Brighton: Prentice Hall/Harvester Wheatsheaf.
Donovan, A. L. 1975. *Philosophical Chemistry in the Scottish Enlightenment*. Edinburgh: Edinburgh University Press.
Dorandi, Tiziano, ed. 2013. *Diogenes Laertius: Lives of Eminent Philosophers*. Cambridge: Cambridge University Press.
Dörrie, Heinrich. 1959. *Porphyrios' "Symmikta zetemata."* Munich: Beck.
Dragona-Monachou, Myrto, 1976. *The Stoic Arguments for the Existence and the Providence of the Gods*. Athens: University of Athens.
Ducheyne, Steffen. 2011. *The Main Business of Natural Philosophy: Isaac Newton's Natural- Philosophical Methodology*. Dordrecht: Springer.
Duhem, Pierre. 1997. *La Théorie physique: Son objet, sa structure*. Rpt., 4th ed., enl. Paris: Vrin.
Dumouchel, Daniel. 2010. "Une Education sentimentale: Sympathie et construction de la morale dans les Lettres sur la sympathie de Sophie de Grouchy." In *Les Lettres sur la sympathie (1798) de Sophie de Grouchy: Philosophie morale et réforme sociale*, by Sophie de Grouchy, ed. Marc AndréBernier and Deidre Dawson. Oxford: Voltaire Foundation, 139–50.
Eamon, William. 1994. *Science and the Secrets of Nature: Books of Secrets in Medieval and Early Modern Culture*. Princeton, NJ: Princeton University Press.
Eastwood, B. S. 1986. "Plinian Astronomy in the Middle Ages and Renaissance." In *Science in the Early Roman Empire: Pliny the Elder, His Sources and Influence*, ed. R. K. French and Frank Greenaway. London: Croom Helm, 1986, 197–251.
Elder, Gregory P. 1996. *Chronic Vigour: Darwin, Anglicans, Catholics and the Development of a Doctrine of Providential Evolution*. Lanham, MD: University Press of America.

Ellsberg, Daniel. 1956. "Theory of the Reluctant Duelist." *American Economic Review* 46(5): 909–23.
Emilsson, Eyjólfur K. 1988. *Plotinus on Sense-Perception: A Philosophical Study*. Cambridge: Cambridge University Press.
Emilsson, Eyjólfur K. 1996. "Cognition and Its Object." In *The Cambridge Companion to Plotinus*, ed. Lloyd P. Gerson. Cambridge: Cambridge University Press, 217–49.
Emilsson, Eyjólfur K. 2007. *Plotinus on Intellect*. Oxford: Oxford University Press.
Emilsson, Eyjólfur K. 2011. "Plotinus on Happiness and Time." *Oxford Studies in Ancient Philosophy* 40 339–60.
Falk, Armin, Ernst Fehr, and Urs Fischbacher. 2007. "On the Nature of Fair Behavior." *Economic Inquiry* 41(1): 20–26.
Fara, Patricia. 1996. *Sympathetic Attractions: Magnetic Practices, Beliefs, and Symbolism in Eighteenth-Century England*. Princeton, NJ: Princeton University Press.
Fiering, Norman. 1976. "Irresistible Compassion: An Aspect of Eighteenth-Century Sympathy and Humanitarianism." *Journal of the History of Ideas* 37: 195–218.
Fizer, John. 1981. *Psychologism and Psychoaesthetics: A Historical and Critical View of Their Relations*. Amsterdam: John Benjamins.
Flashar, Hellmut. 1991. *Aristoteles: Problemata physica*. Berlin: Akademie Verlag.
Fleischacker, Samuel. 2012. "Sympathy in Hume and Smith: A Contrast, Critique, and Reconstruction." In *Intersubjectivity and Objectivity in Adam Smith and Edmund Husserl*, ed. Dagfinn Føllesdal and Christel Fricke. Frankfurt: Ontos, 273–311.
Forget, Evelyn. 2003. "Evocations of Sympathy: Sympathetic Imagery in Eighteenth-Century Social Theory and Philosophy." *History of Political Economy* 35: 282–308.
Forman-Barzilai, Fonna. 2010. *Adam Smith and the Circles of Sympathy*. Cambridge: Cambridge University Press.
Forsythe, Robert, Joel L. Horowitz, N. E. Savin, and Martin Sefton. 1994. "Fairness in Simple Bargaining Experiments." *Games and Economic Behavior* 6(3): 347–69.
Frazer, Michael. 2010. *The Enlightenment of Sympathy: Justice and the Moral Sentiments in the Eighteenth Century and Today*. Oxford: Oxford University Press.
French, R. K. 1986. "Pliny and Renaissance Medicine." In *Science in the Early Roman Empire: Pliny the Elder, His Sources and Influence*, ed. R. K. French and Frank Greenaway. London: Croom Helm, 1986, 252–81.
Frierson, Patrick R. 2006. "Adam Smith and the Possibility of Sympathy with Nature." *Pacific Philosophical Quarterly* 87(4): 442–80.

Furley, David. 1999. "Cosmology." In *The Cambridge History of Hellenistic Philosophy*, ed. Keimpe A. Algra, Jonathan Barnes, Jaap Mansfeld, and Malcolm Schofield. Cambridge: Cambridge University Press, 412–51.

Gaide, Françoise. 2003. "Aspects divers des principles de sympathie et d'antipathie dans les textes thérapeutiques latins." In *Rationnel et irrationnel dans la médecine ancienne et médiévale: aspects historiques, scientifiques et culturels*, ed. Nicoletta Palmieri. Saint-Étienne: Publications de l'Université de Saint-Étienne, 129–44.

Gaillard-Seux, Patricia. 2003. "Sympathie et antipathie dans *l'Histoire Naturelle* de Pline l'Ancien." In *Rationnel et irrationnel dans la médecine ancienne et médiévale: aspects historiques, scientifiques et culturels*, ed. Nicoletta Palmieri. Saint-Étienne: Publications de l'Université de Saint-Étienne, 113–28.

Gallese, V., and A. Goldman. 1998. "Mirror Neurons and the Simulation Theory of Mind-reading." *Trends in cognitive sciences* 2(12): 493–501.

Garrett, Don. 1991. "Spinoza's Necessitarianism." In *God and Nature: Spinoza's Metaphysics*, ed. Yirmiyahu Yovel. Leiden: Brill, 97–118.

Garrett, Don. 1995. "Spinoza's Ethical Theory." In *The Cambridge Companion to Spinoza*, ed. Garrett. Cambridge: Cambridge University Press, 267–314.

Garrett, Don. 2002. "Spinoza's Conatus Argument." In *Spinoza: Metaphysical Themes*, ed. O. Koistinen and J. Biro. Oxford: Oxford University Press, 127–58.

Gatti, Andrea, ed. 1998. *Museo degli strumenti musicali*. Milan: Electa.

Gerson, Lloyd P., ed. 1996. *The Cambridge Companion to Plotinus*. Cambridge: Cambridge University Press.

Gerson, Lloyd P. 2005a. *Aristotle and Other Platonists*. Ithaca, NY: Cornell University Press.

Gerson, Lloyd P. 2005b. "What Is Platonism?" *Journal of the History of Philosophy* 43(3): 253–76.

Gerson, Lloyd P., ed. 2010. *The Cambridge History of Philosophy in Late Antiquity*. Cambridge: Cambridge University Press.

Giannantoni, Gabriele. 1990. *Socratis et socraticorum reliquiae*. Naples: Bibliopolis.

Gildenhard, Ingo. 2011. *Creative Eloquence*. Oxford: Oxford University Press.

Gill, Christopher. 2004. "The Stoic Theory of Ethical Development: In What Sense Is Nature a Norm?" In *Was ist das für den Menschen Gute?*, ed. Jan Szaif and Matthias Lutz-Bachmann. Berlin: De Gruyter, 101–25.

Gill, Michael. 2006. *The British Moralists on Human Nature and the Birth of Secular Ethics*. Cambridge: Cambridge University Press.

Gillies, Anthony S., and Mary L. Rigdon. 2008. "Epistemic Conditions and Social Preferences in Trust Games." Working paper, University of Michigan.

Gilman, Ernest B. 1999. "The Arts of Sympathy: Dr. Harvey, Sir Kenelm Digby, and the Arundel Circle." In *Opening the Borders: Inclusivity in Early Modern Studies:*

Essays in Honor of James V. Mirollo, ed. Peter C. Herman. Newark: University of Delaware Press; London: Associated University Presses, 265–97.

Goldman, A. I. 2006. *Simulating Minds: The Philosophy, Psychology, and Neuroscience of Mindreading*. Oxford: Oxford University Press.

Gouk, Penelope. 2000. "Music in Francis Bacon's Natural Philosophy." In *Number to Sound: The Musical Way to the Scientific Revolution*, ed. Paolo Gozza. Dordrecht: Kluwer Academic, 135–52.

Gould, Stephen J. 2002. *The Structure of Evolutionary Theory*. Cambridge, MA: Harvard University Press.

Goulet-Cazé, Marie-Odile. 1982. "Un Syllogisme stoïcien sur la loi dans la doxographie de Diogène le Cynique: À propos de Diogène Laërce VI 72." *Rheinisches Museum* 125: 214–40.

Goulet-Cazé, Marie-Odile. 1986. *L'Ascèse cynique*. Paris: Vrin.

Grafton, Anthony. 1997. "Giovanni Pico della Mirandola: Trials and Triumphs of an Omnivore." In *Commerce with the Classics: Ancient Books and Renaissance Readers*. Ann Arbor: University of Michigan Press, 93–134.

Gruber, Jacob W. 1960. *A Conscience in Conflict: The Life of St. George Jackson Mivart*. New York: Columbia University Press.

Gueroult, Martial. 1968/1974. *Spinoza*. 2 vols. Paris: Aubier-Montaigne.

Gunkle, George. 1963. "Empathy: Implications for Theatre Research." *Educational Theatre Journal* 15(1): 15–23.

Gurtler, Gary Michael. 1988. *Plotinus: The Experience of Unity*. New York: Peter Lang.

Gurtler, Gary Michael. 2002. "Sympathy: Stoic Materialism and the Platonic Soul." In *Neoplatonism and Nature*, ed. Michael Frank Wagner. International Society for Neoplatonic Studies, vol. 3, Studies in Plotinus' *Enneads*. Albany: SUNY Press, 241–76.

Güth, Werner, Rolf Schmittberger, and Bernd Schwarze. 1982. "An Experimental Analysis of Ultimatum Bargaining." *Journal of Economic Behavior and Organization* 3(4): 367–88.

Guyer, Paul. 2010. "Moral Feelings in the *Metaphysics of Morals*." In *Kant's Metaphysics of Morals: A Critical Guide*, ed. Lara Denis. Cambridge: Cambridge University Press, 130–51.

Hampton, Jean. 1993. "Selflessness and the Loss of Self." In *Altruism*, ed. E. F. Paul, F. Miller, and J. Paul. Cambridge: Cambridge University Press, 135–65.

Hankinson, R. Jim. 1988. "Stoicism, Science, and Divination." *Apeiron* 21(2): 123–60.

Hankinson, R. Jim. 2008. "Philosophy of Nature." In *The Cambridge Companion to Galen*, ed. R. Jim Hankinson. Cambridge: Cambridge University Press, 210–41.

Hanley, Ryan P. 2011. "David Hume and 'the Politics of Humanity.'" *Political Theory* 39: 205–33.
Hanley, Ryan P. 2012. "Rousseau's Virtue Epistemology." *Journal of the History of Philosophy* 50: 239–63.
Hanley, Ryan P. 2014a. "Adam Smith: From Love to Sympathy." *Revue internationale de philosophie* 269(3): 251–73.
Hanley, Ryan P. 2014b. "Pitié développée: Aspects éthiques et épistémiques." In *Philosophie de Rousseau*, ed. B. Bachofen, B. Bernardi, A. Charrak, and F. Guénard. Paris: Classiques Garnier, 2014, 305–18.
Hayek, Friedrich A. 1973. *Law, Legislation and Liberty*. Vol. 1: *Rules and Order*. Chicago: University of Chicago Press.
Hayek, Friedrich A. 1988. *The Fatal Conceit: The Errors of Socialism*. Chicago: University of Chicago Press.
Hayes, Julie Candler. 1991. Identity and Ideology: Diderot, Sade, and the Serious Genre. Amsterdam: John Benjamins.
Heidegger, Martin. 1962 [1927]. *Being and Time*. Trans. John Macquarrie and Edward Robinson. San Francisco: SCM Press.
Helleman, Wendy Elgersma. 2010. "Plotinus as Magician." *International Journal of the Platonic Tradition* 4(2): 114–46.
Helleman-Elgersma, Wypkje. 1980. *Soul-Sisters: A Commentary on Ennead IV.3.1–8 of Plotinus*. Amsterdam: Rodopi.
Henry, John. 1999. "Isaac Newton and the Problem of Action at a Distance." *Revista de Filozofie KRISIS* (8–9): 30–46.
Henry, John. 2010. "Sir Kenelm Digby, Recusant Philosopher." In *Insiders and Outsiders in Seventeenth-Century Philosophy*, ed. G. A. J. Rogers, Tom Sorrell, and Jill Kraye. London: Routledge, 43–75.
Henry, John. 2011. "Gravity and *De gravitatione*: The Development of Newton's Ideas on Action at a Distance." *Studies in History and Philosophy of Science Part A* 42(1): 11–27.
Herdt, Jennifer A. 2001. "The Rise of Sympathy and the Question of Divine Suffering." *Journal of Religious Ethics* 29(3): 367–99.
Hill, W. C. Osman. 1950. "Man's Relation to the Apes." *Man* 50: 161–62.
Hoffman, Elizabeth, Kevin McCabe, Keith Shachat, and Vernon L. Smith. 1994. "Preferences, Property Rights, and Anonymity in Bargaining Experiments." *Games and Economic Behavior* 7(3): 346–80.
Hoffman, Elizabeth, Kevin McCabe, and Vernon L. Smith. 1996. "On Expectations and the Monetary Stakes in Ultimatum Games." *International Journal of Game Theory* 25(3): 289–301.
Holmes, Brooke. 2012. "Sympathy between Hippocrates and Galen: The Case of Galen's *Commentary on Hippocrates 'Epidemics,' Book Two*." In *Epidemics in*

Context: Greek Commentaries on Hippocrates in the Arabic Tradition, ed. Peter Pormann. Berlin: De Gruyter, 49–70.

Holmes, Brooke. 2013. "Disturbing Connections: Sympathetic Affections, Mental Disorder, and the Elusive Soul in Galen." In (ed.), *Mental Disorders in the Classical World*, ed. W. V. Harris. Leiden: Brill, 147–76.

Holmes, Brooke. 2014. "Galen on the Chances of Life." In *Probabilities, Hypotheticals, and Counterfactuals in Ancient Greek Thought*, ed. Victoria Wohl. Cambridge: Cambridge University Press, 230–50.

Hossenfelder, Max. 2003. "Oikeiosis." In *Der Neue Pauly*, ed. Hubert Cancik and Helmuth Schneider, vol. 8 s.v. Leiden: Brill.

Hothersall, David. 1984. *History of Psychology*. Philadelphia: Temple University Press.

Hübner, K. Forthcoming a. "Spinoza on Being Human and Human Perfection." in *Ethics of Spinoza's Ethics*, ed. A. Youpa and M. Kisner. Oxford: Oxford University Press.

Hübner, Karolina. Forthcoming b. "On the Significance of Formal Causes in Spinoza's Metaphysics." *Archiv für Geschichte der Philosophie*.

Hübner, Karolina. Forthcoming c. "Spinoza on Essences, Universals and Beings of Reason," *Pacific Philosophical Quarterly*.

Hübner, Karolina. Forthcoming d. "Spinoza's Unorthodox Metaphysics of the Will." In *The Oxford Handbook on Spinoza*, ed. Michael Della Rocca. Oxford: Oxford University Press.

Hülser, Karlheinz, ed. 1987–88. *Fragmente der Dialektik der Stoiker*. 4 vols. Stuttgart: Frommann-Holzbog.

Hunsdahl, Jørgen. 1967. "Concerning Einfuhlung (Empathy): A Concept Analysis of Its Origin and Early Development." *Journal of the History of the Behavioral Sciences* 3: 180–91.

Hutchison, Keith. 1982. "What Happened to Occult Qualities in the Scientific Revolution?" *Isis* 73(2): 233–53.

Hutton, Sarah, 2004. *Anne Conway: A Woman Philosopher*. Cambridge: Cambridge University Press.

Huzel, James P. 2006. *The Popularization of Malthus in Early Nineteenth-Century England: Martineau, Cobbett and the Pauper Press*. Aldershot, UK: Ashgate.

Ierodiakonou, K. 2006. "The Greek Concept of Sympatheia and Its *Byzantine* Appropriation in Michael Psellos." In *The Occult Sciences in Byzantium*, ed. P. Magdalino and M. Mavroudi. Geneva: Pomme d'or, 97–117.

James, Susan. 1993. "Spinoza the Stoic." In *The Rise of Early Modern Philosophy: The Tension between the New and the Traditional Philosophies from Machiavelli to Leibniz*. Ed. Tom Sorrell. Oxford: Oxford University Press, 289–316.

Janaway, Christopher. 2007. *Beyond Selflessness: Reading Nietzsche's Genealogy*. Oxford: Oxford University Press.
Janiak, Andrew. 2007. "Newton and the Reality of Force." *Journal of the History of Philosophy* 45(1): 127–47.
Janiak, Andrew. 2008. *Newton as Philosopher*. Cambridge: Cambridge University Press.
Jansen, Gemma C. M., Ann Olga Koloski-Ostrow, and Eric M. Moormann, eds. 2011. *Roman Toilets*. Leuven: Peeters.
Johada, Gustav. 2005. "Theodor Lipps and the Shift from Sympathy to Empathy." *Journal of the History of the Behavioral Sciences* 41: 151–63.
Johnston, Sarah I. 2008. *Ancient Greek Divination*. Oxford: Wiley-Blackwell.
Johnston, Sarah I., and Peter T. Struck, eds. 2005. *Mantikê: Studies in Ancient Greek Divination*. Leiden: Brill, 2005.
Karamanolis, George. 2006. *Plato and Aristotle in Agreement? Platonists on Aristotle from Antiochus to Porphyry*. Oxford: Oxford University Press.
Kessler, Eckhard. 2001. "Metaphysics or Empirical Science?" In *Renaissance Readings of the Corpus Aristotelicum: Proceedings from the Conference held in Copenhagen 23–25 April 1998*, ed. Marianne Pade. Copenhagen: Museum Tusculanum, 79–101.
Kinzer, Bruce L., Ann P. Robson, and John M. Robson. 1992. *A Moralist in and out of Parliament: John Stuart Mill at Westminster, 1865–1868*. Toronto: University of Toronto Press.
Kochiras, Hylarie. 2009. "Gravity and Newton's Substance Counting Problem." *Studies in History and Philosophy of Science Part A* 40(3): 267–80.
Kochiras, Hylarie. 2013. "Locke's Philosophy of Science." *The Stanford Encyclopedia of Philosophy*, Fall 2013 ed., ed. Edward N. Zalta. http://plato.stanford.edu/archives/fall2013/entries/locke-philosophy-science/.
Kögler, Hans, and Karsten Stueber, eds. 1999. *Empathy, Agency, and the Problem of Understanding in the Social Sciences*. Boulder, CO: Westview Press.
Koss, Juliet. 2006. "On the Limits of Empathy." *Art Bulletin* 88: 139–57.
Kottler, Malcolm Jay. 1974. "Alfred Russel Wallace, the Origin of Man, and Spiritualism." *Isis* 65: 144–92.
Kranz, Margarita, and Peter Probst. 1998. "Sympathie." In *Historisches Wörterbuch der Philosophie*, ed. Joachim Ritter, Karlfried Gründer, and Gottfried Gabriel. Basel: Schwabe, 10.752–56.
Krause, Sharon. 2008. *Civil Passions: Moral Sentiment and Democratic Deliberation*. Princeton, NJ: Princeton University Press.
Kristeller, Paul O., and Michael Mooney, eds. 1979. *Renaissance Thought and Its Sources* New York: Columbia University Press.

Laerke, M. 2011. "Spinoza's Cosmological Argument in the *Ethics*." *Journal of the History of Philosophy* 49(4): 439–62.

Lamb, Jonathan. 2009. *The Evolution of Sympathy in the Long Eighteenth Century*. London: Pickering and Chatto.

Laurand, Valéry. 2005. "La Sympathie universelle: Union et séparation." In *Les Stoïciens et le monde*, ed. Thomas Bénatouïl and Pierre-Marie Morel. Paris: Presses universitaires de France, 517–35.

Laurent, John, and Geof Cockfield. 2007. "Adam Smith, Charles Darwin and the Moral Sense." In *New Perspectives on Adam Smith's* Theory of Moral Sentiments, ed. Geof Cockfield, Ann Firth, and John Laurent. Cheltenham, UK: Edward Elgar, 141–62.

Lawrence, M. 2005. "Hellenistic Astrology." *The Internet Encyclopedia of Philosophy*. http://www.iep.utm.edu/a/astr-hel.htm.

Lehrich, Christopher I. 2003. The Language of Demons and Angels: Cornelius Agrippa's Occult Philosophy. Leiden: Brill.

Levy, David M. 1978. "Some Normative Aspects of the Malthusian Controversy." *History of Political Economy* 10: 271–85.

Levy, David M. 1999. "Christianity or Malthusianism: The Invisibility of a Successful Radicalism." *Historical Reflections/Réflexions Historiques* 25: 61–93.

Levy, David M., and Sandra J. Peart. 2006. "Charles Kingsley and the Theological Interpretation of Natural Selection." *Journal of Bioeconomics* 8: 197–218.

Levy, David M., and Sandra J. Peart. 2013. "Adam Smith and the State: Language and Reform." In *Oxford Handbook on Adam Smith*, ed. Christopher Berry, Maria Paganelli, and Craig Smith. Oxford: Oxford University Press, 372–93.

List, John, and Todd L. Cherry. 2000. "Learning to Accept in Ultimatum Games: Evidence from an Experimental Design that Generates Low Offers." *Experimental Economics* 3(1): 11–29.

Long, A. A. 2003. "Stoicism in the Philosophical Tradition: Spinoza, Lipsius, Butler." In *Cambridge Companion to the Stoics*, ed. Brad Inwood. Cambridge: Cambridge University Press, 365–92.

Long, Anthony A., and David N. Sedley, 1987. *The Hellenistic Philosophers*. 2 vols, Cambridge: Cambridge University Press.

Look, Brandon C. 2013. "Gottfried Wilhelm Leibniz." In *The Stanford Encyclopedia of Philosophy*, Spring 2013 ed., ed. Edward N. Zalta. http://plato.stanford.edu/archives/spr2013/entries/leibniz/.

Louis, Pierre, ed. 1991. *Aristote: Problèmes*. Vol. 1. Paris: Les Belles Lettres.

Lovejoy, C. Owen. 2009. "Reexamining Human Origins in Light of *Ardipithecus ramidus*." *Science*, 2 October: 74.

Mancosu, P. 1999. *Philosophy of Mathematics and Mathematical Practice in the Seventeenth Century*. Oxford: Oxford University Press.

Mandler, George. 2006. *A History of Modern Experimental Psychology: From James and Wundt to Cognitive Science* Cambridge, MA: MIT Press.

Marshall, David. 1988. *The Surprising Effects of Sympathy: Marivaux, Diderot, Rousseau, and Mary Shelley*. Chicago: University of Chicago Press.

May, Simon. 2011. *Love: A History*. New Haven, CT: Yale University Press.

Mayr, Ernst. 1991. *One Long Argument: Charles Darwin and the Genesis of Modern Evolutionary Thought*. Cambridge, MA: Harvard University Press.

McCabe, Kevin, Stephen Rassenti, and Vernon L. Smith. 1996. "Game Theory and Reciprocity in Some Extensive Form Experimental Games," *Proceedings of the National Academy of Arts and Sciences* 93: 13421–28.

McCabe, Kevin, Mary L. Rigdon, and Vernon L. Smith. 2003. "Positive Reciprocity and Intentions in Trust Games." *Journal of Economic Behavior and Organization* 52(2): 267–75.

McCabe, Kevin, and Vernon L. Smith. 2000. "A Comparison of Naïve and Sophisticated Subject Behavior with Game Theoretic Predictions." *Proceedings of the National Academy of Arts and Sciences* 97(7): 3777–81.

McCabe, Kevin, Vernon L. Smith, and Michael LePore. 2000. "Intentionality Detection and 'Mindreading': Why Does Game Form Matter?" *Proceedings of the National Academy of Sciences* 97(8): 4404–409.

McConnaughey, Gloria. 1950. "Darwin and Social Darwinism." *Osiris* 9: 397–412.

McCracken, Charles. 1998. "Knowledge of the Soul." In *Cambridge History of Seventeenth-Century Philosophy*, ed. D. Garber and M. Ayers. Cambridge: Cambridge University Press, 796–832.

Melamed, Yitzhak. 2012. "Spinoza's Metaphysics of Thought: Parallelisms and the Multifaceted Structure of Ideas." *Philosophy and Phenomenological Research* 86(3): 636–83.

Meltzer, H. 1927. "Lipps' Pre-Gestalt Studies." *Journal of Educational Psychology* 18(2): 131–33.

Menn, Stephen. 1998. *Descartes and Augustine*. New York: Cambridge University Press.

Mercer, Christia. 1998. "Kenelm Digby." In *Routledge Encyclopedia of Philosophy*, ed. E. Craig. London: Routledge, . http://www.rep.routledge.com/article/DA028SECT3.

Mercer, Christia. 2001. *Leibniz's Metaphysics: Its Origins and Development*. Cambridge: Cambridge University Press.

Mercer, Christia. 2002. "Platonism and Philosophical Humanism on the Continent." In *A Companion to Early Modern Philosophy*, ed. Steven Nadler. Oxford: Blackwell, 25–44.

Mercer, Christia. 2012. "Platonism in Early Modern Natural Philosophy: The Case of Leibniz and Conway." In *Neoplatonic Natural Philosophy*, ed. Christoph Horn and James Wilberding. Oxford: Oxford University Press, 103–26.

Mercer, Christia. 2014. "Anne Conway's Metaphysics of Sympathy." In *Feminist History of Philosophy: Recovery and Evaluation of Women's Philosophical Thought*, ed. Eileen O'Neill and Marcy Lascano. New York: Springer.

Merlan, Philip. 1953. "Plotinus and Magic." *Isis* 44: 341–48.

Mills, John A. 2000. *Control: A History of Behavioral Psychology*. New York: New York University Press.

Montes, Leonidas. 2003. "Das Adam Smith Problem: Its Origins, the Stage of the Current Debate, and One Implication for Our Understanding of Sympathy." *Journal of the History of Economic Thought* 35: 63–90.

Montes, Leonidas. 2004. *Adam Smith in Context*. London: Palgrave Macmillan.

Moser-Verrey, Monique. 2007. "Le Discours de la sympathie dans *Les affinités électives*." In *Les Discours de la sympathie: Enquête sur une notion de l'âge classique à la modernité*, ed. Thierry Belleguic, Eric Van der Scheuren, and Sabrina Vervack. Quebec: Les Presses de l'Université Laval, 343–55.

Nadler, Steven, ed. 1993. *Causation in Early Modern Philosophy*. University Park: Pennsylvania State University Press.

Nadler, Steven. 2006. *Spinoza's Ethics: An Introduction*. Cambridge: Cambridge University Press.

Nauert, Charles. 1965. *Agrippa and the Crisis of Renaissance Thought*. Urbana: University of Illinois Press.

Nauert, Charles. 1979. "Humanists, Scientists, and Pliny: Changing Approaches to a Classical Author." *American Historical Review* 84(1): 72–85.

Newlands, Samuel. 2012. "Thinking, Conceiving, and Idealism in Spinoza." *Archiv für Geschichte der Philosophie* 94:31–52.

North, Douglass C. 1990. *Institutions, Institutional Change, and Economic Performance*. Cambridge: Cambridge University Press.

North, Douglass C. 2005. *Understanding the Process of Economic Change*. Princeton, NJ: Princeton University Press.

Nutton, Vivian. 1990. "The Reception of Fracastoro's Theory of Contagion: The Seed That Fell among Thorns?" *Osiris,* 2nd Series 6, *Renaissance Medical Learning: Evolution of a Tradition*: 196–234.

Obbink, Dirk, and Paul A. Vander Waerdt. 1991. "Diogenes of Babylon: The Stoic Sage in the City of Fools." *Greek, Roman and Byzantine Studies* 32: 355–96.

O'Meara, Dominic J. 1996. "The Hierarchical Ordering of Reality in Plotinus." In *The Cambridge Companion to Plotinus*, ed. Lloyd P. Gerson. Cambridge: Cambridge University Press, 66–81.

O'Neill, Daniel I. 2007. *The Burke-Wollstonecraft Debate: Savagery, Civilization, and Democracy*. University Park: Pennsylvania State University Press.

O'Neill, Eileen. 1993. "Influxus Physicus." In , ed., *Causation in Early Modern Philosophy*, ed. Steven Nadler. University Park: Pennsylvania State University Press, 27–55.

O'Neill, Eileen. 1998. "Disappearing Ink: Early Modern Women Philosophers and Their Fate in History." In *Philosophy in a Feminist Voice: Critiques and Reconstructions*, ed. Janet Kournay. Princeton, NJ: Princeton University Press, 17–62.

Opsomer, Jan, 2011. "Virtue, Fortune, and Happiness in Theory and Practice." In *Virtues for the People*, ed. by Geert Roskam and Luc Van der Stockt, 151–73. Leuven: Peeters.

Osborn, Jan, Bart J. Wilson, and Bradley R. Sherwood. Forthcoming. "Conduct in Narrativized Trust Games." *Southern Economic Journal*.

Ospovat, Dov. 1981. *The Development of Darwin's Theory: Natural History, Natural Theology, and Natural Selection, 1838–1859*. Cambridge: Cambridge University Press.

Oxford English Dictionary. 2013. Oxford University Press. http://www.oed.com.

Pagel, Walter. 1982. *Joan Baptista Van Helmont: Reformer of Science and Medicine*. Cambridge: Cambridge University Press.

Palisca, Claude. 2000. "Moving the Affections through Music: Pre-Cartesian Psycho-Physiological Theories." In *Number to Sound: The Musical Way to the Scientific Revolution*, ed. Paolo Gozza. Dordrecht: Kluwer Academic, 289–308.

Papy, Jan. 2011. "Justus Lipsius." *The Stanford Encyclopedia of Philosophy*, Fall 2011 ed., ed. Edward N. Zalta http://plato.stanford.edu/archives/fall2011/entries/justus-lipsius/.

Peart, Sandra J. 2009. "'We Are All Persons Now': Classical Economists and Their Opponents on Marriage, the Franchise and Socialism." *Journal of the History of Economics Society* 31: 3–20.

Peart, Sandra J., and David M. Levy. 2003. "Denying Homogeneity: Eugenics and the Making of Post-Classical Economics." *Journal of the History of Economic Thought* 25: 261–88.

Peart, Sandra J., and David M. Levy. 2005. *The "Vanity of the Philosopher": From Equality to Hierarchy in Post-Classical Economics*. Ann Arbor: University of Michigan Press.

Peart, Sandra J., and David M. Levy. 2008. "Darwin's Unpublished Letter at the Bradlaugh-Besant Trial: A Question of Divided Expert Judgment." *European Journal of Political Economy* 24: 243–53.

Pecorino, Paul, and Mark Van Boening. 2010. "Fairness in an Embedded Ultimatum Game." *Journal of Law and Economics* 53: 263–87.

Pennuto, Concetta. 2008. *Simpatia, fantasia e contagio: Il pensiero medico e il pensiero filosofico di Girolamo Fracastoro*. Rome: Edizioni di storia e letteratura.

Pfeffer, Friedrich. 1976. *Studien zur Mantik in der Philosophie der Antike*. Meisenheim am Glan: Hain.

Pigler, Agnès 2001. "La Réception plotinienne de la notion stoïcienne de sympathie universelle." *Revue de philosophie ancienne* 19(1): 45–78.

Pigman, George. 1995. "Freud and the History of Empathy." *International Journal of Psychoanalysis* 76(2): 237–56.

Pollock, Frederick. 1880. *Spinoza: His Life and Philosophy*. London: Kegan Paul.

Prior, Arthur N. 1947. Review of C. S. Lewis, *Abolition of Man*. *Landfall* 1: 63–67.

Ramelli, Ilaria, ed., and David Konstan, trans. 2009. *Hierocles the Stoic: Elements of Ethics, Fragments, and Excerpts*. Atlanta: Society of Biblical Literature.

Raphael, D. D. 2007. *The Impartial Spectator: Adam Smith's Moral Philosophy*. Oxford: Oxford University Press.

Rapp, Cristof. 2006. "Interaction of Body and Soul: What the Hellenistic Philosophers Saw and Aristotle Avoided." In *Common to Body and Soul*, ed. Richard A. H. King. Berlin: De Gruyter, 186–206.

Reddy, William. 2001. *The Navigation of Feeling: A Framework for the History of the Emotions*. Cambridge: Cambridge University Press.

Reeder, John., ed. 1997. *On Moral Sentiments*. London: Thommes.

Reginster, Bernard. 2000a. "Nietzsche on Selflessness and the Value of Altruism." *History of Philosophy Quarterly* 17(2): 177–200.

Reginster, Bernard. 2000b. "Nietzsche's 'Revaluation' of Altruism." *Nietzsche-Studien Jubiläumsband* 29: 199–219.

Reginster, Bernard. 2006. *The Affirmation of Life: Nietzsche on Overcoming Nihilism*. Cambridge, MA: Harvard University Press.

Reginster, Bernard. 2007. "The Will to Power and the Ethics of Creativity." In *Nietzsche and Morality*, ed. B. Leiter and N. Sinhababu. Oxford: Oxford University Press, 32–56.

Reginster, Bernard. 2012. "Compassion and Selflessness." In *Nietzsche, Naturalism, and Normativity*, ed. C. Janaway and S. Robertston. Oxford: Oxford University Press, 160–82.

Reinhardt, Karl. 1926. *Kosmos und Sympathie: Neue Untersuchungen über Poseidonios*. Munich: Beck.

Richards, Robert J. 1992. *The Meaning of Evolution: The Morphological Construction and Ideological Reconstruction of Darwin's Theory*. Chicago: University of Chicago Press.

Rietz, Thomas A., Roman M. Sheremeta, Timothy W. Shields, and Vernon L. Smith. 2013. "Transparency, Efficiency and the Distribution of Economic Welfare in Pass-Through Investment Trust Games." *Journal of Economic Behavior and Organization* 94: 257–67.

Rigdon, Mary L., Kevin A. McCabe, and Vernon L. Smith. 2007. "Sustaining Cooperation in Trust Games." *Economic Journal* 117(522): 991–1007.

Rizzolatti, G., L. Fogassi, and V. Gallese. 2006. "Mirrors in the Mind." *Scientific American* 295(5): 54–61.

Robson, John M. 1968. *The Improvement of Mankind: The Social and Political Thought of John Stuart Mill*. Toronto: University of Toronto Press.

Ross, Ian S. 2010. *The Life of Adam Smith*. 2nd ed. Oxford: Oxford University Press.

Rothschild, Emma. 2002. *Economic Sentiments: Adam Smith, Condorcet and the Enlightenment*. Cambridge, MA: Harvard University Press.

Rozanova, Olga. 1988 [1918]. "Extracts from Articles." In *Russian Art of the Avant-Garde: Theory and Criticism*, trans. and ed. John E. Bowlt. New York: Thames and Hudson, 148.

Ruse, Michael. 1999. "Afterwards: Two Decades Later." In *The Darwin Revolution: Science Red in Tooth and Claw*. 2nd ed Chicago: University of Chicago Press, 313–38.

Salmon, Timothy C., and Bart J. Wilson. 2008. "Second Chance Offers Versus Sequential Auctions: Theory and Behavior." *Economic Theory* 34: 47–67.

Sambursky, Samuel. 1959. *Physics of the Stoics*. London: Routledge and Kegan Paul.

Sauvé-Meyer, Susan. 2009. "Chain of Causes: What Is Stoic Fate?" In *God and Cosmos in Stoicism*, ed. Riccardo Salles. Oxford: Oxford University Press, 71–90.

Sayre-McCord, Geoffrey. 1994. "On Why Hume's 'General Point of View' Isn't Ideal—and Shouldn't Be." *Social Philosophy and Policy* 11(1): 202–28.

Sayre-McCord, Geoffrey. 2010. "Sentiments and Spectators: Adam Smith's Theory of Moral Judgment." In *The Philosophy of Adam Smith*, ed. Vivienne Brown and Samuel Fleischacker. Abingdon, UK: Routledge, 124–44.

Schadewaldt, Wolfgang. 1973. "Humanitas romana." In *Aufstieg und Niedergang der römischen Welt 1.4*, ed. Hildegard Temporini. Berlin: De Gruyter, 43–62.

Schaefer, W. D. 1967. Introduction to *The Speedy Extinction of Evil and Misery: Selected Prose of James Thomson (B. V.)*. Berkeley: University of California Press.

Scheler, Max. 1970. *The Problem of Sympathy*. Trans. P. Heath. Hamden, CT: Archon.

Schliesser, Eric. 2008. Review of Montes and Raphael. *Ethics* 118: 569–75

Schliesser, Eric. 2011. "Without God: Gravity as a Relational Quality of Matter in Newton's Treatise." In *Vanishing Matter and the Laws of Motion: Descartes and Beyond*, ed. Peter Anstey and Dana Jalobeanu. London: Routledge, 80–102.

Schliesser, Eric. 2012. "Newtonian Emanation, Spinozism, Measurement and the Baconian Origins of the Laws of Nature." *Foundations of Science* 10(3): 1–18.

Schliesser, Eric. 2014. "Sophie de Grouchy, Marquise de Condorcet: Wisdom and Reform between Reason and Feeling." In *Feminist History of Philosophy*, ed. Eileen O'Neill and Marcy P. Lascano. Dordrecht: Springer.

Schliesser, Eric. 2013. "The Piacular, or on Seeing Oneself as a Moral Cause in Adam Smith." In *Contemporary Perspectives on Early Modern Philosophy: Nature and Norms in Thought*, ed. M. Lenz and A. Waldow. Vol. 29. Dordrecht, Netherlands: Springer, 159–77.

Schofield, Malcolm. 1983. "The Syllogisms of Zeno of Citium." *Phronesis* 28: 31–58.

Schofield, Malcolm. 1999. *The Stoic Idea of the City*. 2nd ed. Chicago: University of Chicago Press.

Schweber, S. S. 1977. "The Origin of the Origin Revisited." *Journal of the History of Biology* 10 229–316.

Schweber, S. S. 1980. "Darwin and the Political Economists: Divergence of Character." *Journal of the History of Biology* 13: 195–289.

Sedley, David N. 1999. "Stoic Physics and Metaphysics." In *The Cambridge History of Hellenistic Philosophy*, ed. Keimpe A. Algra, Jonathan Barnes, Jaap Mansfeld, and Malcolm Schofield. Cambridge: Cambridge University Press, 382–411.

Sellers, John. 2011. "Is God a Mindless Vegetable? Cudworth on Stoic Theology." *Intellectual History Review* 21(2): 121–33.

Sharples, Robert W., and Philip J. van der Eijk, trans. 2008. *Nemesius: On the Nature of Man*. Liverpool: Liverpool University Press.

Shermer, Michael. 2002. *In Darwin's Shadow: The Life and Science of Alfred Russel Wallace*. New York: Oxford University Press.

Siegel, Jerrold. 2005. The Idea of the Self: Thought and Experience in Western Europe Since the Seventeenth Century. Cambridge: Cambridge University Press.

Siegel, R. E. 1968. *Galen's System of Physiology and Medicine: An Analysis of His Doctrines and Observations on Bloodflow, Respiration, Tumors, and Internal Diseases*. Basel: Karger.

Simmel, Georg. 1986. *Schopenhauer and Nietzsche*. Trans. H. Loiskandl, D. Weinstein, and M. Weinstein. Amherst, MA: University of Massachusetts Press.

Smith, Vernon L. 2007; 2008. *Rationality in Economics: Constructivist and Ecological Forms*. Cambridge: Cambridge University Press; New York: Cambridge University Press.

Smith, Vernon L. 2013. "Adam Smith: From Propriety and *Sentiments* to Property and *Wealth*." *Forum for Social Economics*, 16 July. http://www.tandfonline.com/doi/abs/10.1080/07360932.2013.798241#.UiizvtIqh8E.

Smith, Vernon L., and Bart J. Wilson. 2013. "*Sentiments*, Conduct, and Trust in the Laboratory." Economic Science Institute Working Paper, Chapman University.
Sobel, Dava. 1995. *Longitude*. New York: Walker.
Sobel, Joel. 2005. "Interdependent Preferences and Reciprocity." *Journal of Economic Literature* 93: 392–436.
Spaulding, S. 2013. "Mirror Neurons and Social Cognition." *Mind and Language* 28(2): 233–57.
Steuer, Daniel. 2002. "In Defence of Experience: Goethe's Natural Investigations." In , ed., *The Cambridge Companion to Goethe*, ed. Lesley Sharpe. Cambridge: Cambridge University Press, 160–78.
Straus, William L., Jr. 1949. "The Riddle of Man's Ancestry." *Quarterly Review of Biology* 24: 200–23.
Struck, P. T. 2007. "A World Full of Signs: Understanding Divination in Ancient Stoicism." In *Seeing with Different Eyes: Essays in Astrology and Divination*, ed. P. Curry and A. Voss. Newcastle: Cambridge Scholars, 3–20.
Swales, Martin. 2002. "Goethe's Prose Fiction." In *The Cambridge Companion to Goethe*, ed. Lesley Sharpe. Cambridge: Cambridge University Press, 129–46.
Taylor, Alfred Edward. 1929. "*A Commentary on Plato's* Timaeus." Oxford: Oxford University Press.
Thomas, Keith. 1971. *Religion and the Decline of Magic: Studies in Popular Beliefs in Sixteenth and Seventeenth Century England*. London: Weidenfeld & Nicolson; New York: Scribner's.
Thorndike, Lynn. 1934. *A History of Magic and Experimental Science*. 8 vols. New York: Columbia University Press.
Tieleman, Teun. 2007. "Panaetius' Place in the History of Stoicism with Special Reference to His Moral Psychology." In *Pyrrhonists, Patricians, Platonizers*, ed. Anna-Maria Ioppolo and David N. Sedley. Naples: Bibliopolis, 103–41.
Tinker, Miles. 1932. "Wundt's Doctorate Students and Their Theses 1875–1920." *American Journal of Psychology* 44(4): 630–37.
Tomlinson, Gary. 1993. *Music in Renaissance Magic*. Chicago: University of Chicago Press.
Turco, Luigi. 1999. "Sympathy and Moral Sense, 1725–1740." *British Journal for the History of Philosophy* 7: 79–101.
Vegetti, Mario. 1983. "La saggezza dell'attore: Problemi dell' etica stoica." *Aut aut* 195–96: 19–41.
Vegetti, Mario. 1996. *L'etica degli antichi*. 4th ed. Rome: Laterza.
Viljanen, Valtteri. 2008. "Spinoza's Essentialist Model of Causation." *Inquiry* 51(4): 412–37.

Vorzimmer, Peter J. 1970. *Charles Darwin: The Years of Controversy*. Philadelphia: Temple University Press.

Waal, Frans de. 2009. *The Age of Empathy*. New York: Harmony.

Wagner, Peter. 2001 "Renaissance Readings of the Corpus Aristotelicum—Not among the Herbalists." In *Renaissance Readings of the Corpus Aristotelicum: Proceedings from the Conference held in Copenhagen 23–25 April 1998*, ed. Marianne Pade. Copenhagen: Eckhard, 167–83.

Wahrman, Dror. 2006. The Making of the Modern Self: Identity and Culture in Eighteenth-Century England. New Haven, CT: Yale University Press.

Walker, D. P. 2000. *Spiritual and Demonic Magic from Ficino to Campanella*. University Park: Pennsylvania State University Press. Orig. 1958, Warburg Institute.

Wallace, Richard. 1996. "'Amaze your Friends!': Lucretius on Magnets." *Greece and Rome* 43: 178–87.

Wear, Andrew. 1998. "Galen in the Renaissance." In *Health and Healing in Early Modern England: Studies in Social and Intellectual History*. Aldershot, UK: Ashgate, I.

White, Michael J. 2003. "Stoic Natural Philosophy (Physics and Cosmology)." In *The Cambridge Companion to the Stoics*, ed. Brad Inwood. Cambridge: Cambridge University Press, 124–52.

Wilks, Ian, 2014. "Efficient Causation in Late Antiquity and the Earlier Medieval Period." In *Efficient Causation: A History*, ed. Tad Schmaltz (New York: Oxford University Press, 83–104.

Wilson, Bart J. 2008. "Language Games of Reciprocity." *Journal of Economic Behavior and Organization* 68: 365–77.

Wilson, Bart J. 2010. "Social Preferences Aren't Preferences." *Journal of Economic Behavior and Organization* 73: 77–82.

Wilson, Bart J. 2012. "Contra Private Fairness." *American Journal of Economics and Sociology* 71: 407–35.

Wilson, Margaret. 1999a. "Objects, Ideas, and 'Minds': Comments on Spinoza's Theory of Mind." In *Ideas and Mechanism: Essays on Early Modern Philosophy*, by Wilson. Princeton, NJ: Princeton University Press, 126–40.

Wilson, Margaret. 1999b. "Spinoza's Causal Axiom (Ethics I, Axiom 4)." In *Ideas and Mechanism: Essays on Early Modern Philosophy*, by Wilson. Princeton, NJ: Princeton University Press, 141–65.

Winch, Donald. 2001. "Darwin Fallen among Political Economists." *Proceedings of the American Philosophical Society* 145: 415–37.

Wispé, Lauren G. 1986. "The Distinction between Sympathy and Empathy: To Call Forth a Concept, a Word Is Needed." *Journal of Personality and Social Psychology* 50(2): 314–21.

Wispé, Lauren G. 2012 [1968]. "Sympathy and Empathy." In the *International Encyclopedia of the Social Sciences*. Detroit: MacMillan, 15.441–47. Republished online, Encyclopedia.com.

Young, Julian. 2005. *Schopenhauer*. London: Routledge.

Zahavi, Dan. 2010. "Empathy, Embodiment, and Interpersonal Understanding: From Lipps to Schultz." *Inquiry* 53(3): 285–306.

Index

Aarsleff, Hans, 187
Abolition movement, 331
Abstraction and Empathy (Worringer), 309
Abstractionism, 308, 309
Accademia dei Lincei, 89
Action at a distance, 7, 10–11, 12–13, 72–73.
    See also Distant action and attraction
Active principle, 9, 9n, 24, 27
Active spirits, 117, 126
Activity, 306
Adrovandi, Ulisse, 92
Aesthetic *Einfühlung*, 301–308
Aesthetics, 221, 290, 293, 296
Aesthetik (Lipps), 309
Affection, 46, 62, 66, 68, 193–194, 230, 328
Affective appearances, 312
Affective reactions, 209
Affinity, 75, 121, 129, 198, 248–249
Affinity of nature, 75–76, 89, 109
Against the Professors (Sextus Empiricus), 26

Agent motivation, 197
Agrippa, Heinrich Cornelius, 78, 79–80, 82, 85, 87, 89
Albertine, 80, 85
Albertus Magnus, 83
Alchemy, 247, 249
Aldrovandi, Ulisse, 92
Alexander of Aphrodisias, 20, 22, 25, 84, 85, 119
Alienation, 309
al-Kindi, 75
Altruism, 256, 259–275, 280, 284
Amadis, 93
Amicitia, 79
Amity, 93
Ammonius Saccas, 37
Analysis of the Phenomena of the Human Mind (Mill), 328
Anatomy, 66, 67
Anfühlung (attentive feeling), 296
Angels, 113

Anger, 218, 311, 312
Animal psychology, 292
Anonymity, 378
Anti-elementalism, 290
Antipater, 20
Antipathy, 84, 89
Antislavery movement, 331
Anxiety, 193
Apes and Man (Mivart), 347
Apollodorus, 26
Appetite, 84
Approbation, 211, 212, 216, 220–232, 241, 245
Appropriation, 34–35
Aquinas, Thomas, 120, 126
Aristotelianism, 53, 114, 115, 118, 120
Aristotle, 4, 16, 22, 52, 57, 63, 68
Arius Didymus, 33
Arrian, 20*n*
Asclepiades of Bithynia, 63, 65
Association, 89, 91, 174, 185
Astral influence, 44–51
Astrology, 44, 75
Atomistic explanation of sympathy, 113, 118
Attic Nights (Aulus Gellius), 17
Attraction, 75, 248. *See also* action at a distance
Attributes, 166–170
Augustinianism, 99, 124
Augustus, 33
Aulus Gellius, 17
Avicenna, 120

Bacon, Francis, 91, 92, 98, 103
Bacon, Roger, 75
Bailey, Michael, 99
Balbus, 26
Bandello, Matteo, 93
Barbaro, Ermolao, 80
Beaumarchais, Pierre-Augustin Caron de, 203
Beauty, 134
Behaviorism, 292
Being, hierarchy of, 123, 123*n*
Beneficence, 373, 374
"Beneficial Restrictions to Liberty of Marriage" (Darwin), 345

Benevolence, 185, 227*n*, 235
Benjamin, Walter, 8, 247
Bentley, Richard, 11
Berkeley, George, 189, 190*n*
Bernier, Marc André, 172
Beroaldo, Filippo, 80
Besant, Annie, 327, 349, 352–356, 358
Beutel, Albrecht, 122*n*
Bias, 238
Binns, William, 323
Birth control, 349
Blameworthiness, 232, 360, 367
"Book of secrets" tradition, 87
Boot, Anselm de, 91
Botanic Garden (Darwin), 331
Bracciolini, Poggio, 77
Bradlaugh, Charles, 327, 340, 349–352
Brain, 68
Breath, 24–25, 26, 33
Brouwer, René, 15, 117
Bruno, Giordano, 108
Burke, Edmund, 180
Butler, Joseph, 178, 179, 195

Cabanis, Pierre, 187
Campbell, Archibald, 195*n*
Cardano, Girolamo, 90
Care, 178, 299, 338
Cassina, Ubaldo, 270, 271–273, 283, 284
Catholics, 97, 122
Causal theory of emanation, 124, 124*n*
Causation, 7, 150*n*, 156, 159, 160
Cavendish, Margaret, 114
Cavendish, Richard, 94
Certaine Tragicall Discourses (Bandello), 93
Charity, 173, 178
Charmides, 16, 18
Cheerfulness, 220
Christianity, 101, 114, 121, 136*n*, 173–174, 341. *See also* Catholics; Protestants
Chrysippus, 20, 22, 23, 26, 30, 33
Cicero, 20, 29, 30, 44, 77
Civil society, 362
Clarke, John, 195*n*
Clarke, Samuel, 11

INDEX

Cleanthes, 16, 21, 28, 30, 32
Cleomedes, 22
Coaffections, 9, 18
Collingwood, R. G., 8
Color, 233
Comfort, 256
Compagni, V. Perrone, 80
Compassion, 178, 193, 260, 266.
    See also Fellow-feeling
  morality of, 254
  Nietzsche on, 255–259, 275–285
  phenomenology of, 269
Concurring nature, 12–13
Condorcet, Marie Louise Sophie de Grouchy, marquise de. See De Grouchy, Sophie
Connection of causes, 167
Connexio idearum, 157–162
Connexio rerum, 146, 152, 155–157, 162–166
Conscience, 362*n*
Consciousness, 263, 265, 289*n*, 314, 362*n*
Consensum, 77
Consequentials, 51
Contagion, 315, 316
Contagious disease, 72, 82
Contareni, Nicolo, 92
Contentment, 256
Continuity hypothesis, 324, 326, 340–345, 358
Contraception, 348, 349
Conway, Anne, 9, 107, 108, 114, 127, 135–138
Cooley, Charles, 298, 318, 319
Cooper, Anthony Ashley, 3rd Earl of Shaftesbury. See Shaftesbury, Earl of
Cooperation, 365
Copenhaver, Brian, 98, 121*n*
Corneille, Pierre, 200, 201
Correspondence, 159, 165
Correspondence theory of truth, 158
Cosmic "sympathy," 146, 149, 156–157
Cosmopolitanism, 28–35
Cosmos, 22, 24, 33, 39–40
Courtesy, 291
Cox, James, 378
Creation, 86
"Creative fire," 24

Crébillon, Prosper Jolyot de, 200
Cri du sang, 200
Critias, 16, 17
Criticism/critique, 247–249
Cudworth, Ralph, 115, 116, 116*n*

d'Alembert, Jean Le Rond, 186, 199
Damascius, 20
Darstellung, 252
Darwall, Stephen, 298, 299, 300, 316, 319
Darwin, Charles, 323–358
  biological background to, 330–335
  on continuity hypothesis, 340–345
  eugenics and, 345–348, 358
  on natural vs. human selection, 335–340, 348–358
Darwin, Erasmus, 330
Darwin, George, 327, 345–348
Debes, Remy, 5, 286
Debru, Armelle, 65*n*
Debus, Allen, 87
"Deception of the imagination," 270
Deck, Cary, 378
De Grouchy, Sophie, 5, 7, 9, 180, 188–189, 204–206
Deindividuated suffering, 283
Della Porta, Giambattista, 89, 90, 97
Della Rocca, Michael, 161*n*, 169*n*
De mirabilibus mundi (Albertus Magnus), 83
Democritus, 83
Demonic, 97, 113
De occultis in re medico proprietatibus (Olmo), 91
De radiis (al-Kindi), 75
Descartes, René, 5, 7, 8, 10, 13, 98, 112, 147, 149*n*, 154, 163
Descent of Man (Darwin), 324, 350
Desire, 77
De sympathia et antipathia rerum (Fracastoro), 82
De triplici vita (Ficino), 79
De Waal, Frans, 15, 15*n*, 16
Diderot, Denis, 202, 203
Die Wahlverwandtschaften (Goethe), 191
Digby, Kenelm, 8, 100, 112, 112*n*, 113

Dilthey, Wilhelm, 298
Diogenes Laertius, 19, 20, 26, 28
Diogenes of Sinope, 32
Disapprobation, 220, 221
Disapproval, 241
Discourse on Metaphysics (Leibniz), 131, 132
Distant action, 4, 9. *See also* Action at a distance
Divination, 28–35, 40, 44, 45, 90
Donne, John, 141
Double activity, 49
Double anonymity, 378, 379n
Double relation, 223
Dreaming, 30
Dualism, 11, 164
Du Bos, Jean-Baptiste, abbé, 202, 203, 206
Duchesne, Joseph, 87
Duncan, Stewart, 11

Eamon, William, 97
Economic behavior. *See* Experimental economic behavior
Economics, 3, 5
Edelstein, Ludwig, 20
Edgeworth, F. Y., 358
Effects, 48–51, 121, 134, 231
Egoism, 194, 262, 263, 265–266, 269, 284
Einfühlung (feeling into), 5, 295–318
  aesthetic, 301–308
  interpersonal, 308–318
Elective affinities, 191, 249, 251
Elective Affinities (Goethe), 248
Elements, 9, 25, 65, 79, 112
The Elements of Theology (Proclus), 125
Eliot, T. S., 106
Emanative causation, 124, 125. *See also* Causation
Emilsson, Eyjólfur K., 7, 36, 115n
Emotions, 4, 32, 65, 93, 176, 199, 201. *See also* Feelings
Empathy, 3, 4, 286, 313
Empedocles, 119
Empirical egoism, 273
Enhanced sympathetic harmony, 137
Enhanced universal sympathy, 127, 138
Enlightenment, 172
Enmity, 89

Enneads (Plotinus), 42, 73
Entretiens sur le Fils naturel (Diderot), 203
Envy, 215
Epictetus, 20, 20n, 115
Epicureans, 12, 57, 118
Epicurus, 16, 18, 19–28, 83
Epidemics II (Hippocrates), 67, 68, 69
Epistemic associationism, 174, 185
Epistemology, 185
Erasmus, Desiderius, 5, 81, 82
Theodicy: Essays on the Goodness of God, the Freedom of Man and the Origin of Evil (Leibniz), 134
Essence, 117, 118, 124–125, 136, 156–158
Ethnic psychology, 290n
Eugenics, 5, 326, 345–348, 358
Evoli, Cesare, 92
Experimental economic behavior, 359–385
  impartial spectator and, 361–364
  principles of action and, 360–361
  traditional game theory and, 364–369
  trust games and, 375–384
  ultimatum games and, 369–375
Experimental psychology, 293
Extortion game, 371

Fadiga, Luciano, 312n
Fairness, 362. *See also* Impartial spectator
Farnese, Alessandro, 82
Fate, 27
Fear, 218
Feelings, 93, 199, 201. *See also* Emotions
Fellow-feeling, 193, 198, 220, 229, 299. *See also* Compassion
Fenlon, Geoffrey, 93
Ficino, Marsilio, 5, 72, 73, 77–80, 85, 106, 109, 122
Fielding, Henry, 196
Figures, 51
Fire, 24, 26, 56, 117
First Truths (Leibniz), 131
Fleischacker, Samuel, 220n
Fogassi, Leonardo, 312n
Folk psychology, 290n
Force, 26, 102, 104–105, 109n, 138, 149, 306
Fordyce, David, 179, 195

Formal reality, 162
Forms, 53, 118, 120, 148*n*
Fracastoro, Girolamo, 5, 82–85, 87, 88, 95, 99
Free will, 151
Freige, Johannes Thomas, 92
Freud, Sigmund, 294, 294*n*, 298, 310
Friendship, 89, 93
Fruits of Philosophy (Knowlton), 349
Frustrated activity, 306

Galen, 4, 56, 57, 58, 60, 61–69, 84–85, 87, 90, 93, 96, 101, 120
Galileo Galilei, 105*n*, 112*n*
Gallese, Vittorio, 312*n*
Galton, Francis, 327, 334, 339, 346, 347, 350
Game theory, 360, 364–369. *See also* Experimental economic behavior
Gangloff, Jacob Heinrich, 119, 120, 121, 123, 126
Garin, Eugenio, 76
Garrett, Don, 159*n*
Gassendi, 112
Geiger, Moritz, 296*n*
General point of view, 234, 236–237, 239–240
Generosity, 366
Gentle sympathy, 120
Gerbino, Giuseppe, 4, 5, 102, 109*n*
Gestalt theory, 310
Gilbert, William, 13
Gillies, Anthony, 379, 380
Glory, 118, 134
Goclenius, Rudolph, 100, 111, 124
God, 10–11, 78, 116–118, 120, 124, 128–130
Goethe, Johann Wolfgang von, 191, 247–253
Golden rule of Christianity, 341
Goodness, 134, 136, 137, 275
Goodwill, 185
Gordian (emperor), 37
"Government" (Mill), 328
Gratitude, 209
Gravity, 10, 72, 130
Greg, W. R., 327, 333, 334, 339
Gulielmus Adolphus Scriborius, 92

Hall, John, 140
Hanley, Ryan Patrick, 13, 14, 171

Happiness, 172, 178, 193–196, 255, 259–261, 282, 325
Harmony, 74, 77, 118, 128
Hartley, David, 5, 185
Hatred, 215, 221, 222
Hayek, Friedrich, 360
Hayes, Julie Candler, 199
Hedonism, 257
Heidegger, Martin, 166*n*
Helvétius, Claude, 187
Henry, John, 12
Heraclitus, 26
Herbal for the Bible (Lemnius), 94
Herder, Johann, 296, 304
Hermeneutic sympathy, 247*n*
Hidden force, 102, 109*n*
Hierarchical emanation, 136
Hierarchy of being, 123, 123*n*
Hierocles, 35, 35*n*
Hippias, 32
Hippocrates, 61, 63, 64, 68, 69
History of Magic and Experimental Science (Thorndike), 90
Hobbes, Thomas, 112, 148, 192, 193, 195
Hoffman, Elizabeth, 372
Hogarth, William, 196
Holmes, Brooke, 4, 61–69
Home, Henry. *See* Kames, Lord
Homopatheia, 59
Horror vacui principle, 63
Hothersall, David, 290*n*
How to Behave towards Relatives (Hierocles), 35
Hübner, Karolina, 13, 14, 146, 174
Huloet, Richard, 94
Human dignity, 317
Humanism, 80
Humboldt, Alexander von, 248, 251, 252
Hume, David, 208–246
  on approbation, 220–228
  on humanity, 181
  on moral judgment, 5, 234–237
  philosophical framework, 209–211
  Scheler's critique of, 313
  simulationist models and, 301
  on sympathy, 7, 43, 196–197, 212–216

Humility, 215, 222, 224
Humoral pathology, 66, 66n, 75
Hutcheson, Francis, 188, 192, 194, 240, 240n
Hutchison, Keith, 97
Hutton, Sarah, 116n
Huxley, Thomas, 344
Huygens, Christian, 10, 130

Idealism, 161
Ideas, 105, 108, 114–116, 157. See also Thought
Identification, 271, 272, 282, 283
Imageless thought, 292
The Image of Nature and Grace (Cavendish), 94
Imagination, 205, 270
Imitation, 305
Imitative-projective process, 302
Immanence, 27n
Immortality of the Soul (More), 125
Impartial spectator, 237, 239, 242–244, 361–364, 380
Indirect passions, 222, 225, 226
Individuation, 268, 273, 274, 283
Infinity of things, 153
Influence, 15, 22–23, 42, 44–51, 75
Influentia, 74
Inherence relations, 150n
Instantaneous effects, 161
Intelligibility, 138, 146, 148–149, 152, 156
Internal perception, 60
Interpersonal *Einfühlung*, 308–318
Introspection, 205, 290, 291, 292
Isomorphism, 152, 159, 165

Jahoda, Gustav, 303, 306
James, William, 289n, 310
Jaucourt, Louis de, 186, 199
Jones, George, 141
Justice, 332, 373, 375
Justinian (emperor), 20
Lipsius, Justus, 115

Kames, Lord, 180, 181
Kant, Immanuel, 180, 181, 185, 254, 265n
Kaske, Carol, 75
Kepler, Johannes, 114, 114n

Kessler, Eckhard, 85n
Kidd, Ian G., 20
King Lear (Shakespeare), 139–145
Knowlton, Charles, 349

La Chaussée, Pierre-Claude Nivelle de, 201
Latin America, 251
Lazzarelli, Ludovico, 79
Lee, Vernon, 293n
Leibniz, Gottfried Wilhelm, 9–11, 107–109, 114, 116, 127, 128–135, 138
Lemnius, Levinus, 94
Leoniceno, Niccolò, 80
Levinus Lemnius, 94, 95
Levy, David M., 5, 323
Libavius, Andreas, 91
Likeness Principle (LP), 7, 8, 9, 11
Lipps, Theodore, 287, 290–294, 297, 301–317, 320
Lives of Eminent Philosophers (Diogenes Laertius), 24
Locke, John, 10
Lodestone, 64, 69, 89. See also Magnetism
Logic, 159n
Logos, 136
Long, Anthony A., 19n
Lotze, Hermann, 296
Love, 75, 77, 121, 129, 184, 221, 222, 224
LP. See Likeness Principle
Luchins, Abraham, 297, 298
Lucretius, 19n, 83
Luther, Martin, 122

Magia naturalis (Della Porta), 89
Magic, 44–51, 71, 73–75, 78, 96, 99, 110
Magical power, 109. See also Power
Magnetism, 13, 72, 100, 148. See also Lodestone
Mairhofer, Matthias, 92
Malebranche, Nicolas, 114
Malthus, T. R., 339, 348, 353, 355
Mandeville, Bernard, 179, 192, 193
Marcus Aurelius, 20
Marshall, David, 204

INDEX

Materialism, 204
Mathematical Principles of Natural Philosophy (Newton), 109
McCabe, Kevin A., 381–383, 383n, 384
McDougall, William, 298
Mead, George, 298, 318, 319–321, 322
Mechanical philosophy, 51, 148
Medicine, 73, 140
Melamed, Yitzhak, 152n
Memory, 205
Mercer, Christia, 14, 107
Mercier, Louis-Sébastien, 179n, 203
Mercuriale, Girolamo, 91
Metaphysical egoism, 272, 273
Metaphysics, 112, 114, 127, 128, 136
Mill, James, 325, 327, 329
Mill, John Stuart, 7, 9, 298, 325–329, 332, 341, 353, 358
Millán, Elizabeth, 247
Mindreading, 295
Minimax strategies, 371n
Mirroring, 159, 312
Mirror neurons, 6, 312, 312n
Mitfühlung, 296
Mivart, St. George, 324, 342–344, 347
Mixed genre, 201
Mizauld, Antoine, 92
Mode, 105, 137, 164, 165, 168
Moderation, 16, 17
Modesty, 291
Molière, 201
Monism, 153, 166–170
Moral approbation, 224, 225, 225n
Moral approval, 226
Moral education, 205
Morality of compassion, 254
Moral judgment
    Hume and Smith on, 209, 232–239
    standard of, 239–245
    sympathy and, 212
Moral philosophy, 70, 72–88, 101
Moral sympathy, 187
More, Henry, 114, 125, 195
Motivation
    altruism and, 280

    by praise, 325, 340
    by praiseworthiness, 327–330
Moyer, Ann E., 5, 70, 108, 109
Mozart, Leopold, 104
"Munich Circle," 294
Murphy, Gardner, 297
Musicology, 5, 102–106
Mutual love, 120, 137

Nachfühlung (responsive feeling), 296
Narcissism, 276
Natural faculties, 63
Natural History (Pliny), 65
Naturalist origins of sympathy, 35
Natural magic, 78, 89–90, 96–97, 99, 110–111
Natural philosophy, 72–88, 96, 101, 138
Natural power, 78, 110n, 147n
Natural selection, 323, 335–340, 348–358
Natural theology, 5
Nature
    affinity of, 75–76, 89, 109
    concurring nature, 12–13
"Negative" eugenics, 346
Neighbor love, 174, 184
Nemesius of Emesa, 21
Neo-Malthusian approach, 354
Neoplatonism, 36
Neo-Stoic ethics, 148
Neurons, 6, 312, 312n
Neuroscience, 3
New Approach to Recently Discovered Occult Causes of Sympathy and Antipathy (Rattray), 118
Newton, Isaac, 10–13, 10n, 94, 109, 114, 129, 130
Newton, Thomas, 94
Nietzsche, Friedrich, 5, 254–285
    on altruism, 259–275
    on compassion, 255–259, 275–285
    on selflessness, 275–285
    on suffering, 255–259
North, Thomas, 94

Objectified self-enjoyment, 309
Objective reality, 162, 164n, 165

Occult, 5, 40, 44–47, 97, 107, 108–113, 138, 147
Olmo, Giovanni Francesco, 91
Olympius of Alexandria, 44*n*
On Common Conceptions (Plutarch), 33
On Divination (Cicero), 20, 29, 30, 77
On Dreams (Chrysippus), 29
On the Life of Plotinus and the Order of His Books (Porphyry), 37
On the Magnetic Curing of Wounds (van Helmont), 111
On the Natural Faculties (Galen), 63, 65, 66, 69
On the Nature of Man (Nemesius of Emesa), 21
On the Nature of the Gods (Cicero), 23, 26
On Nutriment (Hippocrates), 61
On the Origin of Species (Darwin), 326, 335
On the Origin of Things from Forms (Leibniz), 129
On Sympathy (Gangloff), 119
Oration on the Dignity of Man (Pico), 76
Order and connection, 155, 161*n*
Original impressions, 221
"The Origin of Human Races" (Wallace), 332
Ospedale della Pietà, 104
Other-directedness, 176, 177, 192, 194
Otherness, 311, 316
Outline of Psychology (Titchener), 289

Paganism, 97
Panaetius, 30–31, 30–31*n*
Paracelsians, 71, 86, 88, 92, 96, 99
Paracelsus, 86, 89, 90, 111, 117, 121
Parallelism, 132, 152, 169–170
Parasitism, 279
Passions, 218
Passive principle, 24
Pater, Walter, 77
Patrizi, Francesco, 90
Paulus, Julius, 360
Paynell, Thomas, 93
Peart, Sandra J., 5, 323
Pecorino, Paul, 373, 374
Pennuto, Concetta, 85, 85*n*
Pepys, Samuel, 141
Perceptions, 19, 130
Perceptual transmission, 51–60

Perfect harmony, 118, 128
Peripatetics, 57
Perspective taking, 320
Pessimism, 257
Peucer, Caspar, 90
Phenomenological reduction, 314
Phenomenology, 269, 288, 308–318
Philo of Alexandria, 126
Philosophical Enquiry (Burke), 180
Philosophical Lexicon (Goclenius), 124
Physics, 114
Physiology, 184–191
Piaget, Violet, 293*n*
Pico della Mirandola, Giovanni, 76, 77, 78, 79, 109
Pigman, George, 295, 296
Pity, 32, 176, 179, 193, 195
Place, Francis, 348
Plato, 4, 16–18, 38, 55–56, 58, 60, 124
Platonic Theology (Ficino), 74
Platonism
    Darwin and, 339
    Leibniz and, 129
    Plotinus and, 36–37, 55, 121
    in Renaissance, 71, 73, 74, 82
    Spinoza and, 148
    universal sympathy and, 108, 115, 121–128
Pleasure, 224, 225, 226, 227, 304
Plenitude, 125, 133, 134, 136
Pliny, 4, 65, 70, 77, 80–82, 85–87, 96, 99
Plotinus, 36–60
    on astral influence, magic, and prayer, 44–51, 44*n*, 105
    on perceptual transmission, 51–60
    Platonic thought and, 36–37, 55, 121
    precursors to, 38–40
    Renaissance thought and, 72, 73–74, 77, 78, 85
    Stoicism and, 4, 27
    on *sympatheia*, 40–43
    on world soul, 27*n*
Plutarch, 22, 33, 95
Pneuma, 57, 58, 117
Political economy, 6
Political Economy (Mill), 351

Poliziano, Angelo, 80
Pomponazzi, Pietro, 82, 85
Porphyry, 37
Posidonius, 20, 26
"Positive" eugenics, 347
Positivism, 292
Powder of Sympathy, 112–113
Power of signification, 50
Powers
   magical power, 109
   natural power, 78, 110n, 147n
   occult power, 109, 110, 119, 138
   supernatural power, 110, 110n
   sympathetic power, 110, 112, 114, 116, 129, 138
   vital power, 114
Praiseworthiness, 238, 325, 327–330, 360
Prayer, 44–51
Preestablished harmony, 128, 130, 131, 133, 148n
Pride, 215, 222, 224, 291
Primordial otherness, 314
Principle of Sufficient Reason (PSR), 149, 150
Principles of action, 360–361
Principles of Psychology (James), 289n
The Principles of the Most Ancient and Modern Philosophy (Conway), 135
Priscianus Lydus, 20
Problem of other minds, 294, 295, 313, 314
Proclus, 121, 125
Projection, 305
Property dualism, 164
Property rights, 360
Proportion, 134–135
Protestants, 97, 122
Providence, 27
Prudence, 373
Pseudo-Albertine, 80
Pseudo-Plutarch, 25, 33
PSR. *See* Principle of Sufficient Reason
Psychoanalytic theory, 310
Psychological egoism, 275
Psychological Studies (James), 310
Psychology, 3, 286–322
   Einfühlung and, 295–318

historical context, 288–295
social, 318–322
Puccini, Giacomo, 104

Racine, Jean, 201
Racism, 198
Rational capacities, 25, 31–34, 41
Rattray, Sylvester, 118, 119–121, 123
Reason. *See* Rational capacities
Reciprocal beneficence, 377, 380, 382
Recognition, 5, 198, 229, 261, 269
Reddy, William, 200
Reflective impressions, 221
Réflexions critiques sur la poésie et la peinture (Du Bos), 202
Reginster, Bernard, 5, 254
Reid, Thomas, 196
Reik, Theodor, 297
Reinach, Adolf, 294
Reinhardt, Karl, 58n
Religion, 73, 96
Renaissance, 4, 70–101
   attacks on sympathy during, 88–96
   natural and moral philosophy during, 72–88
   sympathies concept expands during, 88–96
Representational parallelism, 165
Resentment, 209, 218, 363
Respect, 215
Retaliation, 363
Rhenanus, Beatus, 81
Rhyff, Walther Hermann, 90
Ribot, Théodule, 298
Ricci, Paolo, 79
Rigdon, Mary L., 379–382, 383, 383n, 384
Rizzolatti, Giacomo, 312n
Roberti, Jean, 111
Rousseau, Jean-Jacques, 179, 185, 189, 196, 203, 206
Rozanova, Olga, 309
Rush, Benjamin, 191

Sabellicus, 80
Sadness, 311

Salmon, Timothy, 372
Sameness, 158–159, 161–162, 164–165, 190
Sayre-McCord, Geoffrey, 14, 197, 208
Scaliger, Joseph Justus, 120
Schegelius, Albertus, 91
Scheler, Max, 294–295, 298, 310, 313–318, 322
Schlegel, Friedrich, 248*n*
Schleiermacher, Friedrich, 247*n*
Schliesser, Eric, 3, 305*n*
Schmitt, Charles, 121*n*
Scholasticism, 121
Schopenhauer, Arthur, 5, 254–285
  on altruism, 259–275
  on compassion, 255–259, 275–285
  on selflessness, 275–285
  on suffering, 255–259
Schwimmer, Johann Michael, 119*n*
Secondary impressions, 221
Sedaine, Michel-Jean, 203
Sedley, David N., 19*n*
Self, 310
Self-absorption, 262
Self-alienation, 309
Self-consciousness, 263, 265
Self-denial, 276, 277
Self-enjoyment, 193
Self-esteem, 276, 278
Self-forgetfulness, 315
Self-government, 339
Self-interest, 144, 173–174, 176, 177–184, 192, 237–238, 281
Selflessness, 260, 275–285
Self-love, 174, 179
Self-observation, 205
Self-other distinction, 307, 315
Self-preservation, 35
Self-sacrifice, 277
Self-sufficiency, 123, 128, 129, 153
Seneca, 20, 32, 115
Sensibility, 186, 199, 205
Sensus communis, 172
Sentimental humanitarianism, 185*n*
Sentimentalism, 199, 204, 208, 211, 230, 245
Severinus, Peter, 87
Sextus Empiricus, 20, 22, 26

Sexual selection, 324, 338, 342, 344
Shaftesbury, Earl of, 192, 193, 194
Shakespeare, William, 5, 139–145
Shuddering, 18
Signification, 50
Simple essence, 117
Simulationist models, 295, 295*n*, 316, 317, 322
Single anonymity, 378
Skwire, Sarah, 139
Smith, Adam, 208–246
  on approbation, 228–232
  de Grouchy's critique of, 204, 205
  on impartial spectator, 145, 359, 362
  on moral judgment, 5, 237–239
  philosophical framework, 209–211, 385
  on reciprocal beneficence, 382
  Scheler's critique of, 313
  on self-interest, 177–178, 185, 196–197
  simulationist models and, 301
  Stein's critique of, 316
  on sympathy, 7, 9, 43, 203, 216–220
  on trust games, 375
  on utilitarianism, 325, 366
Smith, Vernon L., 6, 359, 381–383, 383*n*, 384
Sobel, Joel, 364, 365
Social consciousness, 320
Social Darwinism, 327
Socialization, 320
Social preferences, 366
Social psychology, 288, 318–322
Social Statics (Spencer), 331, 333
Sociology, 6*n*, 313, 318
Socrates, 16, 17, 32
Soul, 21, 25, 27*n*, 28, 38–41, 43, 45, 59, 68
Spencer, Herbert, 298, 319, 331, 332
Spinoza, Baruch, 146–170
  on attributes, 166–170
  on *connexio idearum*, 157–162
  on *connexio rerum*, 155–157, 162–166
  on egoism, 193
  on goodness, 195
  influences on, 153–155
  on monism, 166–170
  Stoicism and, 114, 115*n*
  on sympathy, 13, 174–177

Spirit, 49, 75, 106, 117–118, 120, 126, 141
Spontaneity, 130
Spranger, Eduard, 298
Stanley, Hiram M., 335
Stein, Edith, 294–295, 298, 310, 313–318, 322
Stern, William, 297
Steuer, Daniel, 250
Stewart, Dugald, 327, 328
Stillingfleet, Edward, 10
Stobaeus, 35*n*
Stoicism, 15–35
    cosmopolitanism and, 28–35
    divination and, 28–35
    Epicurus and, 19–28
    Galen and, 61, 63
    internal perception theory, 59
    Leibniz and, 129
    metaphysics, 115
    physics, 24
    Plato and, 16–18
    Pliny and, 82
    Plotinus and, 38, 39, 40, 52, 56, 57, 59
    Smith and, 361
    sympathy as concept in, 4, 87, 101, 108
    theory of the soul, 39
    universal sympathy and, 113–121
Structuralism, 289
Suarez, Francisco, 120
Subjectivity, 263, 265
Substance dualism, 11
Substantial forms, 118, 120, 148*n*
Suffering, 255–259, 267
Superaddition, 12
Supernatural magic, 8, 110
Supernatural power, 110, 110*n*
Superstition, 72, 97, 99
Supreme being assumption, 123, 136
Swales, Martin, 249
Sylva Sylvarum (Bacon), 103
Sympathetic compassion, 180
Sympathetic resonance, 102
Sympathetic vibration, 102, 105
Sympathy
    analysis of, 6–9
    as contagion, 172
    Darwinism and, 323–358
    eighteenth-century context of, 171–198
    as epistemic concept of association, 175, 176
    experimental economic behavior and, 359–385
    French philosophers on, 199–207
    Galen on, 61–69
    Hume on, 208–246
    music and, 102–106
    Nietzsche on, 254–285
    Plotinus on, 36–60
    psychology and, 286–322
    in Renaissance, 70–101
    Schopenhauer on, 254–285
    Smith on, 208–246
    Spinoza on, 146–170, 174–177
    Stoics on, 15–35
    as substituting self for others, 172
    universal, 107–138

Taxonomy of souls, 40
Temple of Nature (Darwin), 330
Tertullian, 21*n*
Theism, 115, 124, 174, 185
Theology, 5
Theoretical egoism, 265
Theoretical philosophy, 295
Theories of influence, 78
The Theory of Moral Sentiments (Smith), 177, 196, 204, 327, 359, 385
Theory Theories, 295
Thevet, André, 93
Thomas, Keith, 141
Thomas Aquinas, 120, 126
Thomasius, Jakob, 115, 116
Thorndike, Lynn, 90
Thought, 16, 28. *See also* Ideas
Thoughtlessness, 260
Three Books on Life (Ficino), 74
Titchener, Edward, 286–292, 294, 297
Traditional game theory, 364–369
Transcendence, 27*n*, 192, 274
A Treatise of Human Nature (Hume), 301
Trithemius, Johannes, 78

True Intellectual System of the Universe (Cudworth), 116
Trust games, 375–384
Truth, 118, 131, 158
Turco, Luigi, 195n
Turnbull, George, 190
Two Treatises (Digby), 112

Ultimatum games, 369–375
Unconscious, 292
Unity of nature, 151
Universal gravity, 10
Universal mindedness, 157, 157n
Universal sympathy, 107–138
    Conway on, 135–138
    Leibniz on, 128–135
    occult and, 108–113
    Platonism and, 121–128
    Stoicism and, 113–121
Unselfing, 283
Urbanization, 183
Urinating, 18
Utilitarianism, 242, 243, 243n, 257, 325, 329, 332, 341, 358
Utilitarianism (Mill), 332

Van Boening, Mark, 373, 374
Van Helmont, Jan Baptiste, 111, 112, 116–121, 123, 126, 130
Vascular network, 62
Vesalius, Andreas, 91
Vibration of strings, 102–106
Vice, 203, 236, 339, 347
Viola d'amore, 103, 105
Virtue, 135, 138, 211, 226
Vischer, Robert, 296–297, 302, 305, 309
Vision, 57, 58, 60, 233
Visual transmission, 55, 57, 59
Vitalism, 135
Vitality, 112, 137
Vital power, 114
Vitruvius, Pollio, 4, 77
Vivaldi, Antonio, 104
Von Winkelried, Arnold, 272, 278, 279

Wahlverwandtschaften (Goethe), 247–253
Wallace, Alfred Russel, 323, 326, 332–334, 337, 342–343
An Inquiry into the Nature and Causes of the Wealth of Nations (Smith), 177
Wedgewood, Josiah, 331
Weigel, Erhard, 114
Well-being, 262
Wilberforce, Samuel, 341, 342
Wilson, Bart J., 6, 359, 372
Wilson, Margaret, 161n
Wispé, Lauren, 298, 299, 300
Wollstonecraft, Mary, 188, 189
World-apart thesis, 131
World-Soul, 27n, 38, 40, 41
Worringer, Wilhelm, 309
Wounds, 100, 110–111, 140
Wundt, Wilhelm, 288, 289, 290, 321

Yawning, 18

Zahavi, Dan, 295n
Zeno, 30
Zero-sum games, 371n
Zorzi, Francesco, 79, 80
Zufühlung (immediate feeling), 296
Zusammenhang, 252